Strong Borders, Secure Nation

PRINCETON STUDIES IN INTERNATIONAL
HISTORY AND POLITICS

SERIES EDITORS

G. John Ikenberry and Marc Trachtenberg

RECENT TITLES

*Strong Borders, Secure Nation: Cooperation and Conflict
in China's Territorial Disputes* by M. Taylor Fravel

The Sino-Soviet Split by Lorenz M. Lüthi

Nuclear Logics: Contrasting Paths in East Asia and the Middle East
by Etel Solingen

Social States: China in International Institutions, 1980–2000
by Alastair Iain Johnston

Appeasing Bankers by Jonathan Kirshner

The Politics of Secularism in International Relations
by Elizabeth Shakman Hurd

Unanswered Threats: Political Constraints on the Balance of Power
by Randall L. Schweller

*Producing Security: Multinational Corporations, Globalization,
and the Changing Calculus of Conflict* by Stephen G. Brooks

*Driving the Soviets up the Wall: Soviet-East German Relations,
1953–1961* by Hope M. Harrison

*Legitimacy and Power Politics: The American and French Revolutions
in International Political Culture* by Mlada Bukovansky

*Rhetoric and Reality in Air Warfare: The Evolution of British
and American Ideas about Strategic Bombing, 1914–1945*
by Tami Davis Biddle

*Revolutions in Sovereignty: How Ideas Shaped Modern
International Relations* by Daniel Philpott

*After Victory: Institutions, Strategic Restraint, and the Rebuilding
of Order after Major Wars* by G. John Ikenberry

Stay the Hand of Vengeance: The Politics of War Crimes Tribunals
by Gary Jonathan Bass

Strong Borders, Secure Nation

COOPERATION AND CONFLICT
IN CHINA'S TERRITORIAL DISPUTES

M. Taylor Fravel

PRINCETON UNIVERSITY PRESS
PRINCETON AND OXFORD

Library of Congress Cataloging-in-Publication Data

Fravel, M. Taylor, 1971–
Strong borders, secure nation : cooperation and conflict in China's
territorial disputes / M. Taylor Fravel.
p.   cm.   —   (Princeton studies in international history and politics)
Includes bibliographical references and index.
ISBN 978-0-691-13608-0 (cloth : alk. paper) —
ISBN 978-0-691-13609-7 (pbk. : alk. paper)
1. China—Boundaries. 2. China—Foreign relations—1949– 3. China—Politics
and government—1949– I. Title.
DS737.F73 2008
327.51—dc22
2008007563

British Library Cataloging-in-Publication Data is available

This book has been composed in Sabon

Printed on acid-free paper. ∞

press.princeton.edu

Printed in the United States of America

10   9   8   7   6   5   4   3   2   1

For Anna

Contents

Illustrations

Tables

Acknowledgments

THE FIRST PERSON I must thank is one who will never read this book, Michel Oksenberg. I would not have pursued an academic career had it not been for Mike. His enthusiasm for the study of contemporary China and his teaching inspired me, like so many others. Although I began my research for this book shortly before he passed away, I continue to learn from his example as a scholar and gentleman. Mike was a mentor and a friend whose fellowship is sadly missed.

While starting this project at Stanford University, I worked with an extraordinary group of advisers. Scott Sagan provided astute suggestions and encouragement in addition to avuncular advice. His support at the early stages was immeasurable, and he never let me lose a step. From our first conversation over a grant application, Jim Fearon provided insights and guidance that have had a lasting impact on my approach to the study of international relations. Jean Oi raised the tough questions that needed to be asked, pushing always for better answers and stronger evidence. I owe a special debt of gratitude to Tom Christensen. His detailed comments improved the quality of the argument, while his moral support arrived at just the right time.

Numerous colleagues and friends offered comments and suggestions on various parts of the manuscript. Their collective wisdom improved the final product. I am indebted to Dennis Blasko, Nisha Fazal, George Gavrilis, Mike Glosny, Hein Goemans, Steve Goldstein, Lei Guang, Ron Hassner, Jacques Hymans, Iain Johnston, Scott Kastner, Andrew Kennedy, Ron Krebs, Milton Liao, Lorenz Luthi, Paul MacDonald, Nikolay Marinov, Quinn Mecham, Evan Medeiros, Alex Montgomery, Kevin Narizny, Daryl Press, Phillip Saunders, Holger Schmidt, David Andrew Singer, Robert Ross, Ed Steinfeld, Monica Toft, Benjamin Valentino, Steven Van Evera, and Xu Xin. I owe special thanks to Allen Carlson, Liselotte Odgaard, Barry Posen, and Alan Wachman, who each read and commented on the entire manuscript with great care.

Along the way, institutions devoted to the study of international relations sustained my research with intellectual community and financial support. This project began at the Center for International Security and Cooperation at Stanford, and I was able to refine the argument at the Olin Institute for Strategic Studies at Harvard University. The Visiting Scholars Program at the American Academy of Arts and Sciences, the Fairbank Center for East Asian Studies at Harvard University, and the

Princeton-Harvard Program on China and the World gave me precious time away from teaching to complete the manuscript. I also thank MIT's Security Studies Program and the Department of Political Science for their support.

Jamie Edwards, Erik Fogg, Brandon Green, Ruijie He, Richard Kraus, Drew Laughlan, Oriana Mastro, and Will Norris provided expert research for the book. Lynne Levine's assistance has been indispensable throughout. Philip Schwartzberg of Meridian Mapping created the many maps, which help simplify the complexity of China's disputed boundaries. At Princeton University Press, I thank Chuck Myers for his continued support of this project. I am also grateful to Will Hively for his excellent copyediting and to Mark Bellis, Dimitri Karetnikov, and the rest of the production team for their assistance. Portions of the book in an earlier form were published in *International Security* (vol. 30, no. 2 and vol. 32, no. 3). I am grateful to the editors for their permission to use the material here.

Long before I started this project, my family supported my intellectual pursuits. I thank all of them, especially my parents, Maris and Judy Fravel, and my sister, Behan Gifford, for their support and encouragement.

Most of all, thank you Anna, without whom this book never would have been written. She has given more love and sustenance than I can ever hope to repay, first moving across an ocean and then a continent so that we may live a life together. Throughout, she made sure that I did not forget what is most important in this world and always put a smile on my face. She is my best friend and much more. Those who have met Anna know how blessed I am to share my life with her.

Abbreviations

AFP	Agence France-Presse
AP	The Associated Press
AMS	Academy of Military Science
ASEAN	Association of Southeast Asian Nations
CC	Central Committee
CCP	Chinese Communist Party
CIA	Central Intelligence Agency
CMC	Central Military Commission
DDZGWJ	Han Nianlong, ed. *Dangdai Zhongguo waijiao* [Diplomacy of Contemporary China]. Beijing: Zhongguo shehui kexue chubanshe, 1990.
DDZGJD	Han Huaizhi and Tan Jingqiao, eds. *Dangdai Zhongguo jundui de junshi gongzuo* [Military Work of Contemporary China's Armed Forces], Vol. 1. Beijing: Zhongguo shehui kexue chubanshe, 1989.
DPP	Democratic Progressive Party
DXPWX3	*Deng Xiaoping wenxuan* [Deng Xiaoping's Selected Works]. Vol. 3. Beijing: Renmin chubanshe, 1993.
EEZ	exclusive economic zone
FEER	*Far Eastern Economic Review*
GLF	Great Leap Forward
GSD	General Staff Department (PLA)
HCC	Sinha, P. B., and A. A. Athale. *History of the Conflict with China*. New Delhi: History Division, Ministry of Defence, Government of India [restricted], 1992.
IB	Intelligence Bureau (India)
JWG	Joint Working Group
KMT	Guomindang (Kuomintang) [Nationalist Party]
LAC	line of actual control
MD	Military District
MFA	Ministry of Foreign Affairs
MR	Military Region
NEFA	North Eastern Frontier Agency
NIE	National Intelligence Estimate
NVDA	National Volunteer Defense Army
NYT	*New York Times*
PAP	People's Armed Police

PBSC	Politburo Standing Committee
PLA	People's Liberation Army
PLAAF	People's Liberation Army Air Force
PLAN	People's Liberation Army Navy
PRC	People's Republic of China
RMRB	*Renmin Ribao* [People's Daily] (Beijing)
ROC	Republic of China (Taiwan)
RVN	Republic of Vietnam
SCO	Shanghai Cooperation Organization
SEATO	Southeast Asia Treaty Organization
SOA	State Oceanographic Agency
TYJ	Waijiao bu, ed. *Zhonghua renmin gongheguo tiaoyue ji* [Treaty Collection of the PRC]. Beijing: Shijie zhishi chubanshe, 1960–1999.
UK	United Kingdom
UN	United Nations
UNCLOS	UN Convention on the Law of the Sea
U.S.	United States
USSR	Union of Soviet Socialist Republics
WP	*White Paper: Notes, Memoranda and Letters Exchanged and Agreements Signed between the Governments of India and China.* 12 editions. New Delhi, Ministry of External Affairs, Government of India, various years.
ZELNP2	Li Ping and Ma Zhisun, eds. *Zhou Enlai nianpu, 1949–1976* [Chronicle of Zhou Enlai's Life]. Vol. 2. Beijing: Zhongyang wenxian chubanshe, 1997.
ZELZ	Jin Chongji, ed. *Zhou Enlai zhuan* [Zhou Enlai's Biography]. 4 vols. Beijing: Zhongyang wenxian chubanshe, 1998.
ZGWJ	Waijiao bu, ed. *Zhongguo waijiao* [China's Diplomacy]. Beijing: Shijie zhishi chubanshe, 1987–2006.
ZYBJ	Jiang Siyi and Li Hui, eds. *ZhongYin bianjing ziwei fanji zuozhan shi* [An Operational History of the China-India Border Counterattack in Self-Defense]. Beijing: Junshi kexue chubanshe [internal circulation], 1994.

Strong Borders, Secure Nation

Introduction

Rising Power, Territory, and War

China is the new great power of the twenty-first century. Whether its rise will be peaceful or violent is a fundamental question for the study and practice of international relations. Unlike many past power transitions, China's current economic growth has occurred largely through its acceptance of the prevailing rules, norms, and institutions of the international system. Nevertheless, ambiguity and anxiety persist around how China will employ the military power that its growing wealth creates.

Amid this historical change, one concern is China's potential for violent conflict with other states over territory. The congressional U.S.-China Economic and Security Review Commission, for example, stated in its 2006 annual report that China might "take advantage of a more advanced military to threaten use of force, or actually use force, to facilitate desirable resolutions . . . of territorial claims."[1] Such concerns have merit. Historically, rapid internal economic growth has propelled states to redefine and expand the interests that they pursue abroad.[2] Economic development funds the acquisition of more robust military capabilities to pursue and defend these interests. Often such expansion results in the escalation of territorial disputes with other states. More generally, the disruption in the balance of power generates uncertainty among the leading states in the system about the security of vital interests and the structure of international order.[3]

In its territorial disputes, however, China has been less prone to violence and more cooperative than a singular view of an expansionist state suggests. Since 1949, China has participated in twenty-three unique terri-

[1] *2006 Report to Congress of the U.S.-China Economic and Security Review Commission,* November 2006, p. 130. Also see Office of the Secretary of Defense, *Annual Report to Congress: The Military Power of the People's Republic of China* (Washington, D.C.: Department of Defense, 2005), 9.

[2] For just a few examples, see Nazli Choucri and Robert Carver North, *Nations in Conflict: National Growth and International Violence* (San Francisco: W. H. Freeman, 1975); Robert Gilpin, *War and Change in World Politics* (New York: Cambridge University Press, 1981); John J. Mearsheimer, *The Tragedy of Great Power Politics* (New York: W. W. Norton, 2001); A.F.K. Organski, *World Politics* (New York: Knopf, 1958).

[3] Given this history of great-power conflict, for example, John Mearsheimer predicts that the "rise of China will not be peaceful at all." John J. Mearsheimer, "The Rise of China Will Not Be Peaceful at All," *The Australian,* November 18, 2005.

torial disputes with its neighbors on land and at sea. Yet it has pursued compromise and offered concessions in seventeen of these conflicts. China's compromises have often been substantial, as it has usually offered to accept less than half of the contested territory in any final settlement. In addition, these compromises have resulted in boundary agreements in which China has abandoned potential irredentist claims to more than 3.4 million square kilometers of land that had been part of the Qing empire at its height in the early nineteenth century. In total, the People's Republic of China (PRC) has contested roughly 238,000 square kilometers or just 7 percent of the territory once part of the Qing.

Although China has pursued compromise frequently, it has nevertheless used force in six of its territorial disputes. Some of these conflicts, especially with India and Vietnam, were notably violent. Others, such as the crises over Taiwan in the 1950s and the clash with the Soviet Union in 1969, were tense moments in the Cold War involving threats to use nuclear weapons. Nevertheless, despite a willingness to use force in certain disputes, China has seized little land that it did not control before the outbreak of hostilities.

The wide variation in China's behavior is puzzling for scholars of international relations and China alike. Leading theories of international relations would expect a state with China's characteristics to be uncompromising and prone to using force in territorial disputes, not conciliatory. Contrary to scholars of offensive realism, however, China has rarely exploited its military superiority to bargain hard for the territory that it claims or to seize it through force.[4] China has likewise not become increasingly assertive in its territorial disputes as its relative power has grown in the past two decades. Contrary to others who emphasize the violent effects of nationalism, which would suggest inflexibility in conflicts over national sovereignty, China has been quite willing to offer territorial concessions despite historical legacies of external victimization and territorial dismemberment under the Qing.[5] And contrary to scholars who stress the role of political institutions, China has escalated only a minority of its territorial conflicts even with a highly centralized, authoritarian political system that places few internal constraints on the use of force.[6]

China's pattern of cooperation and escalation in its territorial disputes may also be surprising for observers and scholars of China. At the end of

---

[4] See, for example, Mearsheimer, *Tragedy*; Fareed Zakaria, *From Wealth to Power: The Unusual Origins of America's World Role* (Princeton, N.J.: Princeton University Press, 1998).

[5] See, for example, Stephen Van Evera, "Hypotheses on Nationalism and War," *International Security*, vol. 18, no. 4 (Spring 1994): 5–39.

[6] See, for example, Bruce Russett, *Grasping the Democratic Peace* (Princeton, N.J.: Princeton University Press, 1993).

the Cold War, many expected that China's numerous territorial disputes would be a leading source of instability in East Asia.[7] With the increased visibility of popular nationalism over the past two decades, other scholars maintain that China harbors broad irredentist claims to land on its periphery that its growing power will allow it to pursue.[8] Similarly, amid the prominence of popular nationalism, China is seen as "prone to muscle-flexing" in its foreign policy in order to deflect attention from growing social unrest.[9] Finally, some scholars maintain that China has a strategic preference for offensive uses of force, especially in zero-sum conflicts such as territorial disputes.[10]

Nevertheless, China has been more likely to compromise over disputed territory and less likely to use force than many policy analysts assert, international relations theories might predict, or China scholars expect. China's varied behavior sparks the questions that this book seeks to answer. Why has China pursued compromise in some disputes but used force in others? More generally, why and when do states cooperate in territorial conflicts? Under what conditions do states escalate disputes to high levels of violence instead of cooperating?

Answers to these questions can help illuminate the trajectory of China's rise as a great power. In an international system composed of sovereign states, behavior in territorial disputes offers a fundamental indicator of whether a state pursues status-quo or revisionist foreign policies.[11] Historically, contested land has been the most common issue over which states collide and go to war.[12] If states are likely to resort to force as a tool of statecraft, it will perhaps be most evident in how they pursue territorial

---

[7] For instance, Richard K. Betts, "Wealth, Power, and Instability: East Asia and the United States after the Cold War," *International Security*, vol. 18, no. 3 (Winter 1993): 34–77; Aaron L. Friedberg, "Ripe for Rivalry: Prospects for Peace in Multipolar Asia," *International Security*, vol. 18, no. 3 (Winter 1993/94), 5–33.

[8] For example, Richard Bernstein and Ross H. Munro, *The Coming Conflict with China* (New York: Knopf, 1997); Maria Hsia Chang, *Return of the Dragon: China's Wounded Nationalism* (Boulder, Colo.: Westview, 2001).

[9] Susan L. Shirk, *China: Fragile Superpower* (New York: Oxford University Press, 2007), 62.

[10] Alastair Iain Johnston, "Cultural Realism and Strategy in Maoist China," in Peter J. Katzenstein, ed., *The Culture of National Security* (New York: Columbia University Press, 1996): 216–270.

[11] On China's status-quo foreign policy in arenas other than territorial disputes, see Alastair Iain Johnston, "Is China a Status Quo Power?" *International Security*, vol. 27, no. 4 (Spring 2003): 5–56.

[12] Kalevi J. Holsti, *Peace and War: Armed Conflicts and International Order, 1648–1989* (Cambridge: Cambridge University Press, 1991); John Vasquez and Marie T. Henehan, "Territorial Disputes and the Probability of War, 1816–1992," *Journal of Peace Research*, vol. 38, no. 2 (2001): 123–138; John A. Vasquez, *The War Puzzle* (New York: Cambridge University Press, 1993).

goals. As China today remains involved in several disputes, these questions are far from academic. Violence over some areas that China claims, such as Taiwan or the Senkaku Islands, would likely result in hostility between China and the United States, which maintains close ties with Taipei and Tokyo.

Answers to these questions are also hard to find. Although research on China's conflict behavior highlights the role of territorial disputes, they have yet to be examined systematically.[13] Instead, individual studies have weighed the legal merits of China's sovereignty claims or examined specific disputes, such as the boundary conflict between China and India.[14] The few comprehensive studies that do exist investigate only China's compromises in the 1960s and were unable to benefit from the flowering of new Chinese-language source materials in the last decade.[15] Finally, no study compares China's willingness to compromise or use force in all these conflicts, analysis that is key to understanding China's behavior.

COOPERATION AND ESCALATION IN TERRITORIAL DISPUTES

My explanation of China's behavior is rooted in two theories that explain how states choose to pursue their territorial claims. One theory examines

---

[13] Alastair Iain Johnston, "China's Militarized Interstate Dispute Behaviour, 1949–1992: A First Cut at the Data," *The China Quarterly*, no. 153 (March 1998): 1–30.

[14] Examples include Luke T. Chang, *China's Boundary Treaties and Frontier Disputes: A Manuscript* (New York: Oceana Publications, 1982); Pao-min Chang, *The Sino-Vietnamese Territorial Dispute* (New York: Praeger, 1986); Chien-peng Chung, *Domestic Politics, International Bargaining and China's Territorial Disputes* (London: RoutledgeCurzon, 2004); George Ginsburgs and Carl F. Pinkele, *The Sino-Soviet Territorial Dispute, 1949–64* (London: Routledge, 1978); Ting Tsz Kao, *The Chinese Frontiers* (Aurora, Ill.: Chinese Scholarly Publishing, 1980); Ying Cheng Kiang, *China's Boundaries* (Lincolnwood, Ill.: Institute of China Studies, 1985); Alastair Lamb, *The Sino-Indian Border in Ladakh* (Canberra: Australian National University Press, 1973); Neville Maxwell, *India's China War* (New York: Pantheon Books, 1970); J.R.V. Prescott et al., *Frontiers of Asia and Southeast Asia* (Carlton: Melbourne University Press, 1977); Tsui Tsien-hua, *The Sino-Soviet Border Dispute in the 1970's* (New York: Mosaic Press, 1983); Byron N. Tzou, *China and International Law: The Boundary Disputes* (New York: Praeger, 1990).

[15] Greg Austin, *China's Ocean Frontier: International Law, Military Force, and National Development* (Canberra: Allen & Unwin, 1998); Mira Sinha Bhattacharjea, "China's Strategy for the Determination and Consolidation of Its Territorial Boundaries: A Preliminary Investigation," *China Report*, vol. 23, no. 4 (1987): 397–419; Harold C. Hinton, *Communist China in World Politics* (New York: Houghton Mifflin, 1966), 273–336; Eric A. Hyer, "The Politics of China's Boundary Disputes and Settlements" (Ph.D. dissertation, Columbia University, 1990); Francis Watson, *The Frontiers of China* (New York: Praeger, 1966). For an important exception, see Allen Carlson, *Unifying China, Integrating with the World: Securing Chinese Sovereignty in the Reform Era* (Stanford, Calif.: Stanford University Press, 2005), 49–91.

the sources of cooperation in territorial disputes, while the other examines the sources of escalation. As detailed in chapter 1, each theory starts with the assumption that states choose among three generic strategies when managing an existing territorial conflict. They can (1) do nothing and delay settlement, (2) offer concessions and compromise, or (3) threaten or use force. Most of the time, a strategy of doing nothing is least risky, due to the costs associated with leaders' potential punishment at home for compromising over national sovereignty and the uncertainty of outcomes when a crisis escalates. Factors that increase the costs that a state bears for contesting territory relative to delaying, then, explain why and when states either compromise or use force in their disputes.

A state is most likely to compromise and offer concessions to counter internal or external threats to its security. Compromise is possible because pressing a claim to another state's land carries some price or opportunity cost, usually unrealized military, economic, or diplomatic assistance. When these costs outweigh the value of the land at stake, compromise becomes more attractive than delay, and a state will trade concessions for aid from a territorial opponent to counter the more processing threat that it faces. External threats to the security or survival of the state are one source of compromise. When engaged in acute competition with a rival, for example, a state can use territorial concessions to form an alliance with a third party against its adversary. Internal threats to the strength and stability of a state offer a second source of compromise. When faced with an armed rebellion, for instance, a state can trade territorial concessions for assistance from neighboring states, such as policing the border or denying safe haven to potential insurgents.

Although a state's overall security environment creates incentives for cooperation, shifts in a state's bargaining power in a territorial dispute explain decisions to escalate these conflicts. A state's bargaining power consists of the amount of contested land that it occupies and its ability to project military power over the entire area under dispute. These two factors shape a state's ability to control contested land and achieve a favorable negotiated settlement. When a state concludes that an adversary is strengthening its relative position in a dispute, inaction becomes more costly than threatening or even using force to halt or reverse its decline. A state that faces a much stronger opponent may also use force when an adversary's power suddenly and temporarily weakens, creating a window of opportunity to seize land and strengthen its otherwise weak negotiating position.

To test these theories, I use a "medium-n" research design that examines China's decisions to cooperate or escalate in each of its twenty-three disputes since 1949. As both types of decision are infrequent, they can all be identified and compared with relative ease. For each dispute, I examine the conditions before and after the change in strategy to identify those factors that vary with decisions to compromise or use force, but not with delay. I then trace the process by which these decisions were made to determine whether these factors have the causal effect that my theories predict.

The chapters that follow exploit untapped Chinese-language sources. These documents include party history materials, oral histories, memoirs of senior leaders, government training manuals, and provincial gazetteers as well as limited materials from a variety of archives. These sources reveal disputes, boundary agreements, and key turning points in high-level negotiations that were previously unknown outside China.

OVERVIEW OF THE BOOK

After outlining my theories of cooperation and escalation, chapter 1 continues with an overview of China's territorial disputes. China's territorial conflicts are intertwined with the varied challenges of maintaining the territorial integrity of a large and multiethnic state. Ethnic geography, or the location and distribution of ethnic groups, largely defines the different goals that China's leaders have pursued in their country's territorial disputes. The PRC's ethnic geography consists of a densely populated Han Chinese core, a large but sparsely populated non-Han periphery, and unpopulated offshore islands. In frontier disputes on their country's land border, China's leaders seek to maintain control over vast borderlands populated by ethnic minorities that were never ruled directly by any past Chinese empire. In homeland disputes, China's leaders seek to unify what they view as Han Chinese areas not under their control when the PRC was established in 1949, namely Hong Kong, Macao, and Taiwan. In offshore island disputes, China's leaders aim to secure a permanent maritime presence among unpopulated rocks and islands far from the mainland.

External threats are one mechanism in my theory of cooperation, but internal threats best explain China's willingness to compromise in its many territorial disputes. China has offered concessions in each and every frontier dispute along its land border but not in any homeland disputes, and in only one offshore island dispute. Ethnic minorities who have maintained strong social and economic ties with neighboring states and harbored aspirations for self-determination live in many of the frontiers near China's borders. When faced with internal threats, especially ethnic unrest in the frontiers, China's leaders have been much more willing to offer concessions in exchange for assistance that strengthens the state's control over these regions, such as denying external support to rebels or affirming Chinese sovereignty over the areas of unrest.

Chapter 2 examines China's efforts to compromise in many frontier disputes in the early 1960s. In 1959, a revolt in Tibet sparked the largest internal threat ever to the PRC's territorial integrity. The outbreak of this revolt dramatically increased the cost of maintaining disputes with Burma, Nepal, and India. China offered concessions in its conflicts with these states in exchange for their cooperation in eliminating external support for the rebels and affirming Chinese sovereignty over Tibet. In the spring of 1962, China faced renewed ethnic unrest in the frontiers, especially Xinjiang, during the economic crisis following the failure of the Great Leap Forward. This combination of internal threats to both territorial integrity and political stability increased the cost of contesting land with its neighbors. China pursued compromise in disputes with North Korea, Mongolia, India, Pakistan, Afghanistan, and the Soviet Union in order to rebuild its economy and consolidate state control by easing external tensions.

How similar internal threats explain China's efforts to compromise in frontier disputes in the 1990s is demonstrated in chapter 3. In 1989, the upheaval in Tiananmen Square posed an internal threat to the stability of China's socialist system of government. This legitimacy crisis, which the weakening of other communist parties worldwide exacerbated, increased the cost of maintaining territorial disputes with the Soviet Union, Laos, and Vietnam. China traded concessions in exchange for cooperation to counter its diplomatic isolation and ensure the continuation of economic reforms. Soon after Tiananmen, ethnic unrest in Xinjiang posed a new internal threat to the state's territorial integrity. The armed uprisings and demonstrations increased the price for pressing claims against neighboring Kazakhstan, Kyrgyzstan, and Tajikistan. China compromised in these disputes in exchange for assistance to limit external support for Uighur separatists.

Although windows of opportunity opened by a rival's temporary weakness offer one mechanism in my theory of escalation, China's own declining bargaining power best explains its willingness to use force in its territorial disputes. Since 1949, China's leaders have demonstrated a keen sensitivity to negative shifts in the state's ability to control disputed land. In most instances, China's behavior reflects such concerns with its own weakness, as China has used force either in disputes with its militarily most powerful neighbors or in conflicts where it has occupied little or none of the land that it has claimed.

Chapter 4 investigates the use of force in its frontier disputes, where China sought to counter challenges from two militarily powerful neighbors, India and the Soviet Union. Domestic instability sharpened perceptions of decline in these cases, as China's leaders concluded that their adversaries sought to profit from the country's internal difficulties. In October 1962, Chinese forces attacked Indian positions all along the contested border after China failed to persuade India to negotiate. China escalated this conflict to halt India's increased military deployments along the contested frontier and its occupation of land in the disputed western sector, decline in China's position in the dispute that the economic crisis after the failure of the Great Leap Forward intensified. For similar reasons, in March 1969 elite Chinese troops ambushed a Soviet patrol near the disputed Zhenbao Island in the Ussuri River. Soviet troop deployments along the border, the Brezhnev doctrine to intervene in the affairs of socialist states, and an aggressive pattern of Soviet patrolling weakened China's position in the dispute, decline that the political instability of the Cultural Revolution heightened.

China's management of homeland disputes, its most important territorial conflicts, is explored in chapter 5. Although China settled disputes over Hong Kong and Macao in the 1980s, it never compromised over the sovereignty of these areas, which were transferred by Britain and Portugal to China in 1997 and 1999, respectively. China has never offered to compromise over the sovereignty of Taiwan, but it has used force to demonstrate its resolve to unify the island with the mainland. In 1954 and 1958, China initiated crises over Nationalist-held coastal islands to deter the United States from further increasing its military and diplomatic support for Taiwan, support that threatened to weaken China's already poor position in this dispute. In 1995 and 1996, China launched a series of provocative military exercises and missile tests when democratization on the island increased popular support for formal independence and Beijing viewed Washington as supporting this goal.

Chapter 6 examines China's offshore island disputes. Although China compromised in one such dispute in 1957, it has never offered territorial concessions in its other island conflicts, owing to their potential economic and strategic value. Moreover, it used force to occupy islands in the Paracels and features such as coral reefs in the Spratlys when its relative position in offshore island disputes began to decline. In the early 1970s, the first wave of offshore petroleum exploration and other claimants' occupation of features in the South China Sea highlighted China's vulnerability in offshore island disputes as control of these islands grew in importance. China used force to strengthen its position in the one area where it could project limited naval power, occupying the Crescent Group in the Paracels. In the late 1980s, China seized features in the Spratlys after Malaysia began to occupy vacant reefs and Vietnam enlarged its presence in the area, further weakening China's position in a dispute where China was the only claimant that did not occupy any disputed land.

In the conclusion, I assess the implications for China's territorial future. Fears that China will pursue broad territorial changes or fight frequently over its territorial claims are overstated. China's rise may still be violent, but territory is not likely to be the leading source of conflict. Overall, then, this book offers relatively good news. If states fight over territory more than any other issue, then China's resolution of seventeen disputes has eliminated many future opportunities for conflict. In addition, in the agreements settling these disputes, China has signaled its acceptance of the sovereignty and territorial integrity of its neighbors and dropped potential irredentist claims to territory that had been part of the Qing empire in the early nineteenth century. As these documents are public, China has "tied its hands" to prevent violations of these settlements in the future.

Nevertheless, China has demonstrated a willingness to fight over territory, both to secure its current boundaries and to regain homeland areas. When vital interests are at stake, China will use force. As it continues to enhance its military capabilities, China will be able to fight more effectively than ever before. In this context, the potential for conflict over Taiwan should not be understated. Yet so long as China's leaders believe that the prospects for unification are not declining over the long term, the odds of violence are low. In its other territorial disputes, China has been much more willing to use force when its bargaining power has declined, not strengthened.

CHAPTER ONE

Cooperation and Escalation in Territorial Disputes

TERRITORIAL DISPUTES BEAR ON a state's national sovereignty and territorial integrity, its core interests. Historically, they have been the most common issue over which states collide and go to war.[1] Decisions to cooperate or escalate in pursuit of a state's territorial claims have enormous consequences for peace and stability in international relations. Why and when do states offer concessions, resolving a conflict that might otherwise escalate to war? Why and when will they use force instead?

China's dispute over Taiwan underscores the importance of answering these questions. Taiwan is China's most important and volatile territorial conflict. At the height of the 1995–96 crisis, the People's Liberation Army (PLA) fired short-range ballistic missiles into target areas abutting the island's two key ports. Since then, scholars, policy analysts, and diplomats have endeavored to understand when the next crisis might erupt and how it might be anticipated, managed, or even prevented. As China's use of force across the Taiwan Strait would likely involve the United States and could easily escalate to high levels of violence, settlement of this dispute would remove the most probable venue for great-power war in East Asia today.

Within the past two decades, a vibrant research program on territorial disputes has emerged. A territorial dispute is defined as a conflicting claim by two or more states over the ownership of the same piece of land. This definition includes offshore islands but excludes disputes over maritime rights, such as exclusive economic zones (EEZs).[2] Through mostly quantitative analysis, scholars have identified important empirical regularities in how states behave in these disputes. Although this research has yielded numerous insights, four factors linked with the settlement and escalation of territorial disputes feature prominently in many studies. Both democracies and alliance partners in a territorial conflict with each other are more

---

[1] Kalevi J. Holsti, *Peace and War: Armed Conflicts and International Order, 1648–1989* (Cambridge: Cambridge University Press, 1991); John A. Vasquez, *The War Puzzle* (New York: Cambridge University Press, 1993).

[2] Paul R. Hensel, "Contentious Issues and World Politics: The Management of Territorial Claims in the Americas, 1816–1992," *International Studies Quarterly*, vol. 45, no. 1 (March 2001): 90; Paul K. Huth and Todd L. Allee, *The Democratic Peace and Territorial Conflict in the Twentieth Century* (Cambridge: Cambridge University Press, 2002), 298.

likely to compromise and often settle their disputes, and less likely to initiate military confrontations, than nondemocratic or nonaligned states in such conflicts with each other. By contrast, all types of states are more likely to use force and less likely to cooperate in disputes over land highly valued for its strategic importance, economic resources, or symbolic significance. Militarily stronger states are also usually more likely to use force to achieve their territorial goals than weaker ones that lack the means to resist or coerce their opponents.[3]

Although this research has deepened general knowledge about territorial disputes, it lacks a complete theoretical account for how states choose to pursue their territorial objectives. These studies illuminate mostly cross-sectional variation in the outcome of disputes, identifying those conflicts that are more likely to be settled or experience the use of force. Nevertheless, although factors such as the value of contested land vary widely across disputes, they are often constant in particular conflicts, which limits their ability to explain how individual states behave over time. If such factors do change, they are likely to shift slowly and therefore unlikely to explain otherwise dramatic decisions to cooperate or escalate. Yet as concern over conflict in the Taiwan Strait highlights, it is precisely these dramatic decisions in specific disputes that animate scholars and policymakers alike.

To explain why and when states use peaceful or violent means in territorial disputes, I shift the analytical focus from dispute outcomes to individual state decisions. Past research has identified which conflicts are most likely to be amenable to settlement or erupt in violence, but why and when states employ such means in any particular dispute requires further investigation. Given an incentive to compromise or escalate, the variables that current research highlights suggest when either outcome may occur. These incentives themselves, however, remain underexamined but critical to explaining how states behave in territorial disputes.

The Taiwan dispute illustrates the limits of existing approaches. As past research would predict, Taiwan is primed for conflict. It is China's most

---

[3] See, for example, Giacomo Chiozza and Ajin Choi, "Guess Who Did What: Political Leaders and the Management of Territorial Disputes, 1950–1990," *Journal of Conflict Resolution*, vol. 47, no. 3 (June 2003): 251–278; Gary Goertz and Paul F. Diehl, *Territorial Changes and International Conflict* (New York: Routledge, 1992); Hensel, "Contentious Issues"; Paul R. Hensel and Sara McLaughlin Mitchell, "Issue Indivisibility and Territorial Claims," *GeoJournal*, vol. 64, no. 4 (December 2005): 275–285; Paul K. Huth, *Standing Your Ground: Territorial Disputes and International Conflict* (Ann Arbor: University of Michigan Press, 1996); Huth and Allee, *Democratic Peace*; Arie M. Kacowicz, *Peaceful Territorial Change* (Columbia: University of South Carolina Press, 1994); Robert Mandel, "Roots of the Modern Interstate Border Dispute," *Journal of Conflict Resolution*, vol. 24, no. 3 (September 1980): 427–454.

important territorial dispute, linked to modern Chinese nationalism and the legitimacy of the Chinese Communist Party (CCP), and is an area of material as well as symbolic importance. Since 1949, China has possessed the military capabilities to attack Taiwan or the territories it controls. Moreover, China's authoritarian political regime has placed few internal constraints on the use of force. Nevertheless, China's willingness to escalate this dispute has varied widely over time, as Beijing initiated major crises in September 1954, August 1958, and July 1995. The importance of the island, China's coercive means, and its nondemocratic political institutions are clearly part of the story, but these constant features fail to explain why China resorted to force at certain moments but not at other times.

To explain such variation, this chapter outlines two general theories that explain how states manage territorial disputes. Although this book examines China's many disputes, I frame the analysis in terms of general theory for several reasons. How states behave in territorial conflicts is a basic problem in international relations with clear relevance beyond China. Likewise, China is only one of many great powers involved in such disputes, which suggests that explanations of its behavior should be rooted in theories of cooperation and escalation. Finally, examining China's disputes in terms of general theory facilitates comparisons with other countries, which can illuminate the dynamics of territorial conflict more broadly.

Building on previous studies, I examine three generic strategies that national leaders can adopt to achieve a state's territorial goals. The selection of a strategy precedes the final outcome of a dispute, which depends on the response of the opposing side. A delaying strategy involves doing nothing, whereby states maintain their territorial claims through public declarations but neither offer concessions nor use force. Importantly, states can delay by participating in negotiations while refusing to compromise. A cooperation strategy excludes the threat or use of force and involves an offer either to transfer control of some or all of the contested land to the opposing side or to drop claims to land held by the other state. Such compromise almost always precedes the final settlement of a dispute in a bilateral treaty or agreement, even in those settlements where one state drops its entire claim. By contrast, an escalation strategy involves the threat or use of force to seize land or coerce an opponent in a territorial dispute.[4]

As China's behavior in the Taiwan conflict demonstrates, states frequently delay and do nothing because the alternatives are costly. Cooperation is costly because concessions over national sovereignty and territory can carry a high domestic political price, which may result in social unrest or creation of a reputation abroad for weakness. Escalation contains

---

[4] See, for example, Huth, *Standing Your Ground.*

many risks as well, including the uncertainty associated with spirals of hostility or domestic political punishment for military defeat in addition to the human and material costs of war. As a result, from a national leader's perspective, continuing a territorial dispute with a delaying strategy is often better than offering concessions or failing to gain disputed land on the battlefield.[5]

Under certain conditions, however, strategies of cooperation or escalation become more attractive than delay. To explain why and when a state shifts from delaying to adopting either of these strategies, the central task is to identify those factors that increase the price a state pays for maintaining a claim when compared to the alternatives. Toward this end, the theories presented below adopt a state-centric approach that Stephen Krasner developed and other scholars have adopted and refined.[6]

Under a state-centric approach, the state is viewed as a unitary actor that exists apart from the society that it governs. The state seeks to maximize its autonomy to ensure both its survival abroad and its self-preservation at home.[7] To achieve these goals, the state must manage varied challenges. They can be external, such as threats from other states in the international arena to its power or territory. They can also be internal, such as coups, revolts, revolutions, secessions, or the collapse of law and order—anything that threatens the authority and control of the state within its borders. In this approach, national leaders craft and implement policy to advance the interests of the state as a whole, not their personal power or private welfare. The survival of the state trumps individual concerns, as any one leader's ability for private gain depends on the continued existence of the state. In the realm of foreign policy, then, national leaders and the executive branch embody the state and act on its behalf.[8]

---

[5] Delaying may also carry specific benefits because it allows a state to buy time to strengthen its tactical military position or maintain domestic support from key constituencies. Delaying is especially useful for states that occupy a majority of disputed land because the passage of time consolidates a favorable status quo. The sources of delay in interstate conflicts such as territorial disputes are a topic that deserves further study.

[6] Stephen D. Krasner, *Defending the National Interest: Raw Materials Investments and U.S. Foreign Policy* (Princeton, N.J.: Princeton University Press, 1978). Also see Thomas J. Christensen, *Useful Adversaries: Grand Strategy, Domestic Mobilization, and Sino-American Conflict, 1947–1958* (Princeton, N.J.: Princeton University Press, 1996); Scott Cooper, "State-Centric Balance-of-Threat Theory: Explaining the Misunderstood Gulf Cooperation Council," *Security Studies*, vol. 13, no. 2 (Winter 2003): 306–349; David A. Lake, "The State and American Trade Strategy in the Pre-hegemonic Era," *International Organization*, vol. 42, no. 1 (1988): 33–58; Michael Mastanduno, David A. Lake, and G. John Ikenberry, "Toward a Realist Theory of State Action," *International Studies Quarterly*, vol. 33, no. 4 (December 1989): 457–474; Fareed Zakaria, *From Wealth to Power: The Unusual Origins of America's World Role* (Princeton, N.J.: Princeton University Press, 1998).

[7] On "self-preservation," see Mastanduno, Lake, and Ikenberry, "Toward," 463.

[8] Krasner, *Defending the National Interest*, 10–11.

At first glance, these assumptions may appear to be too constricting. After all, scholars have demonstrated that societal interest groups, elite factions, leaders' private interests, and bureaucracies can influence foreign policy decisions. Nevertheless, a state-centric approach is well suited for the study of territorial disputes. First, as territorial disputes are conflicts between nations over the control and ownership of land, they involve the core interests of states: the scope of national sovereignty and degree of territorial integrity. Unlike other policy areas, these interests can be deduced from the goals of survival and self-preservation, which require a state's exclusive control over its territory.

Second, by casting the state as an autonomous actor inhabiting both international and domestic arenas, a state-centric approach suggests that a wide range of factors can create incentives for cooperation or escalation in territorial disputes. As the state seeks simultaneously survival abroad and self-preservation at home, foreign policy can be used to advance its internal goals while domestic policy can be employed to enhance its security abroad. Potential explanations of state behavior are not restricted to either the domestic or the international level of analysis, but result from the challenges that the state encounters both at home and abroad. Even though the unit of analysis is the state, it is not a black box whose internal dynamics are assumed away or deemed irrelevant to national leaders' decisions made on behalf of the state.

Third, the emphasis on the state's domestic interests in addition to its foreign ones permits a more nuanced understanding of the sources and degree of state power in international relations. Scholars in the classical and neoclassical realist traditions have recognized the importance of the domestic components of state power that Hans Morgenthau described as the "the quality of government" and "national morale" in addition to standard measures of military and economic capabilities.[9] Scholars of international relations are only now beginning to study the effects of these internal dimensions of state power.[10] A state-centric approach offers one framework for incorporating these more nuanced elements of national power and their effects on foreign policy.

This chapter proceeds as follows. The next three sections outline the theories that form the core of the book. As cooperation and conflict are distinct phenomena of interest in the study of international relations, I

[9] Hans J. Morgenthau, *Politics among Nations: The Struggle for Power and Peace*, 3rd ed. (New York: Knopf, 1960), 110–148. For a detailed discussion, see Randall Schweller, "The Progressiveness of Neoclassical Realism," in Colin Elman and Miriam Fendius Elman, eds., *Progress in International Relations Theory: Appraising the Field* (Cambridge, Mass.: MIT Press, 2003), 311–348.

[10] Randall Schweller, *Unanswered Threats: Political Constraints on the Balance of Power* (Princeton, N.J.: Princeton University Press, 2006).

provide first a theory of cooperation in territorial disputes and then a theory of escalation in territorial disputes. Although strategies of cooperation and escalation are linked, it is useful analytically to examine them individually, as they reflect very different choices that states may make in managing their territorial disputes. I also introduce alternative arguments that may explain the selection of these same strategies in particular conflicts. In the final section of this chapter and in the remainder of the book, I shift the focus to China's territorial disputes, testing my theories and the potential alternatives in twenty-three unique conflicts from 1949 to 2005.

Two phenomena in the study of territorial disputes lie beyond the scope of the theories presented in this book. The first is the sources of the delaying strategy in territorial disputes. To identify those factors that increase the attractiveness of either cooperation or escalation relative to delay, I assume that delaying is the least costly strategy for a state to pursue but I do not seek to explain why and when states might adopt this strategy. The second phenomenon that lies beyond the scope of this project is the initiation of territorial disputes in the first place. Although this is an important question, the theories outlined below and explored in the remainder of this book are limited to explaining decisions to cooperate or escalate in existing disputes.

Cooperation in Territorial Disputes

Although territorial disputes between states are high-stakes contests, compromise is not infrequent. In one major study by Paul Huth and Todd Allee, approximately 50 percent of territorial disputes were settled through a bilateral agreement or arbitration, usually involving compromise by one or both of the contesting states.[11] Compromise is possible because claiming sovereignty over another's land carries some price or opportunity cost for the states involved. When these costs outweigh the value of contested land, compromise becomes more attractive than delay. The key to explaining compromise, then, lies in identifying those events that increase the price a state pays for maintaining a dispute relative to the value of the territory at stake. These factors are most likely to stem from changes in the overall foreign or domestic security environment in which one state pursues and maintains territorial claims against another state.

[11] Todd L. Allee and Paul K. Huth, "When Are Governments Able to Reach Negotiated Settlement Agreements? An Analysis of Dispute Resolution in Territorial Disputes, 1919–1995," in Harvey Starr, ed., *Approaches, Levels, and Methods of Analysis in International Politics* (New York: Palgrave Macmillan, 2006), 14.

Given an active dispute, delaying (maintaining the dispute but doing nothing to compromise or escalate) is usually the least costly strategy for a national leader to adopt. Nevertheless, disputing land controlled or claimed by another state always carries some price. By challenging another state's sovereignty, territorial claims foster uncertainty about the security of the most vital of national interests, territorial integrity, and mistrust about the intentions of the opposing state more broadly. Uncertainty and mistrust, in turn, sustain poor or tense diplomatic relations that limit the willingness of states to engage in or deepen cooperation with each other, creating security, diplomatic, or economic opportunity costs for contesting land.[12] Disputes are also costly because of the aggressive reputation or hostile image that a state may foster by maintaining territorial claims. Other states might be wary of cooperating with a country that challenges another's sovereignty, one of the most basic norms in international society.[13] Finally, maintaining a dispute is costly because the means necessary to defend a state's claim to contested land consume scarce resources at the expense of other national priorities, foreign or domestic, especially once a dispute has been militarized.

The cost a state bears for pressing a territorial claim opens a bargaining space in which concessions over contested land can be exchanged for others goals that a state may seek. The size of the bargaining space depends on changes in the overall security environment in which the dispute occurs, which determines the value of relations with the opposing state relative to the land being contested. When the importance of bilateral ties with the opposing state increases, cooperation in a dispute will become more attractive than continuing to press claims and delay settlement. Given the potentially high stakes that motivate states to claim territory in the first place, only significant or sharp changes in the context of a dispute are likely to raise the benefits of improving ties with the opposing side relative to the importance of contested land. As a result, threats to a state's external security or its internal self-preservation provide the most likely sources of compromise in territorial disputes.

Even though the cost of claiming another's land creates a bargaining space in which concessions can be offered, a state's willingness to compromise depends on the underlying value of the land being contested. The greater the importance of the territory at stake, the higher the price a state will be willing to pay before considering to compromise or offer

---

[12] On economic opportunity costs, see Beth A. Simmons, "Rules over Real Estate: Trade, Territorial Conflict, and International Borders as Institution," *Journal of Conflict Resolution*, vol. 49, no. 6 (December 2005), 823–848.

[13] Hedley Bull, *The Anarchical Society: A Study of Order in World Politics* (New York: Columbia University Press, 1977).

concessions. In most disputes, some bargaining space exists for trading territorial concessions in exchange for improved relations and deepened ties with the opposing side. In some conflicts, however, one or more of the disputants may see no possible trade, which endows the dispute with perceived indivisibility and increases prohibitively the size of side payments necessary for compromise to be more attractive than delay.[14] Such bargaining space is greatly reduced, for example, in disputes over areas populated by co–ethnics of one or more of the disputing states, such as Kashmir.[15] As Huth and Allee have demonstrated, democracies are less likely than authoritarian states to compromise in disputes over land populated by ethnic co-nationals lest the leaders be voted out of office in the next election.[16]

The onset of external or internal threats to a state will not necessarily result in an offer to compromise. A key scope condition for my theory of cooperation is that the opposing side can provide assistance in exchange for territorial concessions. States trade concessions over territory to improve ties with a territorial adversary because they want something in return, usually assistance to counter a more immediate threat that they face. National leaders believe that by compromising over territorial claims, other state goals will be advanced. Unless leaders can expect something in return for their state's territorial concessions, they have no incentive to compromise, even when a threat arises.

External Threats and Cooperation in Territorial Disputes

For scholars of international relations, the logic of external threats as a source of compromise in territorial disputes is relatively straightforward. Anarchic competition among states for survival places a premium on leaders assessing the costs and benefits of different foreign policies so that they can maximize their state's power and influence in the international system.[17] Territorial disputes are no exception, as the net benefit of contesting land depends on other goals that a state pursues. As the external

---

[14] On indivisibility and territory, see Stacie Goddard, "Uncommon Ground: Indivisible Territory and the Politics of Legitimacy," *International Organization*, vol. 60, no. 1 (Winter 2006): 35–68; Ron E. Hassner, "'To Halve and to Hold': Conflicts over Sacred Space and the Problem of Indivisibility," *Security Studies*, vol. 12, no. 4 (Summer 2003): 1–33; Monica Duffy Toft, *The Geography of Ethnic Violence: Identity, Interests, and the Indivisibility of Territory* (Princeton, N.J.: Princeton University Press, 2003); Barbara F. Walter, "Explaining the Intractability of Territorial Conflict," *International Studies Review*, vol. 5, no. 4 (December 2003): 137–153.

[15] Huth, *Standing Your Ground*, 149.

[16] Huth and Allee, *Democratic Peace*, 198–205.

[17] Kenneth N. Waltz, *Theory of International Politics* (New York: McGraw-Hill, 1979).

environment in which a state maintains a dispute changes, so do the costs and benefits of pursuing its claim. When a state confronts threats from abroad, the cost of disputing a piece of land increases if that conflict prevents improved ties with the opposing state in the dispute that might be mobilized to counter such threats.[18]

Two types of external threats to a state's security are likely to create incentives for compromise. External threats to a state's relative power position, especially from the strongest states in the system, are one source of cooperation in territorial disputes. The logic of this explanation draws on the insights of structural realism.[19] These threats occur when an imbalance of power exists that increases the importance of improved ties with a territorial adversary relative to the value of disputed land. A state declining in power relative to other states may pursue compromise to maintain its influence and arrest its decline. A state rising relative to others may offer concessions to prevent the formation of a balancing coalition by stronger states. A state whose power position is steady or static, however, has few incentives to compromise.

Competition with a specific state is a second type of external threat that can be a source of cooperation in territorial disputes. The logic of compromise in this context draws on balance of threat theory and the literature on rivalries.[20] This type of threat arises during the initiation or intensification of security competition with a specific country. During these contests, territorial disputes with third parties become much more costly to pursue when they limit a state's ability to counter its rival through either internal or external balancing efforts, such as expanding its armed forces or forming alliances.

When either type of external threat arises, the cost of maintaining a territorial dispute increases if the conflict limits or blocks assistance that could help counter the external threat. Thus, a state facing external threats is likely to trade territorial concessions in exchange for assistance that enhances its ability to achieve one of several security goals: (1) to form or consolidate an alliance that strengthens its military power and diplomatic influence; (2) to deny potential allies to an adversary or rival by improving ties with third parties; or (3) to facilitate internal balancing

---

[18] One exception here would be disputes over strategic territory that can alter a state's relative position in the international system. See James D. Fearon, "Rationalist Explanations For War," *International Organization*, vol. 49, no. 3 (Summer 1995): 408–409.

[19] On structural realism, see Waltz, *Theory of International Politics*. This logic, however, is not offered as a general test of structural realism, only as a hypothesis for compromise in territorial disputes.

[20] Paul F. Diehl and Gary Goertz, *War and Peace in International Rivalry* (Ann Arbor: University of Michigan Press, 2000); Stephen M. Walt, *The Origins of Alliances* (Ithaca, N.Y.: Cornell University Press, 1987).

through increased bilateral trade or the marshaling of resources for defense. When external threats arise, a state is likely to pursue compromise to capture one or more of these benefits. Cooperation is most likely to occur in disputes that are not an asset in countering the new external threat or that drain military and diplomatic resources away from this threat. In the absence of such external threats, a state will delay settlement and maintain its territorial claims.

Recent history provides a number of examples of external threats creating incentives to compromise in territorial disputes. At the dawn of the Cold War, the Soviet Union suddenly dropped territorial claims against Turkey in 1953 and Iran in 1954. Given the growing global competition with the United States, these disputes became more costly for Moscow to pursue. By dropping its claims, Moscow hoped to improve diplomatic ties with these states to balance against the United States.[21] Likewise, the imperatives of the Cold War had a similar effect on territorial disputes in Western Europe. In October 1956, France, for example, agreed to the incorporation of the Saar region into West Germany, concluding that maintaining the nascent NATO alliance and the cohesion of Western Europe outweighed any potential territorial gains.[22]

Viewing external threats as a source of cooperation in territorial disputes is consistent with some of the empirical findings from the recent literature. According to studies by Huth and Allee, for example, states that are formal alliance partners are more likely to offer concessions and settle their territorial disputes because the need to maintain the alliance and counter a common threat outweighs whatever gains might be achieved in the territorial dispute.[23] Likewise, some studies find that states involved in multiple militarized disputes are more likely to offer concessions.[24] The argument presented here, however, is broader. Based on the context of the dispute, those external threats that increase the value of diplomatic or military aid from an opponent in a territorial dispute should increase the likelihood that a state will offer concessions.

Internal Threats and Cooperation in Territorial Disputes

Unlike external threats, the logic of internal threats as a source of compromise is counterintuitive for most scholars of international relations. Frequently, domestic political conflict within a state is seen as creating

[21] R. H. Dekmejian, "Soviet-Turkish Relations and Politics in the Armenian SSR," *Soviet Studies*, vol. 19, no. 4 (April 1968): 510–525; Basil Dmytryshyn and Frederick Cox, *The Soviet Union and the Middle East* (Princeton, N.J.: Kingston Press, 1987).

[22] Jacques Freymond, *The Saar Conflict, 1945–1955* (London: Stevens, 1960).

[23] Huth, *Standing Your Ground*, 160; Huth and Allee, *Democratic Peace*, 195.

[24] Allee and Huth, "When Are Governments," 27.

strong incentives only for leaders to use force, not to cooperate. In particular, diversionary war theory claims that leaders facing internal threats to their political survival will pursue conflict abroad, a claim presented most recently and forcefully in arguments by Edward Mansfield and Jack Snyder about democratization and war.[25] Nevertheless, threats to a state's domestic position can increase the benefits of compromise in a territorial dispute relative to delay. These are threats to regime security, defined as the strength, stability, and legitimacy of a state's core political institutions.[26]

The logic of internal threats to regime security creating incentives for compromise in territorial disputes advances earlier scholarship on domestic politics and foreign policy. To explain alignment in the developing world, Steven David argues that leaders "omnibalance," forming alliances to balance against the most pressing threat that they face, foreign or domestic.[27] For many national leaders, especially in authoritarian states and new democracies, the most pressing threats to their political survival emanate from internal challenges such as rebellions and coups.[28] To maximize their tenure in office, leaders form alliances, even with external adversaries, to balance against more immediate internal foes.[29]

When internal threats to regime security arise, a state may use foreign policy in addition to domestic tools such as repression to enhance its internal security. It can pursue cooperation in exchange for different types of support from neighboring states: (1) to gain direct assistance in countering internal threats, such as denying material support to opposition

[25] Jack S. Levy, "The Diversionary Theory of War: A Critique," in Manus I. Midlarsky, ed., *Handbook of War Studies* (Boston: Unwin Hyman, 1989), 259–288; Edward D. Mansfield and Jack L. Snyder, *Electing to Fight: Why Emerging Democracies Go to War* (Cambridge, Mass.: MIT Press, 2005).

[26] For an earlier version of this argument, see M. Taylor Fravel, "Regime Insecurity and International Cooperation: Explaining China's Compromises in Territorial Disputes," *International Security*, vol. 30, no. 2 (Fall 2005): 46–83. On regime insecurity, Joe D. Hagan, "Regimes, Political Oppositions, and the Comparative Analysis of Foreign Policy," in Charles F. Hermann, Charles W. Kegley, Jr., and James N. Rosenau, eds., *New Directions in the Study of Foreign Policy* (Boston: Allen Unwin, 1987), 346.

[27] Steven R. David, "Explaining Third World Alignment," *World Politics*, vol. 43, no. 2 (January 1991): 233–256.

[28] On internal insecurity and foreign policy, see Mohammed Ayoob, *The Third World Security Predicament: State Making, Regional Conflict, and the International System* (Boulder, Colo.: Lynne Rienner, 1995); Edward Azar and Chung-In Moon, eds., *National Security in the Third World* (Aldershot: Edward Elgar Publishing, 1988); Brian L. Job, ed., *The Insecurity Dilemma: National Security of Third World States* (Boulder, Colo.: Lynne Rienner, 1992).

[29] For a similar explanation of Egypt's alliances, see Michael N. Barnett and Jack S. Levy, "Domestic Sources of Alliances and Alignments: The Case of Egypt, 1962–73," *International Organization*, vol. 45, no. 3 (Summer 1991): 369–395.

groups; (2) to marshal resources for domestic policy priorities, not external defense; or (3) to bolster international recognition of the regime, leveraging the status-quo bias within international society to delegitimize domestic challengers.[30] In addition, when a state faces internal threats, it may pursue cooperation to enhance its external security by preempting potential attempts by other states to profit from its internal woes. These effects of regime insecurity on foreign policy are thus paradoxical: efforts to consolidate control and authority at home, often through repression, increase its willingness to cooperate abroad. Such behavior is peaceful, but its root cause is not necessarily benign.

Recent scholarship provides general support for identifying regime insecurity as a source of international cooperation. In a broad study of the origins of détente, Jeremi Suri describes how social turmoil in France, Germany, the United States, China, and the Soviet bloc created strong incentives for cooperation among the superpowers.[31] Using quantitative analysis, Giacomo Chiozza and Hein Goemans find that politically insecure leaders are less likely to initiate an international crisis than politically secure ones.[32] Although Chiozza and Goemans do not test directly whether insecure leaders are more likely to compromise in international disputes, the relationship they find between leadership insecurity and conflict avoidance is consistent with the logic of regime insecurity as a source of cooperation. Christopher Way likewise finds that increased political insecurity is linked with elite support for international financial liberalization to facilitate economic development.[33] The imperative to counter shared internal threats to regime security has also been used to explain the formation of regional organizations, such as the Association of Southeast Asian States (ASEAN) and the Gulf Cooperation Council (GCC), to weaken internal communist and Islamist challengers, respectively.[34]

Two types of internal threats to regime security are likely to create incentives for compromise in territorial disputes. Internal threats to territorial integrity provide one source of such cooperation. These threats usually occur as unrest or rebellions that challenge the most basic indicator

---

[30] On external validation as a response to internal insecurity, see Mastanduno, Lake, and Ikenberry, "Toward," 466–467.

[31] Jeremi Suri, *Power and Protest: Global Revolution and the Rise of Detente* (Cambridge, Mass.: Harvard University Press, 2003).

[32] Giacomo Chiozza and H. E. Goemans, "Peace through Insecurity: Tenure and International Conflict," *Journal of Conflict Resolution*, vol. 47, no. 4 (August 2003): 443–467.

[33] Christopher R. Way, "Political Insecurity and the Diffusion of Financial Market Regulation," *The ANNALS of the American Academy of Political and Social Science*, vol. 598, no. 1 (2005): 125–144.

[34] Cooper, "State-Centric"; Michael Leifer, *ASEAN and the Security of South-East Asia* (London: Routledge, 1989).

of a state's authority—administrative control of the territory it governs. When a rebellion or insurgency erupts near international boundaries, territorial disputes with states adjacent to the area of unrest become much more costly to pursue because neighboring states can provide a range of support for rebels or even seek to intervene in the conflict. A state experiencing unrest or rebellion near its borders will be more likely to trade territorial concessions for a neighboring state's direct assistance in crushing the uprising, such as (1) sealing borders; (2) attacking rebel bases; (3) denying refuge or material support to rebels; (4) extraditing rebel leaders; (5) minimizing inadvertent escalation during hot pursuit; (6) providing assurances not to intervene; or (7) affirming the internally threatened state's sovereignty over the region of unrest.[35]

Internal threats to territorial integrity played a prominent role, for example, in an attempt to settle the Iran-Iraq dispute over the Shatt-al-Arab waterway. For most of the twentieth century, Iraq had contested agreements granting Iran partial access to this important line of communication, claiming that the boundary lay on the Iranian bank of the river. In 1975, however, Iraq dropped this claim, agreeing to use the main channel of navigation as the boundary. At the time, the Ba'thist government established in 1968 was seeking to consolidate its control over the country, especially in Kurdish regions that were receiving aid from Iran. Fearing the long-term consequences of this Iranian support for Iraq's territorial integrity, Saddam Hussein traded territorial concessions over the Shatt-al-Arab for an Iranian agreement to cease support for the Kurds.[36]

Internal threats to political stability are a second source of cooperation in territorial disputes. These threats appear in the form of social unrest such as large-scale protests or economic decline that question the legitimacy of a given regime to govern. When such threats arise, even when far from the borders, territorial disputes become much more costly to pursue because they distract national leaders from adequately addressing domestic unrest. A state facing political instability will be more likely to trade territorial concessions for another state's assistance in overcoming internal unrest, such as (1) increasing trade and investment to stimulate economic development, raise living standards, and improve legitimacy; (2) minimizing external tensions so the internally threatened state can marshal its resources for domestic priorities; (3) delegitimizing the threatened state's internal opponents; (4) refraining from attempts to profit from

---

[35] In the absence of a territorial dispute with a neighboring state, one observable implication of this argument is that leaders will offer concessions in other disputes for cooperation to improve regime security.

[36] Jasim M. Abdulghani, *Iraq & Iran: The Years of Crisis* (London: Croom Helm, 1984), 155; Alan J. Day, ed., *Border and Territorial Disputes*, 2nd ed. (Burnt Mill: Longman, 1987), 237–238.

the threatened regime's internal weakness; or (5) affirming externally the threatened state's legitimacy to govern its society.

Argentina and Uruguay, for example, had disputed a 1916 boundary delimitation agreement and the location of the boundary in the Rio de la Plata. In 1971, the embattled Argentine junta under General Alejandro Lanusse compromised in the dispute, resulting in an agreement that Juan Perón signed in 1973.[37] Similarly, political unrest played a role in efforts, which ultimately failed, to settle a long-standing border dispute between Ecuador and Peru. After taking office in the early 1990s, Peru's president Alberto Fujimori faced the twin challenges of an economic crisis and pressure from Shining Path guerrillas who controlled part of the country. In response, in 1992, he proposed a comprehensive settlement to his Ecuadorian counterpart, which included access to the Atlantic Ocean.[38]

Despite the powerful intuition behind diversionary war theory, regime insecurity offers a plausible source of compromise in territorial disputes for several reasons. The first is that the logic underpinning diversionary war theory is intuitively compelling but incomplete.[39] Although the theory posits a domestic benefit for leaders who initiate a conflict abroad, it does not compare escalation to other foreign policies that might be adopted to strengthen a leader's domestic political security. Moreover, arguments in support of the theory fail to specify if leaders take such action when the state's control over society is threatened or only when their own personal power is at risk. Likewise, although tensions in territorial disputes may facilitate efforts by leaders to mobilize societal support, they are arguably the most dangerous type of issue for leaders to manipulate, as failure to achieve the state's territorial objectives would likely result in even greater domestic punishment for the leader. Finally, quantitative analysis has produced strikingly mixed and often contradictory empirical results regarding the correlation between domestic unrest and external conflict that underpins the logic of diversionary war.[40]

[37] Joseph S. Tulchin, *Argentina and the United States: A Conflicted Relationship* (Boston: Twayne, 1990), 136–137.

[38] David Scott Palmer, "Peru-Ecuador Border Conflict: Missed Opportunities, Misplaced Nationalism, and Multilateral Peacekeeping," *Journal of Interamerican Studies and World Affairs*, vol. 39, no. 3 (Autumn 1997): 115–116; Beth A. Simmons, *Territorial Disputes and Their Resolution: The Case of Ecuador and Peru*, Peaceworks no. 27 (Washington, D.C.: United States Institute of Peace, 1999), 11–12.

[39] T. Clifton Morgan and Kenneth N. Bickers, "Domestic Discontent and the Use of Force," *Journal of Conflict Resolution*, vol. 36, no. 1 (March 1992): 25–52.

[40] For examples of studies that find a positive relationship between domestic conflict and dispute escalation, see Kurt Dassel and Eric Reinhardt, "Domestic Strife and the Initiation of Violence at Home and Abroad," *American Journal of Political Science*, vol. 43, no. 1 (January 1999): 56–85; Graeme A. M. Davies, "Domestic Strife and the Initiation of International Conflicts," *Journal of Conflict Resolution*, vol. 46, no. 5 (October 2002): 672–

Second, the majority of territorial disputes in the twentieth century have involved at least one state with an authoritarian political system, where internal threats to regime security are arguably most common.[41] As their power is not secured by popular elections, the rule of law, or constitutional order, authoritarian systems are more prone to extra-constitutional attempts to acquire and maintain political power that directly challenge the state, such as popular uprisings, coups, revolutions, and secession.[42] In the Huth and Allee study, about two-thirds of states coded as challengers in territorial disputes are nondemocracies.[43] Although authoritarian states in this study are on average less likely than democracies to initiate negotiations in territorial disputes, they nevertheless account for the majority of absolute attempts to pursue peaceful settlement. Moreover, authoritarian states are just as likely as democratic ones to offer concessions once negotiations begin, a regularity that existing research cannot explain.[44]

Third, many authoritarian regimes face limits to their state's internal authority or "broadcasting power" within the state's borders. In Africa, for example, limited broadcasting power served as a strong incentive for states not to initiate territorial disputes in the period following decolonization.[45] When broadcasting power is limited, leaders have fewer domestic tools for countering internal threats and the potential for neighbors to influence political stability increases, which creates strong incentives not to initiate territorial claims in the first place.

692; Patrick James and John R. Oneal, "The Influence of Domestic and International Politics on the President's Use of Force," *Journal of Conflict Resolution*, vol. 35, no. 2 (June 1991): 307–332.

For examples of studies that fail to find a positive relationship between domestic political conflict and dispute escalation, see Chiozza and Goemans, "Peace through Insecurity"; Brett Ashley Leeds and David R. Davis, "Domestic Political Vulnerability and International Disputes," *Journal of Conflict Resolution*, vol. 41, no. 6 (December 1997): 814–834; James Meernik and Peter Waterman, "The Myth of the Diversionary Use of Force by American Presidents," *Political Research Quarterly*, vol. 49, no. 3 (September 1996): 575–590.

[41] In one data set, authoritarian dyads account for 43.7 percent of dyad-years, while mixed authoritarian-democratic dyads account for 45.1 percent of dyad-years. See Paul K. Huth and Todd L. Allee, "Domestic Political Accountability and the Escalation and Settlement of International Disputes," *Journal of Conflict Resolution*, vol. 46, no. 6 (December 2002): 754–790, with replication data from http://www.yale.edu/unsy/jcr/jcrdatadec02.htm.

[42] David, "Explaining Third World Alignment."

[43] In the Huth and Allee replication data, democracies are those states with a POLITY net democracy score equal to or greater than 6. Challengers are those states that seek to alter the status quo in a dispute. See note 41.

[44] Democratic targets, however, are more likely to offer concessions than authoritarian ones. Huth and Allee, *Democratic Peace*, 199–201.

[45] Jeffrey Herbst, *States and Power in Africa: Comparative Lessons in Authority and Control* (Princeton, N.J.: Princeton University Press, 2000).

Alternative Explanations for Cooperation

The theory of cooperation outlined above contains two mechanisms that explain why and when states might pursue an otherwise costly policy of compromise in territorial disputes. The first stresses the state's external security environment in which the dispute occurs, namely threats to a state posed by changes in its relative power or by competition with a rival. The second emphasizes changes in the state's domestic security environment, namely internal threats to regime security that revolts or legitimacy crises create. These mechanicisms of cooperation identify factors that increase the cost of contesting land relative to compromising and explain why such factors create incentives for cooperation—because trading territorial concessions for assistance can strengthen the state, either at home or abroad.

In the parlance of contemporary international relations theory, this theory of cooperation may be viewed as rationalist. One important alternative explanation for cooperation is ideational. Tanisha Fazal identifies the emergence in the international system of a norm against territorial conquest from the 1920s, one that became entrenched after World War II.[46] Although Fazal does not examine compromise in territorial disputes, the presence of a norm against conquest suggests that a state may be more likely to offer concessions because the alternative of changing a territorial status quo, through negotiation much less than force, is viewed as increasingly illegitimate and thus more costly.

The evidence supporting the emergence and consolidation of a norm against conquest is persuasive. At the same time, its role in the settlement of territorial disputes is less clear. Although one implication of the norm's emergence is that a state should be less willing to use force in a territorial dispute, one cannot conclude that it will be more willing to offer territorial concessions. Although the norm may be linked with a lower incidence of forceful territorial change, it may also further underpin the value of maintaining a delaying strategy in a dispute. In other words, even if this norm is present, a theory is still required to explain why a state would choose to compromise in its territorial disputes instead of persisting with delay. Also, because such norms are relatively constant once they emerge, they are unlikely to account for the change over time in any given state's

---

[46] Tanisha M. Fazal, *State Death: The Politics and Geography of Conquest, Occupation, and Annexation* (Princeton, N.J.: Princeton University Press, 2007). Similarly, Mark Zacher posits that the consolidation of a territorial integrity norm has led states to become increasingly acceptant of the territorial status quo and less likely to pursue territorial changes through force. Mark W. Zacher, "The Territorial Integrity Norm: International Boundaries and the Use of Force," *International Organization*, vol. 55, no. 2 (Spring 2001): 215–250.

decisions to offer compromises, especially after the norm has become entrenched. My theory of cooperation offers one explanation for the timing and motivation for compromise, even for states that embrace the norm.

Democratic peace theory offers a second alternative explanation for cooperation in territorial disputes. Democracies rarely if ever go to war with each other, including over territory.[47] The pacific tendencies of democratic states suggest that they ought to be more likely to compromise in territorial disputes. Although democratic peace theory details conditions under which the use of force will decline, it does not necessarily follow that democracies will be more likely to offer concessions. Similar to the norm against conquest, democracy might just reinforce a preference for delay. In one comprehensive study of territorial disputes, democracies were more likely to offer concessions in disputes with each other but were no more likely than nondemocracies to offer concessions overall.[48] Instead, a theory is needed to explain why and when both kinds of states offer territorial concessions to nondemocracies.

Theories of economic interdependence provide a final alternative explanation for a state's willingness to offer otherwise costly concessions in territorial disputes. States with high or growing levels of economic interdependence may be more likely to compromise in their disputes in order to increase trade or investment blocked by the presence of a dispute.[49] Arguments about the declining value of territory as a national security asset and a "capitalist peace" strengthen the appeal of this explanation.[50] Nevertheless, interdependence is unlikely to explain individual decisions to compromise. One problem is that asymmetrical interdependence can also be a source of leverage in bargaining over a dispute. Moreover, even when a state does compromise to remove a barrier to trade and investment with a neighbor, this fact alone fails to illuminate a state's motivations. Such actions could easily have been motivated by external or internal threats instead, which increase the value of development as a means to achieve other goals and enhance its security either at home or abroad.

---

[47] Huth, *Standing Your Ground*, 136; Huth and Allee, "Domestic Political Accountability," 251–257; Bruce Russett, *Grasping the Democratic Peace* (Princeton, N.J.: Princeton University Press, 1993).

[48] Hensel, "Contentious Issues," 100; Huth and Allee, *Democratic Peace*, 199–214. Under certain conditions, democracies are even less likely to offer concessions. See Huth and Allee, *Democratic Peace*, 199–201.

[49] Simmons, "Rules."

[50] Stephen G. Brooks, *Producing Security: Multinational Corporations, Globalization, and the Changing Calculus of Conflict* (Princeton, N.J.: Princeton University Press, 2005); Eric Gartzke, "The Capitalist Peace," *American Journal of Political Science*, vol. 51, no. 1 (January 2007): 166–191.

Escalation in Territorial Disputes

The study of territorial disputes generally highlights military power as a key variable in explaining the escalation of these conflicts to high levels of violence. At one level, this finding is unsurprising: one purpose of a military is to seize and secure land from an opposing force. Only states with some military capabilities would be able to use force over territory in the first place. At the same time, this finding leaves many questions unanswered about the causes of escalation in territorial disputes. Although stronger states may more easily employ force to achieve their territorial objectives, it is unclear why and when they do so—whether they are driven by greed or insecurity.

To explain why and when states choose to escalate territorial disputes, I shift the focus from a state's overall security environment to its claim strength or bargaining power in specific conflicts. In examining a state's relative position in a territorial dispute, I extend preventive war theory to a new domain. A preventive war is defined as "a war fought *now* in order to avoid the risks of war under worsening circumstances *later*."[51] As a state's overall power declines, its leaders fear the long-term consequences of their state's weakening position in the international system: a decrease in future bargaining power and a higher risk of war later under worse conditions. As Jack Levy describes, these concerns generate "preventive motivations" to use force, as war sooner rather than later becomes an increasingly attractive alternative for lessening the effects of decline or even maintaining a state's influence.[52] Importantly, war is chosen even though no specific conflict of interest with another state, or *causus belli*, may exist, only uncertainty about the future. In empirical studies, the incentives created by these power shifts are called windows. A "window of vulnerability" is a growing defensive weakness, while a "window of opportunity" is a fading offensive advantage.[53] Both identify different sources of the same "now-is-better-than-later" logic.[54]

---

[51] Jack S. Levy, "Declining Power and the Preventive Motivation for War," *World Politics*, vol. 40, no. 1 (October 1987): 82. Also see Stephen Van Evera, *Causes of War: Power and the Roots of Conflict* (Ithaca, N.Y.: Cornell University Press, 1999), 73–104. For the theory of dynamic differentials that draws heavily on power shifts, see Dale C. Copeland, *Origins of Major War* (Ithaca, N.Y.: Cornell University Press, 2000).

[52] Levy, "Declining Power."

[53] Van Evera, *Causes*, 74.

[54] For applications, see Copeland, *Origins of Major War*, 56–117; Stephen Van Evera, "The Cult of the Offensive and the Origins of the First World War," *International Security*, vol. 9, no. 1 (Summer 1984): 58–107. Also, Victor D. Cha, "Hawk Engagement and Preventive Defense on the Korean Peninsula," *International Security*, vol. 27, no. 1 (2002): 40–78; Jack S. Levy and Joseph R. Gochal, "Democracy and Preventive War: Israel and the

TABLE 1.1
Claim Strength in Territorial Disputes

	Amount of contested territory occupied	
Power projection	Small	Large
High	Strong	Dominant
Low	Inferior	Weak

In territorial disputes, states by definition have conflicting interests, over which they compete to gain advantage. A state assesses its position in a dispute in terms of claim strength, defined as bargaining power in the conflict or the ability of each side to control the land that it contests. Importantly, claim strength does not refer to the merits of a state's sovereignty claim under international law. The first component of claim strength is the amount of contested territory that a state occupies. The greater the proportion of disputed land that a state holds, the stronger its position in a dispute because of the costs for the opposing side to change the status quo by force. The second component of claim strength is the ability to project military power over all contested areas, including those that a state claims but does not control. Even if a state holds only a small proportion of disputed land, it may still be able to project power against its adversary over all contested areas. In this context, power projection refers to the local military balance, not a state's overall position in the international system. As most states face multiple security goals, only a portion of their military assets can be devoted to any particular mission, such as defending a territorial claim.

Both components of claim strength constitute a state's bargaining power in a dispute and shape its ability to achieve a favorable territorial settlement at the negotiating table. Although these components are continuous, extreme values can be used to identify four ideal types outlined in table 1.1. When a state's claim is strong or dominant, its leaders can be optimistic about achieving a favorable resolution through diplomacy. By contrast, when a state's claim is weak or inferior, its leaders are likely to be pessimistic about achieving a preferred outcome through diplomacy.

As discussed below, perceptions of change in claim strength create incentives for states to use force. As a state's claim strength increases over

1956 Sinai Campaign," *Security Studies*, vol. 11, no. 2 (Winter 2001/2002): 1–49. On China, see Thomas J. Christensen, "Windows and War: Trend Analysis and Beijing's Use of Force," in Alastair Iain Johnston and Robert S. Ross, eds., *New Directions in the Study of China's Foreign Policy* (Stanford, Calif.: Stanford University Press, 2006), 50–85. This paper had an important impact on my thinking about China's territorial dispute behavior,

time, it should be more optimistic about the final outcome and less likely to use force.[55] When a state's claim strength declines, however, it should be more pessimistic about its ability to achieve its territorial goals and more likely to use force to halt or reverse its decline. The focus on claim strength also points to a second cause of escalation for a state with a weak or especially an inferior claim in a territorial dispute. Such a state will be tempted to use force if its relative military position in a dispute increases suddenly and temporarily, a shift that creates an opportunity to seize land and strengthen its claim.

As in decisions about cooperation, the salience of disputed land is a critical variable in decisions about escalation. All things being equal, the greater the military, economic, or symbolic value of the territory, the greater the sensitivity of a state to changes in its claim strength. The greater the importance of the territory at stake, the greater the potential gains from using force to acquire or defend it. Nevertheless, because salience changes infrequently and is usually constant in any particular territorial conflict, it offers an incomplete explanation for why and when a state would escalate a dispute. A territory's salience can, however, increase in two ways. The first is through the discovery of natural resources, especially petroleum or minerals, which increases the benefits of escalation, especially for the state with the weaker claim.[56] The second is through "lateral pressure" created by one or both states' economic growth, which in turn increases the value of controlling existing resources in disputed areas.[57]

Either a negative or positive shift in bargaining power in a dispute will not necessarily result in the threat or use of force. A key scope condition for my theory of escalation is that the state facing relative decline or a temporary opportunity possesses a viable military option to either seize at least some of the disputed territory it contests or attack its opponent's forces in the territory that the latter controls. I define this as the ability to execute a limited-aims military operation without risking the destruction of a state's standing army or current fighting power. States with very little military power relative to their opponent are unlikely to use force, as the cost of even a limited-aims operation would be too high.

---

although the sources of preventive logic that I describe as driving escalation in China's territorial disputes focus on bargaining power in a conflict, not China's overall position in the international system.

[55] On the perception of power in international relations, see William Curti Wohlforth, *The Elusive Balance: Power and Perceptions during the Cold War* (Ithaca, N.Y.: Cornell University Press, 1993).

[56] Nils Petter Gleditsch, "Armed Conflict and the Environment: A Critique of the Literature," *Journal of Peace Research*, vol. 35, no. 3 (May 1998): 381–400.

[57] Nazli Choucri and Robert Carver North, *Nations in Conflict: National Growth and International Violence* (San Francisco: W. H. Freeman, 1975).

Negative Power Shifts—Territorial Windows of Vulnerability

Territorial conflicts are dynamic contests. States actively compete to strengthen their claim in a dispute, usually by improving their position in the local military balance. Frequently, states will be able to match each other's moves and maintain their relative position. When one state strengthens its position relative to its opponent, however, the other side is more likely to conclude that it is "losing" in the dispute and more likely to use force to prevent or forestall its decline. Although the rising state in the dispute will be more optimistic about the final outcome and less likely to use force, the declining state should be more pessimistic, which increases the value of using force if it possesses the means to do so. Inaction is viewed as more costly in the long run than using force in the short run.[58]

When a state's claim strength declines relative to that of its adversary, its leaders are more likely to use force along two separate pathways. First, the state can use force to seize land and increase the amount of disputed territory under its control and deny contested land to its opponent. Seizures of land are perhaps most common when states race to occupy disputed territory near the start of a conflict. Second, it can threaten or use force to signal resolve to defend its claim and deter threats to its ability to control disputed land. Signaling resolve is more common for states whose position in a dispute is weak or inferior, especially when they lack the capability to project power over the entire area being contested. By using force in response to their state's declining claim strength, national leaders hope to convey information about their true level of resolve in the dispute.[59]

Changes in either component of claim strength can create perceptions of decline and incentives to escalate. First, as the amount of territory that each side controls in a dispute is often fixed, each side's effort to maximize its position in the local balance is the most likely source of a negative shift in claim strength. Military actions should have the greatest effect on perceptions of decline in bargaining power, including (1) increased troop deployments to the area under dispute; (2) fortification of military positions along contested boundaries; (3) the force posture adopted by the adversary's troops near disputed areas; and (4) one side's development of new capabilities for fighting over disputed areas. Political actions can also shape perceptions of resolve to defend disputed land. Such measures include (1) administrative declarations or acts to incorporate contested

---

[58] For a preliminary version of this argument, see M. Taylor Fravel, "Power Shifts and Escalation: Explaining China's Use of Force in Territorial Disputes," *International Security*, vol. 32, no. 3 (Winter 2007/2008): 44–83.

[59] On information and war, see Fearon, "Rationalist Explanations"; R. Harrison Wagner, "Bargaining and War," *American Journal of Political Science*, vol. 44, no. 3 (July 2000): 469–484.

land into the state; (2) infrastructure projects in disputed areas such as road building designed to increase effective control of disputed territory; and (3) plebiscites and elections intended to increase the legitimacy of one side's claim.

Second, although the amount of territory that each side controls is often fixed, it can change under certain circumstances. Such changes will often be viewed as threatening. At times, disputed territory may not be effectively controlled by any of the states involved. This may occur in new disputes when claimants have not yet deployed troops to areas under dispute, or when both states face operational obstacles to policing or securing the disputed area. These conditions allow one side to seize vacant land through fait-accompli tactics, strengthening its bargaining power in a dispute.

As territorial disputes are by definition conflicting claims to the same piece of land, even policies that one state believes to be defensive are frequently viewed by its adversary as offensive. This inherent volatility stems from the security dilemma, which occurs when "many of the means by which a state tries to increase its security decrease the security of others."[60] Although Robert Jervis examined general security competition under conditions of uncertainty, his insight also applies to concrete conflicts of interest such as territorial disputes, where strictly speaking no dilemma exists. As Thomas Christensen has demonstrated, when sovereignty is contested, the consolidation and defense of a territorial status quo can be viewed as aggressive, especially when it entrenches a disadvantage for one side. As a result, both sides in a dispute may see their own actions as defensive responses to the other side's aggression, resulting in spirals of hostility as each seeks to bolster its claim strength and relative position.[61]

Importantly, the effects of relative decline are independent of a state's initial claim strength in a dispute. States with either strong or weak claims will be sensitive to a decline in their bargaining power in a conflict. For a state with a strong or dominant claim, only the prospect of a sharp decline in bargaining power can produce a powerful motivation to use force. For a state with a weak or inferior claim, perceptions of lesser amounts of decline will have a greater impact on its leaders' beliefs about their state's bargaining power. When a state controls little or none of the contested land, even just political pressure that consolidates such a disadvantageous status quo can appear threatening, as this reduces the long-term ability of the state with an inferior claim to achieve its territorial goals.

---

[60] Robert Jervis, "Cooperation under the Security Dilemma," *World Politics*, vol. 30, no. 2 (January 1978): 167–214.

[61] Thomas J. Christensen, "The Contemporary Security Dilemma: Deterring a Taiwan Conflict," *The Washington Quarterly*, vol. 25, no. 4 (Autumn 2002): 7–21.

Examples of negative shifts in claim strength resulting in the escalation of territorial disputes are easy to find. On July 20, 1974, for example, Turkish troops invaded the island of Cyprus. Only six days before, the Greek junta in Athens had ordered a coup overthrowing the Cypriot president, Archbishop Makarios III, and installing a president who was a strong supporter of Cyprus's unification with Greece. To safeguard the interests of Turkish Cypriots and prevent the stationing of Greek forces on Turkey's southern flank, Ankara used force to maintain its claim strength in the dispute.[62] Likewise, declining claim strength was a key factor in Pakistan's decision to attack India over Kashmir in 1965. Following the 1962 war with China, the Indian Army engaged in a substantial modernization drive, which threatened a long-term shift in the local balance of forces in Kashmir, at Pakistan's expense. Pakistan initiated the 1965 war to strengthen its claim before it would be too late to take military action.[63]

Existing research also supports the role of such preventive logic in explaining why and when states threaten or use force in territorial disputes. Although some studies demonstrate that stronger states are more likely to escalate, the most volatile dyads (measured by the frequency of escalation or highest levels of hostility) are usually those with opponents that are evenly matched in terms of military strength. In many cases, somewhat weaker states initiated the use of force.[64] Under such conditions of rough parity, small military actions should have significant long-term implications for each side's bargaining power in a dispute. Likewise, efforts by one state to change the status quo in a dispute are linked with decisions by the other state to use force.[65] Similarly, during periods of decline, imperial powers have resorted to the use of force to communicate resolve to defend the territorial scope of their empire.[66]

A state's overall security environment can also shape perceptions of decline in claim strength and further increase incentives to escalate a territorial dispute. In my theory of cooperation, the presence of either internal or external threats to a state's security are a key cause of compromise. When its claim strength is stable or increasing, a state facing such internal or external threats is likely to trade concessions in a territorial dispute for military, economic, or diplomatic cooperation to counter the other threats

[62] William Hale, *Turkish Foreign Policy, 1774–2000* (London: Frank Cass, 2000), 150–156.

[63] Sumit Ganguly, *Conflict Unending: India-Pakistan Tensions since 1947* (New York: Columbia University Press, 2001), 37–38.

[64] Hensel, "Contentious Issues," 105; Huth, *Standing Your Ground*, 116.

[65] Huth, *Standing Your Ground*, 122–124.

[66] Charles A. Kupchan, *The Vulnerability of Empire* (Ithaca, N.Y.: Cornell University Press, 1994), 19.

that it faces. When its relative position in a dispute is declining as a result of an opponent's military or political pressure, however, a state facing other internal or external threats will likely magnify the degree of decline it perceives in the territorial dispute. This combination of declining claim strength and a deteriorating security environment creates even stronger preventive motivations to threaten or use force. Under these circumstances, a state is likely to believe the worst about its opponent's intentions—namely that its adversary seeks to profit from its weakness—and believe that it must counter these actions or they will continue. A state may also worry about its ability to counter future pressure applied by its opponent in the dispute, especially if it faces internal threats to its territorial integrity and administrative capacity. Finally, it may fear that failure to respond vigorously could increase internal unrest, adding yet another challenge to the state.

The proposition advanced here must be clarified. I do not claim that either internal or external security threats constitute separate or independent causes of escalation in territorial disputes. As discussed below, alternative arguments based on diversionary war as well as reputation and deterrence advance such claims. Instead, I suggest that the combination of a decline in claim strength and other threats to a state's security is especially deadly. It creates even stronger perceptions of vulnerability, increasing the utility of using force. Without decline in claim strength, however, neither internal nor external threats to a state should create incentives for the escalation of territorial disputes. Instead, as argued in the previous section, a state should pursue territorial concessions if improved ties with the opposing state will yield assistance in countering the threat that it faces.

In early 1980, for example, growing unrest among Iraqi Shi'ites, an internal threat to Saddam Hussein's Iraqi regime, coincided with a revolution in Iran and the rise to power of more radical political forces around Ayatollah Khomeini. Iran's new leaders adopted much more hostile policies toward Iraq, policies that Saddam Hussein viewed as especially threatening because they appeared to provide critical support for Iraq's own Shi'ia majority that could overthrow him.[67] The potential for Shi'ite unrest as an additional source of Iranian power against Iraq was an important factor in Saddam's decision to attack Iran.

Favorable Power Shifts—Territorial Windows of Opportunity

States whose initial claim strength is weak or inferior may use force for a second reason. When a stronger adversary's position in the local military

---

[67] F. Gregory Gause, "Iraq's Decisions to Go to War, 1980 and 1990," *The Middle East Journal*, vol. 56, no. 1 (Winter 2002): 47–70.

balance weakens suddenly for reasons unrelated to the territorial dispute, this increases the weaker state's relative position and creates a window of opportunity for it to improve its claim before the stronger state recovers its strength. This type of window has different properties from those often described in the existing literature on preventive war, as it refers to a fading offensive advantage that both appears suddenly and is expected to last for only a limited period of time.

These windows of opportunity apply only to states whose claim in a dispute is weak or inferior. Such states are especially sensitive to opportunities to improve their otherwise poor position, especially if they occupy little or none of the disputed land. When a state's position in the local military balance suddenly and temporarily improves, the decline in the costs of using force can create incentives to seize territory from the opposing side.[68] By contrast, states with strong claims have a much smaller incentive to use force when a weaker adversary's position declines even further. Instead, strong-claim states can bargain hard at the negotiating table without carrying any of the other risks associated with the use of force in international relations. Nevertheless, even for states with a weak claim, these windows are likely to appear only rarely because of the difficulties states face in assessing changes in the local balance that would ensure the success of a limited-aims military operation to seize disputed land and strengthen a state's claim.[69]

States with weak claims are most likely to perceive favorable shifts in claim strength under two conditions. The first concerns decolonization or state collapse, which can degrade or destroy the ability of one or both sides to project power over a disputed area. Colonial forces may withdraw from a disputed territory, or the process of state collapse might result in the disintegration of one side's military forces. The second set of conditions includes those that lead states to compromise, namely threats in the overall security environment, either instability at home or other conflicts abroad. When the stronger state is countering other threats, the weak-claim state may conclude that its adversary is unwilling or unable to respond, especially to a limited-aims, fait-accompli operation. As Geoffrey Blainey has argued, periods of domestic instability often create the appearance of a shift in the balance of power and a window of opportunity for the weaker state to take military action.[70]

In 1971, for example, Iran seized three offshore islands in the Persian Gulf, islands that it had disputed since the late nineteenth century. The

---

[68] On the initiation of wars by weak states, see T. V. Paul, *Asymmetric Conflicts: War Initiation by Weaker Powers* (Cambridge: Cambridge University Press, 1994).

[69] On this point, see Richard N. Lebow, "Windows of Opportunity: Do States Jump through Them?" *International Security*, vol. 9, no. 1 (Summer 1984): 147–186.

[70] Geoffrey Blainey, *The Causes of War*, 3rd ed. (New York: The Free Press, 1988), 82.

Iranian action occurred just one day before the United Arab Emirates (UAE) achieved its independence from Britain. This created a stark shift in the local balance of forces and a window of opportunity for Iran, as British forces had withdrawn from the area and before the UAE could assert its authority.[71] Similarly, in 1977 Somalia invaded the Ogaden region it had been disputing with Ethiopia. In the few years preceding the invasion, Ethiopia's internal political stability had deteriorated dramatically, resulting in the 1974 coup overthrowing Haile Selassie. Just before the invasion, a revolt intensified in the Eritrean region, sapping the strength of Ethiopian forces and opening a window for Somalia, which controlled none of the land in the dispute.[72]

Alternative Explanations for Escalation

The theory of escalation outlined above offers two mechanisms that explain why and when a state might threaten or use force in a territorial dispute, both of them based on shifts in a state's claim strength. The first stresses how an adversary's relative success in strengthening its claim through military or political means or the occupation of vacant disputed territory can create perceptions of a long-term disadvantage and thus short-term incentives to use force. When a state concludes that its bargaining power in a dispute will continue to decline, it is much more willing to use force to defend its claim and arrest or reverse the decline. The second mechanism highlights the presence of opportunities created by a favorable shift in the local military balance that decreases the costs of using force for a state with a weak claim suddenly but only temporarily.

One alternative explanation draws different conclusions about the incentives for states with strong or dominant claims. According to this argument, these states should be the most likely to use force because they can seize disputed land at an acceptable cost or impose a favorable settlement on their adversary. This explanation draws on offensive realism, a theory asserting that states will expand when they possess the capabilities to do so at an acceptable cost.[73] Accordingly, states in territorial disputes should exploit advantages in relative capabilities to achieve their territorial claims. This explanation is broader than the "windows of opportunity" logic outlined above, as it predicts how all states with strong claims will behave, not just those like Iran whose otherwise weak position improves

[71] Huth, *Standing Your Ground*, 117.

[72] Robert F. Gorman, *Political Conflict on the Horn of Africa* (New York: Praeger, 1981).

[73] John J. Mearsheimer, *The Tragedy of Great Power Politics* (New York: W. W. Norton, 2001); Zakaria, *From Wealth to Power*.

suddenly. A key observable implication of this explanation is that few disputes should exist where there is a great asymmetry in the disputants' military power, as states with strong claims will have settled these disputes at the negotiating table or on the battlefield.

Such an explanation, however, is incomplete. Although a state with a strong claim can more easily use force, especially when diplomacy fails, it has more flexibility in how it can manage a dispute. Because of its strength, a state with a strong claim can be optimistic about achieving a settlement on its terms. Thus, it is unclear why these states would use force except perhaps in disputes viewed as exceptionally salient. Above, I offer an explanation for why states with military advantages use force— when they expect their position in a dispute to weaken in the long run.

A second alternative explanation stresses the role of reputation and the requirements of deterrence. According to this logic, a state will use force in a territorial dispute not because of the importance of the land being contested but because of the need to invest in a general reputation for toughness.[74] One variant of this argument posits that a state will use force in one territorial dispute to create a reputation for resolve and deter its opponents in other territorial disputes. As Barbara Walter argues, a state with multiple territorial conflicts has a strong incentive to build a reputation for toughness that will dissuade states in its other conflicts from demanding concessions or strengthening their relative position. In particular, such a state should not only be less willing to compromise in its disputes, but also more willing to use force against the first territorial opponent that openly threatens its claim in order to deter any subsequent challenges from other states with which it disputes territory.[75]

Another variant of the reputational logic highlights the competitive dynamics of enduring or strategic rivalries. A state might use force in a territorial dispute with a rival not to strengthen its position in the dispute but to signal resolve or coerce its opponent over other interests.[76] The broader dynamics of the rivalry, not more narrow competition over territory, should explain the use of force in territorial disputes between states that are also categorized as rivals.[77] The territorial dispute, then, is a proxy for the rivalry, and it is competition in the rivalry that creates incentives for the use of force. Nevertheless, the applicability of this logic depends on the

[74] For a review of the literature on reputation and deterrence, see Paul K. Huth, "Reputations and Deterrence," *Security Studies*, vol. 7, no. 1 (1997): 72–99.

[75] Walter, "Explaining the Intractability of Territorial Conflict," 149–150.

[76] On rivalries, see Paul F. Diehl and Gary Goertz, *War and Peace in International Rivalry* (Ann Arbor: University of Michigan Press, 2000). On territory and rivalry, see Karen A. Rasler and William R. Thompson, "Contested Territory, Strategic Rivalries, and Conflict Escalation," *International Studies Quarterly*, vol. 50, no. 1 (March 2006): 145-167.

[77] Relative decline in the rivalry, however, might be one reason for the use of force that is consistent with my theory of escalation.

centrality of contested land in a rivalry between two states. If the territorial dispute defines a hostile relationship between two countries, then it would be difficult to separate behavior in the dispute from behavior in the rivalry. In rivalries where states compete over a range of issues apart from contested land, this logic might be more relevant. Yet even when the dispute is a proxy for overall competition in the rivalry, decisions to use force will likely follow shifts in claim strength described above if the dispute becomes the principal focus of competition between the two states.

A third set of alternative explanations examines domestic political incentives for escalating territorial disputes, focusing on logics of mobilization and diversion.[78] As territorial disputes are among the most salient foreign policy issues for a state, they provide an issue over which leaders may rally society to achieve other goals. Domestic-level explanations may illuminate decisions made in particular conflicts, but they are unlikely to explain broad variation in the use of escalation strategies in territorial disputes. As Thomas Christensen notes, the conditions that create incentives for national leaders to manipulate an external conflict to gain popular support for the adoption of a costly a change in grand strategy are likely to be rare. In addition, other external conflicts apart from territory could be used to mobilize society. Likewise, although the notion of diversionary war is intuitive, it has limitations. To start, given the type of threat, leaders possess a range of options, not just force. At the same time, diversion may in fact be less likely in territorial disputes. Even though it could provide a salient issue around which to rally the public, the costs of failure to seize the territory or compel an adversary's concessions would likely cause more problems for an embattled leader than the diversionary gambit would solve. If success is likely because the target is weak, then it is unclear why a leader would need to escalate the dispute.

BRINGING THE THEORIES TOGETHER

The preceding sections outlined two theories, one on the sources of cooperation in territorial disputes and the other on the sources of escalation in these conflicts. As cooperation and escalation are discrete outcomes of interest in the study of international relations, each theory was described separately. Nevertheless, I conclude the book's theoretical discussion by examining how these theories relate to each other. Table 1.2 summarizes the hypothesized effects of the three variables introduced above.

[78] On domestic mobilization, see Christensen, *Useful Adversaries*. On diversionary war, see Levy, "Diversionary Theory," 259–288.

TABLE 1.2
Cooperation and Escalation in Territorial Disputes

	Value of contested land[a]	Claim strength in a dispute[b]	Security environment[c]	(Scope conditions)
Sources of cooperation	A state is more likely to compromise over less valuable land.	A state is more likely to compromise when its relative position in a dispute is stable, strong, or strengthening.	**A state is more likely to compromise when it faces either internal or external threats to its security.**	(An opponent's ability to provide military, economic, or diplomatic support.)
Sources of escalation	A state is more likely to threaten or use force over more valuable land.	**A state is more likely to threaten or use force when its relative position in a dispute is declining.** A state with a weak claim is more likely to use force when its relative position suddenly and temporarily improves.	A state is even more likely to threaten or use force if decline in claim strength coincides with internal or external threats to its security.	(A state's ability to execute a limited-aims operation without destruction of its entire armed forces.)

Note: Principal hypotheses for cooperation and escalation are identified in **boldface** type.
[a] The strategic, economic, or symbolic importance of the land being disputed.
[b] The amount of disputed territory that a state controls and its ability to project military power over the entire area under dispute.
[c] A state's security from internal or external threats to its survival, territory, or power.

The first variable that shapes decisions to cooperate or escalate in a territorial dispute is the underlying value or salience of the contested land. As other scholars have noted, salience plays a critical role in determining the stakes in any conflict and thus the odds that a state will either pursue compromise or threaten or use force. The lower the value of the land being disputed, the more likely a state will consider territorial concessions because it has less to lose through compromise. By contrast, the higher the value of the land at stake, the more likely a state will consider escalation instead because it has more to lose through an unfavorable settlement of the dispute. Although salience does shape the overall stakes in territorial disputes and thus the underlying probability that strategies of cooperation or escalation will be pursued, it is often constant in any particular conflict and thus by itself cannot explain why and when states might adopt either strategy.

Claim strength defined as bargaining power in a dispute also plays a role in decisions to cooperate or escalate. Across different territorial conflicts, states with strong claims will be more likely to compromise than those with weak claims. A strong-claim state can hope to use its power at the negotiating table to achieve a favorable outcome and control over the land under dispute. A state with a weak claim will wait for its relative position to improve in order to achieve a more favorable settlement.

Over time, however, shifts in a state's claim strength create different incentives to cooperate or escalate in specific conflicts. A state whose bargaining power is increasing steadily at its opponent's expense will be less likely to use force because it is even more optimistic about achieving a favorable settlement and thus control over disputed land. By contrast, a state whose position in a dispute is deteriorating relative to its opponent will be more likely to use force to arrest its decline. The greater the rate of decline, the more likely a state will threaten or even use force to defend its claim. The one exception concerns a state with a weak claim whose position improves suddenly and temporarily, which creates a window of opportunity for it to improve its position in the dispute by seizing contested land.

The third variable is the overall security environment in which a state maintains territorial claim against another state. In the absence of either internal or external threats to its security, a state has little reason to pursue cooperation in a dispute and should delay settlement instead. As a state's security environment worsens, however, it should be more willing to pursue compromise to garner military, economic, or diplomatic aid to counter the specific threat that it faces. If a state encounters both decline in its claim strength in a dispute and other threats in its security environment, it may exaggerate the stakes in the conflict and be even more willing to use force than if it was just managing the consequences of relative decline.

Taken together, these variables outline the conditions under which states will most likely shift from a strategy of delaying settlement of a dispute to adopt strategies of either cooperation or escalation. A state is most likely to pursue cooperation in disputes over less salient land, when its claim strength is stable, strong, or strengthening, and when security threats arise abroad or at home that can be countered by improving ties with a territorial adversary. A state is most likely to pursue escalation in disputes over more salient land, when its relative position in the dispute is declining and, at the same time, when it faces either internal or external security threats. By implication, then, a state is most likely to delay in its most important disputes, when its claim strength is stable, strong or strengthening, and it faces a benign security environment abroad and at home.

Explaining China's Territorial Disputes

To test my theories of cooperation and escalation, I use three methods of inference. In this chapter, I compare China's behavior across its disputes to determine if the variation in behavior is consistent with the mechanisms of my theories. In the remainder of the book, I compare the change in China's behavior over time in each dispute, a variant of the method of "structured, focused comparisons."[79] In particular, I compare the adoption of a cooperation or escalation strategy with periods when delay was pursued instead to isolate those factors associated with these important decisions. Finally, I trace the process by which these decisions were made and look for evidence in government documents and statements by Chinese leaders to determine if the reasoning behind these decisions is consistent with the predictions of my theories.[80]

China's territorial disputes provide a fertile environment in which to test theories about cooperation and escalation in territorial disputes for three reasons. First, China has participated in twenty-three unique territorial conflicts, more than any other state since 1945. The characteristics of these disputes differ significantly, including the topography, population density, ethnicity, natural resource stocks, strategic endowments, and historical legacies of the disputed lands as well as the attributes of the states countering China's claims. China has disputed territory on land and at sea, over areas populated by the majority Han group and ethnic minorities, against democratic and authoritarian regimes, and when facing militarily stronger and weaker states, to name just a few. Testing my theories in such a diverse set of disputes should improve its validity and potential application beyond China's numerous conflicts. At the same time, by examining only China, I can hold other factors such as culture and regime type constant, which should help isolate the sources of change in dispute settlement strategies.

Second, while China's disputes reflect a diversity of characteristics, the strategies that China has adopted have also varied widely across space and time. China has pursued compromise in seventeen of its disputes but has nevertheless used force in six of them. Over time, China's willingness to compromise has occurred mostly in the early 1960s and throughout the 1990s, while it has used force in territorial conflicts in each decade since the establishment of the PRC. This wide variation in the use of different settlement strategies facilitates comparisons within and across disputes over time to isolate factors associated with decisions to cooperate or escalate and not delay.

Third, when compared with other countries, China is not an outlier whose behavior requires a special explanation. In one data set of mostly twentieth-century territorial disputes, the PRC's rate of compromise is

[79] Alexander George and Andrew Bennett, *Case Studies and Theory Development in the Social Sciences* (Cambridge, Mass.: MIT Press, 2005), 67–72.

[80] George and Bennett, *Case Studies*, 205–232.

not different in statistical terms from that of other states. Likewise, its rate of threatening force is also not different in statistical terms from that of other states.[81]

A focus on territorial disputes also provides an attractive research design for studying the sources of cooperation and conflict in China's international relations more broadly. Like other countries, China has used force more often over territory than over any other type of foreign policy issue.[82] By limiting this study to one issue area, the potential for bias created by comparing conflicts over dissimilar types of issues in which force might be used is minimized. It may be the case, for example, that what motivates China's use of force over territory differs systematically from what motivates its use of force in pursuit of other interests. At the same time, by examining the entire life cycle of each dispute, the potential for selection bias from examining only instances of cooperation or escalation is reduced, as periods of delay can be compared with times when these alternative strategies were pursued.

An Overview of China's Disputes

Before testing my theories, however, a brief overview of the origins of China's disputes is necessary. For any state, territorial disputes reflect diverse challenges to maintaining territorial integrity. China's territorial disputes are no exception. In particular, a distinctive ethnic geography inherited from its imperial past has shaped the origins of China's many conflicts. This ethnic geography largely defines the different challenges that China's leaders have faced in their attempts to consolidate the territorial integrity of the new state founded in 1949, influencing the goals they have pursued in territorial disputes and the means employed to achieve these objectives.

Ethnic geography refers to the density and distribution of ethnic groups within a state. China's ethnic geography reflects a core-periphery structure. The core, also known as the "central plain" (*zhongyuan*), "inner China" (*neidi*), or "China proper," refers to the densely populated, ethnic Han (Chinese) region that runs from north to south along the coast and that, before industrialization, supported sedentary agriculture such as rice

---

[81] In conflicts where China was coded as a "challenger" after 1949, the PRC compromised at least once in 88 percent of its disputes, while the rate of concessions in all other disputes was 79 percent. In a *t*-test of the two rates, the p-value was .41 (and a p-value above .05 implies that the differences in these rates is statistically insignificant). Likewise, China threatened military force in 38 percent of its disputes, while the rate of threatening force for all other states was 45 percent. The p-value for this *t*-test, .57, is also insignificant. Based on replication data from Huth and Allee, "Domestic Political Accountability," in note 41.

[82] Alastair Iain Johnston, "China's Militarized Interstate Dispute Behaviour 1949–1992: A First Cut at the Data," *The China Quarterly*, no. 153 (March 1998): 1–30.

farming. China proper has constituted the geographic center of every dynasty since the Qin (221 b.c.–206 b.c.), including the Yuan (1271–1368) and Qing (1644–1911) dynasties established by Mongol and Manchu conquerors, respectively. Successive Chinese dynasties, as well as modern regimes seeking to unify China since the Qing's collapse, have all struggled to establish control over this zone.[83]

The periphery, also known as "frontiers" (*bianjiang*) or "outer China" (*waidi*), envelops the Han heartland to the north, west, and southwest.[84] The frontiers are dominated by a variety of non-Han ethnic groups, including Tibetans, Mongols, and various Turkic peoples. Although most of these groups have little in common with one another, they are defined in the eyes of China's current leaders by their cultural, social, and economic differences from the Han majority. For instance, these groups historically did not engage in sedentary agriculture but rather practiced various nomadic and pastoral forms of subsistence. The geographic areas that they occupied were vast, oftentimes larger in total size than China proper.

The rise and fall of the Qing empire illustrates the role that ethnic geography has continued to play in China's territorial integrity after 1949. At its height in the early nineteenth century, the Qing encompassed more than 13 million square kilometers, almost twice the size of its predecessor, the Ming (1368–1644). Moreover, at the Qing's height, its frontiers were larger in total size than the Han core.[85] The Qing expanded primarily through military conquest and the subordination of areas populated by non-Han Chinese ethnic groups. Regions brought under Qing control included present-day Mongolia, China's Xinjiang Uighur Autonomous Region, and Manchuria, as well as parts of present-day Central Asia, the Russian Far East, and Burma.[86]

In the dynasty's last hundred years, the amount of territory under Qing rule decreased dramatically. Overall, the empire shrank by approximately 25 percent as its authority declined in the frontiers. Economic challenges and political unrest strained the empire's administrative capacity and diverted resources from the borderlands to the core. At the same time, for-

---

[83] From the Qin to the Qing, the size of the core gradually increased through the sinicization of non-Han groups residing around the core.

[84] For descriptions of China's frontier areas, see Ma Dazheng and Liu Ti, *Ershi shiji de Zhongguo bianjiang yanjiu: yimen fazhan zhong de bianyuan xueke de yanjin licheng* [China's Borderland Research in the Twentieth Century] (Ha'erbin: Heilongjiang jiaoyu chubanshe, 1998), 1–60; Niu Zhongxun, *Zhongguo bianjiang dili* [China's Frontier Geography] (Beijing: Renmin jiaoyu chubanshe, 1991), 1–7.

[85] Frederick Mote, *Imperial China: 900–1800* (Cambridge, Mass.: Harvard University Press, 1999), 25.

[86] On Qing expansion, see Peter C. Perdue, *China Marches West: The Qing Conquest of Central Eurasia* (Cambridge, Mass.: Belknap Press of Harvard University Press, 2005).

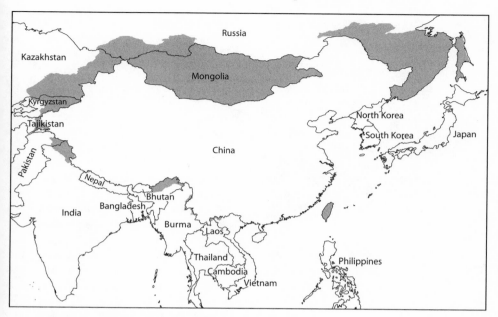

Map 1.1 China's Boundaries in 1820 and 2000
Source: China 2000 County Population Census, China Data Center, University of Michigan, 2003; China Historical GIS, V4, Harvard University.

eign powers stronger than China challenged the Qing on all fronts, eventually establishing zones of extraterritoriality along China's coast and spheres of influence in some of the frontiers. During this period, known in China as the "century of national humiliation" (*bainian guochi*), the Qing ceded large tracts of land through agreements that came to be known as "unequal treaties" (*bu pingdeng tiaoyue*) because of the harsh terms that they contained. As depicted in map 1.1, land ceded in various agreements with foreign powers along with the independence of Mongolia constituted approximately 3.4 million square kilometers of "lost territory" (*shidi*).[87]

When the PRC was established in 1949, the CCP sought to exert sovereignty over the territory recognized to be Qing lands at the empire's collapse in 1911. As demonstrated in map 1.1, this territorial footprint excluded regions that had been ceded in the unequal treaties but nevertheless

---

[87] This was calculated by subtracting China's size in 1820 (13,000,837 square kilometers) from its size today (9,596,960 square kilometers). For data on China's size in 1820, see the GIS shape files available from the China Historical GIS Project, http://www.people.fas.harvard.edu/~chgis/. For data on China's size today, see CIA World Factbook, https://cia.gov/cia//publications/factbook/geos/ch.html. These figures are approximate estimations.

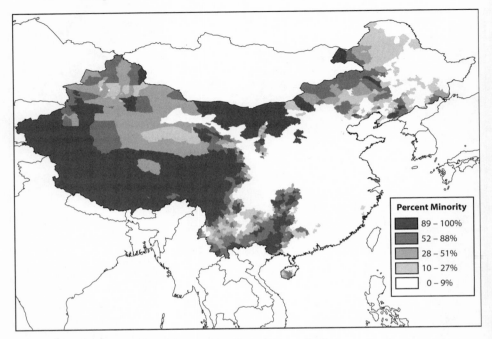

Percent Minority

89 – 100%
52 – 88%
28 – 51%
10 – 27%
0 – 9%

Map 1.2 China's Ethnic Geography (2000)
Source: China 2000 County Population Census, China Data Center, University of Michigan, 2003.
Note: Segments are based on the Jenks optimization method for identifying natural breaks in data.

incorporated many of the late Qing's frontiers, with the important exception of Mongolia. By establishing a state on the rough footprint of the late Qing, China's new leaders sought to consolidate the territorial integrity of an "empire state" that continued the ethnic geography of previous dynasties.[88] As maps 1.2 and 1.3 illustrate, these frontier areas are sparsely populated but dominated by ethnic minority groups. Members of the Han Chinese ethnic group constitute more than 90 percent of China's population and live mostly within China proper, on about 40 percent of the

[88] Owen Lattimore, *Inner Asian Frontiers of China* (New York: American Geographical Society, 1940); Mao Zhenfa, ed., *Bianfang lun* [On Frontier Defense] (Beijing: Junshi kexue chubanshe [internal circulation], 1996); Gerald Segal, *China Changes Shape: Regionalism and Foreign Policy*, Adelphi Paper no. 287 (London: International Institute for Strategic Studies, 1994); Michael D. Swaine and Ashley J. Tellis, *Interpreting China's Grand Strategy: Past, Present, and Future* (Santa Monica, Calif.: RAND, 2000), 21–96; Joseph Whitney, *China: Area, Administration and Nation Building*, Department of Geography Research Paper no. 123 (Chicago: University of Chicago, 1970); Zheng Shan, ed., *Zhongguo bianfang shi* [History of China's Frontier Defense] (Beijing: Shehui kexue wenxian chubanshe, 1995).

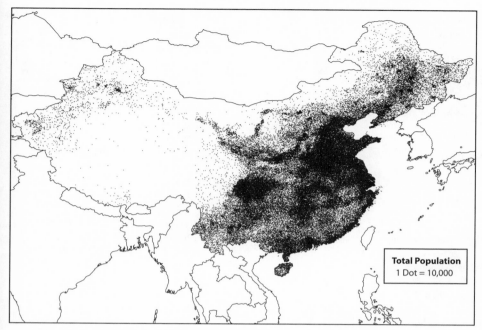

Map 1.3 China's Population Density (2000)
Source: China 2000 County Population Census, China Data Center, University of Michigan, 2003.

total PRC landmass.[89] By contrast, ethnic minorities such as Tibetans or Mongols comprise less than 10 percent of China's population but reside mostly in the frontiers enveloping China proper, which account for roughly 60 percent of the PRC's territory.[90]

China's ethnic geography created varied challenges for the CCP as it sought to establish and maintain the state's territorial integrity. After 1949 these challenges have been reflected in China's many territorial disputes. The origins of each dispute are discussed in the appendix. Based on the existing literature, a territorial dispute is defined as a conflict between China and a neighbor over the control or ownership of a piece of land. This definition includes disputes over offshore islands and other maritime features above the high-tide line such as coral reefs, but excludes disputes over maritime rights such as EEZs as well as subsurface features.[91] As sum-

[89] Bu He, ed., *Minzu lilun yu minzu zhengce* [Nationality Theory and Nationality Policy] (Huhehaote: Neimenggu daxue chubanshe, 1995), 27.

[90] On the frontier areas, see Ma and Liu, *Ershi shiji de Zhongguo bianjiang yanjiu*, 1–60; Niu, *Zhongguo bianjiang dili*, 1–7.

[91] For instance, a potential dispute over Ieo (Suyan) Rock, a subsurface feature where the Chinese and South Korean EEZs overlap, is excluded from the analysis.

TABLE 1.3
Overview of China's Territorial Disputes (1949–2005)

Disputed area	Size (km²)	Salience score[a]	Agreements	Compromise[b]	Force
		Frontier Disputes			
Burma border	1,909	6	1960: BA 1960: BT 1961: BP	Y (82%)	—
Nepal border	2,476 Mt. Everest	3	1960: BA 1961: BT 1963: BP	Y (94%)	—
India border	~125,000	7	1993: MTA 1996: CBM 2005: PriA	Y (74%)	Y
North Korea border	1,165	6	1962: BT 1964: BP	Y (60%)	—
Mongolia border	16,808	4	1962: BT 1964: BP	Y (65%)	—
Pakistan border	8,806 K2 Mt.	6	1963: BA 1965: BP	Y (40%)	—
Afghanistan border	~7,381	2	1963: BT 1965: BP	Y (100%)	—
Russia border (eastern)	~1,000	5	1991: BA 1999: BP	Y (48%)	Y
Bhutan border	1,128	3	1998: MTA	Y (76%)	—
Laos border	18	4	1991: BT 1993: BP	Y (50%)	—
Vietnam border	227	4	1993: PriA 1999: BT	Y (50%)	Y

Key: BA (boundary agreement), BP (boundary protocol), BT (boundary treaty), CBM (confidence-building measures), JD (joint declaration), MTA (maintenance of tranquility agreement), PriA (principles agreement) and SA (supplemental agreement).

[a] Based on Hensel and Mitchell, "Issue Indivisibility."

[b] Compromise refers to the proportion of disputed territory China relinquished.

marized in table 1.3, China's many disputes can be grouped into three categories (frontier, homeland, and offshore island), which refer to their geographical location and which also reflect how Chinese leaders viewed the stakes in these disputes when the PRC was established.

FRONTIER DISPUTES

China has disputed sixteen areas along its land border adjacent to its internal frontiers (see map 1.4). These disputes stem from the challenge of consolidating administrative control over vast borderlands though the

TABLE 1.3 (cont'd)
Overview of China's Territorial Disputes (1949–2005)

Disputed area	Size (km²)	Salience score[a]	Agreements	Compromise[b]	Force
		Frontier Disputes			
Russia border (western)	N/A	3	1994: BA 1999: BP	Y (No data)	—
Kazakhstan border	2,420	5	1994: BA 1997: SA 1998: SA 2002: BP	Y (66%)	—
Kyrgyzstan border	3,656	5	1996: BA 1998: SA 2004: BP	Y (68%)	—
Tajikistan border	28,430	3	1999: BA 2002: SA	Y (96%)	—
Abagaitu and Heixiazi along Russian border	408	6	2004: SA	Y (50%)	—
		Homeland Disputes			
Hong Kong	1,092	11	1984: JD	—	—
Macao	28	11	1987: JD	—	—
Taiwan	35,980	12	—	—	Y
		Offshore Island Disputes			
White Dragon Tail Island	~5	9	n.d.	Y (100%)	—
Paracel Islands	~10	8	—	—	Y
Spratly Islands	~5	8	—	—	Y
Senkaku Islands	~7	7	—	—	—

Key: BA (boundary agreement), BP (boundary protocol), BT (boundary treaty), CBM (confidence-building measures), JD (joint declaration), MTA (maintenance of tranquility agreement), PriA (principles agreement) and SA (supplemental agreement).

[a] Based on Hensel and Mitchell, "Issue Indivisibility."

[b] Compromise refers to the proportion of disputed territory China relinquished.

implementation of direct rule, a goal that no previous Chinese empire ever achieved. In the imperial era, the frontiers were governed indirectly through a variety of arrangements that granted substantial autonomy to local leaders in exchange for their loyalty to the emperor.[92] Then, the frontiers served as strategic buffer zones, shielding the Han core from

---

[92] For an excellent overview of frontier policy during the Qing, see Nicola Di Cosmo, "Qing Colonial Administration in Inner Asia," *The International History Review*, vol. 20, no. 2 (1998): 24–40. For a Chinese account, see Ma Dazheng, ed., *Zhongguo bianjiang jinglue shi* [A History of China's Frontier Administration] (Zhengzhou: Zhongzhou guji chubanshe, 2000), 240–434. Also see Joseph Fletcher, "Ch'ing Inner Asia c. 1800," in John K.

nomadic tribes that periodically attacked and sometimes conquered China proper from the north.[93] Indirect rule was sufficient for governing these buffer zones because it ensured the exclusion of foreign influence and prevented frontier ethnic groups from uniting against the empire, and it did so without the higher costs of direct rule. Many forms of indirect rule were adopted, including the local chieftain system in southwestern tribal areas, military colonies in Xinjiang and parts of Mongolia, a protectorship in Tibet, and vassalage relations in Manchuria and other parts of Mongolia.[94]

After 1949, the CCP confronted numerous challenges in its efforts to consolidate political authority in the vast frontiers. The history of indirect control had bequeathed few institutional links between the central government and more than half of the territory now part of the PRC, territory populated by ethnic groups that harbored aspirations for independence from China. Unlike China proper, the frontiers offered no heritage of direct administration upon which the new state could consolidate its authority and control. The varied authority structures that the Qing had employed in ethnic minority areas also did not provide a single model that could be used in all regions. Because the civil war was waged mostly in China proper, the CCP lacked ethnic minority cadres from the frontier regions, which further limited its ability to create strong political institutions. Finally, China's frontier areas maintained stronger cultural and economic ties with neighboring states than with China proper. Parts of Xinjiang had been ruled or heavily influenced by the Soviet Union for much of the Republican period, as each of the local warlords cultivated stronger ties with Moscow than with Nanjing.[95] India and Nepal maintained a

---

Fairbank, ed., *The Cambridge History of China*, vol. 10 (Cambridge: Cambridge University Press, 1978); Joseph Fletcher, "The Heyday of the Ch'ing Order in Mongolia, Sinkiang and Tibet," in John K. Fairbank, ed., *The Cambridge History of China*, vol. 10 (Cambridge: Cambridge University Press, 1978); Morris Rossabi, *China and Inner Asia: From 1368 to the Present Day* (New York: PICA Press, 1975); Zheng, *Zhongguo bianfang shi*.

[93] Zheng, *Zhongguo bianfang shi*.

[94] On Tibet, see Luciano Petech, *China and Tibet in the Early 18th Century: History of the Establishment of Chinese Protectorate in Tibet* (Leiden: Brill, 1972); Warren W. Smith, *Tibetan Nation: A History of Tibetan Nationalism and Sino-Tibetan Relations* (Boulder, Colo.: Westview, 1996), 115–150. On Xinjiang, see Di Cosmo, "Qing Colonial Administration"; Fletcher, "Ch'ing Inner Asia," 58–90; James Millward, *Beyond the Pass: Economy, Ethnicity and Empire in Qing Central Asia, 1759–1864* (Stanford, Calif.: Stanford University Press, 1998); Rossabi, *China and Inner Asia*, 139–165. On Mongolia, see Fletcher, "The Heyday of the Ch'ing Order"; Rossabi, *China and Inner Asia*, 106–157. On Manchuria, see Rossabi, *China and Inner Asia*, 85–94.

[95] Andrew D. W. Forbes, *Warlords and Muslims in Chinese Central Asia: A Political History of Republican Sinkiang, 1911–1949* (New York: Cambridge University Press, 1986); David N. Wang, *Under the Soviet Shadow: The Yining Incident* (Hong Kong: The Chinese University Press, 1999).

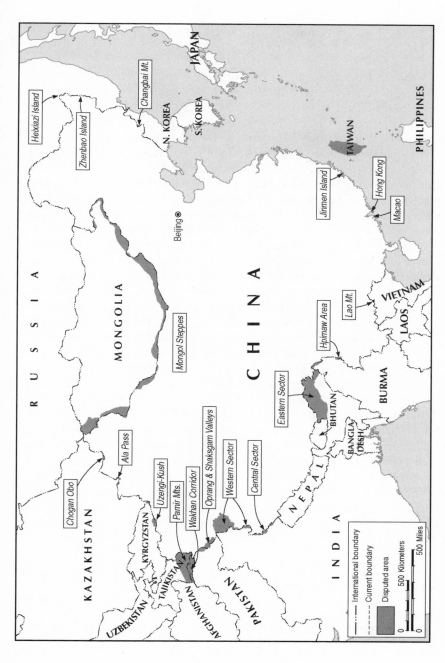

Map 1.4 China's Principal Frontier and Homeland Disputes

network of missions and special trading privileges throughout Tibet.[96] Hill tribes moved freely across China's southwestern borders in Yunnan and Guangxi.[97]

Although frontier disputes are China's most common type of territorial dispute, the contested land itself is not highly valued. Based on an index developed by Paul Hensel and Sara Mitchell to measure the salience of disputed territory, China's frontier disputes average 4.5 on a 12 point scale, almost one standard deviation below the mean in their study.[98] Generally speaking, these areas lack large populations, natural resource stocks, or strategic endowments linked with highly valued land. Instead, frontier disputes are more important to China's leaders because of their potential influence on the political stability of ethnic minority regions near China's boundaries, on the central government's ability to rule these areas, and thus on the control over large tracts of the state.

China's claims in its frontier disputes have been strong. With the exception of Heixiazi (Black Bear) Island, which had been under Russian control since the 1920s, China has controlled at least some of the contested frontier areas. At the same time, with one of the largest standing armies in the world during and after the Cold War, China has been able to defend the territory it controls and project power over most of the areas that it claims but does not occupy. Only the Soviet Union has fielded a ground force larger in size than China's army, and it did so only during the Cold War.

The origins of China's frontier disputes stem mostly from the territorial changes that occurred during the Qing empire's decline, which created ambiguity concerning the extent of China's sovereignty when the People's Republic was established in 1949. Although some portions of the land border had been delimited in prior boundary agreements, these texts were subject to contradictory interpretations even when China acknowledged their validity. In addition, the agreements often lacked detailed maps and the precise language necessary to fix the location of the boundary. The delimitations that they did contain were rarely demarcated on the ground through the placement of boundary markers. Other parts of China's land border had not yet been delimited at all by prior boundary agreements, including China's boundary with Nepal and Mongolia as well as portions

[96] Alastair Lamb, *The McMahon Line: A Study in the Relations between India, China and Tibet, 1904–1914* (London: Routledge & K. Paul, 1966).

[97] Herold J. Wiens, *China's March toward the Tropics* (Hamden, Conn.: Shoe String Press, 1954).

[98] The index is based on (1) the presence of permanent populations, (2) natural resources, (3) strategic endowments, (4) homeland ties, (5) ethnicity, and (6) historical possession. The mean value of territorial disputes in this study is 6.46, with a standard deviation of 2.66. Hensel and Mitchell, "Issue Indivisibility," 278. I coded China's disputes according to these criteria. The mean value was 6.0 with a standard deviation of 2.76.

of the boundary with the Soviet Union. In some cases, third parties had sought to delimit portions of China's border, as happened in 1895, for example, with the agreement between Russia and Britain to establish a buffer zone in the Pamir Mountain region of present-day Tajikistan.

HOMELAND DISPUTES

In contrast to the frontiers, the maintenance of territorial integrity in China proper was least problematic for China's new leaders in 1949. The Han core was relatively easy to govern because the CCP had inherited an administrative system of direct rule that began in the Ming dynasty and vertically integrated townships and provinces with the central government.[99] In effect, the new state grafted itself onto these existing institutions by establishing party committees at each level of government within the provincial system. Through the protracted civil war in China proper, the CCP cultivated a large pool of Han cadres to consolidate its control of the political institutions it had inherited. Although devastated by the Japanese occupation and the civil war, the economy of the core was largely self-sustaining and sheltered from international trade, which provided a basis for pursuing socialist transformation.

Nevertheless, China has disputed three areas linked to its consolidation of the Han Chinese core, or homeland. The main challenge to territorial integrity here has been to control those parts of China proper not under PRC control when it was established in 1949. These disputes include China's most contentious conflicts over Taiwan, Hong Kong, and Macao. China's new leaders sought to regain these areas and complete the modern project of national unification begun by Sun Yat-sen, a goal intertwined with the very legitimacy of the CCP. As a result, China's homeland disputes are its most important, with an average salience score of 11.3 on the Hensel-Mitchell index, almost two standard deviations above the mean.[100]

Some might object to grouping Taiwan, China's most important territorial dispute, with Hong Kong and Macao. First, Taiwan was not always treated by past dynasties as part of the Han Chinese core. The early Qing viewed the island as a frontier region, and it was not incorporated as a province until 1885.[101] According to this view, Taiwan might be seen as a frontier dispute. Nevertheless, as noted above, the size of China proper

[99] For a discussion of China's administrative structure, see Charles O. Hucker, *A Dictionary of Official Titles in Imperial China* (Stanford, Calif.: Stanford University Press, 1985), 71–96.

[100] Hensel and Mitchell, "Issue Indivisibility," 278.

[101] John Robert Shephard, *Statecraft and Political Economy on the Taiwan Frontier, 1600–1800* (Stanford, Calif.: Stanford University Press, 1993); Emma Teng, *Taiwan's Imagined Geography: Chinese Colonial Travel Writing and Pictures, 1683–1895* (Cambridge, Mass.: Harvard University Press, 2004).

has evolved over time to include many former frontiers. When the PRC was established in 1949, both Nationalist (KMT) and CCP elites alike viewed the island as a part of China's core. As Allen Carlson notes, all three of these disputes bear on the PRC's jurisdiction over large populations.[102] The common goal of unification that PRC leaders have pursued in these disputes reflects their view of Taiwan's status as a homeland area. A second possible objection is that national identity on Taiwan is hotly contested: more people there now self-identify as "Taiwanese" rather than solely "Chinese."[103] This shift in identity lies at the heart of the dispute today. Nevertheless, even though subgroups exist within the Han ethnic category, such as the Cantonese, these differences are seen as small when compared with the ethnic, religious, and cultural differences between Han and non-Han groups.[104] Thus, I group Hong Kong, Macao, and Taiwan together for the analytical task of explaining how China has behaved in homeland disputes.

The variation in China's claim strength in each dispute reflects the utility of grouping these three homeland areas together. What has varied is not their status as components of the core but China's ability to project power over these areas. Although Hong Kong remained under British control and Macao under Portuguese control after 1949, China has maintained the ability to conquer these areas with little or no resistance. By contrast, China's claim over Taiwan has been weak or inferior. It has not controlled any of the area that it claims in the dispute and, especially after the outbreak of the Korean War in June 1950 and the 1954 U.S.–Republic of China [ROC] Mutual Defense Treaty, it has faced great difficulty in projecting power across the Taiwan Strait and over Nationalist-held areas.

OFFSHORE ISLAND DISPUTES

As noted in map 1.5, China has disputed four offshore island groups. In addition to the well-known Spratly (Nansha) Islands in the South China Sea, China has also claimed the Paracel (Xisha) Islands, the Senkaku (Diaoyu) Islands, and White Dragon Tail (Bailongwei) Island. In these disputes, the challenge has been to establish a maritime presence in offshore areas where none existed before, and thus complete the PRC's consolidation of territorial integrity around its ocean perimeter as well as its land frontiers. With the exception of the early Ming dynasty, imperial

---

[102] Allen Carlson, *Unifying China, Integrating with the World: Securing Chinese Sovereignty in the Reform Era* (Stanford, Calif.: Stanford University Press, 2005), 49–91.

[103] Melissa J. Brown, *Is Taiwan Chinese? The Impact of Culture, Power, and Migration on Changing Identities* (Berkeley: University of California Press, 2004).

[104] For an examination of the changing salience of Taiwan for Chinese leaders, see Alan M. Wachman, *Why Taiwan? Geostrategic Rationales for China's Territorial Integrity* (Stanford, Calif.: Stanford University Press, 2007).

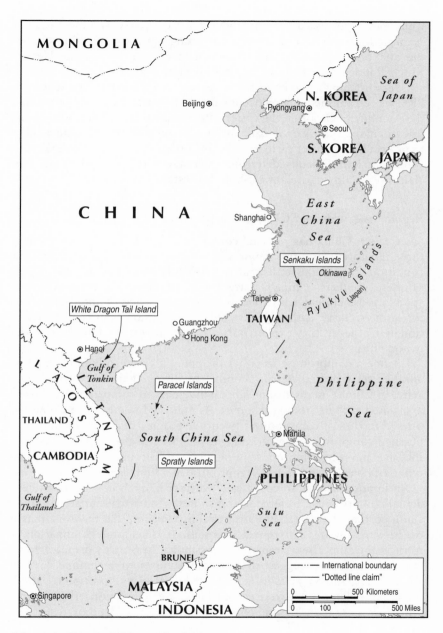

Map 1.5 China's Offshore Island Disputes

China never possessed a formidable maritime force. Given these islands' strategic locations and their role in asserting rights to natural resources, the offshore disputes are highly salient, averaging 8.0 on the Hensel-Mitchell index, less than one standard deviation above the mean.[105]

Overall, China's claims in these disputes have been weak. When the PRC was established, China occupied only White Dragon Tail Island and the Amphitrite Group in the eastern Paracels. China did not occupy any features in the Spratly or Senkaku islands. In addition, it lacked any ability to project naval power from its coast over these areas. With a weak navy, China has had difficulty deterring other states from strengthening their claims or occupying vacant offshore real estate.

Regime Insecurity and China's Compromises

Since 1949, China has pursued compromise in seventeen of its twenty-three territorial disputes. China's willingness to cooperate created the conditions for a final settlement through bilateral agreements in fifteen of these conflicts. China's pattern of compromise and delay corresponds most closely with the presence or absence of internal threats to regime security. Although external threats are one source of cooperation in my theory, they explain only a small fraction of China's territorial concessions.

I define a compromise as either dropping a claim to land claimed by another state or transferring control of disputed territory to another state. In China's many disputes, its willingness to compromise is closely associated with its frontier disputes. As indicated in table 1.4, China has offered territorial compromises twenty-five times since 1949. China has pursued compromise in each and every frontier dispute. By contrast, the PRC has pursued compromise in only one of its four offshore island disputes and has never pursued compromise in a homeland dispute.

An important issue to consider is whether China's concessions reflect actual compromises. In territorial disputes, a state may inflate its initial claim so that it receives its "reservation point" or the territory that it really wants in any subsequent negotiations. This strategic inflation of territorial claims always remains a possibility. In China's disputes, however, several factors suggest that its compromises were genuine. First, if China exaggerated its claims, it contested only a small portion of land it might have claimed if it were engaged in strategic inflation. Although the Qing lost more than 3.4 million square kilometers of land in its last one hundred years, China has disputed only 238,000 square kilometers of territory with its neighbors since 1949—less than 10 percent of what it might have claimed. Second, China's concessions were debated within

---

[105] Hensel and Mitchell, "Issue Indivisibility," 278.

TABLE 1.4
Summary of Findings for China's Compromises in Territorial Disputes (1949–2005)

Compromise			Sources of cooperation			Outcome
Date	Country	Description	Ethnic unrest	Political instability	External rivalry	Assistance gained by China
1956 (Nov.)	Burma	Concession over Nam-Wan tract			Tensions with the U.S. over SE Asia	Improved ties with a key nonaligned country
1957 (May)	North Vietnam	Transfer of White Dragon Tail Island			Tensions with the U.S. over SE Asia	Strengthened ally in rivalry with the U.S. in SE Asia
1960 (Jan.–Aug.)	Burma	Concessions over watershed in the north and size of Hpimaw area	Revolt in Tibet			Acknowledgment of sovereignty over Tibet; stable border adjacent to Tibet; joint military operations against KMT irregulars in Burma from Nov. 1960 to Feb. 1961
1960 (Mar.)	Nepal	Concessions over 10 sectors and Mt. Everest	Revolt in Tibet			Acknowledgment of sovereignty over Tibet; demilitarization of the border; military operations in Nepal against Tibetan rebels in 1960 and 1964
1960 (Apr.)	India	"Package deal" trading eastern sector for western sector	Revolt in Tibet			None (desired elimination of support for Tibetan rebels in India and affirmation of sovereignty over Tibet)
1962 (Feb.–July)	India	Additional concessions in the western sector	Revolt in Tibet	Economic crisis after Great Leap		None (desired elimination of support for Tibetan rebels in India and affirmation of sovereignty over Tibet)
1962 (Oct.)	North Korea	Concessions over Changbai (Paektu) Mt. and crater lake		Economic crisis after Great Leap		Pressure on Soviets to settle dispute with China

TABLE 1.4 (*cont'd*)
Summary of Findings for China's Compromises in Territorial Disputes (1949–2005)

	Compromise			Sources of cooperation			Outcome
Date	Country	Description	Ethnic unrest	Political instability	External rivalry		Assistance gained by China
1962 (Nov.–Dec.)	Mongolia	Concessions over Hongshanzui, Bogeda Mt., Qinghe, Beita Mt., and steppe areas	Migration in Xinjiang	Economic crisis after Great Leap			Sealed and stable border along eastern Xinjiang; pressure on Soviets to settle dispute with China
1962 (Dec.)	Pakistan	Concessions over Oprang Valley, K2 Mt., and 6 passes	Migration in Xinjiang	Economic crisis after Great Leap			Sealed and stable border along southwestern Xinjiang; pressure on India to settle with China
1963 (July)	Afghanistan	Dropping of claim to Wakhan Corridor	Migration in Xinjiang	Economic crisis after Great Leap			Sealed and stable border with southwestern Xinjiang; pressure on Soviets to settle with China
1964 (May–July)	Soviet Union	Compromise in the eastern sector, discussion of Central Asian sector	Migration in Xinjiang	Economic crisis after Great Leap			None (desired sealed border with Xinjiang)
1990 (Feb.)	Laos	Division of disputed areas on land border		Tiananmen legitimacy crisis			Validation of China's socialist system; improved ties with remaining socialist states; increased cross-border trade
1990 (June)	Soviet Union	Agreement to reach sector-by-sector settlements, starting with the eastern sector	Violence in Xinjiang	Tiananmen legitimacy crisis			Validation of China's socialist system; improved ties with remaining socialist states; increased cross-border trade
1990 (Aug.)	Bhutan	Offer "package deal" for sectors along western portion of Bhutan's border	Demonstrations in Tibet				Stable border adjacent to Tibet; acknowledgment of sovereignty over Tibet
1993 (Aug.)	Vietnam	Maintenance of status quo and affirmation of the 1895 agreement		Tiananmen legitimacy crisis			Validation of China's socialist system; improved ties with remaining socialist states; increased cross-border trade

TABLE 1.4 (cont'd)
Summary of Findings for China's Compromises in Territorial Disputes (1949–2005)

Compromise			Sources of cooperation			Outcome
Date	Country	Description	Ethnic unrest	Political instability	External rivalry	Assistance gained by China
1993 (Oct.)	Kazakhstan	Division of Ala Pass and concessions in other sectors	Violence in Xinjiang			Improved border security; denial of external support to Uighurs; increased cross-border trade
1994 (Jan.)	Russia	Agreement for western sector	Violence in Xinjiang	Tiananmen legitimacy crisis		Consolidation of ties with Russia
1995 (Sept.)	Kyrgyzstan	Concessions over Khan-Tengri and Irkeshtam	Violence in Xinjiang			Improved border security; denial of external support to Uighurs; increased cross-border trade
1997 (Jan.)	Kazakhstan	Compromise over Khan-Tengri	Violence in Xinjiang			Improved border security; denial of external support to Uighurs; repatriation of Uighurs; increased cross-border trade
1997 (Aug.)	Vietnam	Division of areas along land border		Tiananmen legitimacy crisis	Competition with the U.S.	Improved ties with remaining socialist state
1997 (Oct.)	Tajikistan	Dropping of claim to Uzbel Pass and division of Markansu Valley	Violence in Xinjiang			Improved border security, increased cross-border trade
1998 (May)	Kyrgyzstan	Division of Uzengi-Kush	Violence in Xinjiang			Improved border security; denial of external support to Uighurs; increased cross-border trade
1998 (June)	Kazakhstan	Division of Sary-Childy and Chogan Obo	Violence in Xinjiang			Improved border security; denial of external support to Uighurs; increased cross-border trade
2001 (Dec.)	Tajikistan	Large concession over Pamir Mts.	Violence in Xinjiang			Improved border security; increased cross-border trade
2002	Russia	Division of Heixiazi and Abagaitu			Competition with the U.S.	Improved ties to counter the U.S.

the elite, as some in the late 1950s believed that China should not offer concessions in its disputes, debate which suggests that the claims it did pursue were viewed internally as genuine and not inflated. Third, in the 1990s, the Chinese sought to conceal the content of its territorial settlements from the public, indicating that the government believed that it had made concessions (or would be perceived as having made concessions).

Several factors explain China's willingness to compromise in frontier disputes but not others. First, the land being disputed along the frontiers is generally less valuable than offshore or homeland territory. All things being equal, states are more likely to cooperate in their less important disputes. China is no exception here. Second, China's strength in the local military balance along the frontier has reduced the potential risks of compromising. With a large standing army, China has greater leverage in disputes on its land border, where it can most easily project power, decreasing the chance that other states will perceive territorial concessions as a sign of weakness. Although the low value of contested land and high level of military power indicate why China has more frequently pursued compromise over its frontiers than over offshore islands or homeland areas, neither factor can account for the variation over time in China's willingness to compromise or explain why, in each case, China chose to do so. The value of contested land and the PRC's claim strength have been mostly constant in China's frontier disputes since 1949, but its willingness to compromise has varied widely.

China has pursued cooperation in two distinct periods of time. From 1960 to 1964, China attempted compromise in eight disputes, reaching boundary treaties with six neighbors. From 1990 to 1999, China pursued compromise in most remaining frontier disputes, signing boundary agreements in nine additional disputes. These two waves of compromise correspond closely with periods of acute regime insecurity for China's leaders. Ethnic revolt near China's borders is the first type of internal threat linked with compromise attempts in these two periods. As shown in figure 1.1, data from the Minorities at Risk project demonstrate the link between ethnic rebellions in Chinese provinces that have an international boundary and the two periods in which China pursued compromise frequently in its territorial disputes. When a rebellion peaked in Tibet in 1959, China moved to compromise in disputes with Burma, Nepal, and India in 1960. After ethnic unrest erupted in Xinjiang in 1962, China pursued compromise with Mongolia, Pakistan, Afghanistan, and the Soviet Union. In the 1990s, sustained ethnic violence in Xinjiang coincided with compromises in disputes with Kazakhstan, Kyrgyzstan, and Tajikistan.

One episode of ethnic rebellion, the 1969 Nyemo revolt in Tibet, failed to produce any efforts to compromise. The revolt was small compared to the rebellion of the late 1950s, involving perhaps only several hundred

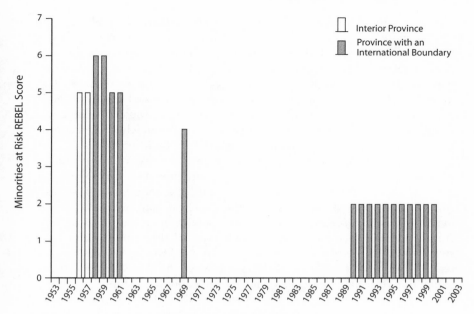

Figure 1.1 Ethnic Rebellion in China (1953–2003)
Source: Minorities at Risk Project (2005), College Park, Md.: Center for International Development and Conflict Management.
Note: Each year includes the highest score measuring the intensity of rebellion by ethnic minorities against the state.

rebels, and occurred on the outskirts of Lhasa, not near the border with India. It also was short-lived, lasting less than a month and quickly suppressed. Finally, China's leaders likely concluded that India would be unwilling to provide any assistance.[106]

Political instability is the second type of internal threat linked with efforts to compromise in frontier disputes. In the aftermath of the Great Leap Forward in the early 1960s, concerns about consolidating political authority throughout the country created additional incentives to compromise in disputes with Mongolia, Afghanistan, Pakistan, and the Soviet Union as well as North Korea. Following the 1989 Tiananmen massacre and worries about the viability of its socialist system, China pursued compromise in disputes with its socialist neighbors Laos, the Soviet Union, and Vietnam, and it reached agreements reducing border tensions with India and Bhutan.

---

[106] Tsering Shakya, *The Dragon in the Land of the Snows: A History of Modern Tibet since 1947* (New York: Penguin Compass, 1999), 344–346. During the summer and fall of 1969, Tibet witnessed repeated armed conflict between primarily Han-Chinese Red Guard factions and PLA units in Tibet. See, for example, *NYT*, 16 November 1969, 6.

A third period of political instability during the early phase of the Cultural Revolution (1966–69) failed to produce any efforts to compromise. China's senior leaders, however, created this chaos deliberately. It did not initially reflect a threat to the regime's security. Instead, it was an upheaval that China's leaders, especially Mao, inspired and stoked. When events moved beyond control of these leaders during 1967 and 1968 and perhaps did become an internal security threat, China could not have responded with any change in foreign policy, because much of the central government ceased to operate, including the Foreign Ministry.[107]

In the absence of internal threats to regime security, China's leaders have generally avoided compromise. China attempted compromise only twice in disputes before 1960. Likewise, China did not offer new concessions in any territorial disputes from the mid-1960s until 1990.[108] Moreover, China's territorial compromises in the 1960s and the 1990s do not correspond closely with periods of high external threat to the state. Instead, the two periods most threatening to the PRC witnessed few attempts to compromise. In the early 1950s, when the United States fought China to a stalemate on the Korean Peninsula and then established a network of alliances in the region to contain the PRC, China attempted compromise in only two disputes despite the clear external threat that it faced and the potential to use concessions to gain allies. After China's split with the Soviet Union in the mid-1960s resulted in intense military competition on its northern border that lasted for almost two decades, China did not offer any new concessions in its remaining territorial disputes.[109] Thus, in China's disputes, internal threats to the state have trumped external ones as a source of compromise.

Likewise, the two waves of territorial compromise do not correspond clearly with an acceptance of a norm against conquest. China pursued compromise in numerous disputes in the early 1960s when it upheld a revolutionary and expansionist socialist ideology clearly at odds with such beliefs. Moreover, China frequently used force over territorial issues in the 1950s and the 1960s.[110] Even after China's opening to the West and

---

[107] Barbara Barnouin and Yu Changgen, *Chinese Foreign Policy during the Cultural Revolution* (New York: Kegan Paul International, 1998); Roderick MacFarquhar and Michael Schoenhals, *Mao's Last Revolution* (Cambridge, Mass.: Belknap Press of Harvard University Press, 2006).

[108] In 1979, Deng Xiaoping did repeat Zhou Enlai's 1960 offer of a "package deal" settlement in its dispute with India. See chapter 3.

[109] For arguments that China settled its disputes to balance against external threats, see Eric A. Hyer, "The Politics of China's Boundary Disputes and Settlements" (Ph.D. dissertation, Columbia University, 1990); Francis Watson, *The Frontiers of China* (New York: Praeger, 1966).

[110] Johnston, "China's Militarized Interstate Dispute Behaviour," 24.

economic reform under the leadership of Deng Xiaoping, its seizure of land in disputes as late as 1994 casts doubt on the degree to which such a norm might explain China's efforts to compromise at the same time.[111]

In addition, democratic political institutions and economic interdependence cannot explain these two waves of compromise. Since its founding in 1949, China has always had an authoritarian political system but nevertheless frequently pursued compromise in many of its territorial disputes, despite lacking democratic norms of conflict resolution. Trade as a percentage of a state's gross domestic product (GDP) is one indicator of economic interdependence. Yet in the two periods in which China compromised, China's economic integration with the world varied widely, as merchandise trade accounted for 9 percent of GDP in 1960 but 33 percent in 1990.[112] As trade's share of GDP grew in the 1990s, it is possible that interdependence could account for the second wave of compromises, but the case studies fail to support this argument and indicate that increased support for trade, especially in border regions, resulted from an effort to bolster regime security.

The nature of frontier disputes suggests why regime insecurity creates incentives for settlement. Securing one of the longest land borders in the world poses a logistical challenge for China's armed forces even under optimal conditions.[113] The presence of ethnic minorities, many of whom aspire to secede, intertwines territorial integrity with political stability.[114] In addition, the weakness of the state in the frontiers increases the potential influence of China's neighbors within these borderlands, creating an opportunity for China to trade territorial concessions for support in governing its frontiers. As Deng Xiaoping foreshadowed in 1950 when describing China's southwestern frontier, "on a border this long . . . if the issue of ethnic minorities is not resolved, then the matter of national defense cannot be settled."[115]

Likewise, Chinese military publications link the defense of China's frontiers against external threats with internal political stability. These

---

[111] For an argument that China's moderation in territorial disputes in the 1990s was based partly on an increasing acceptance of such norms, see Carlson, *Unifying China*, 49–91.

[112] World Bank, World Development Indictors, online database. Merchandise trade understates the total amount of trade, but it is the only trade indicator available for 1960.

[113] M. Taylor Fravel, "Securing Borders: China's Doctrine and Force Structure for Frontier Defense," *Journal of Strategic Studies*, vol. 30, nos. 4–5 (2007): 705–737.

[114] Of the 135 counties adjacent to China's international frontiers, 107 are ethnic autonomous regions. Bu, *Minzu lilun yu minzu zhengce*, 27.

[115] *Deng Xiaoping wenxuan* [Deng Xiaoping's Selected Works], vol. 1 (Beijing: Renmin chubanshe, 1994), 161. Also, see Zhang Zhirong, *Zhongguo bianjiang yu minzu wenti: dangdai Zhongguo de tiaozhan jiqi lishi youlai* [China's Frontier and Nationality Problems: Contemporary China's Challenge and Their Historical Origins] (Beijing: Beijing daxue chubanshe, 2005).

studies assert that insecure borders promote ethnic unrest by increasing external influence within China, revealing suspicions that neighbors may manipulate ethnic tensions to create instability.[116] Indeed, diplomatic relations with neighboring states are consistently highlighted as a key tool for maintaining internal control over frontiers in addition to border security, economic development, and political mobilization. Benefits of cooperation with neighbors include policing rebel activity, limiting the potential for miscalculation during pacification campaigns, and expanding cross-border trade, among others.[117]

Nevertheless, internal threats to regime security leave unexplained three attempts by China to compromise. First, China and Burma held negotiations in 1956 after border patrols clashed in late 1955. Even though China offered to exchange some disputed areas, the impetus for the talks was to enhance China's standing with non-aligned states and reduce the potential for escalation, as Nationalist troops in Burma periodically raided the border of Yunnan Province. Second, in 1957, China transferred White Dragon Tail Island in the Tonkin Gulf to North Vietnam. Newly available sources indicate that Mao Zedong ordered this compromise to aid Hanoi in its conflict with the United States, reflecting the role of external threats in this case.[118] Third, in October 2004, China and Russia agreed to divide control of two disputed river islands, Abagaitu in the Argun River and Heixiazi, at the confluence of the Amur and Ussuri rivers. As no internal threats to regime security preceded this agreement, China's compromise most likely stemmed from external factors, especially the need to deepen ties with Russia.[119]

Declining Claim Strength and China's Uses of Force

To test my theory of escalation, I limit the analysis to China's uses of force in pursuit of territorial goals. Since 1949, China has used force in six of its twenty-three territorial disputes. China's pattern of escalation and delay

[116] See especially Li Xing, ed., *Bianfang xue* [The Science of Frontier Defense] (Beijing: Junshi kexue chubanshe, 2004); Mao, *Bianfang lun*, 232–234, 256–261. Also see Cai Xiru, ed., *Bianfang lilun* [Theory of Frontier Defense] (Beijing: Jingguan jiaoyu chubanshe [internal circulation], 1996); Wei Zhongli and Song Xianchun, eds., *Guonei anquan baowei* [Safeguarding Internal Security] (Beijing: Jingguan jiaoyu chubanshe [internal circulation], 1999), 180–191.

[117] Mao, *Bianfang lun*, 241–255; Wang Wenrong, ed., *Zhanlue xue* [The Science of Military Strategy] (Beijing: Guofang daxue chubanshe, 1999), 270.

[118] Li Dechao, "Bailongwei dao zhengming" [Rectification of White Dragon Tail Island's Name], *Zhongguo bianjiang shidi yanjiu baogao*, vols. 1–2, no. 3 (1988): 21–23; Mao, *Bianfang lun*, 137.

[119] "Russian Foreign Minister Gives TV Interview Focusing on Ties with Neighbors," Moscow NTV in Russian, 14 November 2004, FBIS# CEP-2004-1114-000063.

corresponds most closely with declining claim strength and negative shifts in bargaining power in its disputes. Although windows of opportunity are one source of escalation in my theory, this mechanism does not explain any of China's uses of force.

As table 1.5 notes, China has initiated the use of force sixteen times in six different disputes. Following the Correlates of War project, I define the use of force to include a blockade, an occupation of territory, a raid, a clash, or war.[120] To limit the analysis to escalations clearly authorized by China's top leaders, I examine only episodes in which at least one battalion of troops or its naval equivalent was employed in the use of force. As a result, I exclude small-scale clashes among border guards or naval patrols, even those that resulted in casualties, unless China seized disputed territory.

Two potential cases are excluded from the analysis because territorial goals were not the objective that China pursued in the use of force. The first is the 1965 mobilization and subsequent clashes along the Chinese-Indian border, which reflected China's efforts to support Pakistan in its war with India.[121] The second is China's 1979 invasion of Vietnam, which was motivated primarily by a desire to deter Soviet and Vietnamese expansion in Southeast Asia, not by the territorial disputes between China and Vietnam.[122] The 1995–96 Taiwan Strait crisis, which I include as a use force, might be viewed as a borderline case. Although it conducted numerous live ammunition exercises, China did not engage in combat operations against Taiwan. Nevertheless, the March 1996 missile tests effectively blockaded the island's two key ports. I also exclude the occupation of territory before states define their competing claims, especially during the process of state formation. For example, China's occupation of parts of the western sector disputed with India when units from the People's Liberation Army (PLA) deployed to Xinjiang and Tibet in 1950 is not counted as a use of force.

Across China's disputes, two characteristics of its use of force are consistent with negative power shifts and a decline in claim strength. First, in its frontier disputes on its land border, China has escalated those conflicts where it faced militarily powerful opponents, the only states that could possibly challenge its otherwise strong claims. In these disputes, China

---

[120] Daniel M. Jones, Stuart A. Bremer, and J. David Singer, "Militarized Interstate Disputes, 1816–1992: Rationale, Coding Rules, and Empirical Patterns," *Conflict Management and Peace Science*, vol. 15, no. 2 (August 1996): 173.

[121] John W. Garver, *Protracted Contest: Sino-Indian Rivalry in the Twentieth Century* (Seattle: University of Washington Press, 2001), 200-204.

[122] Robert S. Ross, *The Indochina Tangle: China's Vietnam Policy, 1975–1979* (New York: Columbia University Press, 1988); Zhang Xiaoming, "China's 1979 War with Vietnam: A Reassessment," *The China Quarterly*, no. 184 (December 2005): 851–874.

TABLE 1.5
Summary of Findings for China's Uses of Force in Territorial Disputes (1949–2005)

Use of force			Sources of escalation			Goal
Year	Country	Description	Territory controlled	Power projection	Regime security	Chinese objective
1950–54	Taiwan	Battles over coastal islands	KMT attacks on coastal islands	KMT operations along mainland coast		Achieve control of coastal front line in Taiwan dispute
1954 (Sept.–Oct.)	Taiwan	Shelling of Jinmen	—	Improved U.S.-Taiwan military ties; prospect of security treaty		Deter the U.S. from signing treaty with Taiwan
1955 (Jan.)	Taiwan	Attack on Yijiangshan	—	Signing of U.S.-ROC treaty		Probe scope of U.S.-ROC Taiwan alliance; control coastal islands
1958–59 (Aug.–Jan.)	Taiwan	Shelling of Jinmen and Mazu	—	Improved U.S.-Taiwan military ties; stalemated talks with the U.S.		Signal resolve in dispute; compel Jinmen evacuation; mobilize support for Great Leap
1959–61	India	Occupation of additional territory in Western sector	—	India's clarification of western sector claim; India's support for Tibet	Revolt in Tibet	Seal Tibet's borders; secure Xinjiang-Tibet highway
1962 (Oct.–Nov.)	India	Offensive against Indian positions	Indian gains in Western sector	Indian deployments in both sectors; creation of IV Corps	Revolt in Tibet; crisis after Great Leap	Eliminate Indian military pressure on border and potential influence in Tibet
1967 (Sept.–Oct.)	India	Nathu and Cho La clashes	—	India's deployment of mountain divisions; Indian fortifications in central sector	Instability of Cultural Revolution	Deter Indian forward posture along border
1969 (March)	USSR	Zhenbao Island ambush	Soviet effort to deny Chinese access to disputed river islands	Increased Soviet troop deployments to Far East; forward posture; assertive patrolling	Instability of Cultural Revolution	Deter future Soviet pressure in dispute; deter Soviet invasion of China

TABLE 1.5 (cont'd)
Summary of Findings for China's Uses of Force in Territorial Disputes (1949–2005)

	Use of force			Sources of escalation		Goal
Year	Country	Description	Territory controlled	Power projection	Regime security	Chinese objective
1974 (Jan.)	Vietnam	Seizure of Crescent Group in Paracels	Philippine and S. Vietnam moves into Spratlys	S. Vietnamese and Philippine oil exploration; worldwide assertion of maritime rights		Strengthen position in all offshore island disputes
1980 (Oct.)	Vietnam	Assault on Luojiapingda Mt.	Vietnamese control of hilltop	—		Deter increased Soviet influence in SE Asia
1981 (May)	Vietnam	Assault on Faka and Koulin mts.	Vietnamese control of hilltops	—		Deter increased Soviet influence in SE Asia
1984 (Apr.)	Vietnam	Assault on Lao and Zheyin mts.	Vietnamese control of hilltops	—		Deter increased Soviet influence in SE Asia
1986 (June)	India	Occupation of Sumdurong Chu	Indian building of post near Thag La	Indian forward positions in eastern sector		Deter future Indian occupations in neutral zones
1988 (Jan.–Mar.)	Vietnam, Philippines	Occupation of 6 Spratlys features; clash with Vietnam	Philippine, Malaysian, and Vietnamese occupations in Spratlys	China's naval modernization in the 1980s		Gain control of some territory in Spratlys dispute
1994 (Dec.)	Vietnam, Philippines	Occupation of Mischief Reef in Spratlys	Vietnamese occupation of 7 reefs	Vietnamese and Philippine oil exploration efforts and maritime claims		Control territory in eastern part of Spratlys dispute
1995–96	Taiwan	Missiles tests and military exercises	—	Taiwan's democratization and growing support for independence from China; U.S. policy toward Taiwan	Violence in Xinjiang	Deter support in Taiwan for independence; limit U.S. support for Taiwan

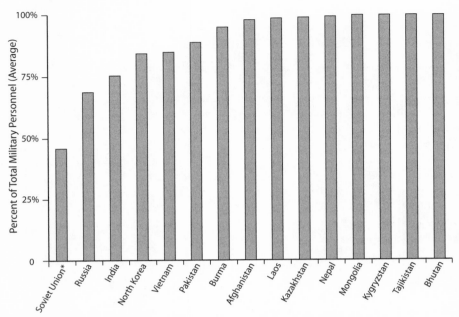

Figure 1.2 China's Military Power in Frontier Disputes (1949–2002)

Source: Correlates of War Project, military personnel variable, from EuGene program (v. 3.040).

Note: Each bar represents China's share of total military personnel. Figures greater than 50 percent indicate a Chinese advantage in the total military balance with the opposing state.

* Includes Russia, Kazakhstan, Kyrgyzstan, and Tajikistan before 1992.

has been sensitive to potential decline in its bargaining power. The local military balance in a conflict is difficult to measure. Nevertheless, as figure 1.2 demonstrates, China has on average been vastly stronger in the overall military balance than most of its land neighbors with which it has disputed territory. Although this chart compares aggregate military capabilities, these numbers indicate that only a few countries possessed sufficient forces to shift the local military balance on China's borders. Not coincidentally, these are the same countries against which China has used force. In 1969, China ambushed Soviet forces in the Ussuri River when China was clearly weaker militarily. China was stronger than India at the start of the 1962 border war, but India had the second-largest army on China's border. China was also stronger than Vietnam during the battles over border hilltops in the 1980s, but Vietnam, as demonstrated by its performance in the 1979 war, possessed a large, capable fighting force and an alliance with China's most powerful neighbor, the Soviet Union.

Second, China has also used force in those disputes where its claims were inferior, especially where it occupied little or none of the land that it contested. In these disputes, China has been sensitive to any further decline in its bargaining power. In offshore island disputes, China clashed with Saigon over the Crescent Group of the Paracels in 1974 and with Hanoi over features in the Spratlys in 1988, as well as occupied without Vietnamese or Philippine resistance Mischief Reef in 1994. In the Taiwan dispute, China used force to initiate major crises in 1954, 1958, and 1995–96. Both components of claim strength have contributed to China's weakness in these disputes. In 1949, China controlled less than half of the offshore island areas it claimed and none of the Taiwan areas under Nationalist control. China also faced real challenges in projecting military power from its coast over distant offshore islands in the East and South China Seas and across the Taiwan Strait against Nationalist forces backed by the United States.

The fact that China has seized only small amounts of territory through force is also consistent with the logic of declining claim strength. It is difficult to determine with much precision the amount of disputed territory that China has occupied on the battlefield. China occupied several thousand square kilometers of land in the western sector of its dispute with India in the late 1950s. After the war in 1962, China may have gained control over an additional 1,000 square kilometers of territory. China gained small amounts of territory after a series of clashes with Vietnam (1974, 1980, 1981, 1984, 1988) and occupied Mischief Reef in 1994. Overall, however, this reflects only a small portion the total amount of territory that China has disputed.

Several alternative explanations are inconsistent with the general pattern in China's use of force across its territorial disputes. One alternative is that windows of opportunity, not vulnerability, explain China's use of force. This logic only applies to those disputes where China's weakness stemmed from a significant advantage that its territorial adversary, namely the Soviet Union, enjoyed in the local military balance. Only in such disputes would a favorable change in the local military balance arise, creating an opportunity for China to seize land through force. In March 1969, however, China did not ambush the Soviets on Zhenbao under such conditions. Instead, as described in chapter 4, it did so after Moscow had doubled the number of Soviet divisions in the Far East. Moreover, when the Soviet Union collapsed in 1991, China did not seek to take advantage of its strengthened position in these disputes to use force. Similarly, China has not sought to profit from the U.S. involvement in other military conflicts such as the 2003 Iraq War and its aftermath to adopt an increasingly belligerent posture in the Taiwan conflict.

For similar reasons, arguments based on China's relative military superiority also fall short. Growing naval capabilities did enable China's occupation of features in the Paracels and the Spratlys, but as discussed in chapter 6 these actions were sparked by fears that China's position in these disputes was declining relative to those of the other claimants. Improved military capabilities allowed China to take action but were not the primary reason for China's decisions to use force. More importantly, China has not used force in those disputes where it has enjoyed its most significant military advantages, namely frontier disputes with smaller states such as Burma or Kazakhstan. Instead, it has often offered substantial concessions at the negotiating table.[123]

Rivalry dynamics do account for China's decisions to attack and seize Vietnamese-held hilltops on the China-Vietnam border in the 1980s, especially the 1984 assault on Lao and Zheyin mountains. No negative or positive shift in bargaining power in the territorial dispute is associated with this use of force. Instead, it likely reflected China's ongoing coercive diplomacy against the Soviet Union and its client Vietnam in Southeast Asia and a continuation of the 1979 war.[124] Broader concerns about the Chinese-Soviet rivalry were an additional factor in the 1969 ambush on Zhenbao. By contrast, although China-India relations may be viewed as a rivalry, especially in the 1960s and 1970s, the rivalry stemmed from their large territorial dispute, not other conflicts of interest. This logic also implies that China should have used force more frequently over Taiwan or against other U.S. allies in East Asia such as Japan as a means to signal its determination to counter U.S. containment before rapprochement in the 1970s, which China did not do.

Finally, domestic explanations for escalation such as mobilization and diversion are not strongly associated with China's decisions to use force in its territorial disputes. Domestic mobilization to generate support for the ambitious goals of the Great Leap helps explain why Mao sought to initiate a crisis over Taiwan in August 1958, but it has not been a factor in other disputes.[125] Likewise, China has frequently compromised during periods of internal threat to the state, a pattern of behavior that poses a strong challenge for diversionary war arguments.[126] Although domestic

---

[123] Fravel, "Regime Insecurity," 55–62.

[124] One could argue that this reflected China's efforts to counter potential decline at the strategic level, namely by blocking Soviet efforts to encircle China from the north, west, and south.

[125] Christensen, *Useful Adversaries.*

[126] Fravel, "Regime Insecurity." Also, see Johnston, "China's Militarized Interstate Dispute Behaviour," 18–20. On diversionary war, see Jack S. Levy, "The Diversionary Theory of War: A Critique," in Manus I. Midlarsky, ed., *Handbook of War Studies,* (Boston: Unwin Hyman, 1989), 259–288.

unrest is linked with China's uses of force in 1962 and 1967 against India and in 1969 against the Soviet Union, it magnified perceptions of decline created by India and Soviet military actions, respectively.

CONCLUSION

This chapter began by outlining two theories to explain why and when states make dramatic decisions either to compromise or to threaten or use force in territorial disputes. In the last section, I showed that, in China's disputes, internal threats to regime security and negative shifts in claim strength are closely correlated with China's decisions to cooperate or escalate in its territorial disputes. In the chapters that follow, I further test my theories by comparing the use of these strategies within each dispute and tracing the process by which these decisions were made. These chapters demonstrate two clear correlations: (1) between the onset of internal threats to regime security and a willingness to compromise, and (2) between the appearance of decline in claim strength in a dispute and a willingness to use force. Using newly available Chinese sources, these chapters also demonstrate that China's leaders made decisions that the logics of regime insecurity and declining claim strength predict. In the absence of internal threats to the regime and when China's bargaining power in its disputes was stable or strengthening, China has adopted a delaying strategy, deferring settlement of its disputes.

CHAPTER TWO

Cooperation in Frontier Disputes in the 1960s

FROM THE ESTABLISHMENT of the People's Republic until 1960, China pursued compromise in only one of its sixteen frontier disputes. In 1956, China held negotiations with Burma following a clash between border patrols in November 1955. Yet throughout the 1950s, many neighbors on its land border sought to enter into boundary talks with China, but each and every time these requests were rebuffed, as China preferred instead to delay the resolution of these disputes. In early 1960, China's approach shifted: it initiated talks and offered substantial concessions in disputes with three neighbors from January to April. By the summer of 1964, China had offered concessions in frontier disputes with eight neighbors and concluded bilateral boundary agreements resolving six disputes.

Regime insecurity best explains China's shift from delay to cooperation in the 1960s. China adopted a delaying strategy in all but one frontier dispute for more than a decade and then, suddenly, embraced cooperation. This shift corresponds with the onset of severe and repeated internal threats to the CCP-led government. In 1959, a major revolt swept through Tibet, a region bordering four countries. Although the central government had faced ethnic unrest from the mid-1950s in interior provinces such as Sichuan or Gansu, this marked the first instance of sustained armed rebellion in an area abutting China's borders. China offered concessions in territorial disputes with Tibet's neighbors in exchange for assistance in suppressing the revolt and bolstering domestic stability. In early 1962, China's leaders confronted an economic crisis and famine following the Great Leap Forward along with ethnic unrest in Xinjiang. Tensions in disputes with India and Taiwan only added to the insecurity of this period. Facing these challenges to territorial integrity, China compromised again. In both rounds of compromise in the 1960s, improved ties with neighbors were more important than holding out for maximal claims on its land border.

This chapter demonstrates how the onset of these internal threats created incentives for territorial compromise. I also show how other factors cannot account for the frequency of cooperation in the early 1960s. China faced real external threats at this time, especially from the United States, threats that could have also created strong incentives for cooperation in territorial disputes. Following the stalemate on the Korean Peninsula, the

United States pursued a containment strategy in the Asia-Pacific targeting China, forming bilateral alliances and implementing an economic embargo. Yet as the U.S. threat grew during the 1950s, resulting in hostilities across the Taiwan Strait described in chapter 6, China did not seek to cooperate in many territorial disputes, even when its neighbors demonstrated a willingness to engage China. Instead, with just one exception (Burma) it pursued a delaying strategy—until the outbreak of internal threats to its territorial integrity and political stability.

THE 1959 TIBETAN REVOLT

Before the revolt erupted in Tibet, China deferred opportunities to open negotiations with its neighbors over disputed territory. In 1954, Chinese premier Zhou Enlai and Indian prime minister Jawaharlal Nehru touched on the issue of their Himalayan boundary in their consultations, but agreed not to pursue the subject.[1] In 1956, Nepal sought to discuss its disputed border with China, but Beijing demurred.[2] Negotiations with Burma in 1956 stalled when China would not accede to demands over four disputed areas.[3] Yet from January to April 1960, China initiated talks and offered substantial compromises in disputes with each of these neighbors.

Regime insecurity best explains the change in China's willingness to compromise. The key difference between early 1960 and the previous decade was the outbreak of a large-scale rebellion in Tibet, which constituted the single largest revolt against the CCP. Moreover, it was the largest revolt China had faced in its frontiers, involving somewhere between 23,000 and 87,000 rebels, and it threatened the state's control over an area comprising almost 13 percent of the country. The revolt and the internal vulnerability that it reflected increased the costs for China of being in disputes with Tibet's neighbors. As the Chinese government moved to suppress the rebels, stable ties with neighboring states became much more important than before. China dropped large claims, seeking in exchange affirmations of its sovereignty over Tibet and assistance in suppressing the rebels. Without the Tibetan revolt in 1959, China proba-

---

[1] *ZELZ*, vol. 3, 1492. For a list of abbreviations, see page xv.

[2] S. D. Muni, *Foreign Policy of Nepal* (New Delhi: National Publishing House, 1973), 104.

[3] *ZELZ*, vol. 3, 1292–1324; Dorothy Woodman, *The Making of Burma* (The Cresset Press: London, 1962), 535–536; Yao Zhongming, "Zhou Enlai zongli jiejue ZhongMian bianjie wenti de guanghui yeji" [Premier Zhou Enlai's Glorious Achievement in Settling the Chinese-Burmese Border Problem], in Pei Jianzhang, ed., *Yanjiu Zhou Enlai: waijiao sixiang yu shijian* [Studying Zhou Enlai: Diplomatic Thought and Practice] (Beijing: Shijie zhishi chubanshe, 1989), 94–111.

bly would not even have entered into negotiations with India, Nepal, and Burma in 1960, much less offered to compromise in these disputes.

The Frontier Control Problem in Tibet

For China, control of Tibet was strategic. As Mao Zedong noted in 1949, "although Tibet's population is small, its international position is extremely important and we must occupy it."[4] Mao further emphasized the region's position as a strategic gateway leading into China's southwest, its valuable natural resources, and potential British or American ambitions.[5] As an elevated plateau, bounded by the Himalayas to the south, Tibet has been termed China's "soft underbelly" abutting Xinjiang as well as Qinghai, Sichuan, and Yunnan provinces. Domination or control of the plateau by a foreign power would put these other regions at risk, linking the physical security of China's southwest with the exclusion of foreign influence in Tibet. Without Tibet, for example, the only link between China and Xinjiang would be through the Gansu corridor, which was later threatened when the Soviet Union moved troops to the Chinese-Mongolian border in the late 1960s.[6] As a result, occupation and control of Tibet was necessary for "consolidating frontiers and national defense."[7]

Following the end of World War II, the prospect of foreign and especially Western control of such a large and vital region required that it be incorporated into the new state. Preparations to occupy Tibet began in the fall of 1949 when the Second Field Army defeated Nationalist forces in Sichuan. In the fall of 1950, the PLA defeated ethnic Tibetan forces in the Changdu (Qamdo) region in the eastern part of present-day Tibet and moved to open negotiations with the Tibetan government in Lhasa. In May 1951, an agreement was reached under a threat of an invasion of Tibet proper that provided for its incorporation into the PRC.[8]

---

[4] "Mao Zedong guanyu you xinanju chouhua jinjun ji jingying Xizang wenti de dianbao (1950 nian 1 yue 2 ri)" [Mao Zedong's Telegram on Problems Regarding the Southwest Bureau's Plans to Enter and Administer Tibet (2 January 1950)], in Ni Fuhan and Huang Ke, eds., *Heping jiefang Xizang* [The Peaceful Liberation of Tibet] (Lasa: Xizang renmin chubanshe [internal circulation], 1995), 47.

[5] "Shiba jun dangwei guanyu jinjun Xizang gongzuo zhishi (jielu) (1950 nian 2 yue 1 ri)" [Instructions for the 18th Army Party Committee for Work on Entering Tibet (excerpt) (1 February 1950)], in Ni and Huang, *Heping jiefang Xizang*, 59.

[6] This paragraph draws on John W. Garver, *Protracted Contest: Sino-Indian Rivalry in the Twentieth Century* (Seattle: University of Washington Press, 2001), 34–39.

[7] Ni and Huang, *Heping jiefang Xizang*, 59. Also see Zhao Shenying, *Zhang Guohua jiangjun zai Xizang* [General Zhang Guohua in Tibet] (Beijing: Zhongguo zangxue chubanshe, 2001), 9.

[8] Ni and Huang, *Heping jiefang Xizang*; Tsering Shakya, *The Dragon in the Land of the Snows: A History of Modern Tibet since 1947* (New York: Penguin Compass, 1999), 33–91.

Despite securing a Tibetan surrender, the new Chinese state faced three challenges to the consolidation of its authority in the region. First, as Tibet had been a Qing protectorate, the CCP inherited no institutions of direct rule that could strengthen its control over the area.[9] Under the Qing, two *ambans* or officials were stationed in Lhasa along with a small garrison.[10] The local Tibetan government administered the region, while the Qing *ambans* had nominal control over foreign affairs and, for a few decades, the financial system. After the collapse of the Qing, the last *ambans* left Lhasa in 1913.[11] From then until 1934, when Nationalist general Huang Musong visited Lhasa, no Chinese official set foot in Tibet. In 1939, the Republican government opened a small mission under the name of the Mongolian and Tibetan Affairs Commission, but it was not officially recognized by the Tibetan government and was expelled in 1949.[12] After 1949, the CCP had difficulty recruiting Tibetans, the most religious ethnic group that it sought to govern after 1949. Buddhist beliefs and Tibet's feudal hierarchy contradicted the basic tenets of communism, a contrast that was only sharpened by the dominance of religion in Tibetan culture and government. Reflecting this institutional weakness, eight years after its incorporation into the PRC, the region had only 875 ethnic Tibetan Communist Party members.[13]

Second, Tibet lacked communication links with China proper and Xinjiang. In 1949, no motorable roads connected Tibet with any of the other regions controlled by the CCP. Indeed, one of the principal reasons for the PLA's delayed entry into Tibet was the lack of suitable roads for logistical support.[14] Even after three roads connecting Tibet to Qinghai, Gansu, and Xinjiang were constructed in the 1950s, transportation difficulties remained, as many of the roads were not passable in winter and were often in disrepair. Moreover, most of Tibet's traditional lines of communication linked it not with China proper but with its Himalayan neighbors, especially India and Nepal, which had enjoyed special trading privileges under the Qing. India, for example, maintained a mission in Lhasa, trade

---

[9] On China's relations with Tibet before 1949, see A. Tom Grunfeld, *The Making of Modern Tibet: Revised Edition* (Armonk: M. E. Sharpe, 1996), 7–106; Dawa Norbu, *China's Tibet Policy* (London: Curzon Press, 2001), 15–178; Warren W. Smith, *Tibetan Nation: A History of Tibetan Nationalism and Sino-Tibetan Relations* (Boulder, Colo.: Westview, 1996), 81–264.

[10] Norbu, *China's Tibet Policy*, 78; Luciano Petech, *China and Tibet in the Early 18th Century: History of the Establishment of Chinese Protectorate in Tibet* (Leiden, Netherlands: Brill, 1972).

[11] Throughout this period, however, China did not relinquish its claims to sovereignty over Tibet. Norbu, *China's Tibet Policy*, 102–109.

[12] Shakya, *Dragon*, 5–6.

[13] Shakya, *Dragon*, 255.

[14] DDZGJD, 208–212; ZYBJ, 47–59.

agencies, postal and telegraphic infrastructure, and military escorts.[15] Indeed, during the first part of the 1950s, Chinese officials often traveled to Tibet via India, and almost all of Tibet's trade was conducted with India and Nepal, including the procurement of supplies for PLA units stationed in the region.[16]

Third, most Tibetans never viewed themselves as part of the Chinese state that was established in 1949. Following the Qing's collapse in 1911, Tibet functioned as an independent country, conducting a limited foreign policy without China's involvement and maintaining a small armed force to guard its borders. In the late 1940s, as the prospect of Chinese occupation loomed closer, the Tibetan government moved to declare its formal independence and sought diplomatic recognition. Of course, the prospect of British or American influence in Tibet only increased China's fears about the security of its southwest frontier and was a key reason why Mao concluded that China had to control the region. In the late 1940s, the United States, Britain, and ultimately India rebuffed Lhasa's efforts to gain international recognition.[17]

Facing these internal challenges to its control of a large frontier area, the CCP implemented indirect rule. Short of coerced reform, which did occur after the 1959 revolt, the CCP had few options. The outline of the indirect approach was contained in the May 1951 "17-Point Agreement" that specified the terms of Tibet's incorporation into the PRC.[18] In this agreement, Beijing pledged not to alter the existing political system in Tibet or change the status of the Dalai Lama. China's central government assumed responsibility for the defense and foreign relations of Tibet, while the government led by the Dalai Lama administered Tibet proper. Senior military and party leaders established a military and administrative committee (*junzheng weiyuanhui*) and Tibetan military headquarters (*silingbu*) through which to implement the agreement and safeguard the state's interests.

This indirect approach to governing Tibet stands in stark contrast to the establishment of CCP authority elsewhere in China and underscores the degree of the frontier control problem in Tibet. By ruling through the Dalai Lama and existing Tibetan institutions, the CCP hoped to build support over time for the state's authority and institute a gradual transition to direct rule. The indirect approach also allowed the central

---

[15] Neville Maxwell, *India's China War* (New York: Pantheon Books, 1970), 78.

[16] Garver, *Protracted*, 85–86.

[17] Grunfeld, *Making*, 82–106.

[18] Shakya, *Dragon*, 449–452. The agreement is formally known as the "Agreement between the Central People's Government and the Tibetan Local Government on Measures for the Peaceful Liberation of Tibet" (*zhongyang renmin zhengfu yu Xizang difang zhengfu guanyu heping jiefang Xizang banfa de xieyi*).

government to focus on upgrading the region's infrastructure, especially roads, in order to facilitate centralized control and enhance border security. In addition, through biding its time, the central government hoped to nurture a cohort of Tibetan cadres and use economic development to gain legitimacy.

Rebellion in the Southwest

Indirect rule never erased the fundamental contradiction between Tibetan culture and the CCP's utopian vision of communism. China's leaders viewed indirect rule as a means of preparing a feudal society for an eventual transition to socialism. Tibetans viewed the 17-Point Agreement as the best possible deal that they could make to maintain their customs, given the lack of U.S., British, and Indian support for their independence. This fragile balance did not last long. An armed revolt against Chinese rule began in Tibet proper in 1958 and spread following a series of demonstrations and their suppression in Lhasa in March 1959. By highlighting the weakness of the Chinese state in the region and its vulnerability to external influence, the revolt created strong incentives for China's leaders to compromise in territorial disputes with adjacent states.

REVOLT AGAINST CHINESE RULE

The revolt within Tibet proper stemmed from brewing unrest in ethnic Tibetan areas in adjacent provinces. Although sporadic uprisings against the government had occurred as early as 1952, the introduction of political reforms in 1954 and 1955, especially land reform, threatened traditional Tibetan culture and sparked isolated pockets of armed resistance. As parts of Chinese provinces, the Kham and Amdo Tibetan regions were not subject to the autonomy guarantees in the 17-Point Agreement, which led to the introduction of political reforms in these regions that were deferred within Tibet proper. In early 1956, the PLA siege of the Lithang monastery in Sichuan sparked a widespread uprising known as the Kanding revolt.[19] Although it was eventually suppressed, more than 10,000 Khampas joined the conflict, which lasted from March to June.[20] At the same time, similar revolts erupted in Qinghai, Gansu, Yunnan, and Xinjiang, which resulted

---

[19] On the background to the revolt, see Grunfeld, *Making*, 131–150; Norbu, *China's Tibet Policy*, 210–227; Shakya, *Dragon*, 131–211. For a Chinese account, see Li Peisheng and Li Guozhen, eds., *Pingxi Xizang panluan* [Suppression of the Tibetan Rebellion] (Lasa: Xizang renmin chubanshe [internal circulation], 1995).

[20] *Gongan budui: zongshu, dashiji, biaoce* [Public Security Troops: Summary, Chronology, Statistics] (Beijing: Jiefangjun chubanshe [military circulation], 1997), 46.

in sustained pacification campaigns.[21] By the end of 1958, the government had suppressed more than 230,000 ethnic Tibetans involved in revolts in these areas, mostly outside of Tibet proper.[22]

The violent suppression of the Kham uprisings united various Tibetan resistance groups that had formed to fight CCP rule. As PLA units counterattacked, rebels fled west to escape capture, congregating in Lhasa and the surrounding areas. In 1957, a Khampa trader, Gompo Tashi Andrugstang, formed a pan-Tibetan resistance movement and rallied support while traveling the country to raise funds for a golden throne to commemorate the Dalai Lama.[23] In March 1958, Andrugstang convened a meeting of Khampa leaders, who decided to unite their efforts to oppose the Chinese. In June 1958, all the disparate armed groups merged to form the National Volunteer Defense Army (NVDA), which then began to conduct raids against PLA outposts and convoys around Lhasa in southern Tibet.[24]

Estimates of rebel strength within Tibet proper have varied widely. Chinese sources indicate that the number of armed rebels (*panluan wuzhuang*) in Tibet in early 1959 ranged from 23,000[25] to 40,000[26] to 87,000.[27] Whatever their numbers, the rebels controlled much of the region apart from Lhasa and the main roads. A large number were based in Lhoka (Shannan), a heavily forested area between Lhasa and Tibet's borders with India and Bhutan. In August 1958, the NVDA conducted its first large-scale attack against the PLA with more than seven hundred rebels.[28] Raids and ambushes continued throughout the fall against PLA

[21] Yang Chengwu, "Xizang panluan" [The Tibetan Rebellion], in *Zongcan moubu: huiyi shiliao* [General Staff Department: Recollections and Historical Materials] (Beijing: Jiefangjun chubanshe [military circulation], 1997), 534.

[22] Yang, "Xizang panluan," 535. This figure refers to the total number of individuals killed, wounded, captured, surrendered, and disarmed.

[23] *Zhonggong Xizang dangshi dashiji, 1949–1966* [A Chronicle of Major Events in the Party History of the CCP in Tibet, 1949–1966] (Lasa: Xizang renmin chubanshe, 1990), 72.

[24] Kenneth Conboy and James Morrison, *The CIA's Secret War in Tibet* (Lawrence: University of Kansas Press, 2002), 72; John Kenneth Knaus, *Orphans of the Cold War: America and the Tibetan Struggle for Survival* (New York: Public Affairs, 1999), 150–151.

[25] *Zhou Enlai waijiao wenxuan* [Zhou Enlai's Selected Works on Diplomacy] (Beijing: Zhongyang wenxian chubanshe, 1990), 273; Li and Li, *Pingxi*, 17.

[26] Yang Qiliang, *Wang Shangrong jiangjun* [General Wang Shangrong] (Beijing: Dangdai Zhongguo chubanshe, 2000), 403.

[27] Jamyang Norbu, "The Tibetan Resistance Movement and the Role of the CIA," in Robert Barnett, ed., *Resistance and Reform in Tibet* (London: Hurst and Company, 1994), 189. Norbu cites a document published by the Political Department of the Tibetan MD. Another source notes that more than 90,000 people participated in the revolt within Tibet proper but that the core participants numbered only 23,000. "Zhengge Xizang pingpan san nian" [Three Years of Suppression throughout Tibet], *Zhongguo diming*, vol. 1, no. 115 (2004): 40.

[28] Li and Li, *Pingxi*, 217.

outposts, armories, and warehouses as well as checkpoints on the Sichuan-Tibet and Qinghai-Tibet roads, two of the main lines of communication.[29] In December 1958, for example, rebels ambushed a unit of the PLA's 155th regiment, killing fifty–six soldiers including the regiment's deputy commander.[30]

By March 1959, the situation within Tibet proper was tense. The residents of Lhasa and the Tibetan government feared an imminent crackdown. An influx of refugees was straining the already burdened local economy, while stories of Chinese brutality in other regions only redoubled local suspicion of the CCP's intentions. The Tibetan government itself was split between those who wanted to support the rebels and those, including the Dalai Lama, who sought to find some compromise with Beijing to avoid further violence. From the Chinese perspective, the spread of armed uprisings from Kham to Tibet proper was ominous. The attacks themselves demonstrated the fragility of the central government's authority in a key frontier area and the failure of indirect rule. Although China's leaders initially did not want to suppress the rebels in Tibet proper, which would alienate what little support remained, they increasingly viewed the Dalai Lama and his administration as aligned with the resistance and either unwilling or unable to stop its spread.

Within this turbulent environment, an otherwise innocuous invitation for the Dalai Lama to attend a dance performance at the PLA headquarters sparked the Lhasa uprising of March 1959. Although the invitation was originally extended in early February, the Dalai Lama had not chosen to discuss it publicly. Some of the Dalai Lama's junior advisers believed that the invitation was a trap to kidnap or perhaps assassinate their leader.[31] To prevent him from leaving his residence, these advisers spread rumors that the Dalai Lama would be abducted when he visited PLA headquarters on March 10. To protect him, crowds surrounded the Norbulinkga palace, escalating into various demonstrations with as many as 30,000 people.[32] The demonstrations quickly spun out of control as members of the Tibetan government began to distribute arms to the demonstrators and rebels inside the city occupied key strategic points.[33] On March 12, fifty Tibetan officials established a "People's Assembly," declared Tibet's independence, and renounced the 17-Point Agreement.[34] As

---

[29] *Zhonggong Xizang*, 78–85; Knaus, *Orphans*, 152–156; Shakya, *Dragon*, 179–180.

[30] Li and Li, *Pingxi*, 220.

[31] Shakya, *Dragon*, 186–191.

[32] Roger E. McCarthy, *Tears of the Lotus: Accounts of Tibetan Resistance to the Chinese Invasion, 1950–1962* (Jefferson, N.C.: McFarland & Company, 1997), 180.

[33] Contrary to subsequent Chinese claims, the events in Lhasa were not directed by the NVDA or the CIA-trained rebels. Shakya, *Dragon*, 201–202.

[34] Shakya, *Dragon*, 197.

the demonstrations grew, clashes between Chinese troops and protesters began on March 17, the day that the Dalai Lama secretly fled Lhasa. On the morning of March 20, the PLA launched a full-scale assault to regain control of the city, which by then contained more than 7,000 rebels.[35]

Following these events in Lhasa, the central government moved quickly to consolidate its authority through suppression of the revolt and the implementation of direct rule. Counterinsurgency operations within Tibet were the focus of this effort. In April 1959, the Central Military Commission (CMC) deployed units from the Lanzhou and Chengdu Military Regions (MR) to assault rebel base areas in Lhoka, starting a pacification campaign that ended in late 1961. As a district was pacified, reforms (including land reform, the settling of nomads, and the elimination of monasteries) were implemented.[36] During this process, known as "suppressing while reforming" (*yibian pingxi, yibian gaige*), Tibet's traditional political institutions were dismantled and replaced by a county and prefecture system similar to that of China proper.

EXTERNAL VULNERABILITY

The revolt highlighted the state's internal weakness and its exposure to external influence in a strategic region. At the time, China's border with India, Nepal, and Burma was largely undefended by the PLA. Before 1959, frontier defense had been the responsibility of the Tibetan army, a small force that remained in existence after 1951.[37] One noted military historian describes the role of PLA units in Tibet as being limited to "guarding key points [and] defending communication lines," that is, securing only key cities and the roads connecting them, not the border.[38] Although PLA units were garrisoned at a few points along the frontier, the border was largely undefended prior to the start of pacification operations in 1959.[39] Only after pursuing rebels fleeing south from Lhasa did large numbers of PLA troops deploy to the border. Reflecting this vulnerability, the CMC in April instructed units to "Seal rapidly the border [and] control important points near the undelimited 'McMahon Line' on the

[35] Li and Li, *Pingxi*, 28–29; Shakya, *Dragon*, 203; Yang, "Xizang panluan," 541.

[36] For Chinese accounts of these campaigns, see *DDZGJD*, 423–441; Li and Li, *Pingxi*; Yang, "Xizang panluan," 532–548.

[37] Wu Lengxi, *Shinian lunzhan: 1956–1966 ZhongSu guanxi huiyilu* [Ten Years of Polemics: A Recollection of Chinese-Soviet Relations from 1956 to 1966] (Beijing: Zhongyang wenxian chubanshe, 1999), 212.

[38] Xu Yan, "Jiefang hou woguo chuli bianjie chongtu weiji de huigu he zongjie" [A Review and Summary of Our Country's Handling of Border Conflicts and Crises after Liberation], *Shijie jingji yu zhengzhi*, vol. 3 (2005): 17.

[39] *ZYBJ*, 86. For a description of the few checkpoints that were garrisoned, see Yang Gongsu, *Cangsang jiushi nian: yige waijiao teshi de huiyi* [Ninety Years of Great Changes: A Special Envoy's Recollections] (Haikou: Hainan chubanshe, 1999), 235.

China-India border and China-Bhutan border and key communication lines across the borders."[40] A CMC circular issued in October 1961 stated that successful suppression of the revolt "further consolidated our country's strategic rear [and] safeguarded the security of our southwestern frontier defense."[41]

China's leaders believed that the rebellion had received external support, especially from India. The Chinese government had long maintained that the Indian border town of Kalimpong served as a base not only for Tibetan émigrés but also for U.S. and Nationalist agents who supported the Tibetan resistance (map 2.1). As early as 1956, Zhou raised China's concerns about these activities in letters and conversations with Nehru.[42] Even then, Zhou sought Nehru's assistance, linking events inside Tibet to diplomatic ties with India. Zhou stated that "if we get hold of any evidence of US espionage activities in Kalimpong, we will inform the Indian Government in order that you might be able to take some action."[43] Zhou also suggested that China would be prepared to acknowledge the McMahon Line in the eastern sector, which although not a formal concession shows how regime insecurity creates incentives for states to compromise. After the revolt, Zhou concluded that "without external encouragement and incitement, this kind of rebellion would not have erupted."[44]

Zhou's concerns were not unfounded. The CIA recruited its first Tibetan agents in Kalimpong, and rebels purchased weapons and supplies in the town. Moreover, by the outbreak of the revolt, China's leaders were probably well aware of the CIA's operation "ST Circus" to train and supply Tibetan rebels.[45] In December 1957, six Khampas trained on Saipan by the CIA parachuted into Tibet in two separate insertions, after which limited arms and supplies were delivered. In early 1958, the PLA captured one of these rebels, who no doubt revealed the details of this operation.[46] In March 1958, Zhang Guohua and Tan Guansen, the top CCP officials in Lhasa, accused the Tibetan government of relying on American support and mentioned that they knew of the secret radio station on a mountain peak near Lhasa, which had been established after

---

[40] "Zhongyang junwei dui Xizang shannan diqu pingpan ji dangqian gongzuo de zhishi (1959 nian 4 yue 23 ri)" [CMC Instructions for Current Work in Suppressing Rebellion in the Tibetan Shannan Area], in Li and Li, *Pingxi*, 99.

[41] Li and Li, *Pingxi*, 105.

[42] WP, I, 60–63, 66.

[43] Mushirul Hasan, ed., *Selected Works of Jawaharlal Nehru*, second series, vol. 36 (New Delhi: Oxford University Press, 2005), 605.

[44] *Zhou Enlai waijiao wenxuan*, 272.

[45] Conboy and Morrison, *CIA's Secret War*; Knaus, *Orphans*; Shakya, *Dragon*, 175–180, 281–286.

[46] Shakya, *Dragon*, 175.

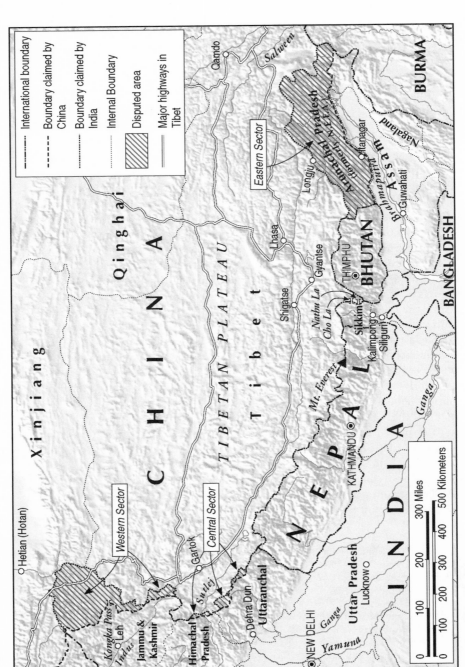

Map 2.1 China-India Border

the first CIA insertion.[47] Although the CIA's support never came close to altering the balance of power between the rebels and the PLA in Tibet, the Chinese leaders' knowledge of external support, especially from the United States, no doubt had a strong psychological impact on their sense of China's internal vulnerability to external influence.[48]

The Tibetan revolt dramatically altered the context of the territorial dispute between China and India and hardened perceptions on both sides. China's leaders concluded that India harbored intentions to maintain special influence in Tibet.[49] As Zhou explained in May 1959 to ambassadors from socialist countries, "their goal is for Tibet to stagnate, not reform, as a 'buffer state' under India's sphere of influence, becoming its protectorate."[50] Zhou then elaborated on how India pursued these goals by supporting the leaders of the Tibetan revolt.[51] On May 6, the *People's Daily* in Beijing published a scathing editorial highlighting the link between the Tibetan rebels and the Indian government.[52]

During the course of the rebellion in Tibet, various Indian actions enhanced this perception. First, only days after the revolt erupted, on March 22, 1959, Nehru sent a letter to Zhou further detailing India's territorial claims, focusing on the western sector as well as the McMahon Line in the east.[53] In light of the revolt, Nehru's demands were viewed not merely as part of an interstate dispute but also as an effort to profit from China's current weakness and strengthen India's influence within Tibet. India's demands in the western sector required that China cede control over one of only three roads connecting Tibet to other parts of China, the Xinjiang-Tibet highway. This road was especially important during the pacification operations because it entered Tibet from the west, not the east where rebel

---

[47] Shakya, *Dragon*, 176.

[48] The CIA's support of Tibetan rebels occurred in two phases. First, from December 1957 to the spring of 1961, the CIA inserted ten teams of Tibetans that had been trained in Saipan and Colorado to coordinate activities with local rebels groups. During this period, the CIA provided almost six hundred tons of supplies and material through thirty-seven different airdrops over Tibet. After 1961, when the PLA had eliminated all rebel groups inside Tibet, the focus of attention shifted to several thousand Tibetan irregulars who established a base area in the Mustang region of Nepal. See Conboy and Morrison, *CIA's Secret War*; Knaus, *Orphans*; Shakya, *Dragon*, 175–180, 281–286.

[49] Wang Hongwei, *Ximalaya shan qingjie: ZhongYin guanxi yanjiu* [Himalayan Sentiments: A Study of Chinese-Indian Relations] (Beijing: Zhongguo zangxue chubanshe, 1998), 129–154. For a detailed examination of India's role in Tibet from a Chinese perspective, see Yang Gongsu, *Zhongguo fandui waiguo qinlue ganshe Xizang difang douzheng shi* [History of China's Struggle against Foreign Aggression and Intervention in Tibet] (Beijing: Zangxue chubanshe, 1992), 249–325.

[50] *Zhou Enlai waijiao wenxuan*, 270.

[51] *Zhou Enlai waijiao wenxuan*, 273–274.

[52] *RMRB*, 6 May 1959, 1.

[53] *WP*, I, 55–57.

attacks were frequent. India's claims in the east would give it control of other vital passes and trade routes between the two countries that were used by Tibetan refugees and rebels, thereby strengthening India's influence in Tibet.

Second, in April 1959, India began to embargo trade with Tibet by banning the export of foodstuffs. In the months that followed, more items such as steel, kerosene, and spare parts for cars were embargoed. By 1960, Indian imports to Tibet had dropped by 91 percent, while Tibetan exports to India dropped by 96 percent.[54] Given the importance to Tibet's economy of trade with India, China's leaders viewed the embargo as an attempt to strangle the Tibetan economy at a moment of internal instability and perhaps to give India leverage in negotiations.

Third, also in April, the Indian government granted asylum to the Dalai Lama, who had crossed the border on March 30. Although Nehru clearly stated that the Dalai Lama would not be permitted to conduct political activities in India, he was treated with great sympathy by the Indian government, Parliament, and the general public. To Chinese eyes, the Dalai Lama was welcomed as a valiant hero. India's treatment of the Dalai Lama not only struck China as disingenuous but also raised the specter of a second government-in-exile in addition to the Nationalists on Taiwan, supported by outside powers challenging the CCP's sovereignty over China.

As perceptions hardened on both sides, stability on the border deteriorated. When PLA units moved south in pursuit of Tibetan rebels fleeing to India, Bhutan, and Nepal, they approached the international border and began to secure the frontier. As Zhou stated in September 1959, "for the purpose of preventing remnant armed Tibetan rebels from crossing the border back and forth . . . the Chinese government has in recent months dispatched guard units to be stationed in the southeastern part of the Tibet region of China."[55] At the same time, the Indian Army deployed additional troops to the frontier to deal with the influx of refugees and defend against possible Chinese incursions, which led China to conclude that India was supporting the rebels. Over the summer of 1959, numerous confrontations occurred between Chinese and Indian forces along the McMahon Line as well as in areas of the western sector.[56]

On August 25, the first armed clash between Chinese and Indian forces occurred at Longju (Langjiu), a small hamlet under Indian control near the McMahon Line. Based on conflicting interpretations of the precise location of the line, both sides claimed that this hamlet lay on their side. When the fighting was over the following day, two Indian soldiers had

[54] Yang, *Cangsang*, 232–233.
[55] *WP*, II, 32.
[56] *WP*, I, 33–43.

been killed.[57] The clash itself highlighted for China's leaders the dangers of external conflict during a period of internal turmoil and unrest. For the first time, Chinese troops had needed to engage not only the rebels but also Indian forces, who were more organized and better supplied than the insurgents. As this incident appears to have been a clash resulting from increased patrolling by both sides, China's leaders did not view it as part of a larger effort by India to strengthen its claim in the territorial dispute. Instead, it underscored the possibility of future conflict on the border and the negative implications such conflict would have for stability within Tibet.

China Compromises

Before 1960, China had rebuffed efforts by neighboring states to open negotiations over disputed territory. The Tibetan revolt, however, increased the cost of contesting land with India, Nepal, and Burma. To achieve its domestic goals of pacification and political reform in Tibet, China required peaceful ties with its neighbors. By compromising over territorial claims and securing its borders, China sought to limit external support for the revolt and gain recognition of its sovereignty over Tibet. Peaceful borders would also ensure external stability, so that more resources could be used to support internal reform. To consolidate its control and authority over Tibet, China would need a secure border to prevent foreign influence and to marshal resources for internal consolidation, not external defense.

The Longju clash produced a substantial change in China's policy toward its dispute with India. Immediately following the incident, Zhou ordered an investigation. On September 8, 1959, Mao convened a Politburo meeting to discuss the investigation and China's policy toward India. According to one participant, the Politburo agreed that China should seek a negotiated settlement to the dispute with India and that before holding negotiations, China should suggest that both sides maintain the status quo.[58] In early October 1959, Mao told Nikita Khrushchev that "the McMahon line with India will be maintained and the border conflict will end. . . . We will solve the border question with India through negotiations."[59] China did not immediately seek to open talks with India, but Mao did order a cessation of all polemics against India in the official

[57] For conflicting accounts, see *ZYBJ*, 96; *HCC*, 33.

[58] On the details of the meeting, see Wu, *Shinian*, 212.

[59] "Record of Conversation of Comrade Khrushchev N.S.," in David Wolff, " 'One Finger's Worth of Historical Events?' New Russian and Chinese Evidence on the Sino-Soviet Alliance and Split, 1948–1959," *Cold War International History Project Working Paper*, no. 30 (2000): 67.

press.[60] At the same time, Mao Zedong and Liu Shaoqi met with Ajoy Ghosh, a leading Indian communist, in Beijing. They reportedly told Ghosh that China planned to hold negotiations with India and, foreshadowing Zhou's "package deal," was prepared to trade the eastern sector for the western sector.[61]

The Politburo probably also agreed to open negotiations with Tibet's other Himalayan neighbors, Burma and Nepal. Many refugees and rebels had fled to Nepal in particular. Settlement of territorial disputes with these states would not only improve stability on the border but also pressure India to enter into talks with China. On September 24, Zhou wrote to General Ne Win, then Burma's interim prime minister, stating his interest in reopening talks based on earlier correspondence between the two sides.[62] Negotiations with Burma had been stalled since early 1957, largely because of China's reluctance to agree to Burmese demands. Zhou's letter represented the first time in two years that China had seized the initiative in this dispute. A few weeks later, Zhou moved to open negotiations with Nepal. On October 9, Zhou met with Tulsi Giri, a Nepalese minister who was representing his country at China's national day celebrations. In their discussions, Zhou expressed China's willingness to enter into talks with Nepal over their border dispute, a message conveyed to Prime Minister Bishweshwar Koirala.[63] Nepal's desire to consult with India delayed the final designation of a date.[64]

On October 21, 1959, Chinese and Indian forces clashed again, this time in the eastern sector around the Kongka Pass. Nine Indian soldiers and one Chinese were killed.[65] In response, Mao convened an informal working meeting of senior leaders on November 3 in Hangzhou.[66] Although the local PLA commanders in Tibet sought permission to assault Indian positions, Mao refused their request. Instead, he instructed Zhou to issue two new proposals to India: the creation of a forty-kilometer demilitarized buffer zone, by means of a twenty-kilometer withdrawal by

[60] Wu, *Shinian*, 215.

[61] Arthur Cohen, *The Sino-Indian Border Dispute*, I, DD/I Staff Study POLO XVI [Top Secret] (Washington, D.C.: Central Intelligence Agency, 1963), 40.

[62] Specifically, Ne Win's 4 June 1959 letter and Zhou's last letter from June 1958. Woodman, *The Making of Burma*, 536–536.

[63] *ZELNP2*, 260; Leo E. Rose, *Nepal: Strategy for Survival* (Berkeley: University of California Press, 1971), 223.

[64] Fang Jianchang, "ZhongNi bianjie chutan" [A Preliminary Investigation of the Chinese-Nepalese Border], *Zhongguo bianjiang shidi yanjiu baogao*, nos. 3–4 (1992): 20.

[65] For conflicting accounts, see *ZYBJ*, 96; *HCC*, 34–35.

[66] For a detailed recollection of this meeting, see Lei Yingfu, *Zai zuigao tongshuaibu dang canmou: Lei Yingfu huiyilu* [Staff Officer at the Supreme Command: General Lei Yingfu's Recollections] (Nanchang: Baihuazhou wenyi chubanshe, 1997), 201–203.

each side from the line of actual control, and the initiation of high-level talks between prime ministers.[67]

On November 7, Zhou wrote a letter to Nehru outlining these two proposals. Zhou asked specifically that "Prime Ministers from the two countries hold talks in the immediate future."[68] When Nehru replied, however, he agreed in principle to such talks but offered a different formula for withdrawal that would apply only to Chinese forces in the western sector, which Beijing rejected.[69] On December 17, Zhou again wrote to Nehru, proposing to hold talks in Rangoon on December 26. Zhou stated that China had decided to stop patrolling along all sectors of the border, not just in the eastern sector as Nehru has suggested in an earlier note.[70] Nehru again demurred. On December 20, Zhou met with India's ambassador in Beijing to further press for the opening of talks.[71] When Nehru requested a Chinese summary of the facts in the dispute, Zhou sent a twenty-two-page letter detailing China's claims.[72]

In January 1960, as Zhou waited for Nehru to reply to his request to open talks, the Politburo Standing Committee (PBSC) discussed the Chinese-Indian border dispute during a ten-day working meeting in Hangzhou. The committee agreed that the conflict with India should be settled swiftly and outlined China's general approach: to seek a peaceful settlement through negotiations based on the principle of "give and take" (hu-liang hurang). As one participant recalled, "China should make some concessions, India should make some concessions, [and] in this way reach an agreement through mutual compromise."[73] The PBSC also agreed to adopt a similar approach to China's other border disputes and stated that China should strive for a quick settlement with Burma and Nepal.

Internal government documents demonstrate that China's leaders linked internal stability in the frontier regions with stable and secure borders. In May 1960, the PLA's General Staff Department (GSD) issued "Southwest Region Frontier Defense Regulations" (xinan diqu bianfang shouze), which outlined the general policy direction for securing the area. The regulations stated that "to stabilize our southwestern border region quickly, we must not only bring stability to the interior (neibu), but also

---

[67] ZELNP2, 265–266.

[68] WP, III, 46.

[69] In essence, this formula would have had China withdraw from the western sector without any corresponding withdrawal by Indian from the eastern sector, which China claimed but did not occupy.

[70] WP, III, 52–57.

[71] ZELNP2, 274.

[72] WP, III, 60–82.

[73] Wu, Shinian, 248.

to the exterior (*waibu*)."[74] An internal army publication stressed the same theme, noting that "the PLA must work hard to make our southwest and northwest regional borders peaceful and secure. This is the best way to settle the problem of our border regions."[75] The document further stressed the importance of continuing to implement regulations designed to contain any potential for escalation of the conflict with India.

As noted previously, China's first attempt to compromise with Burma reflected a response to external threats, not internal ones. The two sides held talks in 1956 after patrols clashed in a disputed area when PLA units were pursuing Nationalist irregulars based in Burma at the end of 1955. The prospect of worsened relations with Burma, a key nonaligned state linked to China's efforts to improve ties with nonaligned nations and its enunciation of the Five Principles of Peaceful Coexistence, was sufficient to increase the costs of contesting land with Burma and led to the opening of talks and initial concessions. Nevertheless, Zhou Enlai felt no pressure to reach an agreement quickly with Burma. Official talks stalled in 1957, though intermittent correspondence continued without producing any progress, as China would not met Burmese demands concerning the size of the Hpimaw area to be transferred to China and the location of the boundary in the north.

Following the PBSC meeting in January 1960, Zhou moved to engage in new talks with Burma. On January 12, Zhou invited Ne Win to visit Beijing. Zhou's letter stated that if Ne Win could quickly come to China, the Chinese government would explain its principles for resolving the Chinese-Burmese dispute and conduct negotiations to remove differences between the two sides.[76] When Ne Win arrived on January 23, 1960, the two sides moved quickly to settle their dispute. The timing of the talks and China's accession to previous Burmese demands suggest that this agreement stemmed from China's ongoing effort to consolidate control over Tibet through a settlement of the Chinese-Indian dispute. Impetus for China's attempts to cooperate with Burma also grew from heightened Chinese sensitivity to the potential impact of remnant Nationalist troops still based in Burma (see map 2.2).

Following three rounds of talks, Zhou and Ne Win achieved rapid progress. On January 28, 1960, they signed a boundary agreement that outlined a comprehensive framework for settling the territorial dispute.[77]

---

[74] *ZYBJ*, 458.

[75] J. Chester Cheng, ed., *Politics of the Chinese Red Army* (Stanford, Calif.: Hoover Institution Publications, 1966), 191.

[76] *ZELNP2*, 278.

[77] *TYJ*, 1960, 65–67.

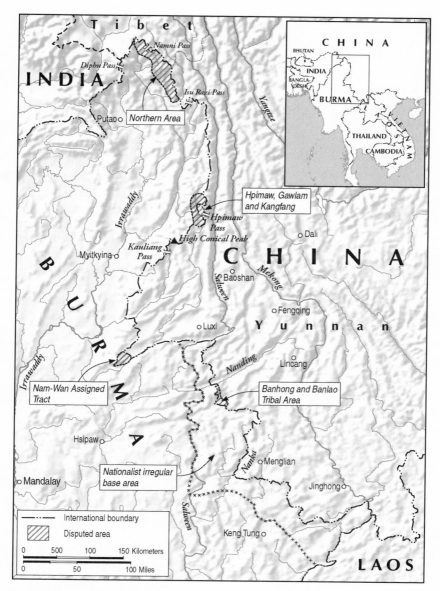

Map 2.2 China-Burma Border

China met several Burmese demands raised by U Nu in early 1957 and again by Ne Win in 1959. First, China agreed to transfer the Nam-Wan area to Burma, which encompassed the only motorway linking the Kachin and Wa states. In exchange, Burma agreed to transfer two villages in the Banhong (Panghung) area in the Wa state to China (map 2.2). Second, China agreed to use the watershed as the "customary boundary" in the north between Isu Razi Pass and the Diphu Pass at the Burmese-Indian-Chinese trijunction, conceding approximately 1,000 square kilometers to Burma. China had originally sought to make exceptions to the watershed in this area, which Burma had opposed.[78] Third, China agreed to transfer its stake in the Lufeng salt mine to Burma. Fourth, China agreed to accept the Salween watershed as the boundary between Isu Razi Pass and the High Conical Peak. In addition, the two sides maintained the 1956 bargain that Burma would return three villages to China around Hpimaw that the British had seized in 1913. During negotiations over the treaty, however, China acceded to the Burmese position concerning the size of the area to be returned to China, accepting far less than it had initially demanded.[79]

The timing of the January agreement and the compromises that it contained reflected China's efforts to reach a similar compromise with India. Zhou invited Ne Win to Beijing in early January after attempting to start talks with Nehru the previous November. Indeed, only five days after the agreement with Burma was announced, Nehru finally agreed to meet with Zhou and invited him to visit New Delhi. Before traveling to India in April 1960, Zhou stopped in Rangoon to celebrate the signing of the January agreement. Zhou repeatedly mentioned that China's settlement with Burma would "establish a model for Asian countries" and "would be advantageous for discussing the problem with India."[80] As a February editorial in the *People's Daily* asked, "The Chinese-Burmese agreement on the boundary issue set a new example for Asian countries of living in harmony. Why cannot events that have happened between China and Burma also occur between China and other Asian countries?"[81] By negotiating with Burma, Zhou hoped to convince India to accept a similar compromise.

[78] *ZELZ*, vol. 3, 1318–1319. Also see *Burma Weekly Bulletin*, vol. 9, no. 1 (5 May 1960): 6.

[79] In 1956, China asked for 482 square kilometers for the three villages in the Hpimaw area, but Burma offered only 145 square kilometers. In the final treaty, Burma transferred only 153 square kilometers of the Hpimaw area, conceding 8, not 329, square kilometers to China. The final compromise mirrored Burma's original position, not China's. See *ZELZ*, vol. 3, 1314, 1317; Daphne E. Whittam, "The Sino-Burmese Boundary Treaty," *Pacific Affairs*, vol. 34, no. 2 (Summer 1961): 180–181; Woodman, *The Making of Burma*, 533, 538.

[80] *ZELZ*, vol. 3, 1513.

[81] *RMRB*, 2 February 1960, 1.

The content of the January agreement outlined the nature of the compromise that China would pursue with India. The northern portion of the Chinese-Burmese border mostly followed the 1914 McMahon Line. In the agreement, China unequivocally accepted this alignment, though of course it did not refer to it as the McMahon Line but rather the "customary boundary." This clearly signaled to India that China would be willing to accept the direction of the McMahon Line in that dispute as well. In April, before traveling to India to conduct talks with Nehru, Zhou told U Nu, knowing that this message would be passed along to New Delhi: "we can completely solve the Chinese-Indian border problem according to the principles for solving the Chinese-Burmese border problem."[82]

In addition to concerns about the Chinese-Indian border, China had a second reason to compromise with Burma. At the time, China faced a threat to internal stability from irregular Nationalist (KMT) troops that had established base areas in Burma along the Yunnan portion of the border. Although some of these troops had been repatriated in 1954, the tempo of their harassment operations increased when the rebellion erupted in Tibet. In February 1959, China received intelligence that Chiang Kai-shek had ordered the Nationalist general in Burma, Liu Yuanlin, to take advantage of the situation in Tibet and start a rebellion in Yunnan.[83] Reportedly, Chiang ordered Liu to "use attacks to create violence, use violence to create chaos."[84] In response, Mao ordered the Yunnan provincial committee as well as the Kunming MD to increase its level of alert, prepare for the Nationalist threat, and study China's policy options.[85] On May 5, 1959, Mao dispatched General Yang Chengwu, then deputy chief of staff, to investigate the situation.[86] By early 1960, China's leaders learned that the Nationalist forces were strengthening, as Liu had constructed an airfield near Meng-Pao to receive supplies and special forces personnel from Taiwan. In April, Zhou complained about U.S.-backed KMT flights from Burma to Tibet, suggesting that this airfield might have also been used to supply Tibetan rebels as well as KMT troops.[87] Along with those who

[82] Quoted in *ZELZ*, vol. 4, 1514.

[83] *Jianguo yilai Mao Zedong wengao* [Manuscripts of Mao Zedong since the Founding of the Nation], vol. 8 (Beijing: Zhongyang wenxian chubanshe [internal circulation], 1993), 245–246.

[84] Quoted in Wang Shangrong, "Xin Zhongguo dansheng hou jici zhongda zhanzheng" [Several Major Wars after the Emergence of New China], in Zhu Yuanshi, ed., *Gongheguo yaoshi koushushi* [An Oral History of the Republic's Important Events] (Changsha: Henan renmin chubanshe, 1999), 269.

[85] *Jianguo yilai Mao Zedong wengao*, vol. 8, 245–246.

[86] *DDZGJD*, 374.

[87] *ZELNP2*, 304.

returned from Laos and Thailand, the strength of these KMT forces grew to approximately 9,400 troops.[88]

The boundary negotiations with Burma gave China an opportunity to deal with the Nationalist troops. In the spring of 1960, China began to link completion of the border negotiations to Burmese cooperation against the Nationalist troops, culminating in a joint military operation that began in late 1960. As the two sides prepared to negotiate the division of several disputed sectors, Zhou Enlai in an April 1960 meeting with Ne Win raised the issue of the KMT activities in southern Burma and asked that the two sides cooperate to shoot down KMT planes.[89] In late June, during the first meeting of the Chinese-Burmese boundary joint working group, China raised an additional demand. Zhou instructed China's chief representative, Yao Zhongming, to obtain Burma's agreement for military operations against the Nationalist irregulars.[90] Wang Shangrong, then the head of the GSD's Operations Department, likewise recalls that Zhou linked final negotiations on the boundary treaty to Burmese cooperation against the Nationalists.[91]

Burma readily agreed to China's request for two reasons. First, the Nationalist troops had been a constant source of tension in Chinese-Burmese relations, causing the original clash between Burmese and Chinese forces in November 1955. Elimination of this force would stabilize Burma's ties with China. Second, the Burmese government had had its own reasons for wanting to evict the Nationalists, who had established effective control over a large part of northeastern Burma and were also supporting the Kachin ethnic group, who sought independence. Alone, the weak Burmese armed forces could not challenge the Nationalists and therefore welcomed Chinese cooperation.[92] Military operations from November 1960 to February 1961 destroyed the primary Nationalist base areas and forced those troops not killed or captured into Laos. Approximately 741 Nationalist soldiers were killed or wounded while PLA units suffered 230 casualties.[93]

On October 10, 1960, Zhou Enlai and Prime Minister U Nu signed a boundary treaty. This document stipulated the basic direction of the Chinese-Burmese border and incorporated the compromises outlined

---

[88] *DDZGJD*, 375; Ma Jinan, "Zhongguo jundui jingwai de yichang mimi zhanzheng" [The Chinese Military's Secret War across the Border], *Dongnanya zongheng*, no. 1 (2001): 12.

[89] *ZELNP2*, 303–304.

[90] Yao, "Zhou Enlai," 100–101.

[91] Wang, "Xin Zhongguo," 270. Also see Ma, "Zhongguo jundui," 14.

[92] Yao, "Zhou Enlai," 100.

[93] *DDZGJD*, 369–379.

above.[94] Approximately one year later, after extensive surveys, Zhou and U Nu signed a boundary protocol with detailed maps of the Chinese-Burmese boundary, which outlined the location of 244 boundary markers that had been placed along the border.[95]

NEPAL

On March 11, 1960, Nepalese prime minister Koirala arrived in Beijing for high-level talks on the Chinese-Nepalese border dispute. During three rounds of negotiations, the two sides exchanged maps and discussed the details of areas where actual jurisdiction conflicted on each other's maps. On March 21, 1960, the two sides reached a preliminary agreement to use the customary boundary and actual control of border areas as the basis for a final settlement.[96] Although discrepancies were acknowledged, both sides reached consensus on the general direction of the customary boundary and agreed to establish a joint boundary commission to deal with remaining differences. During a meeting with Koirala, Mao proposed that sovereignty over disputed Mount Everest be divided equally.[97]

During the talks, one of the key topics was how to deal with Tibetan rebels along the Chinese-Nepali border. Zhou stated that Nepal could arrest them, give them asylum, or return them to China.[98] Subsequently, sometime in 1960, Nepal allowed China to conduct military operations against rebel groups stationed in Nepal, perhaps for the same reasons that Burma allowed China to conduct operations against the Nationalist forces.[99] According to a Chinese diplomat, the PLA conducted additional operations against Tibetan rebels in Nepal in June 1964.[100]

Final terms of the border settlement were negotiated over the next fourteen months during four sessions of the joint commission. On October 5, 1961, Liu Shaoqi and King Mahendra signed a boundary treaty.[101] Again, as it had done with Burma, China acceded to most of Nepal's demands. In the final settlement, Nepal received control over ten of the eleven disputed sectors, totaling approximately 2,331 square kilometers.[102] By contrast,

---

[94] *TYJ*, 1960, 68–79.

[95] *TYJ*, 1961, 52–232.

[96] *TYJ*, 1960, 63–65.

[97] *Mao Zedong waijiao wenxuan* [Mao Zedong's Selected Works on Diplomacy] (Beijing: Shijie zhishi chubanshe, 1994), 395.

[98] ZELNP2, 293.

[99] Garver, *Protracted*, 148.

[100] Yang, *Zhongguo*, 324–325.

[101] *TYJ*, 1962, 45–50.

[102] For Chinese sources, see ZELNP2, 293–296, 315; Wang Taiping, ed., *Zhonghua renmin gongheguo waijiao shi, 1957–1969* [Diplomatic History of the People's Republic of China, 1957–1969] (Beijing: Shijie zhishi chubanshe, 1998), 99–100; Yang, *Zhongguo*, 320–325. For English sources, see Arthur Lall, *How Communist China Negotiates* (New

China received control over the other disputed sector, which was approximately 145 square kilometers. Regarding Mount Everest, it was agreed that the boundary would "pass through the peak," a stipulation that implied a division of sovereignty but allowed the Nepali leader to maintain his country's claim.[103]

When the Tibetan revolt threatened China's territorial integrity, the strategic context of China's territorial dispute with Nepal fundamentally changed. Now, a stabilized border and friendly relations with Himalayan states were much more important than any territory that had been disputed. Although China conceded much of what it had claimed, it gained improved relations with an important Himalayan neighbor, secured a vulnerable portion of Tibet's international boundary, and placed additional pressure on India to seek a similar agreement in its upcoming talks.

Three aspects of China's negotiations with Nepal support this interpretation. First, the timing of China's negotiations with Nepal was linked to Zhou's efforts to seek a compromise settlement with India. After the Politburo decision to pursue a negotiated settlement with India in September 1959, Zhou invited Nepalese leader Koirala to visit Beijing in October 1959. After Zhou agreed in February 1960 to travel to India in April, he opened high-level talks with Nepal and signed an agreement on the principles for resolving the Chinese-Nepalese dispute. By signing agreements with two neighboring states before arriving in New Delhi, Zhou aimed to build momentum for a similar settlement with India. Zhou praised the January 1960 agreement with Burma because it "created a new model for developing unity and friendship among Asian and African countries."[104] Likewise, after the signing of the March 1960 agreement with Nepal, a *People's Daily* editorial stated that "this is strong proof that any unresolved conflict between Asian and African countries can be settled."[105]

Second, the boundary line in the 1961 Chinese-Nepalese treaty conformed with the direction of the McMahon Line in the eastern sector of the Chinese-Indian border, again indicating China's willingness to accept India's position in exchange for Indian recognition of China's claim in the west. Given the close ties between New Delhi and Kathmandu, India was no doubt well aware of the terms that China would be willing to accept in India's own dispute.

York: Columbia University Press, 1968), 194–201; J.R.V. Prescott, *Map of Mainland Asia by Treaty* (Carlton: Melbourne University Press, 1975), 265–267; Rose, *Nepal*, 224–229, 235–236.

[103] See article 11 of the treaty.

[104] *RMRB*, 29 January 1960, 2.

[105] *RMRB*, 25 March 1960, 1.

Third, reflecting the internal insecurity in Tibet, China took additional measures to eliminate tensions with Nepal on its border. In the March 1960 negotiations, the two sides agreed to withdraw twenty kilometers from each side of the border to create a demilitarized zone. Nevertheless, on June 28, 1960, Chinese and Nepalese forces clashed in the Mustang region of Nepal. At the time, PLA units were pursuing Tibetan rebel groups near the border, violating the terms of the March 1960 agreement. Chinese troops killed a Nepali border patrol officer and captured fifteen others, which threatened to become a cause for Nepal to jettison the boundary agreement. Zhou immediately issued an apology, and China paid an indemnity for the incident.[106] In August 1961, the two sides signed an additional agreement to ban cross-border movement of border-area residents, which was designed to prevent Nepalese border areas from supporting Tibetan rebels.[107]

After the boundary treaty was signed, a joint boundary commission began to survey the border and erect boundary markers. On January 20, 1963, Chen Yi and Tulsi Giri signed a boundary protocol, which signified the completion of the demarcation phase. Survey and demarcation teams placed ninety-nine boundary makers along seventy-nine different points on the border.[108] Much of the protocol described the direction of the boundary across various Himalayan peaks.[109]

INDIA

After Nehru's February 1960 invitation to Zhou to visit New Delhi, the two sides agreed to meet in early April following China's negotiations with Burma and Nepal. Although the talks failed spectacularly, little information about the discussions has been revealed to date. Newly available sources from China, which include summaries of each meeting between Zhou and Nehru, permit a reconstruction of the negotiations for the first time.[110] These materials demonstrate China's efforts to outline a framework for compromise similar to those reached with Burma and Nepal. Although the talks failed to produce a written agreement or even an informal consensus, these new sources nevertheless reveal China's attempts to seek a cooperative solution to the dispute.

Before departing for New Delhi, Zhou personally drafted a plan that outlined China's objectives in the talks with Nehru. The document, titled

---

[106] FEER, 29 September 1960, 697.

[107] Guy Searls, "Communist China's Border Policy: Dragon Throne Imperialism?" Current Scene, vol. 11, no. 12 (15 April 1963): 13.

[108] Department of State, "China-Nepal Boundary," International Boundary Study, no. 50 (May 30, 1965): 5.

[109] TYJ, 1963, 67–121.

[110] The two principal sources are ZELZ, vol. 3, 1515–1530; ZELNP2, 302, 306–314.

"Plan for the Chinese-Indian Premier Talks on the Border Problem (draft)," describes Zhou's intention to ease tensions between the two sides and establish a framework for settling the dispute, in particular the principle of compromising over conflicting claims. Before he departed, Zhou stated that his most optimistic assessment was that China could reach an agreement "the same as with Burma and Nepal."[111]

Even before Nehru agreed to talks with Zhou, China had decided to compromise. In his November 7 letter to Nehru, Zhou repeated China's policy of not dispatching troops beyond the McMahon Line to disputed sectors in the east. Previously, Zhou had mentioned several times to Nehru that he would be willing to accept a border delimited by the McMahon Line, though of course he would not "acknowledge" (*chengren*) the line itself.[112] During a meeting with the Soviet ambassador in early November, Zhou stated that "although China does not acknowledge the McMahon Line, the McMahon Line can still be used as a boundary line."[113] Moreover, China's acceptance of the McMahon Line in its agreement with Burma and affirmation of that line's direction along the Himalayas in its agreement with Nepal suggested that China would also accept the McMahon Line in a compromise with India, thus addressing India's largest concern.

Newly available sources indicate that during the talks themselves, Zhou proposed a territorial swap that Nehru's official biographer denies ever occurred.[114] According to a recently declassified CIA report, a circular distributed to Indian embassies stated that, in the meetings, "It was . . . obvious that if we accepted the line claimed by China in Ladakh, [the Chinese] would accept the McMahon line."[115] In their first meeting, Zhou discussed the McMahon Line, stating that the area south of the line was once part of Tibet but that China would be "practical" and was not seeking to raise new demands to this territory.[116] In their fifth meeting, Zhou stated that the customary line of actual control should be used as the basis for a settlement, which implied a compromise based on exchanging China's position in the west for India's position in the east. In the sixth meeting, Zhou stated: "In the eastern sector, we recognize the line reached

---

[111] Zhou Enlai quoted in *ZELNP2*, 302; Shi Zhongquan, *Zhou Enlai de zhuoyue gongxian* [Zhou Enlai's Great Contributions] (Beijing: Zhongong zhongyang dangxiao chubanshe, 1993), 393.

[112] As others have noted, China's usage of the word "acknowledge" caused great confusion and may very well have increased India's own suspicions about China's intentions.

[113] *ZELZ*, vol. 3, 1511.

[114] Sarvepalli Gopal, *Jawaharlal Nehru: A Biography* (London: Jonathan Cape, 1984), 136.

[115] Cohen, *Sino-Indian*, II, 47.

[116] For Chinese accounts of the six meetings, see *ZELZ*, vol. 3, 1517–1523; *ZELNP2*, 304–314.

by India's administrative jurisdiction. In the western sector, India should recognize the line of China's administrative jurisdiction."[117] This approach later became known as the "package deal" for settling the dispute.

The only result of the talks was the establishment of an expert working group to determine precise areas of disagreement through mutual examination of each side's maps and historical documents. A lengthy report was published in 1961, but no progress was achieved in settling the dispute.[118] Nevertheless, although the Zhou-Nehru talks were fruitless, China's effort to compromise should not be overlooked. Prior to his meetings, Zhou had every expectation that he would be able to use the same type of compromise agreement that had settled disputes with Burma and Nepal. He publicly and privately stated his intention to reach such an agreement. Yet China clearly overestimated the efficacy of such a cooperative posture. By compromising publicly with Burma and Nepal, China may have encouraged Nehru to bargain hard with China in order to maximize India's gains.

In the absence of an agreement, China moved to stabilize the Tibetan frontier unilaterally. First, it withdrew from its forward positions in the east to reduce the potential for clashes or conflicts between Chinese and Indian frontier defense troops. At the same time, to secure the Xinjiang-Tibet highway, it began to establish more posts in the western sector of its claim line. Second, the GSD issued "Southwest Region Frontier Defense Regulations" in May 1960. The rationale for these regulations clearly acknowledged the link between external border security and internal political stability: according to an internal PLA history, the regulations "were designed to avoid conflict with neighboring states and to make our southwestern border peaceful."[119] They banned patrolling, demolition, exercises, live fire, and other types of potentially provocative actions.[120] China also moved to seal its border with India, largely to stop the cross-border movement of rebels.

After the failed talks, China continued to press for the package deal that Zhou had outlined to Nehru. In July 1960, Chen Yi approached Indian diplomats in Beijing, stating that China was prepared to negotiate based on Zhou's formula. Chen further stated that Zhou would be willing to visit India again to sign an agreement. At the same time, China sought

---

[117] ZELNP2, 312.

[118] *Report of the Officials of the Governments of India and the People's Republic of China on the Boundary Question* (New Delhi: Ministry of External Affairs, 1961).

[119] ZYBJ, 458.

[120] For a detailed description, see Wang Shangrong, "ZhongYin bianjing ziwei fanji zuozhan shijian de zongcan zuozhanbu" [The GSD's Operations Department during the Chinese-Indian Border Counterattack in Self-Defense], in *Zongcan moubu: huiyi shiliao* [General Staff Department: Recollections and Historical Materials] (Beijing: Jiefangjun chubanshe [military circulation], 1997), 551–552.

to send messages through Burmese leader U Nu, who maintained a close working relationship with Nehru. In November 1960, Zhou repeated to U Nu China's willingness to drop its claim in the eastern sector in exchange for India's acceptance of China's position in the west, especially the territory it already controlled.[121] In April 1961, the Chinese embassy in New Delhi probed whether India would support the appointment of an arbitrator to settle the dispute. In June 1961, on the sidelines of the Geneva Conference on Laos, the Chinese delegation indicated that Chen Yi desired to discuss the dispute with Krishna Menon.[122]

External Threats?

The other mechanism in my theory of cooperation in territorial disputes, external threats, offers the most plausible alternative explanation for China's willingness to compromise in its disputes with Burma, Nepal, and India in 1960. This explanation asserts that China settled not to consolidate its domestic authority within Tibet but to balance against external threats posed by various rivals, including the United States, the Soviet Union, and India.[123] To start, the absence of compromise before 1960 should be stressed. Although the United States remained China's primary adversary throughout the 1950s and into the early 1960s, China did not pursue compromise in those disputes that might have strengthened its position vis-à-vis the United States. If that had been China's goal, it might have engaged in cooperative efforts with other nonaligned countries with which it disputed territory in the 1950s, as well as with allies of the United States, such as Pakistan or Afghanistan. Indeed, as discussed in the next section, China did pursue compromise with these states a few years later, but in response to new internal threats, not external ones.

Likewise, despite the emerging Chinese-Soviet split, China's compromise attempts in the early 1960s were not designed to improve China's position in its growing rivalry with the Soviet Union. China's initial offers to compromise with Burma, Nepal, and India occurred in late 1959 and early 1960, when relations between China and the Soviet Union remained cordial despite disagreement over policy toward the United States and other issues that surfaced in 1958. Most importantly, China's efforts to compromise from January to April 1960 occurred before the Soviet Union's July 1960 decision to withdraw its remaining experts working in

---

[121] Cohen, *Sino-Indian*, II, 66.

[122] Cohen, *Sino-Indian*, III, 3–4.

[123] See, for example, Eric A. Hyer, "The Politics of China's Boundary Disputes and Settlements" (Ph.D. dissertation, Columbia University, 1990); Francis Watson, *The Frontiers of China* (New York: Praeger, 1966).

China and its decision in the middle of 1961 to provide India with limited military assistance.[124]

Finally, China's attempts to compromise with Burma and Nepal were not part of an effort to balance against growing Indian power. Although India was more threatening to China after 1959, this was not because of increased Indian activity in the region or a rise in Indian power. Instead, China's leaders viewed India as threatening because of their own insecurity in Tibet and their beliefs about India's ambitions in the area. More generally, if China was seeking to counter India's growing influence in the region, territorial compromise with India probably would not have furthered this objective. If China and India were really only competing for influence over buffer states such as Nepal and to a lesser extent Burma, China probably would have adopted a much more assertive policy in the territorial dispute with India and not pursued compromise. Instead, China's leaders were countering internal threats to territorial integrity, which they believed that India could exacerbate or exploit. To crush the rebellion and consolidate direct rule of Tibet, China ironically needed secure borders and improved ties with its neighbors.

THE 1962 TERRITORIAL CRISIS

Even before the widely publicized agreements with Burma and Nepal in 1960, many of China's other neighbors had hoped to hold talks over their disputed boundaries. In October 1959, for example, President Ayub Khan stated that Pakistan would approach China to settle any territorial disputes.[125] Through its ambassador in Beijing in February 1960 and then through a March 1961 diplomatic note, Pakistan again sought to hold boundary talks with China.[126] Likewise, Mongolia first approached China in 1957 to open negotiations on the border and raised the issue again during Zhou Enlai's 1960 state visit.[127] North Korea also reportedly sought to hold boundary talks with China in the early 1950s and again in 1961.[128]

---

[124] Allen S. Whiting, *The Chinese Calculus of Deterrence: India and Indochina* (Ann Arbor: University of Michigan Press, 1975), 73.

[125] Anwar Hussain Seyd, *China and Pakistan: Diplomacy of Entente Cordiale* (Amherst: University of Massachusetts Press, 1974), 82.

[126] Shen Bingnian, ed., *Xinjiang tongzhi: waishi zhi* [Xinjiang Gazetteer: Foreign Affairs] (Wulumuqi: Xinjiang renmin chubanshe, 1995), 306.

[127] Wang Yinqing and Zhaori Getu, eds., *Neimenggu zizhiqu zhi: junshi zhi* [Inner Mongolian Autonomous Region Gazetteer: Military Affairs] (Huhehaote: Neimenggu renmin chubanshe, 2002), 473.

[128] Interview, Beijing, June 2002. All interviews for this project were conducted on a non-attribution basis.

In each instance, China rebuffed its neighbor's request. Yet in early 1962, China quickly changed its approach. Between February and June, China moved to open talks with Pakistan, Mongolia, and North Korea. China also redoubled efforts to hold talks with the Soviet Union and readily agreed to enter into boundary negotiations when approached by Afghanistan at the end of the year. China offered compromises in disputes with each country, signing four boundary agreements and holding unprecedented negotiations with the Soviet Union.

Regime insecurity best explains this dramatic change in China's approach to many of its remaining frontier disputes. In the spring of 1962, China's leaders confronted a perfect storm of insecurity created first by the political instability associated with the economic crisis and famine after the Great Leap Forward and then by ethnic unrest in Xinjiang, like Tibet a vital frontier region. Challenges from India and Taiwan in other disputes only increased the importance of maintaining territorial integrity and consolidating the state's internal control. Although each event by itself may have been insufficient to create incentives to compromise in so many territorial disputes, the combination of these threats, in the same two-month period, against the backdrop of the Great Leap, alarmed China's leaders. This combination of internal threats to both territorial integrity and political stability increased the cost of maintaining frontier disputes with its neighbors. As the crisis deepened, China moved to open talks and offer concessions in many of its frontier disputes.

Political Instability in China Proper

This period of regime insecurity began with the dramatic failure of the Great Leap Forward (GLF), which spawned a severe crisis of legitimacy for China's leaders. In 1958, the GLF represented Mao's idealistic plan for the rapid industrialization of a largely agricultural economy.[129] The approach was to use organizational and mobilization techniques to achieve ambitious growth targets, such as producing 30 million tons of

---

[129] For two review articles on this period, see Nicholas Lardy, "The Chinese Economy under Stress, 1958–1965," in John King Fairbank and Roderick MacFarquhar, eds., *The Cambridge History of China*, vol. 14 (Cambridge: Cambridge University Press, 1987), 360–397; Kenneth Lieberthal, "The Great Leap Forward and the Split in the Yenan Leadership," in John King Fairbank and Roderick MacFarquhar, eds., *The Cambridge History of China*, vol. 14 (Cambridge: Cambridge University Press, 1987), 293–359. On the origins of the Great Leap, see David M. Bachman, *Bureaucracy, Economy, and Leadership in China: The Institutional Origins of the Great Leap Forward* (Cambridge: Cambridge University Press, 1991); Roderick MacFarquhar, *The Origins of the Cultural Revolution*, vol. 2 (New York: Columbia University Press, 1983); Frederick C. Teiwes and Warren Sun, *China's Road to Disaster: Mao, Central Politicians and Provincial Leaders in the Unfolding of the Great Leap Forward, 1955–1959* (Armonk, N.Y.: M. E. Sharpe, 1999).

steel when output in the previous year had been only 5.5 million.[130] In a matter of months, massive communes were established to increase both agricultural and industrial production, while local officials were permitted to use any means necessary, however unscientific, to achieve their unrealistic production targets.

Rather than catapult China into the modern industrial age, the GLF propelled China backward. The economic and human costs were staggering and unprecedented in the PRC's history. The emphasis on rapid industrialization shifted rural resources away from agriculture, which led to a decrease in production that bad weather exacerbated. Simultaneously, more grain was extracted from the countryside for urban areas, further compounding the crisis. This combination of misguided agricultural policies, bad weather, and bureaucratic incompetence led to the starvation of somewhere between 20 and 30 million people from 1959 to 1962. Grain production in 1960 was only 75.5 percent of that in 1958. Industrial output also decreased significantly.[131] China's GDP dropped by 27 percent in 1961 alone.[132] No period of economic decline since 1949 parallels the one that occurred at this time.

The aftermath of the GLF had dramatic political consequences for China's leaders. Domestically, the senior leadership focused on rebuilding the economy and consolidating the state's internal strength. On November 3, 1960, the Central Committee (CC) of the CCP issued a "Twelve Article Emergency Decree" designed to restore agricultural production through the dismantling of the commune system. On November 15, the CC issued another emergency directive to halt mass mobilization efforts. Retrenchment became official policy at the Ninth Plenum in January 1961 with the slogan "readjustment, consolidation, replenishment and raising standards" (*tiaozheng, gugong, changshi, tigao*).[133] Mao himself became increasingly isolated from day-to-day policy making as Liu Shaoqi and Deng Xiaoping moved to repair the economy.[134] To relieve pressure in urban areas, and presumably to prevent potential unrest, the CC decided to reduce China's urban population and preempt unrest by sending 20 million people to the countryside.[135]

The CCP's focus on regime consolidation required a stable external environment. Relations with the United States were "generally tranquil" during this period, as China participated in the second Geneva Confer-

---

[130] Lieberthal, "Great Leap Forward," 309.

[131] Lieberthal, "Great Leap Forward," 318.

[132] World Bank, World Development Indicators, online database.

[133] ZELNP2, 392.

[134] Roderick MacFarquhar, *The Origins of the Cultural Revolution*, vol. 3 (New York: Columbia University Press, 1997), 1–121.

[135] MacFarquhar, *Origins*, vol. 3, 32.

ence on Laos in July 1961 and continued the ambassadorial talks in War-saw.[136] In December 1961, China stopped shelling Jinmen Island with live ammunition, switching to propaganda leaflets instead.[137] The Chinese-Indian border remained stable without armed clashes, probably as a result of China's conflict-avoidance procedures instituted in early 1960. Despite growing tensions in relations with the Soviet Union following the July 1960 withdrawal of Soviet economic advisers from China, the tenor of the polemics had abated. In 1961, the two sides discussed limited economic cooperation and the potential sale of MiG-21 fighter aircraft.

Government documents, however, connect this foreign policy orientation with China's domestic economic crisis. In early 1962, Wang Jiaxiang, head of the CCP's International Liaison Department, which played a key role in China's foreign policy in this period, wrote several internal reports in which he proposed further moderation in China's external relations.[138] The essence of Wang's proposals were contained in a February 27, 1962, letter to Zhou Enlai, Deng Xiaoping, and Chen Yi that he coauthored with Liu Ningyi and Wu Xiuquan. Wang argued that because of China's internal economic difficulties and diplomatic "struggles" with the United States and the Soviet Union, China should relax its foreign policy and buy time to improve the country's internal economic situation. Wang argued, in particular, that China should seek to avoid becoming America's primary target, be alert to Khrushchev's efforts to isolate China, and find a way to break the stalemate with India, noting that Nehru was not an enemy of the Chinese nation.[139]

In September 1962, Mao harshly criticized Wang at a preparatory meeting for the Tenth Plenum of the Eighth Central Committee, linking moderation abroad with "revisionism" at home. Nevertheless, Wang's ideas reflected China's general approach to foreign affairs as it began to pursue compromise agreements in many frontier disputes in the spring of 1962. In February, for instance, Chinese diplomats in New Delhi informed left-leaning journalists in India that China would allow joint use of the Xin-

---

[136] Zhang Baijia, "The Changing International Scene and Chinese Policy Toward the United States, 1954–1970," in Robert S. Ross and Jiang Changbin, eds., *Re-examining the Cold War: U.S.-China Diplomacy, 1954–1973* (Cambridge, Mass.: Harvard University Press, 2001), 60.

[137] Wang Ziwen, ed., *Fujian shengzhi: junshi zhi* [Fujian Provincial Gazetteer: Military Affairs] (Beijing: Xinhua chubanshe, 1995), 291.

[138] Xu Zehao, ed., *Wang Jiaxiang nianpu* [Chronicle of Wang Jiaxiang's Life] (Beijing: Zhongyang wenxian chubanshe, 2001), 486–489. Two of these reports were subsequently openly published. See *Wang Jiaxiang xuanji* [Wang Jiaxiang's Selected Works] (Beijing: Renmin chubanshe, 1989), 444–460.

[139] Wang's February 27 letter is summarized and excerpted in Xu, *Wang Jiaxiang nianpu*, 488 and Xu Zehao, *Wang Jiaxiang zhuan* [Wang Jiaxiang's Biography] (Beijing: Dangdai Zhongguo chubanshe, 1996), 563.

jiang-Tibet highway, recognize the McMahon Line in the east, and form a joint commission to delimit the border in the western sector.[140] Wang noted the domestic imperative for external moderation in another report in March, writing that "especially because our country remains in a period of emergency [*feichang shiqi*], we should deal with matters even more cautiously and not exceed our limits."[141] Although scholars have long speculated that Wang's reports represented divisions within China's senior leadership, no strong evidence exists of such fissures at the time that they were written. Mao's attack was more opportunistic than anything else, as Wang provided an easy target.[142] Moreover, even after Mao's attack, China continued to pursue compromise in its frontier disputes.

Unrest in the Northwest

Against the backdrop of the Great Leap's failure and the resulting retrenchment effort, China faced renewed internal threats to its territorial integrity when ethnic Kazakhs began to flee in large numbers from Xinjiang to the Soviet Union. From early April to late May of 1962, more than 60,000 people fled across the border into the Soviet Republic of Kazakhstan, a flight that resulted in a large and violent riot in the town of Yining (Kulja) on May 29, 1962, as China moved to seal the border. Subsequently called the "Yita incident" (*shijian*), these events signaled the spread of frontier instability from Tibet into Xinjiang, China's single largest administrative region comprising 17 percent of the country.

Similar to the Tibetan revolt, the migration and demonstrations in Xinjiang highlighted the vulnerability of China's large and multiethnic state to external influence and the importance of cooperation with neighbors in maintaining internal stability. The first and primary source of vulnerability was Soviet influence within China. From the mid-1880s, Russia played an influential role in Yining. During the Republican period, the Soviets exerted an exceptionally high degree of influence over various Han Chinese warlords in Xinjiang, especially Sheng Shicai.[143] After the end of

---

[140] Cohen, *Sino-Indian*, III, 24.

[141] Xu, *Wang Jiaxiang nianpu*, 488. For more on Wang Jiaxiang and Mao, see Li Jie, "Changes in China's Domestic Situation in the 1960s and Sino-US Relations," in Robert S. Ross and Jiang Changbin, eds., *Re-examining the Cold War: U.S.-China Diplomacy, 1954–1973* (Cambridge, Mass.: Harvard University Press, 2001), 301–306; MacFarquhar, *Origins*, vol. 3, 269–273.

[142] One informant believes that Mao seized upon Wang Jiaxiang simply as a means to return to a more active position in Chinese politics. Wang was an easy target because Mao did not have the standing to criticize the domestic policies of Liu and Deng, who were then in charge of the day-to-day affairs. Interview, Beijing, February 2004.

[143] Andrew D. W. Forbes, *Warlords and Muslims in Chinese Central Asia: A Political History of Republican Sinkiang, 1911–1949* (New York: Cambridge University Press, 1986).

World War II, Moscow supported the founding of the East Turkestan Republic (1946–49), established in three prefectures abutting Kazakhstan.[144] Following the PRC's establishment, Soviet influence lingered. Over 103,000 Soviet citizens lived in Xinjiang, and many of them, who were ethnic Kazakhs, served in the local government and military units. The Russian language was more common than Mandarin, dominating the local press. School textbooks, for example, were imported from Moscow, describing the Soviet Union, not the PRC, as the "motherland."[145] The Soviet Union maintained four consulates in Xinjiang, all of which predated the establishment of the PRC.[146]

A second source of vulnerability was the weakness of central government institutions in the region. Like Tibet, Xinjiang lacked political institutions linking it with the central government that the CCP could use to consolidate its authority after 1949. Under the Qing dynasty, Xinjiang had been ruled as a military colony and was not integrated into the centralized provincial system of administration.[147] During the Republican era, a string of ethnic Han Chinese warlords controlled the area, but they governed in almost complete independence of the Nationalist government and usually maintained far closer administrative and economic ties with the Soviet Union than with China proper. As few non-Han cadres were available to help the CCP maintain authority in the region, the central government had to rely on local officials who had either served in the East Turkestan Republic or had served the Russians or various warlords.[148]

Xinjiang's relative isolation from China proper was a third source of vulnerability. When the PRC was established in 1949, few motorable roads linked Xinjiang with the rest of the country. Indeed, to facilitate the CCP's control of these areas, the Soviet Union airlifted more than 14,000 PLA troops from Jiuquan in Gansu Province to Urmuqi in the fall of 1949 because no suitable roads were available to transport them.[149] At the same

---

[144] Linda Benson, *The Ili Rebellion: The Moslem Challenge to Chinese Authority in Xinjiang, 1944–1949* (Armonk, N.Y.: M. E. Sharpe, 1990).

[145] Li Danhui, "Dui 1962 nian Xinjiang Yita shijian qiyin de lishi kaocha (xu)" [Historical Investigation of the Origins of the 1962 Yita Incident in Xinjiang (cont.)], *Dangshi yanjiu ziliao*, no. 5 (1999): 1–22.

[146] Shen, *Xinjiang tongzhi: waishi zhi*, 49–63.

[147] Xinjiang was incorporated as a province in 1884 as the Qing empire collapsed. On Xinjiang under the Qing, see Joseph Fletcher, "Ch'ing Inner Asia c. 1800," in John K. Fairbank, ed., *The Cambridge History of China*, vol. 10 (Cambridge: Cambridge University Press, 1978); James Millward, *Beyond the Pass: Economy, Ethnicity and Empire in Qing Central Asia, 1759–1864* (Stanford, Calif.: Stanford University Press, 1998); Peter C. Perdue, *China Marches West: The Qing Conquest of Central Eurasia* (Cambridge, Mass.: Belknap Press of Harvard University Press, 2005).

[148] Li Danhui, "Dui 1962 nian Xinjiang Yita shijian."

[149] *DDZGJD*, 168.

time, most of Xinjiang's trade was conducted with adjacent Soviet republics, not with the provinces of China proper.[150]

A fourth source of vulnerability that the Yita incident highlighted was the PRC's undefended border in the region. Throughout the 1950s, China's borders with the USSR and Mongolia were basically unguarded, known as "having a border without defense" (*you bian wu fang*).[151] At the height of the Chinese-Soviet alliance, socialist idealism downplayed the importance of secure borders between "fraternal states," leading to the deployment of few guards and frequent unregulated crossings by local residents. According to a PLA history, only 628 soldiers guarded more than 11,800 kilometers of border adjacent to the Soviet Union and Mongolia in the 1950s and early 1960s. Along the Xinjiang sector, 110 troops manned only eight frontier defense stations (*bianfang zhan*).[152] In the Yili Prefecture, where the Yita incident occurred, only two frontier defense posts and one checkpoint had been established. Of the 300 kilometers of international border in that region, only 30 percent could be patrolled every few days, while some areas were patrolled only once a week, if at all.[153] Along the Mongolian sector, only two frontier defense stations had been established, with twenty-six guards.[154]

For China's leaders, Soviet actions highlighted the state's weakness in this frontier. In an exchange of letters and notes following the Yita incident, China's leaders consistently sought to blame the Soviet Union for the crisis.[155] Although there had been as many as 103,000 Soviet citizens resident in Xinjiang in the early 1950s, the vast majority of them had been repatri-

---

[150] On Xinjiang-Russian trade, see Li Sheng, *Xinjiang dui Su(E) maoyi shi (1600–1990)* [Xinjiang's Trade with the Soviet Union (Russia) (1600–1990)] (Wulumuqi: Xinjiang renmin chubanshe, 1993).

[151] Li Danhui, "Dui 1962 nian Xinjiang Yita shijian," 5.

[152] *Gongan budui*, 78. This deployment stands in contrast to deployments on China's other borders during the period. Along the border with Burma and Laos, for example, China had stationed more than 20,000 troops from thirteen regiments and seven battalions.

[153] Li Danhui, "Dui 1962 nian Xinjiang Yita shijian," 5.

[154] *Gongan budui*, 78.

[155] See, for example, the following documents from the Russian archives. "Record of Conversation with the Vice–Foreign Minister of the PRC Zhang Hanfu," 24 April 1962 ["Zapis besedy s zamestitelom ministra inostrannykh del KNR Chzhan Khan-fu," 24 aprelya 1962 goda], *AVP RF*, fond 0100, opis 55, delo 6, papka 480, pp. 119–120; "Statement of the Government of the PRC from 24 April 1962" ["Zayavlenie pravitelstva KNR ot 24 aprelya 1962 goda"], *AVP RF*, fond 0100, opis 55, delo 2, papka 480, pp. 37–39; "Reply of the Government of the PRC on the Memorandum of the Government of the U.S.S.R. from 29 April 1962," 19 May 1962 ["Otbet pravitelstva KNR na pamyantnuyu zapisku Pravitelstva SSSR ot 29 aprealya 1962 goda," 19 maya 1962 g.], *AVP RF*, fond 0100, opis 55, delo 2, papka 480, pp. 44–48. I am grateful to Lorenz Luthi for sharing his translations of these documents with me. All documents are from the Foreign Policy Archive of the Russian Federation.

ated by end of the decade.[156] China charged that Soviet diplomats had issued false identification papers in 1960 and 1961 and then encouraged holders of these cards, many of whom were ethnic Kazakhs, to flee across the border. To facilitate their flight, Soviet border guards had reportedly opened wide holes in border fences, dispatched trucks to transport refugees from the border into the Soviet Union, and spread a steady stream of print and radio propaganda to encourage such migration.[157]

From the Chinese perspective, the USSR was deliberately seeking to destabilize a region where the central government's control was already quite tenuous. The flight of so many people had hollowed out the population of nearby counties. In Tacheng County, 68 percent of the population had fled across the border, while in Yumin County more than 50 percent had fled.[158] This depopulation had dramatically reduced the labor force in these areas and included many ethnic Kazakh officials and military officers, the loss of which threatened further instability. The migration had caused a failure of crops from 60,000 *mu* of abandoned farmland and resulted in the loss of more than 230,000 head of livestock, both of which were critical to the local economy.[159]

These events brought into stark relief China's own weaknesses in Xinjiang as well as the latent challenge of Soviet influence. Moreover, the Yita incident dramatically changed the context of China's unresolved disputes with its northern neighbors. Maintaining stability in Xinjiang required securing its undefended and undemarcated frontier with the Soviet Union and Mongolia. Whatever territorial gains China sought in this region paled in comparison to the challenge of maintaining internal control over a restive ethnic minority population far from Beijing.

To consolidate the regime's authority in Xinjiang, China pursued both unilateral measures and diplomacy. First, after the exodus, the government moved quickly to strengthen its control of the border. Members of the paramilitary Xinjiang Production and Construction Corps were dispatched to patrol the border and erect checkpoints. In July, the CC ordered the creation of thirty-eight border farms in Yili, Tacheng, and

[156] Shen, *Xinjiang tongzhi: waishi zhi*, 95. By 1959, 91,499 Soviet citizens had been repatriated along with 41,000 family members, or roughly 88 percent of the total living in Xinjiang since 1949.

[157] Li Danhui, "Dui 1962 nian Xinjiang Yita shijian"; Zhang Zhouxiang, *Xinjiang bianfang gaiyao* [Overview of Xinjiang's Frontier Defense] (Wulumuqi: Xinjiang renmin chubanshe, 1999), 357–359.

[158] Li Fusheng, ed., *Xinjiang bingtuan tunken shubian shi* [History of the Xinjiang Production and Construction Corps' Development and Defense of the Frontier] (Wulumuqi: Xinjiang renmin chubanshe, 1997), 712; Zheng Zhiyun and Li Min, eds., *Yumin xianzhi* [Yumin County Gazetteer] (Wulumuqi: Xinjiang renmin chubanshe, 2003), 438.

[159] Zhang, *Xinjiang*, 358–359.

other areas under the Xinjiang Production and Construction Corps. These farms comprised more than 11,000 square kilometers of land and formed a 30-kilometer-wide buffer between Xinjiang and the Soviet Union along key communication routes.[160] In September 1962, the GSD issued new regulations for the administration of the Chinese-Soviet and Chinese-Mongolian borders.[161] By the end of 1963, more than 11,200 soldiers had been deployed to garrison more than 201 frontier defense headquarters, stations, and checkpoints, almost a twentyfold increase in the number of border guards.[162] Finally, China closed all Soviet consulates in Xinjiang as well as those in Shanghai and Harbin and ceased all border trade in Xinjiang with the Soviet Union and Mongolia.[163]

Second, China moved to settle disputes with neighboring states. In the spring of 1962, the Ministry of Foreign Affairs (MFA) began to plan for talks with the Soviet Union, China's most powerful neighbor and the one with which it shared the longest border.[164] Given the length of the border and its complex history of changes, however, the MFA needed time to prepare for any talks. To support these negotiations, China moved first to open talks with Mongolia and North Korea, its other northern neighbors and fellow socialist states. In late March, Zhou Enlai supervised preparatory meetings with Chinese experts responsible for the Mongolian and North Korean border talks.[165] On April 13, China moved to open negotiations with Mongolia, proposing a series of measures to maintain stability on the border pending a final agreement.[166] When Mongolia did not reply, Zhou Enlai met with the Mongolian ambassador in Beijing in early May to press again for talks.[167]

Other Threats to Territorial Integrity

Amid all the internal threats to regime security, China faced increasing pressure in two of its most important territorial disputes with India and Taiwan. These challenges, especially from India, further underscored

---

[160] Su Yongwen, Qiu Xinyan, and Xia Zhongchun, *Aletai diqu zhi* [Altay Prefecture Gazetteer] (Wulumuqi: Xinjiang renmin chubanshe, 2004), 324–325; Zhuang Chaoqun, ed., *Xinjiang tongzhi: shengchan jianshe budui zhi* [Xinjiang Gazetteer: Production and Construction Corps] (Wulumuqi: Xinjiang renmin chubanshe, 1998), 726–727.

[161] Feng Qingfu, ed., *Bianjing guanli xue* [The Science of Border Management] (Beijing: Jingguan jiaoyu chubanshe [internal circulation], 1999), 70–71.

[162] *Gongan budui*, 73, 78.

[163] Li Jiasong, ed., *Zhonghua renmin gongheguo waijiao dashiji, di er juan* [Diplomatic Chronology of the PRC: Volume 2] (Beijing: Shijie zhishi chubanshe, 2001), 234, 239, 244.

[164] Interviews, Beijing, June 2002.

[165] ZELNP2, 468, 481.

[166] Wang, *Zhonghua renmin gongheguo waijiao shi, 1957–1969*, 101.

[167] ZELNP2, 477.

the need for improved ties with neighboring states to maintain territorial integrity.

The first threat came from India. As described more fully in chapter 4, India in November 1961 adopted a major change in its policy toward China, a "forward policy" of establishing sentries and border posts in contested areas not under Chinese control. From Beijing's perspective, the new Indian policy posed a direct challenge to the stability of Tibet and its southwestern frontier. Since the October 1959 Kongka Pass clash, the border had been relatively stable: in 1960 and 1961, few confrontations occurred and no armed clashes erupted, as both sides sought to limit the potential for escalation. Moreover, the forward policy was adopted just as China's leaders had consolidated their authority in Tibet. At the end of 1961, the CMC declared that Tibet had been pacified and central authority restored.[168] In February 1962, the CMC decided that the troops in Tibet "should move from taking pacification as the priority to taking internal consolidation as the priority." Mobile units were instructed to continue to focus on frontier defense, while the remaining troops were instructed to shift to production.[169]

When PLA commanders realized the full extent of the Indian challenge, tactical countermeasures were adopted. China resumed patrols in disputed sectors and ordered border defense units to fortify their positions and erect outposts to block further Indian advances.[170] At the same time, China moved to stabilize other borders in the region, starting with Pakistan. On February 27, 1962, two days before sending its first demarche to India over the forward policy, China replied to Pakistan's 1961 note and stated its willingness to sign a provisional boundary agreement. On May 3, as India continued to expand the forward policy, China and Pakistan released a joint communiqué stating their intention to enter into negotiations.[171] In addition to stabilizing this border, China's opening with Pakistan was clearly aimed at India. After the talks were announced, a Chinese diplomatic note to India asked, "Since the Government of Pakistan has also agreed with the Chinese government to negotiate a boundary settlement, why is it that the Indian government cannot negotiate and settle its boundary question with the Chinese government?"[172]

As discussed in chapter 4, Taiwan provided the second territorial threat for China's leaders. In late December 1961, Chiang Kai-shek stated that 1962 would be a "decisive" year.[173] At the end of March, Chiang stated

---

[168] Li and Li, *Pingxi*, 234.
[169] *ZYBJ*, 463.
[170] *WP*, VI, 101; *ZYBJ*, 465.
[171] *DDZGWJ*, 151–153.
[172] *WP*, VI, 101.
[173] *NYT*, 26 December 1961, 3.

that "we can no longer vacillate or hesitate to perform our duty . . . there is no doubt that we can annihilate the Communists, reunify our country, and restore freedom to the people on the mainland."[174] From early March to early May, the Nationalist government issued a conscription mobilization decree to increase manpower, adopted a special budget to fund wartime mobilization efforts, and imposed a "return to the mainland" tax.[175] At the same time, Beijing viewed a slew of high-level U.S. officials who visited Taiwan as providing additional support for an attack.[176]

By mid-May, China's leaders concluded that the threat from Taiwan was real and moved quickly to respond.[177] In early June, the CMC instructed adjacent coastal provinces to undertake war preparations, while five first-grade divisions were ordered to arrive at the front line by June 20, 1962, and existing units were placed on high alert.[178] The CMC directed Deng Xiaoping to oversee military production and Li Xiannian to supervise food supplies. The crisis began to dissipate after a meeting between U.S. and Chinese ambassadors in Warsaw on June 23, when the Chinese delegation was told in no uncertain terms that the United States did not encourage Chiang's current "return to the mainland" efforts and would provide no military support in the event of a Nationalist assault.[179]

Although the Taiwan crisis had no direct impact on China's decision to compromise in its frontier disputes, it nevertheless played a key role in shaping the attitudes of China's leaders toward the depth and breadth of challenges to China's territorial integrity. The crisis demonstrated that outsiders viewed China as weak and sought to take advantage of this weakness. In May, a meeting of the CMC's strategy research small group (*zhanlue yanjiu xiaozu*) chaired by Marshal Liu Bocheng concluded that Chiang Kai-shek sought to take advantage of this period of economic difficulty in China. According to the recollection of one participant, Chiang viewed the difficulties in China as an "extremely rare opportunity" (*qian zai nan feng*).[180]

---

[174] *NYT*, 30 March 1962, 2.

[175] On this period, see Melvin Gurtov and Byong-Moo Hwang, *China under Threat: The Politics of Strategy and Diplomacy* (Baltimore: Johns Hopkins University Press, 1980), 127–128; Harold C. Hinton, *Communist China in World Politics* (New York: Houghton Mifflin, 1966), 280–272; Whiting, *Calculus*, 62–72.

[176] In fact, these officials were dispatched to dissuade Chiang from taking such action. Whiting, *Calculus*, 64–65.

[177] For a discussion of Chinese decision making during this period, see Yang, *Wang Shangrong*, 484–492.

[178] Wang, "Xin Zhongguo," 278.

[179] For a detailed account of the talks, see Wang Bingnan, *ZhongMei huitan jiunian huigu* [Reflections on Nine Years of Chinese-American Talks] (Beijing: Shijie zhishi chubanshe, 1985), 85–90.

[180] Wang, "Xin Zhongguo," 277–278.

The Xinjiang unrest and migration might have been an isolated incident, but the new Indian pressure on Tibet and Taiwan's plans to attack constituted a dangerous trend in the minds of China's leaders. As Xinjiang party secretary Wang Enmao remarked in June 1962, these varied challenges "were absolutely not accidental." The Soviet actions in Xinjiang, for example, "sought to increase our difficulties by creating great losses in production, manpower, livestock, and capital."[181] In response to these pressures, Zhou chaired a meeting in mid-May with China's senior military commanders, Luo Ruiqing and Yang Chengwu, to discuss the entire border situation (*quanguo bianjing qingkuang*).[182] This is one of the few meetings about border security on record convened by China's civilian leaders during the 1950s and 1960s. The holding of such a meeting demonstrates the depth of the 1962 territorial crisis because it occurred amid escalating tensions on multiple borders, several weeks before the decision was made to mobilize across from Taiwan, and several months before the first armed clash with India. In June, General Su Yu likewise observed that Chiang was seeking to profit from "our three continuous years of serious natural disasters, food shortages, and economic difficulties."[183]

As tensions with India and Taiwan increased, China continued to pursue compromise with Mongolia, North Korea, and Pakistan. In June, China sent a formal diplomatic note to Mongolia along with a map depicting a proposed boundary delimitation consistent with the line of actual control between the two sides.[184] In the same month, Zhou met with the North Korean ambassador to discuss the Chinese–North Korean border.[185] Although the details of this conversation are not public, it is likely that China pressed for talks. In July, China and Pakistan exchanged maps of their border and discussed procedures for upcoming talks.[186] As noted below, all these efforts led to the opening of talks with Mongolia, North Korea, and Pakistan in late September and early October, precisely the same period when China was seeking to hold similar talks with India.

---

[181] *Wang Enmao wenji* [Wang Enmao's Collected Works] (Beijing: Zhongyang wenxian chubanshe, 1997), 389.

[182] Liu Wusheng and Du Hongqi, eds., *Zhou Enlai junshi huodong jishi, 1918–1975 (xia)* [Chronicle of Zhou Enlai's Military Activities, vol. 2] (Beijing: Zhongyang wenxian chubanshe, 2000), 564.

[183] *Su Yu wenxuan* [Su Yu's Selected Works], vol. 3 (Beijing: Junshi kexue chubanshe, 2004), 414.

[184] Cai Xiru, ed., *Bianfang lilun* [Theory of Frontier Defense] (Beijing: Jingguan jiaoyu chubanshe [internal circulation], 1996), 11; DDZGWJ, 151; Wang, *Zhonghua renmin gongheguo waijiao shi, 1957–1969*, 101.

[185] ZELNP2, 486.

[186] Seyd, *China*, 86.

As soon as the Taiwan crisis abated, the dispute on the Himalayan frontier began to intensify even further. Reflecting the increasing tensions on the border, the first armed clash since 1959 occurred on July 21, 1962, in the Chip Chap Valley (see map 4.1). Throughout the summer of 1962, China sought to hold talks as it nevertheless prepared to counter the growing Indian presence. In late July, Zhou instructed Chen Yi to arrange a meeting with Krishna Menon, the Indian defense minister, on the sidelines of the Geneva Conference. Chen was to "explain China's consistent position to settle the dispute through negotiations and discuss arrangements for resuming negotiations."[187] In his discussions with Menon, Chen indicated that China would be willing to consider further adjustments in Ladakh based on the territory that each side controlled, representing more concessions than Zhou had offered in 1960.[188] After this meeting, China proposed holding negotiations on three occasions: on August 4, after Nehru indicated a willingness to talk; on September 13, following a standoff over Thag La in the eastern sector; and on October 3. Each time, however, India replied that it would negotiate only if China first withdrew from disputed areas in the west. This precondition required China to abandon approximately 33,000 square kilometers of territory claimed by India without a corresponding move by India, and such a withdrawal would leave the Xinjiang-Tibet highway exposed.

China Compromises

In the short term, events on the Himalayan frontier propelled China's attempts to settle territorial disputes with North Korea, Mongolia, and Pakistan through compromises. China began negotiations with all three states in September or October 1962, after it had offered to enter into talks with India but before the outbreak of the 1962 war. The speedy conclusion of these boundary negotiations in late 1962 and early 1963 were used by China to influence the Colombo talks on the Chinese-Indian dispute held after the war.

More generally, all these agreements were linked as well to China's efforts to settle its dispute with the Soviet Union. China proposed talks with Moscow when it announced the start of talks with Afghanistan in March 1963. China's agreements with its socialist neighbors to the north were also designed to pressure the Soviet Union to agree to similar terms, while its agreements with Pakistan and Afghanistan secured China's

[187] Liu and Du, *Zhou Enlai junshi huodong jishi (xia)*, 567.
[188] Arthur Lall, *The Emergence of Modern India* (New York: Columbia University Press, 1981), 156.

southern borders in Central Asia before engaging the Soviet Union over the thorny issue of the Pamir Mountains.

MONGOLIA

After receiving Soviet approval, Mongolia agreed to talks with China in August 1962, and negotiations began on October 12 in Ulaanbaatar. After thirty-two days, the two sides reached a preliminary agreement, publishing a summary of the talks on November 17 just as the second Chinese offensive against India began in the Himalayas.[189] On December 16, Zhou invited Mongolian leader Yumjaagiin Tsedenbal to visit Beijing for a signing ceremony. After a second round of talks, the two sides finalized an agreement on December 25, 1962, that was signed the following day.[190]

China's sudden willingness to compromise with Mongolia highlights the combined effects of ethnic unrest and core legitimacy concerns. Without those incentives, China had maintained a delaying strategy. In 1956, after a conflict erupted over grazing rights around Hongshanzui, a mountain pass in the west, local officials held informal and inconclusive talks in July over the location of the border in this area (map 2.3).[191] On November 22, 1957, Mongolia sent a diplomatic note to China proposing to negotiate the boundary. China agreed in principle in March 1958 to hold talks, but no progress was achieved. In July 1958, Mongolia sent a second note, claiming sovereignty over Baogeda Mountain and grazing areas around the Chagang River in the Qinghe area.[192] During Zhou's May 1960 trip to Ulaanbaatar, Mongolia again expressed its desire to settle the territorial dispute.[193] Yet only in April 1962, five years after Mongolia's initial request, did China push for talks.

Newly available sources now make it possible to understand the broad parameters of the compromise that occurred. During the 1962 negotiations, talks focused on those areas where maps from each side diverged: overall, 16,808 square kilometers, including 506 square kilometers where the two sides agreed to mutual adjustments, was disputed.[194] Various comparisons of maps all demonstrate that China relinquished most of its claims, most of which were over stretches of the steppes.[195] Another Chinese source indicates that the size of this area was slightly smaller, approx-

[189] Wang, *Zhonghua renmin gongheguo waijiao shi, 1957–1969*, 101–102.

[190] *TYJ*, 1962, 19–37.

[191] Shen, *Xinjiang tongzhi: waishi zhi*, 284.

[192] Wang and Getu, *Neimenggu zizhiqu zhi: junshi zhi*, 473. Baogeda Mountain is also called Bogeda Mountain.

[193] Shen, *Xinjiang tongzhi: waishi zhi*, 235.

[194] Wang, *Zhonghua renmin gongheguo waijiao shi, 1957–1969*, 102.

[195] See Alastair Lamb, *Asian Frontiers: Studies in a Continuing Problem* (New York: Praeger, 1968), 200, 202; Prescott, *Map*, 94; Watson, *Frontiers*, 173–174.

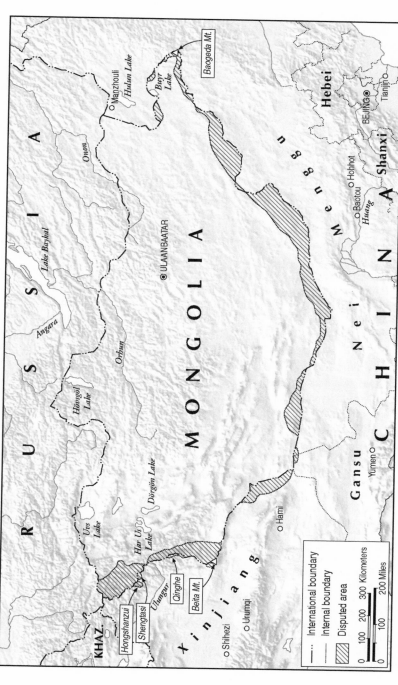

Map 2.3 China-Mongolia Border

imately 16,329 square kilometers, with Mongolia receiving 10,709 square kilometers and China 5,620.[196] In its analysis, the U.S. State Department concluded that "throughout, the agreement favored the traditional Mongolian version [of the boundary]."[197]

China's willingness to compromise is reflected in the division of specific disputed areas. In the Hongshanzui region, where tensions over grazing areas had occurred in 1956, China conceded to Mongolia 190 square kilometers of territory, or 37 percent of the area under dispute. Mongolia received 75 percent of the Qinghe grazing area that it had demanded in 1958. In the dispute over the northern slope of Beita Mountain, China retained only 26 percent of the 836 square kilometers.[198] Mongolia dropped its claim to 300 square kilometers around Shengtasi, while China agreed to Mongolia's demand for Baogeda Mountain.[199]

The timing of the final agreement was linked to China's other frontier disputes. Again, China seized the initiative by inviting Tsedenbal to Beijing. At this time, China was still seeking to settle the dispute with India, withdrawing its troops after the November 1962 offensive and agreeing to Ceylon's mediation. During his meeting with Tsedenbal, Zhou stated: "A reasonable settlement of the border question between China and Mongolia will be an example and encouragement for border negotiations with other countries."[200] More broadly, however, Zhou noted that the treaty would "contribute to the resolution of the border questions with our other neighboring countries," clearly referring to the Soviet Union as well as India. During the signing ceremony, Chairman Liu Shaoqi similarly stated, "China hopes to settle its boundary question with other socialist countries on the basis of the same principles," which could refer only to Moscow given the agreement with Pyongyang.[201] At the same time, Politburo member Peng Zhen noted that the agreement with Mon-

---

[196] Wang and Getu, *Neimenggu zizhiqu zhi: junshi zhi*, 474. A 1964 *Christian Science Monitor* article, citing interviews with Mongolian officials, states that of the approximately 17,000 square kilometers that were disputed, Mongolia received approximately 12,000 square kilometers and China received 5,000 square kilometers. See *Christian Science Monitor*, 2 January 1964, 2.

[197] Department of State, "China-Mongolia Boundary," *International Boundary Study*, no. 173 (August 14, 1985): 10.

[198] Su, Qiu, and Xia, *Aletai diqu zhi*, 947.

[199] Qu Xing, *Zhongguo waijiao 50 nian* [50 Years of Chinese Diplomacy] (Nanjing: Jiangsu renmin chubanshe, 2000), 221.

[200] "Record of Conversation (from East German archives) between Chinese Premier Zhou Enlai and Mongolian leader J. Zedenbal, Beijing, 26 December 1962," Cold War International History Project Virtual Archive, http://cwihp.si.edu/.

[201] *DDZGWJ*, 151. Liu could only be referring to the Soviet Union, as China and Vietnam agreed in 1958 to delay talks in their land border dispute.

golia constituted a "major contribution to strengthening the unity of the socialist bloc."[202] Given the close relationship between the Soviet Union and Mongolia, China hoped that its treaty with Mongolia would send a strong signal to its other northern neighbor.

Over the next two years, China and Mongolia implemented the various terms of the treaty. On March 25, 1963, instruments of ratification were exchanged. The joint survey commission to demarcate the boundary held its first meeting on April 16, 1963. One year later, in June 1964, the two sides signed a boundary protocol, which completed the demarcation process. The protocol, which includes a description of 639 boundary markers, was the longest boundary agreement that China signed in the 1960s, totaling more than 181 pages.[203]

NORTH KOREA

As China has never publicized its treaty with North Korea, very little information is available about the agreement and the compromises it contains. Nevertheless, newly available sources confirm the conclusion of a treaty and the role of Chinese concessions. After Zhou's June 1962 meeting with the North Korean ambassador, negotiations over the border began sometime in September. By October 3, vice–foreign ministers from both countries had initialed minutes of talks over the territorial dispute.[204] On October 12, Zhou Enlai and North Korean communist leader Kim Il-sung signed a boundary treaty in Pyongyang.[205] The two sides agreed to divide the disputed Changbai Mountain through the crater lake, which formed the crux of the dispute (map 2.4). As Zhou later explained to President Richard Nixon, "We finally solved the question by dividing and sharing the lake."[206] As a result of this delimitation, a Korean scholar estimates that China received roughly 40 percent of the disputed area while North Korea received 60 percent, though China appears to have

---

[202] *RMRB*, 27 December 1962, 1.

[203] *TYJ*, 1964, 78–259. For a detailed discussion of the border demarcation, see Bai, *Xinjiang tongzhi: waishi juan*, 240–249.

[204] Cai, *Bianfang*, 9.

[205] Cai, *Bianfang*, 8–9; Feng, *Bianjing*, 20–21; Han Zheshi, ed., *Changbai chaoxianzu zizhixian zhi* [Changbai Korean Autonomous County Gazetteer] (Beijing: Zhonghua shuju chubanshe, 1993), 312; Liu Shufa, ed., *Chen Yi nianpu* [Chronicle of Chen Yi's Life] (Beijing: Zhongyang wenxian chubanshe, 1995), 938; Pei Jianzhang and Feng Yaoyuan, eds., *Zhou Enlai waijiao huodong dashiji* [Record of Zhou Enlai's Diplomatic Activities] (Beijing: Shijie zhishi chubanshe, 1993), 338.

[206] "Memorandum of Conversation between Richard Nixon, Henry Kissinger, Zhou Enlai, et al., 23 February 1972, 2:PM–6:PM," 26, from the National Security Archive, George Washington University, Washington D.C., http://www.gwu.edu/~nsarchiv/nsa /publications/DOC_readers/kissinger/nixzhou/13–01.htm.

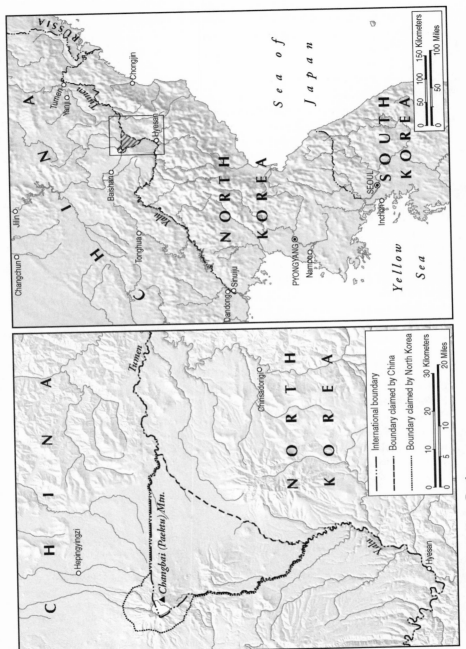

Map 2.4 China–North Korea Border

made additional concessions over the mountain's eastern slope.[207] The treaty determined that elsewhere the boundary would run along the Yalu and Tumen rivers or their tributaries and that the rivers would be shared equally by both sides. The islands and shoals in these rivers were also divided. In the Tumen River, for example, North Korea received 56 percent of the islands and shoals.[208]

The timing of China's compromise and the apparent swiftness of negotiations with North Korea reflect concerns about regime security. As China realized its vulnerability along the Soviet border, it moved to seek settlements with other socialist states, both to pressure Moscow to reach a similar settlement and prevent any cross-border subversion similar to what had occurred in Xinjiang. If the Chinese–North Korean treaty had been publicly announced, it is likely that it would have also been used, as was the treaty with Mongolia, to support China's efforts to negotiate with the Soviets. Moreover, China's interactions with Mongolia closely parallel China's efforts with North Korea, suggesting the operation of a similar calculus. Nevertheless, the secrecy surrounding the latter agreement makes definitive conclusions difficult to draw. Interviews and archival research suggests that North Korea did not want the terms of the agreement publicized. In a conversation with the Mongolian leader Tsedenbal in December 1962, Zhou explained that China was "still waiting for an answer from North Korea and therefore [has] not yet made a public announcement to the press."[209] Kim was apparently reluctant to have the treaty discussed publicly because he had to compromise over the sovereignty of his alleged birthplace, which would have weakened his nationalist credentials.[210]

Over the next two years, the two sides moved to implement the terms of the 1962 treaty. A joint boundary survey commission was established, which began in May 1963 to survey the border, erect boundary markers, and allocate the ownership of islands and shoals in the rivers, completing its work in November 1963.[211] On March 2, 1964, the two governments signed a boundary protocol in Beijing, but, like the 1962 treaty, it was never openly published.[212]

---

[207] "DPRK-PRC Border Pact Said Confirmed," Seoul Yonhap News Agency, FBIS# FTS19991019001881.

[208] *Yanbian Chaoxianzu zizhizhou zhi* [Yanbian Korean Autonomous Prefecture Gazetteer] (Beijing: Zhonghua shuju chubanshe, 1996), 498.

[209] "Record of Conversation (from East German archives) between Chinese Premier Zhou Enlai and Mongolian leader J. Zedenbal."

[210] Interview, Beijing, June 2002.

[211] *Yanbian Chaoxianzu*, 497. For a detailed discussion of the work of the joint boundary commission in one county bordering North Korea, see Han, *Changbai chaoxianzu*, 312–314.

[212] Cai, *Bianfang*, 9.

PAKISTAN

When China sought to reopen negotiations with India in September and early October 1962, it also entered into talks with Pakistan. The talks, which were held in Beijing, began on October 12, the same day that Zhou signed the boundary treaty with North Korea. On December 28, soon after the Chinese-Mongolian boundary treaty was signed, China and Pakistan issued a joint communiqué stating that both sides had reached an agreement "in principle . . . on the location and alignment of the boundary actually existing between the two countries."[213] After additional discussions in February 1963, foreign ministers Chen Yi and Zulfikar Ali Bhutto signed a provisional boundary agreement on March 2, 1963, in Beijing.[214]

China maintained control over more of the disputed territory, but the agreement overall was more favorable to Pakistan. China kept roughly 5,309 square kilometers it contested in the Shaksgam Valley (map 2.5).[215] However, it transferred control of some 1,942 square kilometers of territory in the Oprang Valley to Pakistan, which also maintained control over an additional 1,554 square kilometers of territory it already held. On balance, Pakistan seems to have gained more from the deal, as the final borderline followed closely the line of actual control advocated by Pakistan. China not only abandoned its claims to the Hunza, but Pakistan also received grazing areas in the Prang and Bund Darwaza valleys, the Kharachanai salt mine, and the town of Sokh Bulaq. In addition, Pakistan kept control over three-fourths of K2 as well as six of seven disputed mountain passes. Finally, Pakistan transferred no territory already under its control to China.[216]

More than any other dispute, China's compromise with Pakistan was linked to the China-India conflict. Upon discovering the forward policy, China moved to open talks with Pakistan despite rebuffing earlier Pakistani efforts toward negotiation dating from the late 1950s. While China was seeking to open talks with India in September and October 1962, Pakistan and China conducted negotiations. As the Colombo process began after the 1962 war, China and Pakistan announced their agreement. The December 1962 joint statement pointedly declared that "conducting peaceful consultations on the basis of mutual respect and goodwill is an

[213] Quoted in *Peking Review,* no. 52 (28 December 1962), 8.

[214] Mujtaba Razvi, *The Frontiers of Pakistan: A Study of Frontier Problems in Pakistan's Foreign Policy* (Karachi-Dacca: National Publishing House, 1971), 174–176. The agreement was provisional pending the final resolution of the status of Kashmir. See *TYJ,* 1963, 64–67.

[215] Watson, *Frontiers,* 166.

[216] Razvi, *Frontiers,* 177; Seyd, *China,* 87.

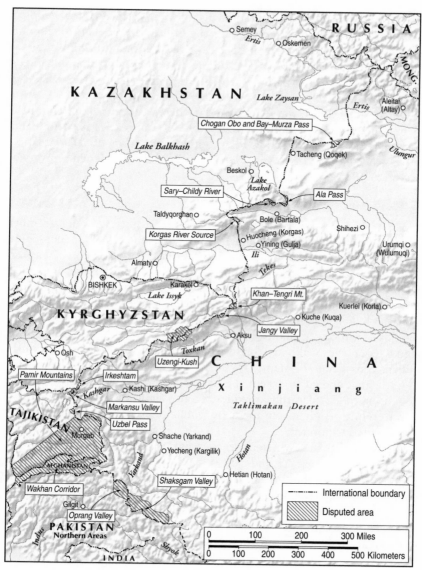

Map 2.5 China's Central Asian Borders

effective way of solving international disputes."[217] According to a *People's Daily* editorial, "Now is the time for the Indian government to respond actively to China's peaceful proposals."[218] Additionally, China's agreement with Pakistan helped to consolidate the southern portion of China's Central Asian frontier before it entered into talks with the Soviets the following spring.

On May 31, 1963, the joint boundary demarcation commission held its first meeting.[219] Based on the Chinese-Pakistani treaty, four field teams surveyed the border, erecting forty boundary markers.[220] Demarcation work was completed two years later, when both sides signed a protocol in March 1965.

AFGHANISTAN

When Afghanistan proposed holding boundary negotiations in December 1962, China readily agreed. On March 2, 1963, the same day that China signed a provisional agreement with Pakistan, China and Afghanistan announced their intention to enter into formal talks on settling their territorial dispute. From China's perspective, the crux of the negotiations was the determination of the Afghan-Soviet-Chinese tripoint, which itself was linked to China's claim to the Pamir Mountains controlled by the Soviet Union. Afghanistan sought Chinese recognition of its sovereignty over the Wakhan Corridor, which PRC maps had previously indicated as Chinese (map 2.5). In the talks, which began on June 17, 1963, China agreed to accept the line of actual control as the basis for delimiting the border, thus abandoning any claim to the Wakhan Corridor. In return, Afghanistan made no public references to the location of the disputed tripoint.[221]

On August 1, the two sides reached agreement on a draft treaty. On November 22, Chen Yi and Al-Qayyum signed a boundary treaty in Beijing.[222] Overall, the agreement favored Afghanistan. The boundary line contained in the treaty largely followed the line set by Russia and Britain in 1895, which had allocated the Pamir Mountains to Russia. Through the treaty, China abandoned any claims to the Wakhan area. After the signing of the treaty, a joint survey team was established to survey the border, erect

[217] *FEER*, 10 January 1963, 55.

[218] *RMRB*, 29 December 1962, 1.

[219] P. L. Bhola, *Pakistan-China Relations: Search for Politico-Strategic Relationship* (Jaipur: R.B.S.A. Publishers, 1986), 101.

[220] Department of State, "China-Pakistan Boundary," *International Boundary Study*, no. 85 (May 30, 1968): 5.

[221] On the talks, see Wang, *Zhonghua renmin gongheguo waijiao shi, 1957–1969*, 105.

[222] *TYJ*, 1963, 122–124.

boundary markers, and draw new maps. A boundary protocol was signed in March 1965 at the conclusion of the demarcation process.[223]

On its own, China's dispute with Afghanistan was unimportant. China had not occupied any of the areas that it claimed for at least fifty years, and few people lived on either side of the line of actual control. The treaty, however, did play an important role in China's solution to the 1962 territorial crisis. Overall, the treaty served as another signal to the Soviet Union and India of China's willingness to compromise in its outstanding territorial disputes. During the first session of negotiations, the head of the Chinese delegation stated, "the resolution of the Chinese-Afghan boundary problem will become another example for all neighboring countries to settle problems between them peacefully through negotiations."[224]

Most importantly, the agreement with Afghanistan supported China's efforts to secure its border with the Soviet Union. The treaty was signed after Moscow had agreed to China's proposal for talks in May 1963. Again, from China's perspective, a successful settlement with Afghanistan would help to ensure a similar agreement with the USSR. Moreover, while the tripoint was not mentioned by name, it was quite clear in the treaty, which was published on the front page of the *People's Daily*, that the borderline was consistent with the status quo of actual control over the Pamir Mountains.[225] The line accepted by China in the Chinese-Afghan treaty followed the 1895 Russo-British agreement. China thus signaled its willingness to compromise in its boundary disputes with the Soviets by accepting their position on the Pamirs. If China still intended to press claims to the Pamirs, it would not have declared its own border with Afghanistan to be fully demarcated and settled.

SOVIET UNION

After resolving disputes with North Korea, Mongolia, Pakistan, and Afghanistan, China attempted to settle its dispute with the Soviet Union through compromise in early 1964. Chinese and Western scholars alike have maintained that these talks made no progress and deteriorated into polemics.[226] Newly available materials, however, indicate that both sides

---

[223] Waijiao bu, ed., *Zhonghua renmin gongheguo bianjie shiwu tiaoyue ji: ZhongA Zhong-Ba juan* [Collection of Treaties on the PRC's Boundary Affairs: China-Afghanistan, China-Pakistan] (Beijing: Shijie zhishi chubanshe [internal circulation], 2004), 22.

[224] *RMRB*, 20 June 1963, 1. On the link to the Pamirs, see Hyer, "Politics," 300.

[225] *RMRB*, 23 November 1963, 1.

[226] One exception is Ginsburgs and Pinkele, who cite a 1974 Polish article. See George Ginsburgs and Carl F. Pinkele, *The Sino-Soviet Territorial Dispute, 1949–64* (London: Routledge, 1978), 95–131. On the whole, however, assessment of these negotiations has followed the line carried by Soviet propaganda statements—that no progress was achieved, because of Chinese stubbornness.

achieved far more progress in settling their numerous disputes than was previously believed.[227] Although the talks produced no final agreement, both sides reached a consensus on how to delimit the Chinese-Soviet border in the eastern sector that was almost identical to the agreement signed in 1991. Issues in the more complicated western sector, especially the Pamirs, were also discussed but not resolved. China concluded that a stable border with the USSR was more important than marginal additions to its territory.

In September 1960, China had previously approached the Soviet Union to hold talks over one sector of the disputed border in Central Asia. In 1956, confrontations over grazing areas northeast of the Boziaigeer (Potzuaikerh) Pass in Xinjiang's Atushi (Artux) County adjacent to present-day Kyrgyzstan occurred. At the time, border defense guards from each side agreed to maintain the status quo pending a final resolution of the China-Soviet boundary dispute. As Chinese-Soviet relations soured in the summer of 1960, similar confrontations between Soviet troops and Chinese herders occurred in the same area.[228] On September 21, 1960, the Chinese Foreign Ministry sent a diplomatic note to the Soviet Embassy in Beijing suggesting that the two sides hold negotiations over this sector. As this incident occurred during a period of ethnic instability in Tibet, it is unknown whether China would have compromised had negotiations with the Soviet Union occurred (they did not). China did, however, agree to withdraw its herders by the end of the month in an effort to minimize future tensions, action that is consistent with the effects of regime insecurity as a source of compromise.[229]

Although preparations for negotiations with Moscow began in 1960, China made no move to open comprehensive boundary talks until April 1963. In the interim period, however, stability on the border continued to deteriorate, and a number of polemics exchanged between the two sides mentioned border issues. In particular, a March 1963 *People's Daily* editorial discussed publicly for the first time the "unequal treaties" in which the Qing had ceded vast tracts of land to tsarist Russia.[230] The

---

[227] Li Lianqing, *Lengnuan suiyue: yibo sanzhe de ZhongSu guanxi* [Hot and Cold Times: The Twists and Turns of Chinese-Soviet Relations] (Beijing: Shijie zhishi chubanshe, 1999), 323–324; Tang Jiaxuan, ed., *Zhongguo waijiao cidian* [Dictionary of China's Diplomacy] (Beijing: Shijie zhishi chubanshe, 2000), 725; Wang, Zhonghua renmin gongheguo *waijiao shi, 1957–1969*, 254–256. Interviews, Beijing, July 2001, January 2002, and June 2002.

[228] On the confrontations, see Meng Zhaobi, ed. *Xinjiang tongzhi: junshi zhi* [Xinjiang Gazetteer: Military Affairs] (Wulumuqi: Xinjiang renmin chubanshe, 1997), 338; He Jihong, ed., *Kezilesu keerkezi zizhizhou zhi* [Kezilesu Kyrgyz Autonomous Region Gazetteer] (Wulumuqi: Xinjiang renmin chubanshe, 2004), 1091.

[229] On the diplomatic note, see Shen Bingnian, ed. *Xinjiang tongzhi: waishi zhi* [Xinjiang Gazetteer: Foreign Affairs] (Wulumuqi: Xinjiang renmin chubanshe, 1995), 284–285.

[230] *RMRB*, 8 March 1963, 1.

reference to these agreements was a response Khrushchev's remarks in December 1962 that Hong Kong and Macao were "remnants of colonialism [that] remained untouched on [Chinese] territory."[231] From the Soviet perspective, however, the Chinese editorial revealed a willingness to pursue irredentist claims to "lost" territory and overturn past agreements.

As in its diplomacy with India, China used negotiations with other states to convince the Soviet Union to settle the dispute. After it had signed treaties or agreements with North Korea, Mongolia, and Pakistan and announced its intention to negotiate with Afghanistan, China sent a diplomatic note to Moscow in April 1963 urging that the two sides hold talks over their disputed territory.[232] By negotiating with smaller states first, China sought to reduce its vulnerabilities in other frontier regions and signal its intention to reach a similar compromise settlement with the Soviet Union. As leader of the socialist bloc, Moscow was presumably well informed of the compromises in China's agreements with North Korea and Mongolia. The agreement with Pakistan was openly discussed in the press, especially the division of disputed areas between the two sides.

In May 1963, the USSR replied to China's offer to hold talks. Moscow stated, in particular, that it was willing to engage in limited discussions about specific problems on the border as opposed to talks encompassing the entire boundary.[233] In August, China replied with a six-point proposal for maintaining the status quo on the border pending a final settlement. Correspondence between the two sides continued in the fall as the scope of the talks was discussed. Beijing pressed for the inclusion of the entire border, while Moscow agreed only to discuss certain disputed sectors.[234]

Negotiations finally began on February 23, 1964, when a Soviet delegation arrived in Beijing. Overall, eight plenary sessions were held along with more than thirty meetings of experts from each side. During the first two months, the talks focused on the nature of the unequal treaties signed during the Qing dynasty. China had stated that it would use the delimitations in past treaties as the basis for negotiations but nevertheless sought Soviet acknowledgment of their "unequal" status.[235] The Soviets

---

[231] Dennis J. Doolin, *Territorial Claims in the Sino-Soviet Conflict: Documents and Analysis* (Stanford, Calif.: Hoover Institution, 1965), 28.

[232] Wang, *Zhonghua renmin gongheguo waijiao shi, 1957–1969*, 254.

[233] Li, *Lengnuan suiyue*, 323–324; Wang, *Zhonghua renmin gongheguo waijiao shi, 1957–1969*, 254.

[234] George Ginsburgs, "The End of the Sino-Russian Territorial Disputes? " *The Journal of East Asian Studies*, vol. 7, no. 1 (1993): 68–82.

[235] For a firsthand Chinese account, see Ma Xusheng, "Takan bianjie tanpan jiaofeng: zhaohui shiluo de guojie xian (er)" [On-the-Spot Survey of Battles in Boundary Negotiations: Retrieving Lost National Boundaries (2)], *Shijie zhishi*, no. 12 (2001): 42–43.

feared that such an acknowledgment would open the door for further Chinese demands, especially in light of the March 1963 *People's Daily* editorial. According to an official diplomatic history, China stated that it did not seek the return of land ceded in the unequal treaties and instead wanted to discuss only discrepancies created by the implementation of those treaties.[236] The Soviets refused to acknowledge that the prior treaties were "unequal" and did not want to use them as a basis for negotiations. Part of the Soviet position at the time was that the 1860 Treaty of Peking had determined that the border lay on the Chinese bank of the rivers, not in the main channel of navigation.

In May, the two sides agreed to shift from questions of principle to substantive issues. Negotiators exchanged maps depicting the shared boundary and identified more than twenty disputed sectors where the maps diverged.[237] As talks progressed, the two sides reached a consensus on the eastern sector.[238] According to Russian and Chinese sources, the draft 1964 agreement was almost identical to the one reached in 1991.[239] In the river areas, both sides agreed to place the border through the middle of the rivers, not on the Chinese bank. In the Amur and Ussuri rivers, the *thalweg* principle, or main channel of navigation, determined the border, thereby allocating four hundred islands comprising 600 square kilometers to China. In the Argun River, the use of the middle line as the border transferred approximately 200 square kilometers of islands to China. Agreement was also reached over Manzhouli and the land border adjacent to Heilongjiang and Jilin provinces. Only two areas in the eastern sector were not resolved by the draft agreement, namely Heixiazi (Black Bear) Island, where both sides disputed the direction of the main channel at the confluence of the Amur and Ussuri rivers, and the Abagaitu Shoal, where changes in the direction of the Argun River created ambiguity over the location of the boundary (see map 3.1).[240] According to one Russian source, Moscow refused to initial the draft treaty because it did not resolve the dispute over these two islands that the Soviet Union controlled.[241]

---

[236] Tang, *Zhongguo waijiao cidian*, 725.

[237] Li, *Lengnuan suiyue*, 324. Also see Genrikh Kireyev, "Demarcation of the Border with China," *International Affairs*, vol. 45, no. 2 (1999): 100. Kireyev was the head of the Russian delegation to the Joint Boundary Demarcation Commission in the 1990s.

[238] Kireyev, "Demarcation," 100.

[239] Kireyev, "Demarcation," 99–100; Li, *Lengnuan suiyue*, 323–324; Tang, *Zhongguo waijiao cidian*, 725; Wang, *Zhonghua renmin gongheguo waijiao shi, 1957–1969*, 254–255.

[240] Wang, *Zhonghua renmin gongheguo waijiao shi, 1957–1969*, 255; Wang and Getu, *Neimenggu zizhiqu zhi: junshi zhi*, 471–472.

[241] Kireyev, "Demarcation," 100.

During these meetings, other topics related to border issues were discussed. Importantly, border management and utilization, including ocean access rights via the Tumen River as well as fishing and navigation rights, were key agenda items. In addition, the two sides discussed their competing claims in Central Asia. According to a retired diplomat, China sought to link its acceptance of Soviet control over the Pamirs to the two disputed islands in the eastern sector.[242]

The talks collapsed in the summer of 1964. On July 10, Mao met with a visiting delegation from Japan's Socialist Party. During the meeting, Mao referred to the treaties signed by the Qing and stated that "we have yet to settle this account with them" (*women hai meiyou gen tamen suan zhege zhang ne*).[243] Although this comment was made in the context of Japan's own dispute with the Soviet Union over the Kurile Islands, Moscow viewed it with great trepidation and viewed China as making sweeping territorial claims. Mao subsequently stated that he had sought to scare Khrushchev, "firing empty cannons" (*fang kongpao*), perhaps to expedite the conclusion of an agreement.[244] Moscow suggested in August that the two sides take a temporary break and resume negotiations in the USSR on October 15.[245] On October 14, however, Khrushchev fell from power, and the negotiations never resumed.

External Threats?

As with China's territorial compromises during the Tibetan revolt, external threats provide the most compelling alternative explanation for China's behavior. As the Chinese-Soviet split was growing, this explanation asserts that China used territorial compromise to gain allies. Nevertheless, China did not seek to settle with these same states during earlier periods of tension with the Soviet Union, especially after the withdrawal of Soviet advisers in 1960. Chinese-Soviet ties were relatively stable in 1961, as economic cooperation continued and the sale of MiG fighter aircraft was broached. Moreover, China also held substantive territorial negotiations with the Soviet Union, which is inconsistent with balancing against a Soviet threat, as such actions might be viewed as signaling weakness. If China were balancing against the Soviet Union, its best strategy might

[242] Interview, Beijing, June 2001.

[243] Yang Kuisong, *Mao Zedong yu Mosike de enen yuanyuan* [Personal Feelings between Mao Zedong and Moscow] (Nanchang: Jiangxi renmin chubanshe, 1999), 509. Yang cites the actual speech based on a Central Archives document. For an English version based on a translation of the Japanese news report of Mao's statement, see Doolin, *Territorial Claims*, 42–44.

[244] Yang, *Mao Zedong*, 510.

[245] Wang, *Zhonghua renmin gongheguo waijiao shi, 1957–1969*, 255.

have been to strengthen border security, while downplaying the presence of a dispute to bide time to improve its military position. This is precisely what China did after the open split in 1965. Finally, many of the states with which China compromised offered little leverage in its dispute with the Soviet Union. Pakistan was a member of the Southeast Asia Treaty Organization (SEATO), an anticommunist alliance, while Afghanistan was not part of the Soviet orbit at the time.

China's attempts to settle with Mongolia and North Korea are the easiest cases for a Soviet balancing argument. Both were members of the socialist bloc and maintained strong ties with Moscow, and thus were likely objects for diplomatic competition between China and the Soviet Union. Nevertheless, while the Soviet factor surely played a role in China's considerations, the Soviet balancing argument is insufficient to explain China's attempts to compremise. Moscow began to improve ties with Mongolia at China's expense in the late 1950s as the Chinese-Soviet split began.[246] Yet despite the Soviets' diplomatic initiatives, China did not seek to settle its territorial dispute with Mongolia until 1962. Moreover, Mongolia had sought to settle with China repeatedly during this period, and if China had responded promptly it would be an easy case for an argument based on external threats. Instead, China attempted to settle the dispute only after the outbreak of the Yita incident, clashes on the China-Mongolia border, and broader concerns about frontier stability that emerged in early 1962, events that carried clear implications for stability in Xinjiang and Inner Mongolia, which bordered Mongolia. Soviet influence in Mongolia may have made China more concerned about stability in its frontiers, but it was China's internal threats that prompted compromise in the spring of 1962. The Soviet factor in the North Korean dispute is difficult to assess owing to the lack of information about this dispute. But given the timing of China's negotiations with Mongolia and North Korea, it is likely that the Soviet factor was not the driving reason for China's attempt to settle this dispute in 1962 either.

Conclusion

From 1960 to 1964, China attempted to compromise in all its frontier disputes except for those with Bhutan, Laos, and Vietnam. At the time, China did not maintain diplomatic relations with Bhutan, which had delegated its foreign policy and defense to India in a 1949 treaty. China did not seek to settle disputes with Laos and Vietnam for two reasons. Areas

---

[246] Robert A. Rupen, "Mongolia in the Sino-Soviet Dispute," *The China Quarterly*, no. 16 (1963): 75–85.

in Guangxi and Yunnan adjacent to these countries did not witness ethnic unrest or political instability that might have prompted compromise. At the same time, both countries were allies in China's struggle against the United States. Although this shared threat failed to create incentives for China to compromise in these disputes, China could nevertheless rely on their diplomatic support.[247]

In its other frontier disputes, regime insecurity best explains China's pattern of delay in the 1950s and cooperation in the 1960s. China's leaders compromised when faced with internal threats to regime security—the revolt in Tibet, the instability following the Great Leap Forward, and unrest in Xinjiang. The timing of compromise efforts, official documents, and statements by China's leaders demonstrate that internal threats, not external ones, explain why and when China pursued cooperation. Almost three decades would pass before China faced similar levels of regime insecurity and pursued compromise in its remaining frontier disputes in the 1990s.

[247] As discussed in chapter 6, China did compromise in its dispute with North Vietnam over White Dragon Tail Island, which it transferred to its ally in 1957.

CHAPTER THREE

Cooperation in Frontier Disputes in the 1990s

THE END OF THE COLD WAR presents a paradox. Until the late 1980s, the main military threat to China came from the Soviet Union. In the 1970s, Moscow doubled the number of troops based in the Far East to more than fifty divisions. By the early 1980s, more than 600,000 Soviet troops were deployed along the Chinese-Soviet frontier, a force that included nuclear-tipped SS-20 missiles.[1] With the end of the Cold War, China for the first time in more than forty years did not face the threat of invasion.

The rapid shift in the global balance of power created an unparalleled opportunity for China to bargain hard over territory that it had long contested in the region, threaten the use of force, or even seize some disputed areas on the cheap. Russia was weaker militarily than the Soviet Union had been, while none of the newly independent Central Asian states or Mongolia maintained military forces of any significance.[2] Moreover, all these states were in the throes of establishing new political regimes and institutions. Nevertheless, China was not more assertive or belligerent in this period. Instead, it attempted to compromise in all its remaining frontier disputes. From 1991 to 1999, China signed eleven boundary agreements resolving part or all of seven frontier disputes. China today still contests territory with India and Bhutan, but these two conflicts were largely neutralized in the beginning of this decade.

Internal threats best explain why China pursued compromise, not aggression, in its frontier disputes after the end of the Cold War. Although its external security environment improved dramatically, the collapse of the Soviet Union coincided with and at times exacerbated a period of unparalleled regime insecurity. The demonstrations in Tiananmen highlighted popular dissatisfaction with the CCP's rule and paramount leader Deng Xiaoping's economic reform program. The violent suppression and subsequent crackdown further alienated the state from the society it sought to govern. Almost simultaneously, ethnic unrest erupted in Xinjiang and Tibet, threatening again the stability and territorial integrity of China's vast frontiers.

---

[1] AP, 25 September 1986 (Lexis-Nexis).

[2] On Chinese perceptions of these changes, see Bonnie S. Glaser, "China's Security Perceptions: Interests and Ambitions," *Asian Survey*, vol. 33, no. 3 (1993): 252–271.

External events aggravated this internal insecurity. The collapse of socialism in Eastern Europe and the disintegration of the Soviet Union underscored the vulnerability of China's own socialist system to political change and left China's leaders with few diplomatic sources of support for their increasingly embattled regime. At the same time, rapidly deteriorating relations with Western states, especially the United States, threatened to undermine further reform by blocking access to foreign markets and capital.

The dramatic improvement in China's external security following the end of the Cold War suggests that external threats to the state cannot explain China's frequent territorial compromises in the 1990s. As Jiang Zemin noted in 1993 in a key speech on military strategy, "Our country's peripheral security environment continues to improve. Friendly relations with neighboring countries are *the best* since the nation's founding" (emphasis added).[3] Despite some concerns about the United States as the sole remaining superpower, the main threat to the Chinese state was internal, not external. China sought to maintain access to U.S. markets while simultaneously rebuffing American demands for political change, thereby increasing regime security by continuing Deng's economic reforms without pursuing political liberalization.

Before proceeding, one caveat is necessary. The data sources on Chinese foreign policy decision making in the 1990s are scarcer than those available for the 1960s. The release of party history documents remains limited to the Mao era and the early years of Deng's rule. Likewise, many of the diplomats who were involved in the boundary negotiations in the 1990s are still active officials or have not yet written memoirs. As a result, it is more difficult to determine the precise timing of China's compromises. Although it is possible to identify the rough division of territory in different agreements, it is also more challenging to pinpoint exactly when offers were made by both sides. Nevertheless, given the demands of negotiating and drafting a boundary agreement, offers of compromise often occur a year or more before the signing of a formal agreement.

TIANANMEN UPHEAVAL

In the 1980s, before the demonstrations in Tiananmen, three of China's socialist neighbors—the Soviet Union, Laos, and Vietnam—sought to normalize their diplomatic relations with the PRC. During the late 1970s, bilateral ties with all three had been downgraded as Chinese-Soviet com-

---

[3] *Jiang Zemin wenxuan* [Jiang Zemin's Selected Works], vol. 3 (Beijing: Renmin chubanshe, 2006), 279.

petition intensified. China, however, remained wary of such normalization, especially before it achieved its long-standing diplomatic objectives of reducing Soviet pressure on its periphery. Unwillingness to compromise in its territorial disputes with these states in the 1980s reflected such reluctance. Yet in 1991, China signed boundary agreements with all three neighbors, making significant progress toward the final resolution of these territorial disputes.

The difference between delay since in the mid-1980s and compromise in the early 1990s was the appearance of internal threats to the political stability of China's communist regime that occurred during and after the 1989 demonstrations in Tiananmen Square. Cumulatively, the demonstrations in April and May were the largest and longest unsanctioned protests against the government in the PRC's history.[4] At their height, as many as 300,000 people marched daily in and around the square as demonstrations also occurred in other cities. When the government moved to crush dissent after June 4, poor diplomatic relations with its socialist neighbors became much more costly, and now leaders of these states all shared the same goal of resisting pressure for political change. By compromising in its territorial disputes, China sought to bolster other socialist states and thus the legitimacy of its own regime.

Legitimacy Crisis at the Core

Although the causes of the Tiananmen protests will not be covered extensively in this chapter, they stemmed largely from a desire for greater accountability in China's governance.[5] In the mid-1980s, urban residents had become increasingly dissatisfied with the side effects of economic reform, including inflation, the scarcity of consumer products, economic mismanagement of state enterprises, and corruption within all levels of the CCP. Participatory democracy was not an initial demand of the student demonstrators, but widespread consensus existed for greater accountability and openness, including within the CCP.

On April 15, 1989, the death of Hu Yaobang provided a spark for this underbrush of discontent. Hu was a reformist CCP general secretary who had been dismissed for mismanaging a series of student demonstrations in late 1986. Students who gathered in Tiananmen Square to mourn his passing soon began to demand a reevaluation of his legacy and the rehabilitation of individuals purged during earlier campaigns against spiritual

[4] The mass campaigns of the Mao era were of course much larger, at times in the millions, but these were led by the CCP, not against it.

[5] For a detailed discussion, see Richard Baum, *Burying Mao: Chinese Politics in the Age of Deng Xiaoping* (Princeton, N.J.: Princeton University Press, 1994), 225–244.

pollution and bourgeois liberalization. On April 22, more than 100,000 people defied a government prohibition and spontaneously entered the square during Hu's official memorial.[6] Five days later, 150,000 people marched to the square, and a similar number returned days later to mark the seventieth anniversary of the May Fourth Movement.[7] At the end of May, more than 300,000 entered the square to witness the unveiling of the Goddess of Democracy, a plastic-foam model that resembled the Statue of Liberty.[8]

From the start, China's leaders were divided on how to respond to the Tiananmen crisis. Hard-liners as well as Deng sought to nip the opposition in the bud, which led to a harsh *People's Daily* editorial in late April that labeled the movement as unpatriotic and counterrevolutionary "turmoil" (*dongluan*).[9] Reformers led by Premier Zhao Ziyang pushed for a more conciliatory approach and hoped to use the protests to deepen political reform. A leadership struggle ensued, which Zhao ultimately lost with his purge at the end of May. On May 19, approximately eight PLA divisions were instructed to enter the capital as Premier Li Peng announced the Politburo's decision to implement martial law. As the soldiers deployed, a popular uprising involving more than one million people erected barricades to stop the PLA from entering the city.[10] Although troops withdrew temporarily to the suburbs, they were ordered to clear the square of protestors on the evening of June 3. By the time the smoke cleared, between 1,000 and 2,600 people had been killed, ironically mostly urban residents and not students.[11]

The protests in Tiananmen were not the first time since 1949 that citizens in Beijing demonstrated directly against the central government. Nevertheless, in terms of size and duration, they were by far the largest series of protests, involving on a daily basis at their peak hundreds of thousands of people, permanent occupation of the square, and open defiance of the government. Prior demonstrations in 1976 and 1986 hardly matched this magnitude. In 1976, two days of demonstrations occurred on April 4 and 5 as people flocked to the square to mourn the death of Zhou Enlai.[12] Protestors numbered in the tens of thousands, but the police quickly as-

---

[6] Baum, *Burying Mao*, 248.

[7] Baum, *Burying Mao*, 253; Timothy Brook, *Quelling the People: The Military Suppression of the Beijing Democracy Movement* (Stanford, Calif.: Stanford University Press, 1992), 33.

[8] Baum, *Burying Mao*, 273.

[9] *RMRB*, 26 April 1989, 1.

[10] Baum, *Burying Mao*, 265; Brook, *Quelling the People*, 48–54.

[11] Brook, *Quelling the People*, 164–169.

[12] Baum, *Burying Mao*, 34; Jonathan Spence, *The Search for Modern China* (New York: Norton, 1990), 612.

sumed control of the square. The next major protests occurred in December 1986, when students in major cities protested for "freedom" and "democracy." The unrest in Beijing was limited, however, to several days in late December and early January, involving perhaps twenty thousand students who entered the square only once.[13] The geographic scope of these demonstrations was wider than in 1976, but the numbers of students involved and the duration of unrest were both smaller than in 1989.[14]

The crisis of public confidence in the government reflected in the 1989 events was national, not local. Demonstrations occurred in 123 Chinese cities, including Shanghai, Chengdu, Nanjing, and Xian.[15] From May 4 to May 19, for example, more than 1.5 million people demonstrated in eighty cities, a figure that doubled the following week.[16] Likewise, the social base of the protesters expanded from students to other segments of society. Initial student protests had been tolerated because students were seen as part of society's elite, viewed as a loyal opposition of sorts for the CCP. The inclusion of workers, especially the organization of an autonomous national union of workers, Gongzilian, revealed that events in Tiananmen represented much broader dissatisfaction with the party. Moreover, such dissatisfaction permeated the CCP itself. More than 800,000 party members were reported to have joined the students and workers, which demonstrated the degree of regime insecurity.[17]

Paradoxically, the crackdown in the name of social stability only increased the regime's insecurity. The violent suppression of the demonstrations and the senior leaders' unwillingness to meet the students' demands for better government further alienated the CCP from China's urban society, its key base of support. In the crackdown that followed the massacre on June 4, approximately 4,000 people were arrested, many of them students, which only increased popular resentment.[18] The CCP and the PLA implemented rectification campaigns to cleanse their ranks, though relatively few cadres were punished.[19] The government retained control of the city, but popular support for the regime continued to drop.

An additional source of regime insecurity was the growing ethnic unrest in the frontiers. In March 1989, then party secretary Hu Jintao imposed martial law in Lhasa following violent demonstrations on the eve of the

[13] *NYT*, 2 January 1987, 2.

[14] Baum, *Burying Mao*, 203; Julia Kwong, "The 1986 Student Demonstrations in China: A Democratic Movement?" *Asian Survey*, vol. 28, no. 9 (September 1988): 970–985; Spence, *Search for Modern China*, 683–684.

[15] Baum, *Burying Mao*, 276.

[16] Baum, *Burying Mao*, 253.

[17] Baum, *Burying Mao*, 276.

[18] Baum, *Burying Mao*, 290.

[19] Baum, *Burying Mao*, 304–307.

thirtieth anniversary of the 1959 revolt. In April 1990, the Baren uprising in southwestern Xinjiang sparked a decade of riots, bombings, assassinations, and armed clashes between separatist groups seeking independence and local security forces. The occurrence of unrest in the frontiers was especially worrying for China's leaders: it demonstrated the breadth of dissatisfaction with the current regime and raised the specter of renewed frontier instability during a period of political unrest at the core, a second perfect storm of regime insecurity comparable to the 1962 territorial crisis discussed in chapter 2. The effects of this unrest are explored in more detail in the second half of this chapter.

International Isolation and Regime Insecurity

The international isolation that China encountered as a result of the worldwide condemnation of the violent crackdown magnified the degree of threat posed by the internal political instability. China's leaders saw the Western sanctions and censure, especially from the United States, as an assault on the CCP itself that threatened to undermine the continuation of Deng's economic reforms keyed to foreign markets and capital. The collapse of socialism in Eastern Europe and disintegration of the Soviet Union left China's leaders with few ideological allies abroad at the time—world trends were moving against China's system of government precisely when it faced internal crisis. China's external security was not greatly threatened by its isolation, as its territory had never been more secure from other countries. What really mattered was the effects of international pressure on China's leaders, who saw international isolation and external pressure as threatening the CCP's political survival.[20]

Tiananmen was a watershed in China's relations with the West, especially the United States. In the first decade since normalization in 1979, a shared adversary—the Soviet Union—provided a basis for cooperation.[21] American leaders viewed Chinese leaders as reformers who were nudging their country toward economic and political liberalization. Deng Xiaoping even graced the cover of *Time* magazine as "Man of the Year." For China, improved ties with the United States were key to its modernization drive, providing a huge market for Chinese exports and an important

[20] Chinese sources refer explicitly to the concept of "political security" (*zhengzhi anquan*) in contrast to territorial security and economic security. See Yan Xuetong, "Shiyan Zhongguo de anquan huanjing" [Preliminary Analysis of China's Security Environment], *Dangdai guoji wenti yanjiu*, no. 4 (1994): 35–41.

[21] On U.S.-China relations during this period, see Harry Harding, *A Fragile Relationship: The United States and China since 1972* (Washington, D.C.: The Brookings Institution, 1992), 107–214; Robert S. Ross, *Negotiating Cooperation: The United States and China, 1969–1989* (Stanford, Calif.: Stanford University Press, 1995), 163–245.

source of capital and technology. Although many bumps existed in the relationship, especially over Taiwan and nuclear proliferation, China's leaders viewed the United States as supporting their regime and its reforms, not opposing it. American leaders for the most part viewed China as liberalizing and playing an important role in the Cold War by tying down the Soviet Union in the Far East.

After Tiananmen, perceptions on both sides changed dramatically. For the United States, China's leaders were not visionary reformers but ruthless dictators. The violence, in short, was viewed as an affront to American values and beliefs. President George Bush tried to prevent a complete break in the relationship, but ties nevertheless soured. The United States publicly condemned the crackdown, gave refuge to China's most prominent dissident, Fang Lizhi, and instituted sanctions designed to punish the regime. In the following years, internal political change in China became one of the main benchmarks for assessing U.S. "China policy."[22] Key issues such as human rights, Tibet, most-favored-nation status, and market transparency were designed to bring about political change in China, directly challenging the CCP's domestic authority.

Likewise, China's leaders no longer viewed the United States as a strategic partner, cooperating against the Soviet threat and providing key support for Deng's economic reforms. Deng, for example, blamed the United States for seeking to bring about regime change through "peaceful evolution."[23] In Deng's typically blunt words, "the West really wants turmoil in China."[24] Deng himself blamed the United States for supporting the demonstrators and viewed U.S. sanctions as directed not against the Chinese state but against the socialist system as part of a broader U.S. effort to bring down socialist regimes.[25] A July 1989 *People's Daily* editorial emphasized the party's insecurity, noting that "certain foreign forces" wanted to "turn China into a bourgeois republic dependent on the West."[26]

The collapse of socialism in Eastern Europe and the disintegration of the Soviet Union further deepened China's international isolation and regime insecurity. As described by one Chinese policy analyst, the end of Cold War was "a big political and psychological shock."[27] The shock

---

[22] On U.S.-China relations during this period, see David M. Lampton, *Same Bed Different Dreams: Managing U.S.-China Relations, 1989–2000* (Berkeley: University of California Press, 2001); Robert L. Suettinger, *Beyond Tiananmen: The Politics of U.S.-China Relations, 1989–2000* (Washington, D.C.: The Brookings Institution, 2003).

[23] *DXPWX3*, 325.

[24] *DXPWX3*, 325.

[25] *DXPWX3*, 330–333.

[26] *RMRB*, 22 July 1989, 1.

[27] Chen Qimao, "New Approaches in China's Foreign Policy: The Post–Cold War Era," *Asian Survey*, vol. 33, no. 3 (March 1993): 238.

began with Nicolai Ceausescu's fall in Romania in December 1989. In the following two years, the remaining socialist regimes in Eastern Europe collapsed, culminating with the disintegration of the Soviet Union itself. The rapid collapse of so many socialist states not only deprived China's leaders of key diplomatic support during a period of political instability but also highlighted the vulnerability of China's own political system and the broad-based support for deeper political and economic change.

The collapse of socialism aggravated China's regime insecurity in two additional ways. It first increased apprehension about U.S. intentions. Some feared that China would become the next target, as it was the largest remaining socialist state.[28] Deng reportedly remarked in 1990 that "everyone should be very clear that under the present international situation all enemy attention will be concentrated on China. They will use every pretext to cause trouble, to create difficulties and pressure for us."[29]

The fall of the Soviet Union also sparked a global wave of national self-determination movements, which placed additional pressure on the regime for change. In many of the former socialist republics, democratic political forces emerged in stark contrast to the communist dictatorships that they replaced. Self-determination further undermined the socialist model that China upheld, enhancing the threatening nature of the post–Cold War world environment for China's political system. Moreover, the rise of democratic political forces provided encouragement for ethnic minorities within China seeking to enhance their autonomy or secede.[30] China's leaders explicitly linked the collapse of the Soviet Union and the rise of self-determination movements to the increased unrest in frontier areas, especially Xinjiang, Tibet, and Inner Mongolia—all internal threats to the regime.[31]

Stability, Continued Reform, and Foreign Policy Moderation

Facing political instability at home and an external environment hostile to its political system, China's leaders moved to strengthen the regime. Domestically, Deng pushed for continued reform, which served as the basis for maintaining regime legitimacy. Externally, Deng implemented a moderate foreign policy designed to support these internal goals by limiting external threats to the regime and ensuring access to foreign markets

---

[28] Chen, "New Approaches," 240; John W. Garver, "The Chinese Communist Party and the Collapse of Soviet Communism," *The China Quarterly*, no. 133 (March 1993): 1–26.

[29] Quoted in Garver, "Chinese Communist Party," 19.

[30] See, for example, Wei Zhongli and Song Xianchun, eds., *Guonei anquan baowei* [Safeguarding Internal Security] (Beijing: Jingguan jiaoyu chubanshe [internal circulation], 1999), 180–192.

[31] Chen, "New Approaches," 238; Yan, "Shiyan Zhongguo," 40.

necessary for continued reform. Compromise in territorial disputes reflected this broader shift in China's foreign policy.

The primary focus of China's response to the regime insecurity created by Tiananmen and the end of the Cold War was internal. Foreign policy was grounded in the imperative of ensuring the CCP's survival.[32] Deng's primary goal was to maintain internal stability, a foundation for continued economic reform. As he told Richard Nixon in October 1989, "stability overrides everything" (*wending yadao yiqie*).[33] Deng urged the continuation of reform, arguing that it was key to achieving the Four Modernizations, defending Chinese socialism, and increasing public support for the CCP.[34] As Deng noted, "without reform and opening, there is no hope."[35] Tiananmen, however, exposed divisions within the senior leadership over the pace and scope of reform. Conservative leaders including Chen Yun argued for a more gradual approach. Until his vaunted "southern tour" in the spring of 1992, Deng battled to ensure the continuation of an aggressive reform program.

Foreign policy was structured to support these domestic priorities. In the summer and fall of 1989, Deng articulated a foreign policy strategy to bolster the regime in the face of collapsing socialism and international isolation. The goals of this policy were to strengthen the CCP within China, continue the opening and reform policy, and resist Western pressure for political change (*dingzhu xifang yali*). As Deng instructed in September 1989, "In brief, as for the international situation, it can be summarized in three sentences: First, observe coolly. Second, hold our ground. Third, be cool-headed. Don't be impatient. We must not be impatient. Be calm, calm and more calm, and quietly immerse ourselves in practical work to accomplish something—something for China."[36] In the months that followed, this approach became known as the "20-character policy": "observe things coolly, manage things calmly, hold one's ground, hide our capacities and bide our time, get some things done" (*lengjing guancha, chenzhuo yingfu, wenzhu zhenjiao, taoguang yanghui, yousuo zuowei*).[37]

---

[32] On the link between domestic challenges and foreign policy, see Zhang Baijia, "Jiushi niandai de Zhongguo neizheng yu waijiao" [China's Domestic Politics and Diplomacy in the 1990s], *Zhonggong dangshi yanjiu*, no. 6 (2001): 29–34.

[33] *DXPWX3*, 331.

[34] *DXPWX3*, 302–315.

[35] *DXPWX3*, 320. For more on the domestic politics of this period and Deng's southern tour, see Baum, *Burying Mao*, 275–368; Joseph Fewsmith, *China since Tiananmen: The Politics of Transition* (Cambridge: Cambridge University Press, 2001), 21–74.

[36] *DXPWX3*, 315–321.

[37] For an authoritative statement of these phrases, see Qian Qichen's entry in Wang Taiping, ed., *Deng Xiaoping waijiao sixiang yanjiu lunwenji* [Collected Papers on the Study of Deng Xiaoping's Diplomatic Thought] (Beijing: Shijie zhishi chubanshe, 1996), 4–10. This is also sometimes referred to as the 28-character policy, with the addition of "remain free of

Foreign policy should buy time for regime consolidation (in the short run) and the continuation of reform (in the longer run). As described by one Chinese scholar, this policy direction was characterized by the four "don'ts" and the two "transcends": don't carry the flag, don't take the lead, don't antagonize, don't make enemies, transcend ideology, transcend partisanship.[38]

Moreover, Deng's foreign policy was not linked to external security threats or dramatic changes in the structure of the international system. Indeed, this policy was formulated immediately following Tiananmen in the summer and fall of 1989, well before the August 1991 coup that led to the collapse of the Soviet Union and Cold War bipolarity. Moreover, the objective of the policy was not to balance against any one state but rather to balance against threats to the regime's authority and control. As leading Chinese scholars have indicated, this foreign policy was linked first and foremost to supporting reform and protecting the regime in an uncertain international environment containing elements that were hostile to China's economic reform and internal stability.[39]

Deng's foreign policy strategy had three principal components. The first was to improve relations with neighboring states through the good-neighbor policy (*muling zhengce*).[40] The declining importance of the Soviet Union and deterioration of relations with the United States increased the importance of China's ties with its immediate neighbors, as potential trade partners and diplomatic buffers for the regime. Li Peng's 1993 work report instructed that "actively developing friendly relations with neighboring countries and striving for a peaceful peripheral environment is the focal point of our country's diplomatic work."[41] Following Tiananmen,

---

ambition, by no means take a lead" (*shanyu shouzhuo, juebu dangtou*). No public record of Deng using either all of the 20 or 28 characters exists, in particular the "taoguang yanghui" phrase by which this policy is widely known. Most likely, it appears that these traditional expressions were used to capture the essence of Deng's September 4 remarks quoted above, which have roughly the same meaning. For one of the first scholarly Chinese articles to describe this policy, see Qu Xing, "Shilun DongOu jubian he Sulian jieti hou de Zhongguo waijiao zhengce" [On China's Foreign Policy after the Sudden Change in Eastern Europe and the Disintegration of the Soviet Union], *Waijiao xueyuan xuebao*, no. 4 (1994): 16–22. Also see Wei Ling and Sun Jiewan, *Deng Xiaoping waijiao sixiang tanjiu* [Research on Deng Xiaoping's Diplomatic Thought] (Beijing: Zhongyang wenxian chubanse, 2000), 215–227.

[38] Qu, "Shilun DongOu," 19.

[39] See, for example, Qu Xing, *Zhongguo waijiao 50 nian* [50 Years of Chinese Diplomacy] (Nanjing: Jiangsu renmin chubanshe, 2000), 505–545; Xie Yixian, *Zhongguo dangdai waijiao shi (1949–1995)* [History of China's Contemporary Diplomacy (1949–1995)] (Beijing: Zhongguo qingnian chubanshe, 1997), 457–477; Zhang, "Jiushi niandai de Zhongguo."

[40] This rubric follows Chen, "New Approaches."

[41] Li Peng, "Zhengfu gongzuo baogao (1993)" [Government Work Report], 15 March 1993, http://www.npc.gov.cn/.

China established diplomatic relations or normalized ties with ten states in the region (apart from the Soviet successor states), including South Korea, Indonesia, Singapore, Vietnam, and Laos. As will be described in more detail below, China's willingness to compromise in territorial disputes was a key component of the good-neighbor policy.[42]

The second component was an "omnidirectional" (*quanfangwei*) orientation designed to improve ties with the developed and the developing worlds. In addition to stabilizing China's diplomatic position, the omnidirectional policy ensured the continued success of reform, as new or invigorated diplomatic relations would identify additional export markets and sources of foreign investment.[43] Key targets were the principal Western states, including the United States and Japan. Contrary to systemic explanations, China sought to improve ties with the United States after Tiananmen and the collapse of the Soviet Union even though it was the only pole in the international system.[44] Despite the added ideological pressure on the regime due to the collapse of communist states and the advance of Western-style democracies and capitalism elsewhere, China chose not to ignore ties with Western states, which were key to the success of reform.

The third component was limited but increased participation in the international community, especially trade-related organizations. China maintained its participation in the UN system, continued with its application to join the World Trade Organization, and began to join as an observer in regional organizations such as the ASEAN. These efforts were all linked to the goal of supporting continued economic reform.[45]

---

[42] On the link between regime security and the good-neighbor policy, see Zhang, "Jiushi niandai de Zhongguo," 30, 34. For descriptions of the good-neighbor policy, see Liu Hongxuan, *Zhongguo mulin shi: Zhongguo yu zhoubian guojia guanxi* [History of Good-Neighborliness: China's Relations with Peripheral States] (Beijing: Shijie zhishi chubanshe, 2001); Shi Yuanhua, "Lun xin Zhongguo zhoubian waijiao zhengce de lishi yanbian" [On the Historical Evolution of New China's Peripheral Foreign Policy], *Dangdai Zhongguo shi yanjiu*, vol. 7, no. 5 (2000): 38–50; Zhu Tingchang, "Lun Zhongguo mulin zhengce de lilun yu shijian" [On the Theory and Practice of China's Good-Neighbor Policy], *Guoji guancha*, no. 2 (2001): 12–18; Zhu Tingchang, ed., *Zhongguo zhoubian anquan huanjing yu anquan zhanlue* [China's Peripheral Security Environment and Security Strategy] (Beijing: Shishi chubanshe, 2002).

[43] See James C. Hsiung, "China's Omni-Directional Diplomacy: Realignment to Cope with Monopolar U.S. Power," *Asian Survey*, vol. 35, no. 6 (June 1995): 573–586; Zhang Baijia, "Cong 'yi bian dao' dao 'quan fang wei': dui 50 nianlai Zhongguo waijiao geju yanjin de sikao" [From 'Lean to One Side' to 'Omnidirection': Reflections on the Evolution of China's Foreign Policy Structure over the Past 50 Years], *Zhonggong dangshi yanjiu*, no. 1 (2000): 21–28; Zhang, "Jiushi niandai de Zhongguo," 29–34.

[44] *DXPWX3*, 350–351; Robert S. Ross, "The Diplomacy of Tiananmen: Two-Level Bargaining and Great-Power Cooperation," *Security Studies*, vol. 10, no. 2 (Winter 2000/2001): 139–178.

[45] Chen, "New Approaches," 243–244; Hsiung, "China's Omni-Directional Diplomacy," 581–584; Zhang, "Jiushi niandai de Zhongguo," 32–33.

China Compromises

China's efforts to settle outstanding territorial disputes were an important part of Deng's overall foreign policy strategy. In the wake of regime instability, such disputes had become much more costly to pursue because they blocked the external cooperation that China sought to support its domestic consolidation effort. The presence of unresolved territorial disputes was a key obstacle to the normalization or deepening of diplomatic ties with many of China's neighbors. In addition, given Deng's commitment to reform, active territorial disputes limited the development of cross-border trade, which was part of China's overall economic reform program but also particularly vital for frontier regions, whose development lagged behind that of the coastal areas. Compromising in territorial disputes allowed China to both improve ties with its neighbors, thereby increasing external diplomatic support for the regime, and promote its own economic development.

In response to the regime insecurity after Tiananmen, China attempted to settle frontier disputes with three socialist states: the Soviet Union, Laos, and Vietnam. China signed a boundary treaty with Laos, a delimitation agreement with Russia for the eastern sector, and two temporary agreements with Vietnam. Since these states were kindred communist regimes, improved ties with them increased diplomatic support for China's own regime and strengthened the position of socialism during a period of turbulence in Eastern Europe. Since they were land neighbors, improved ties also supported the good-neighbor policy of stabilizing China's periphery and increasing trade. Without the internal upheaval around Tiananmen and the external pressure on socialist states for domestic reform, China's leaders would have been much less willing to compromise in these territorial disputes.

THE SOVIET UNION AND RUSSIA

The most important settlement achieved during this period was with the Soviet Union. The impetus for the 1991 agreement, however, came not from Beijing but from Moscow. Amid intensified competition with the United States in the early 1980s, the Soviet Union faced an economic crisis that increased the cost of maintaining its empire. In this context, the Soviet Union's territorial disputes with China became much more costly to maintain because they tied down more than 600,000 troops and blocked the normalization of ties with China. The Soviet Union could not afford both a second arms race with the United States and a significant military presence on the China-Soviet border. By normalizing ties, Mikhail Gorbachev hoped to arrest any further decline in the Soviet Union's international position.

Facing these pressures, Gorbachev took the first step toward compromise. In a July 1986 Vladivostok speech, he proposed the normalization of Chinese-Soviet relations and troop reductions. For China, the massive Soviet deployment on its border, which was linked to the ongoing dispute, was one of three obstacles to improved relations.[46] Gorbachev also indicated that where a river constituted the border, the Soviet Union would accept the main channel of navigation, or the *thalweg* principle, as the means for delimiting the eastern sector, which represented a major concession. The Soviet Union had claimed previously that the river border ran along the Chinese bank, not the river's midpoint.[47] Moreover, Gorbachev's speech signaled that the Soviet Union would accept the 1964 consensus over the eastern sector, which had been based on the *thalweg* principle. Two months after the speech, China and the Soviet Union agreed to resume negotiations over disputed areas that had been suspended in 1979.[48]

With this Soviet concession, progress toward settling the dispute began. During the first round of talks in February 1987, the two sides agreed to focus first on the eastern sector, indicating that negotiations would resume based on the 1964 consensus.[49] In August 1987, the two sides agreed to settle disputes in the eastern sector on the basis of the "existing relevant treaties," namely the "unequal" treaties signed in the nineteenth century, and to use the *thalweg* principle or the median line to delimit the boundary line in rivers. They also established a joint working group of experts to draft a boundary delimitation agreement.[50] Nevertheless, China was not eager to sign an agreement only for the eastern sector, which the Soviet Union favored. Instead, China sought a comprehensive settlement to all disputed areas, which increased its leverage over the complex disputes in the western sector.[51] As Qian Qichen stated in a 1987 press conference, "there can be no separate agreements. *We must have the whole*" (emphasis added).[52]

---

[46] The three obstacles were the Soviet occupation of Afghanistan, the militarization of the Chinese-Soviet border, and Soviet support for Vietnam's occupation of Cambodia.

[47] As discussed in chapter 2, the Soviet Union had also accepted the main channel of navigation in the 1964 negotiations. Genrikh Kireyev, "Demarcation of the Border with China," *International Affairs*, vol. 45, no. 2 (1999): 100.

[48] AP, 25 September 1986 (Lexis-Nexis).

[49] AP, 23 February 1987 (Lexis-Nexis).

[50] Xinhua, 21 August 1987 (Lexis-Nexis).

[51] Interview, Beijing, June 2001. Also see Xing Guangcheng, "China and Central Asia: Towards a New Relationship," in Yongjin Zhang and Rouben Azizian, eds., *Ethnic Challenges beyond Borders: Chinese and Russian Perspectives of the Central Asia Conundrum* (New York: St. Martin's Press, 1998), 46.

[52] Quoted in Jim Abrams, "Chinese, Soviets Agree on Committees to Review Borders," AP, 22 August 1987 (Lexis-Nexis).

Progress continued in the next round of talks held in October 1988. According to a Soviet spokesman, the two sides "reached an understanding on the larger part of [the eastern] section of the border."[53] As rivers constitute most of the border in this region, the prior acceptance of the *thalweg* principle determined the boundary line and the allocation of most of the disputed islands. Nevertheless, the sticking point was the same as in 1964, namely Heixiazi Island at the confluence of the Amur and Ussuri rivers as well as Abagaitu Shoal in the Argun River (map 3.1). Although Heixiazi had been under Soviet control since the 1920s, China maintained that both areas were located on the Chinese side of the main navigation channel as indicated in maps exchanged after the 1860 treaty. The two sides also agreed to start discussions over the western sector, including the Pamir Mountains, and conduct a joint aerial survey.[54]

In retrospect, this progress is unsurprising. In essence, the two sides resurrected a consensus reached in 1964, which had also excluded Heixiazi Island. In addition, this consensus indicates that China's desire to compromise with the Soviet Union was not driven by relative power considerations and growing Soviet weakness: China endorsed the same agreement in two periods when its power relative to the Soviet Union was quite different. China was much stronger in 1988, while the Soviet Union was mired in crisis, yet China agreed to the same terms both times. Although China's desire for a comprehensive settlement might suggest that it was leveraging its strength at the negotiating table, it pursued a similar settlement in 1964.

In May 1989, China and the Soviet Union normalized relations during Gorbachev's visit to Beijing amid the Tiananmen demonstrations. Gorbachev had pressed for such a summit for two years, a capstone of his engagement of China. Before the summit, significant progress had been made toward settling outstanding territorial disputes. The two sides had reached a consensus over most of the eastern sector and had begun to tackle the Central Asian areas. Nevertheless, both sides were still quite far from the comprehensive settlement that China sought. Although the joint communiqué called on both sides to "speed up" discussions, no breakthrough was reached despite the consensus that appeared to emerge in 1988. The summit would have been an ideal time to sign an agreement, especially since a consensus had been reached over most of the eastern sector.[55]

[53] Quoted in "China, Soviet Union Agree on Part of Eastern Border," Reuters, 31 October 1988 (Factiva).

[54] Reuters, 31 October 1988 (Factiva).

[55] Xinhua, 18 May 1989 (Lexis-Nexis).

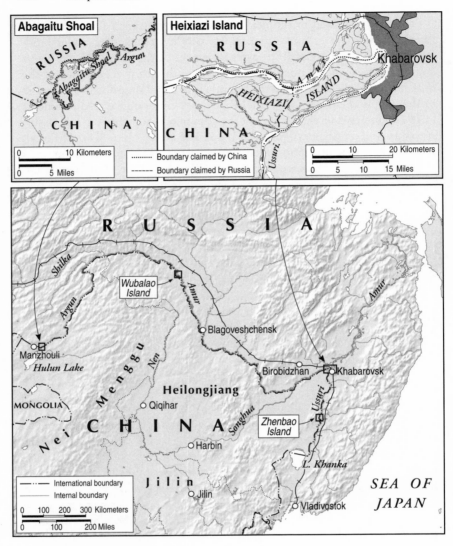

Map 3.1 China-Russia Border (Eastern Sector)

After Tiananmen, however, the pace quickened. The reason was not renewed impetus from Gorbachev's visit but the regime insecurity that China's leaders now faced, which increased the importance of ties with the Soviet Union. At the fourth round of negotiations in October 1989, China's first concession was to drop its earlier demand for a comprehensive package settlement, a direct reversal of Qian Qichen's 1987 statement that "we must have the whole." Instead, China agreed to sign sector-specific deals. The timing of this concession reflects the role of internal threats—it occurred after Tiananmen but well before the August 1991 coup and the disintegration of the Soviet Union. China's second concession was to sign an agreement that excluded the two disputed islands. China did not drop its claim but offered to reach an agreement for the eastern sector that excluded the islands. According to interviews, China had hoped to use the islands as leverage in negotiations over the western sector, which were never completed, owing to the collapse of the Soviet Union.[56] Given the imperatives of China's internal problems, an agreement for most of the eastern sector, which would improve Chinese-Soviet relations, was better than no agreement at all.

With these concessions, negotiators moved to sign an agreement. In June 1990, vice–foreign ministers decided to affirm existing areas of agreement in a legal document, a decision that produced the 1991 eastern sector agreement.[57] In October 1990, the joint working group began the necessary legal work for signing a final agreement.[58] Over the next six months, eight rounds of talks were held by the joint working group, consisting of a joint drafting group and a joint survey working group.[59] The two sides reached a draft agreement in March 1991.[60] In between, negotiations continued over the two islands as well as the western sector, but the two sides did not reach any agreements.[61]

To consolidate Chinese-Soviet ties, a boundary agreement was a key deliverable during Jiang Zemin's first trip as general secretary to the Soviet Union in May 1991. This trip was part of a much broader effort to strengthen diplomatic ties with socialist states.[62] On May 16, Qian Qichen and Soviet foreign minister Alexander Bessmertnykh signed a boundary

[56] Interview, June 2001.

[57] Tian Zengpei, ed., *Gaige kaifang yilai de Zhongguo waijiao* [China's Diplomacy since Reform and Opening] (Beijing: Shijie zhishi chubanshe, 1993), 328. One source states that China and the Soviet Union reached an agreement over the eastern sector in 1989, presumably at the October 1989 meeting. If this is true, then it provides even stronger evidence for the effects of regime insecurity on China's decisions to compromise. See Li Fenglin, "ZhongSu bianjie tanpan qinli ji" [Record of My Personal Experiences in the Chinese-Soviet Boundary Negotiations], *Zhonggong dangshi ziliao*, no. 4 (2003): 34.

[58] *ZGWJ*, 1991, 235.

[59] *ZGWJ*, 1991, and *ZGWJ*, 1992, 233–234.

[60] *ZGWJ*, 1993, 233.

[61] One Soviet source states that by the end of 1990 the two sides had agreed on 90 percent of the border. However, it appears that he was referring to areas where both sides had agreed to use existing treaties, which cover most of the western sector. See Alexei Voskresensky, "Some Border Issues Unsolved," *New Times*, no. 19 (1991): 27.

[62] On the importance of Jiang Zemin's first trip to the Soviet Union, see Elizabeth Wishnick, *Mending Fences: The Evolution of Moscow's China Policy from Brezhnev to Yeltsin* (Seattle: University of Washington Press, 2001).

agreement for the eastern sector.[63] The document outlined the alignment of the boundary in the eastern sector, most of which ran through the main channel or the median line of the Amur, Ussuri, and Argun rivers. Article 5 stated that river islands and shoals would be allocated according to the recommendations of a joint commission.

The disintegration of the Soviet Union did not prevent the ratification or implementation of this agreement. Demarcation began in late 1991 with the establishment of a small group of demarcation experts to conduct preparatory work.[64] The Chinese-Russian joint demarcation commission was formed in June 1992, and actual demarcation of the eastern sector started in 1993.[65] The detailed delimitation of the border, including the allocation of disputed islands, was finished in November 1997 with the placement of 1,183 boundary markers and twenty-four buoys in Lake Khanka.[66] Disputed territory was divided almost evenly between the two sides. A Chinese source states that China received 765 disputed islands or approximately 53 percent of the total.[67] A Russian sources states that China received 1,281 of 2,444 disputed river islands and shoals, or approximately 52 percent.[68] Overall, the two sides split the roughly 1,000 square kilometers of disputed territory in this sector almost evenly.[69] The final protocol demarcating the boundary and accompanying maps comprised more than two thousand pages of documentation, making this the most detailed border agreement that China has reached with any of its land neighbors.[70]

During the demarcation process, local Russian officials objected to the division of territory contained in the 1991 agreement. These conflicts garnered a good deal of attention in the press and implied incorrectly that

---

[63] *TYJ*, 1991, 266–277.

[64] *ZGWJ*, 1992, 234.

[65] *ZGWJ*, 1993, 234.

[66] Kireyev, "Demarcation," 108.

[67] Xue Jundu and Lu Nanquan, *Xin Eluosi: zhengzhi, jingji, waijiao* [New Russia: Politics, Economics, Diplomacy] (Beijing: Zhongguo shehui kexue chubanshe, 1997), 410.

[68] Interfax, 10 April 1999 (Factiva).

[69] Very little information is available concerning the size of the disputed islands. An official Chinese source puts the total at 800 square kilometers, with 600 square kilometers in the Amur and Ussuri rivers and 200 square kilometers in the Argun River. Other sources refer to only 600 square kilometers, but this figure most likely refers only to the Amur and Ussuri sections. For the Chinese estimate, see Tang Jiaxuan, ed., *Zhongguo waijiao cidian* [Dictionary of China's Diplomacy] (Beijing: Shijie zhishi chubanshe, 2000), 725. For other estimates, see George Ginsburgs, "The End of the Sino-Russian Territorial Disputes? " *The Journal of East Asian Studies*, vol. 7, no. 1 (1993): 267; Yakov Zinberg, "The Vladivostok Curve: Subnational Intervention into Russo-Chinese Border Agreements," *Boundary and Security Bulletin*, vol. 4, no. 3 (1996): 78.

[70] Kireyev, "Demarcation," 109.

China was making additional demands.[71] These included Menkeseli Island in the Chita region along with areas near Khasan (3 square kilometers), Ussuriik (9 square kilometers) and Khanka (3 square kilometers) in the Maritime Province, and many river islands.[72] Menkeseli was returned to China as planned, but an agreement for joint use of the islands was signed in 1997 to accommodate local Russian farmers.[73] Ussuriik was also returned to China per the 1991 agreement but was believed to be Russian because of a tsarist boundary marker that was placed on the Chinese side of the river.[74] The disputed areas near Khasan and Khanka were divided between the two sides, with China receiving 50 percent and 74 percent of the contested areas, respectively, even though under the original agreement all of these areas would have been transferred to China.[75] As the head of the Russian delegation stressed, these changes did not result from subsequent negotiations but from the implementation of the 1991 agreement, which itself was based on the delimitation of the 1860 treaty.[76]

After the disintegration of the Soviet Union, the new Central Asian states inherited most of the disputes in the western sector of the Chinese-Soviet border, as discussed later in this chapter. All that remained between China and Russia was a 55-kilometer stretch of land between the Mongolia-Russia-China tripoint and the Kazakhstan-Russia-China tripoint. An agreement over this area was concluded during a series of meetings held by working groups in the first half of 1994.[77] In September 1994, Qian Qichen and Andrei Kozyrev signed the western sector boundary agreement.[78] Demarcation of this sector was completed in 1997 with the placement of two boundary markers. Otherwise, the border follows the watershed in the region.[79]

---

[71] For an excellent study of the demarcation of the eastern sector, see Akihiro Iwashita, *A 4,000 Kilometer Journey along the Sino-Russian Border* (Sapporo: Slavic Research Center, Hokkaido University, 2004). Negotiations continued over the unresolved islands but not over other areas. On local opposition, see Wishnick, *Mending Fences*, 176–181.

[72] This section is based on Yutaka Akino, "Moscow's New Perspectives on Sino-Russian Relations," in Tadayuki Hayashi, ed., *The Emerging New Regional Order in Central and Eastern Europe* (Sapporo: Slavic Research Center, Hokkaido University, 1997); Kireyev, "Demarcation," 106–107; Zinberg, "The Vladivostk Curve," 76–86.

[73] *TYJ*, 1997, 266–276.

[74] Genrikh Kireyev, "Strategic Partnership and a Stable Border," *Far Eastern Affairs*, no. 4 (1997): 19–20; Kireyev, "Demarcation," 106.

[75] Kireyev, "Demarcation," 106.

[76] Kireyev, "Strategic Partnership," 8–22; Kireyev, "Demarcation," 98–109.

[77] *ZGWJ*, 1995, 274.

[78] *TYJ*, 1994, 706–708.

[79] Kireyev, "Demarcation," 108.

China's many territorial disputes with Russia were not finally settled until October 2004. As discussed above, two areas were excluded from the 1991 eastern sector agreement, Heixiazi Island and the Abagaitu Shoal, and they remained in dispute throughout the 1990s. During President Putin's 2004 visit to China, he and Jiang Zemin signed a supplemental boundary agreement for the eastern sector. In the document, China and Russia agreed, in the words of one Chinese scholar, "to divide [them] . . . equally."[80] According to interviews, the decision to compromise was reached sometime in 2002.[81] No increase in regime insecurity is associated with this decision, as Chinese politics remained relatively stable. Instead, it is likely that it stemmed from an external logic, namely a desire to consolidate the "strategic partnership" declared in the 2001 Chinese-Russian treaty and solidify the bilateral relationship amid what appeared to be growing U.S. power after September 11 with the attacks against Afghanistan and Iraq.

LAOS

Laos had sought to normalize ties with China as early as 1985. Although the two sides had exchanged ambassadors in 1988, progress toward normalization remained slow. After Tiananmen, however, China pushed for rapprochement as part of its broader effort to engage socialist states and stabilize its periphery.[82] Normalized ties with Laos would also help to improve relations with Vietnam, China's traditional adversary in the southeast. China's attempt to settle its territorial dispute with Laos was a key part of this broader foreign policy initiative.

In the summer of 1989, Li Peng invited Kaysone Phomvihane, general secretary of the Lao People's Revolutionary Party, to visit China. In July, the Laotian leader had expressed public support for China's handling of the Tiananmen demonstrations.[83] His visit in October 1989 marked the first summit between party leaders since 1976. Since Phomvihane was one of the first world leaders to visit China after Tiananmen, his visit launched China's effort to implement Deng's new foreign policy strategy.[84] During the summit, Chinese leaders stressed the importance of maintaining their socialist system. Moreover, as Phomvihane was head of the Laotian communist party, his visit reflected the restoration of party-to-party as well as state-to-state ties, which underscored efforts to bolster the beleaguered CCP.

---

[80] Zhang Lijun, "Building Peaceful Borders," *Beijing Review*, vol. 49, no. 25 (June 2006): 10.

[81] Interview, February 2004, Beijing.

[82] Zhou Liming, "Lengzhan hou Laowo de duihua zhengce" [Laotian China Policy after the Cold War], *Dangdai yatai*, no. 9 (2000): 19.

[83] Xinhua, 3 July 1989 (Lexis-Nexis).

[84] Zhou, "Lengzhan hou," 20.

Progress on the territorial dispute between the two states formed the basis for normalization. During Phomvihane's visit, one of the deliverables was a temporary agreement on border affairs. Importantly, the agreement affirmed that the status quo created by the prior Chinese-French treaties should be maintained pending a final settlement, a clear signal that China would not pursue additional claims. The agreement also covered functional issues, such as consular work and the regulation of cross-border trade.[85] The timing of Li Peng's invitation to Phomvihane and the swift progress toward a temporary agreement reflect the effect of political instability on China's willingness to compromise. Although Laos had sought to normalize ties since 1985, China responded only after Tiananmen, when the value of relations with Laos increased. Attempts to settle the dispute indicate that improved ties were more important than hard bargaining over disputed land.

Formal negotiations over the border began the following year. In August 1990, the first round of talks was held in Vientiane, where the two sides signed a provisional agreement to delimit the Chinese-Laotian border on the basis of existing treaties and to conduct a joint aerial survey, reaffirming China's early position in the temporary agreement.[86] A group of experts began meeting the following month to compare maps and prepare for the survey.[87] By February 1991, experts from the two sides had reached a consensus on the location of the watershed and the direction of the border. In August 1991, during the third round of expert meetings, the two sides reached a consensus on the treaty, which was initialed by Vice–Foreign Ministers Liu Huaqiu and Soulivong Phrasithideth.[88]

Like China's eastern sector agreement with Russia, the signing of the treaty with Laos was a key deliverable during a high-level visit. In October 1991, Premiers Li Peng and Khamtay Siphandone signed a boundary treaty.[89] In essence, the treaty affirmed the boundary line derived from the original Chinese-French treaties, and the 18-square-kilometer area under dispute was divided almost evenly between the two sides.[90] In January 1992, demarcation work to survey the border and place boundary markers began.[91] A detailed boundary protocol, which identified the location of forty-five boundary markers, was signed in 1993.[92]

---

[85] TYJ, 1989, 93–103.
[86] Lao National Radio, 24 August 1990 (Lexis-Nexis).
[87] Lao National Radio, 26 September 1990 (Lexis-Nexis).
[88] ZGWJ, 1990, 52; ZGWJ, 1991, 54; ZGWJ, 1992, 53.
[89] TYJ, 1991, 62–66.
[90] Interview, Beijing, July 2001.
[91] ZGWJ, 1993, 55–56, 544.
[92] TYJ, 1993, 89–114.

VIETNAM

In a sequence similar to the rapprochement between Laos and China, Vietnam first pushed to normalize ties with China in 1988. China demurred, partly because Vietnam had not yet withdrawn its troops from Cambodia, which Vietnam had invaded in 1978. Following Tiananmen, China played a much more active role in Cambodia as part of Deng's good-neighbor policy. Beijing walked a fine line between reducing Vietnamese influence in Cambodia (one of the main reasons for China's 1979 war with Vietnam) and enhancing its position in the region by improving ties with Vietnam and facilitating a peace agreement in Cambodia. Although China used Vietnam's desire for normalization as leverage to settle the Cambodia issue, both objectives stemmed from the same impulse to stabilize China's diplomatic position after Tiananmen.

In May 1990, Chinese and Vietnamese diplomats began a series of quiet talks over Cambodia and normalization. Both leaders had strong incentives to improve ties, as each was seeking to strengthen an internally threatened communist party. In early September 1990, senior Vietnamese leaders, including General Secretary Nguyen Van Linh, Prime Minister Do Muoi, and former prime minister Pham Van Dong, secretly traveled to China.[93] Although not an official summit, this trip was the first meeting of the two parties' leaders since 1976. In the talks, Vietnam agreed to the peace plan for Cambodia being promoted by China and other members of the UN Security Council.[94] The following summer, as the situation in Cambodia eased, the two sides agreed to normalize ties through another series of secret and official visits to China by Vietnamese officials. In November 1991, Jiang Zemin and Do Muoi, now the general secretary of Vietnam's communist party, held a summit in Beijing and declared the normalization of relations.

Progress on the territorial disputes between the two sides was an integral part of normalization. Because of mistrust that lingered since the 1979 war, settlement of the disputes would reduce suspicions and facilitate closer ties. In their 1991 joint communiqué, Jiang and Do agreed to maintain "peace and tranquility" along the border and to settle the territorial disputes peacefully.[95] During the summit, the two sides signed a temporary agreement on border affairs, which outlined the practicalities of normalization, including a commitment to maintain the status quo pending a final settlement. Reflecting the importance of increasing cross-border trade and developing frontier regions, the agreement also identified twenty-four ports to be opened on the border to increase trade and communications.[96]

[93] AP, 17 September 1990 (Lexis-Nexis).
[94] Kyodo News Service, 20 October 1990 (Lexis-Nexis).
[95] Xinhua, 10 November 1991 (Lexis-Nexis).
[96] *TYJ*, 1993, 85–93.

Following normalization, China and Vietnam began formal talks on the land border. In February 1992, the two sides formed an expert working group to determine the principles for settling disputes. After three rounds of negotiations, two at the expert working-group level and one at the vice-ministerial level, China and Vietnam signed an agreement in October 1993 outlining the principles for settling disputes over the land border and the Tonkin Gulf demarcation. In the document, the two sides agreed to take the 1887 and 1895 Chinese-French agreements as the basis for negotiations and use the principle of "give and take" to settle disputes, which again signaled China's willingness to compromise. A joint working group was formed to identify the location of the boundary line, determine areas where actual control and the boundary line differed, and resolve these disputed areas.[97]

Despite the October 1993 agreement, progress toward settling the land dispute was slow. By the end of 1996, thirteen rounds of negotiations had been held, nine at the working-group level and four at the vice-ministerial level, yet the only real breakthrough was an agreement in October 1996 to begin an aerial survey of the border.[98] Three factors prevented further progress. The first was the presence of multiple disputes: the land border, the delimitation of the Tonkin Gulf, the Paracel Islands, and the Spratly Islands. China sought to focus only on the land border and the Tonkin Gulf, both of which were linked to economic issues, while Vietnam sought to negotiate the resolution of all four disputes through a comprehensive agreement that might enhance its leverage. Interviews indicate that Vietnam's insistence on linking all four disputes limited progress on the land border.[99] In 1994, China partly accommodated Vietnam's wishes when it agreed to discuss the Spratly Islands as part of a settlement of the land border dispute.[100] Although China's leaders did face domestic threats after Tiananmen, their effects were not strong enough to create incentives to compromise in all four disputes with Vietnam, especially over the offshore islands.

The second obstacle was the reluctance of some officials on both sides to pursue compromise seriously. Hard feelings lingered in both countries. With memories of 1979 still fresh, many Vietnamese were naturally quite suspicious of China's intentions. Likewise, after losing perhaps tens of thousands of lives in the 1979 war, the PLA reportedly refused to partici-

---

[97] Waijiao bu, ed., *Zhonghua renmin gongheguo bianjie shiwu tiaoyue ji: ZhongYue juan* [Collection of Treaties on the PRC's Boundary Affairs: China-Vietnam] (Beijing: Shishi chubanshe [internal circulation], 2004), 49–52.

[98] *ZGWJ*, 1997, 804.

[99] Interview, Beijing, June 2002.

[100] *ZGWJ*, 1995, 44. For a detailed review, see Ramses Amer, "The Sino-Vietnamese Approach to Managing Boundary Disputes," *Maritime Briefing*, vol. 3, no. 5 (2002).

pate in China's delegation to the negotiations.[101] The final obstacle was practical, namely the need to clear minefields placed on the border during repeated clashes in the 1980s. Mine-clearing efforts were held in 1994 and 1999, though work reportedly still continues.

A renewal of political will on both sides was necessary for a breakthrough. During their July 1997 summit, Jiang and Do mandated that the two countries settle the land border dispute by the end of 1999, a move directed against internal opponents to compromise. China may have also wanted to limit U.S. influence in Southeast Asia, which had normalized ties with Vietnam in 1995. On December 30, 1999, Foreign Ministers Tang Jiaxuan and Nguyen Manh Cam signed a boundary treaty one day before the deadline expired.[102] Overall, the two sides held twenty-four rounds of negotiations, including two at the expert level, sixteen at the working-group level, and six at the vice-ministerial level.[103] On balance, the agreement divided disputed territory evenly. China received 114 square kilometers, or 50.2 percent of disputed territory, while Vietnam received the remainder.[104]

Unlike China's post-treaty work with Russia and Laos, the demarcation process with Vietnam has been just as protracted as the original negotiations. More than three years after the land border agreement, the joint demarcation commission had erected only 6 of 1,533 boundary markers that it planned to place.[105] To date, the commission has met seventeen times, demarcating roughly half of the border. During President Hu Jintao's visit to Vietnam in November 2005, the two sides agreed to complete demarcation by 2008, nine years after the boundary treaty was signed.[106]

Clearly, the regime insecurity perceived by China's leaders was not strong enough to produce a rapid settlement of the boundary dispute with Vietnam. Nevertheless, the 1991 and 1993 provisional agreements gave China's leaders most of what they wanted—improved ties with an important socialist neighbor and increased border trade during a period of political instability.

External Threats?

External threats, one mechanism in my theory of cooperation in territorial disputes, provides an alternative explanation for China's behavior during

---

[101] Interview, Beijing, January 2002.

[102] *TYJ*, 1999, 218–239. Originally, the two sides had hoped to include the agreement as part of Zhu Rongji's early December trip to Vietnam, but negotiators apparently worked feverishly just to meet the 1999 deadline.

[103] *ZGWJ*, various years.

[104] *Nhan Dan*, 16 September 2002 (Factiva).

[105] *Vietnam Economic News*, 20 February 2003 (Lexis-Nexis).

[106] Xinhua, 2 November 2005 (Lexis-Nexis); *ZGWJ*, 2006, 324.

this period: China sought to balance against increasing U.S. power after the Cold War, not bolster the security of its socialist regime. This argument posits that the collapse of the Soviet Union and the resulting era of U.S. unipolarity increased China's willingness to compromise in its territorial disputes in the 1990s to strengthen its relative position in the international system. Several factors, however, weigh against this interpretation. In the early 1990s, China's security policy, including defense spending, military ties, and military training, did not keep pace with the dramatic shift in the global balance of power following the Soviet Union's collapse.[107] If China's compromise attempts were the result of balancing against the United States, they were exceptional from the perspective of Chinese security policy at the time. Second, China's decisions to compromise with the Soviet Union preceded the USSR's collapse by several years. Although the initiative for these talks stemmed from Moscow, the pace quickened dramatically after Tiananmen but before the Soviet collapse. The 1991 Chinese-Soviet agreement was drafted in 1990, before the full extent of Soviet weakness was known, and signed in April 1991, before the August revolution that set in motion the collapse of the Soviet Union. Likewise, China signed an agreement with Laos and opened talks with Vietnam before the disintegration of the Soviet Union.

In addition, it might be argued that China pursued territorial settlements and normalization with Laos and Vietnam to counter increased U.S. power. At the time, however, Chinese leaders were more concerned about the future of the CCP in China than about U.S. threats to their country's security. Furthermore, the timing of efforts to compromise with Laos and Vietnam also fails to support an external-balancing explanation. Washington and Vientiane resumed limited ties in 1982, well before the regime insecurity created by Tiananmen. Although U.S.-Vietnamese normalization might have influenced the 1997 mandate to reach a border agreement by 1999, 1997 was a year of U.S.-China cooperation, not conflict, as reflected in Jiang's first summit with President Bill Clinton.

Norm Internalization?

The territorial agreements that China reached during this period largely confirmed the status quo on its land border. Although China has not released precise details on the amount of land transferred in these settlements, the agreements with the Soviet Union, Laos, and Vietnam were

---

[107] Alastair Iain Johnston, "Realism(s) and Chinese Security Policy in the Post–Cold War World," in Ethan B. Kapstein and Michael Mastanduno, eds., *Unipolar Politics: Realism and State Strategies after the Cold War* (New York: Columbia University Press, 1999), 261–318.

based on prior boundary treaties. As such, it might be the case that these new agreements reflect an internalization of a norm against conquest. Nevertheless, several factors weigh against this explanation. First, many territorial disputes, not just those involving China, are settled without drastic changes in the amount of disputed territory that each side controls. Unless compelled, states can always delay and refuse to settle. As a result, affirmation of the status quo in a dispute's settlement is not a clear indicator of norm internalization. Second, and more importantly, China's efforts to compromise in these disputes correspond in particular with the onset of intense political vulnerability following Tiananmen. In the norms argument, it is unclear what would explain these compromises at that time, namely 1990 and 1991, even if, over the prior decades, China had become increasingly acceptant of the norm. Moreover, in statements released during the signing of these agreements, Chinese leaders did not stress support for the status quo in their decisions to settle these disputes. Third, in China's case, especially in its dispute with Vietnam, this explanation is suspect because of the sustained use of force on the land border throughout the 1980s as discussed in chapter 4, as well as the occupation of reefs in the Spratlys in 1988 and 1994, actions that are inconsistent with a norm against conquest.

Democracy or Economic Interdependence?

Other potential alternative explanations also cannot account for China's willingness to compromise in territorial disputes after Tiananmen. Arguments based on the democratic peace and norms of pacific conflict resolution are clearly not relevant, given the authoritarian nature of the Chinese state reflected in the violent crackdown in Tiananmen. Likewise, while China did seek to increase trade during this period, and the settlement of disputed land borders facilitated the opening of ports for trade, it also falls short of explaining China's behavior. China sought to continue Deng's economic reforms after the events of 1989 because economic development would increase the state's legitimacy, which had been badly damaged by the use of force against its own citizens.

XINJIANG UNREST

The collapse of the Soviet Union might have presented China with an ideal opportunity to regain the more than 34,000 square kilometers of territory it had claimed in Central Asia. The newly independent states of Kazakhstan, Kyrgyzstan, and Tajikistan, struggling to secure their independence, lacked the military and diplomatic resources to resist Chinese demands. Nevertheless, despite this clear opportunity to press for the land that it claimed, China pursued compromise instead. Although China's military position was quite strong, it offered concessions in disputes with its new Central Asian neighbors, signing six boundary agreements in the 1990s as well as a supplemental agreement with Tajikistan in 2002.

Regime insecurity best explains why China compromised despite its newfound military superiority on its Central Asian frontier. From 1990, violent ethnic unrest in Xinjiang sparked another internal threat to the territorial integrity of the PRC. Mounting grievances among Uighur and other minority groups against the central government resulted in an unprecedented number of demonstrations, bombings, assassinations, and revolts. Although the scale of unrest was small compared with the Tibetan revolt, it was nevertheless a source of considerable concern for China's leaders, especially after the political instability of Tiananmen. Attempts to settle outstanding territorial disputes were a central component of China's engagement of the region in this period, including the formation of the Shanghai Cooperation Organization. For China's leaders, territorial disputes had become much more costly to maintain because they blocked assistance that China sought to bolster Xinjiang's internal stability. China needed cooperation with its neighbors to prevent the spread of pan-Islamic and pan-Turkic groups, limit external support for separatists within Xinjiang, and increase cross-border trade as part of a broader strategy to maintain stability through economic development.

Instability in the Northwestern Frontier

Political stability in China's western frontiers began to unravel in the late 1980s. Tibet saw the first signs of unrest in September 1987, when a small group of monks rallied for Tibetan independence. In March 1989, a large demonstration in Lhasa turned violent after security forces used live ammunition to disperse the crowd. Fearing additional unrest on the thirtieth anniversary of the Tibetan revolt, the government soon imposed martial law.[108] Although certainly a source of concern, this limited revival of ethno-nationalism in Tibet was not especially threatening by itself. China's control of the area was much stronger than it had been in the 1950s, unrest was limited to one city, and it was mostly nonviolent.

After Tiananmen, however, China's leaders became much more concerned about ethnic unrest in the frontiers. In May 1989, Tiananmen fever spread to Urumqi, where several thousand university students marched in support of their colleagues in Beijing. The gathering mushroomed into

---

[108] Solomon M. Karmel, "Ethnic Tension and the Struggle for Order: China's Policies in Tibet," *Pacific Affairs*, vol. 68, no. 4 (1995): 485–508.

a riot when religious students joined the march to protest against a book on sexual customs.[109] Although the government did not violently suppress this event, it provided an early indication of a much more explosive combination of latent Uighur nationalism and growing Islamic radicalism. What had started as an isolated demonstration in Tibet now appeared to be part of a much broader trend portending "separatism" throughout the frontiers. In the fall and winter of 1989, for example, leaflets calling for the end of Chinese rule began to appear throughout Xinjiang.[110]

In the context of Tiananmen, China's leaders were increasingly sensitive to potential threats to the state in the frontiers. In August 1989, Public Security Minister Wang Fang conducted an inspection tour of Xinjiang, warning against "conspiratorial separatist activities."[111] In November 1989, Premier Li Peng visited the region, stressing "national unity," the official code for opposing separatism.[112] A meeting of the State Nationalities Affairs Commission in February 1990 highlighted the challenge of separatism.[113] In the same month, Xinjiang party chief Song Hanliang identified eliminating the separatist threat as "the key to Xinjiang's political and social stability."[114]

In April 1990, armed uprisings in several southwestern Xinjiang towns in confirmed the worst fears of China's leaders. The locus of unrest was in Baren near Kashgar (map 2.5), where two to three hundred armed men attacked government buildings, taking hostages and besieging a township office building into which People's Armed Police (PAP) forces had retreated to protect local officials. Security forces who rushed to the scene were reportedly attacked and killed in their vehicles.[115] New government restrictions on the building of mosques in the region had incensed the local population and sparked the attack. As the crowd swelled to more than two thousand people, they began calling for a "holy war," the expul-

[109] Felix K. Chang, "China's Central Asian Power and Problems," *Orbis*, vol. 41, no. 3 (Summer 1997): 408–409; Michael Dillon, *Xinjiang: Ethnicity, Separatism and Control in Central Asia*, Durham East Asian Papers, no. 2 (Durham, UK: Durham University, 1995), 19; *FEER*, 3 August 1989, 36; Yitzhak Shichor, "Separatism: Sino-Muslim Conflict in Xinjiang," *Pacifica Review*, vol. 6, no. 2 (1994): 74.

[110] AP, 24 March 1990 (Lexis-Nexis).

[111] Xinhua Xinjiang Regional Service, 26 August 1989, BBC Summary of World Broadcasts, 1 September 1989, FE/0550/B2/1 (Lexis-Nexis).

[112] Xinhua Xinjiang Regional Service, 27 November 1989, BBC Summary of World Broadcasts, 30 November 1989, FE/0628/B2/1 (Lexis-Nexis).

[113] Xinhua, 13 February 1990 (Lexis-Nexis).

[114] Xinhua Xinjiang Regional Service, BBC Summary of World Broadcasts, 9 February 1990, FE/0684/B2/1 (Lexis-Nexis).

[115] Amnesty International, *Secret Violence: Human Rights Violations in Xinjiang* (New York: Amnesty International, 1992); Chang, "China's Central Asian Power," 409; Dillon, *Xinjiang*, 21; Shichor, "Separatism," 74–75. For the official report of the incident, see "Tomur Dawamat Reports on April Rebellion in Xinjiang," *Xinjiang Ribao*, 26 May 1990, BBC Summary of World Broadcasts, 20 July 1990, FE/0821/B2/1 (Lexis-Nexis).

sion of Han Chinese from Xinjiang, and the establishment of an East Turkestan state. Rioters reportedly attacked the small detachment of PAP forces inside the township building with small arms and explosives. After additional PAP troops arrived, a violent crackdown followed. Somewhere between twenty-two and fifty people were killed, while more than one thousand were detained. This uprising was led by Zahideen Yusuf, a religious student who had built a small following in the region and acquired some smuggled arms.[116] Similar uprisings and demonstrations occurred in other southern Xinjiang cities at the time.[117]

The Baren uprising sparked a decade of ethnic unrest and instability in Xinjiang that challenged the regime's authority in this vast frontier. Increasing levels of violence highlighted the continued weakness of the central government, which many in Xinjiang still viewed as an occupying force. China's leaders were keenly aware of the state's tenuous legitimacy in the area. Sections of Xinjiang had enjoyed independence briefly in the 1860s and the 1940s, while periodic demonstrations were always linked to desires for more autonomy, including the 1962 Yita incident, an April 1980 riot in Aksu County, and an October 1981 riot in Kashgar.[118] These latent desires for greater autonomy and the flowering of Islam in Xinjiang from the mid-1980s created a volatile mix. Local grievances included the steady influx of Han migrants to the region, which was viewed as eroding local identity and exploiting local resources, along with China's restrictive family planning policy and nuclear testing in Lop Nor. By 1993, unrest had reached all parts of Xinjiang. Ulema were advocating revolt from within mosques, while ethnic minority party members and government officials participated in separatist activities.[119]

Xinjiang witnessed three different types of ethnic-related violence. The first was an increasing number of protests, demonstrations, and riots directed against government policies and institutions. Many of these demonstrations were spontaneous, often in response to a local crackdown on religious leaders or suspected separatists. Some gatherings were peaceful, but others erupted in violence or riots and were brutally suppressed. After the Baren uprising, the most serious demonstration occurred in Yining, where several days of rioting and clashes with police follwed the arrest of suspected separatists in February 1997.[120]

---

[116] Michael Winchester, "Beijing vs. Islam," *Asiaweek*, vol. 23, no. 42 (1997): 31.

[117] Erkin Alptekin, "The April 1990 Uprising in Eastern Turkestan," *Journal of Muslim Minority Affairs*, vol. 11, no. 2 (1990): 255–256; Shichor, "Separatism," 75. Also see AP, 23 April 1990; Central News Agency (Taiwan), 18 April 1990 (Lexis-Nexis).

[118] *Xinjiang tongzhi: gongan zhi* [Xinjiang Gazetteer: Public Security] (Wulumuqi: Xinjiang renmin chubanshe, 2004), 64, 66.

[119] Winchester, "Beijing."

[120] For details on violence in this period, see *Xinjiang tongzhi: gongan zhi*, 79–111, 845–862.

The second type of unrest was terrorist-style attacks, including bombings of public places and assassinations of local officials. Bombing campaigns, which were sporadic, started in 1991 and usually targeted buses or government buildings in Han-dominated areas, often in response to police crackdowns. In reaction to the 1997 Yining riots, for example, three bombs exploded on buses in the Han-dominated capital, Urumqi, on the day of Deng Xiaoping's February 1997 memorial service. Local officials supporting the central government, including Uighur and other religious leaders viewed as pro-Beijing, have been key targets for assassination throughout Xinjiang, especially in southwestern areas.

The third type of unrest was conflict between armed insurgent groups and government security forces, especially the PAP. Although no unified resistance ever congealed in Xinjiang, many small armed groups formed, sharing roughly the same goal of expelling the Han Chinese.[121] Some of these groups were probably responsible for the bombings and assassinations, but detailed information is lacking. Nevertheless, these insurgents were the targets of police crackdowns, which often resulted in deadly armed clashes. Some of these groups also launched attacks on police stations, prisons, PAP checkpoints, and PLA outposts, reminiscent of the unrest in Tibet thirty years earlier.

In absolute terms, the rebellion in Xinjiang never posed a grave threat to the state. Separatist groups did not organize in large numbers, nor did the disparate groups act in concert against central authorities. Unlike the Tibetan rebels, they never controlled large amounts of territory, in part because the PLA and police forces had been well established in the region since the 1960s. Nevertheless, China's leaders viewed the unrest in Xinjiang with great concern, linking separatist movements with Western pressure for political liberalization. Li Peng captured this sensitivity in February 1990 before the Baren uprising when he called on the government to "eliminate separatist activities in the embryonic stage."[122] During his October 1990 tour of Xinjiang, Jiang Zemin stressed the external threats to its stability. In a speech to PLA troops, Jiang noted that "following the changes in the international and domestic climate and following the sudden changes in Eastern Europe and the disturbances in the Soviet Union, domestic national separatists and international hostile forces have colluded with each other to accelerate plots and activities to split the motherland. This has become the main danger to the stability of Xinjiang." Jiang emphasized that "especially under current circumstances, safeguarding

---

[121] On these groups, see Dewardric L. McNeal, *China's Relations with Central Asian States and Problems with Terrorism* (Washington, D.C.: Library of Congress, Congressional Research Service, 2001).

[122] *RMRB*, 21 February 1990, 1.

stability and calm in Xinjiang will have a decisive influence on the stability of the entire nation."[123]

As violence and instability increased in the 1990s, China's senior leaders took action. In 1996, the Politburo Standing Committee (PBSC) convened to discuss stability in Xinjiang. The minutes summarizing the meeting and its decisions reflected China's leaders' insecurity, echoing Jiang's earlier sentiments. As the document noted, "Today, ethnic [nationalist] separatism and illegal religious activities are the main threats to stability in Xinjiang."[124] If not contained, they will "affect the stability of . . . the whole nation."[125] Moreover, the PBSC linked internal unrest with Xinjiang's external environment, noting that "with each passing day, the outside national separatists are joining hands and strengthening the infiltration into Xinjiang of sabotage activities."[126] Although China's leaders have often been quick to blame proverbial "hostile foreign forces" for domestic problems, the charge had some merit in Central Asia. Official statements, scholarly analysis, and internal reports all link Xinjiang's stability with the external environment. China's leaders viewed the global wave of national self-determination following the Cold War, the rise of Islamic radicalism, and the creation of new states in the region as inspiring ethnic groups in Xinjiang to seek their own independence.[127] A book issued by the Xinjiang government similarly highlighted the threats to stability in Central Asia created by the spread of pan-Islamic fundamentalism and Pan-Turkic nationalism in the wake of the Soviet Union's disintegration. The chief concern was that similar ideas could spill across the border into Xinjiang, inspiring more unrest and antigovernment activity, a theme repeated by other scholars.[128] The Islamic resurgence in Afghanistan was of particular concern, as that country borders China and

---

[123] Jiang Zemin, *Lun guofang he jundui jianshe* [On National Defense and Army Building] (Jiefangjun chubanshe, 2003 [internal circulation]), 12.

[124] "Zhongyang zhengzhiju changweihui guanyu weihu Xinjiang wending de huiyi jiyao, zhongfa [1996] 7 hao" [Record of the Politburo Standing Committee Meeting on Maintaining Stability in Xinjiang, Central Committee Document (1996) No. 7]. For a summary of the document, see *Xinjiang tongzhi: gongan zhi*, 96. For a full translation, see Human Rights Watch, "China: State Control of Religion, Update No. 1" (New York: Human Rights Watch, 1998): Appendix I (hereafter Central Committee, "Document [1996] No. 7").

[125] Central Committee, "Document (1996) No. 7." For a discussion of the document by one of Xinjiang's leading officials, see Tomur Damawat, *Lun minzu gongzuo yu minzu wenhua* [On Nationality Work and Culture] (Beijing: Zhonggong zhongyang dangxiao chubanshe, 2005), 455.

[126] Central Committee, "Document (1996) No. 7."

[127] *Xinjiang Ribao*, 19 October 1990, BBC Summary of World Broadcasts, 22 November 1990, FE/0928/B2/1 (Lexis-Nexis).

[128] Wang Shuanqian, ed., *Zouxiang 21 shiji de Xinjiang: zhengzhi juan* [Xinjiang Moving toward the 21st Century: Politics] (Wulumuqi: Xinjiang renmin chubanshe, 1999), 197–203. Also see Xing, "China and Central Asia," 44–45.

Tajikistan.[129] The leader of the Baren uprising was reportedly inspired by events in Afghanistan, while other Uighur separatists had received military training abroad.[130]

More specifically, China's leaders believed that neighboring states were providing crucial material support for separatist groups within China. A number of Uighur political parties were active in Kazakhstan and Kyrgyzstan in the early 1990s, including the Uighur Liberation Organization, For a Free Uighuristan, and the International Uighur Union, all of which sought the establishment of an independent Uighur state.[131] Organizations from these states, as well as other countries, also funded private religious schools established in the 1980s, which many Xinjiang officials believed were used to fuel the growing ethno-nationalism. All these organizations were viewed as providing critical support for separatist activity within China.[132]

The final external link was Xinjiang's long and porous border with all its Central Asian neighbors. China's leaders viewed external cooperation as necessary, not only to deny separatist groups access to base areas abroad, but also to prevent the smuggling of weapons, propaganda, and people across the border. After the Baren uprising, for example, Li Peng asked Gorbachev to seal the Soviet Union's Central Asian border with China.[133] Arms used in the 1990 uprisings had entered China from Afghanistan, however, reflecting the porous nature of all the borders in this region.[134]

Frontier Stability through Cooperation

In the early to mid-1990s, the central government adopted a mix of domestic and foreign policies to maintain stability in Xinjiang and crush the brewing ethno-nationalism. The thrust of China's efforts to address unrest in Xinjiang was internal, but China also required cooperation from neighboring states to contain separatist activity, prevent smuggling, and promote cross-border trade.

China's domestic response to Xinjiang's ethnic unrest consisted of three components. The first was a series of measures designed to strengthen

---

[129] *Xinjiang Ribao*, 19 October 1990, BBC Summary of World Broadcasts, 22 November 1990, FE/0928/B2/1 (Lexis-Nexis).

[130] Winchester, "Beijing," 31.

[131] Dillon, *Xinjiang*, 24.

[132] See, for example, Xing Guangcheng, "China and Central Asia," in Roy Allison and Lena Jonson, eds., *Central Asian Security: The New International Context* (Washington, D.C.: The Brookings Institution, 2001), 163.

[133] Alptekin, "The April 1990 Uprising," 255; Shichor, "Separatism," 79.

[134] *The Guardian* (London), 10 May 1990 (Lexis-Nexis); *Xinjiang tongzhi: gongan zhi*.

administrative control. After the 1990 Baren uprising, the leadership focused on strengthening party control at the local level, including villages and townships, and rectifying party ranks to eliminate separatists.[135] A campaign to regulate religious activity was launched, increasing controls on religious teaching, the building of mosques, and other activities. By 1993, more than 10 percent of Xinjiang's 25,000 religious leaders had been removed from their positions.[136]

The second thrust of the domestic response was a swift and often brutal crackdown against suspected separatists. The first wave occurred immediately after the Baren uprising, focusing mostly on southwestern areas. The single largest crackdown occurred as part of the 1996 national "Strike Hard" anticrime drive, in which separatists in Xinjiang were added to the list of criminals targeted.[137] In April 1996, for example, 1,700 suspected separatists were arrested.[138] Security forces conducted similar dragnets in following years, detaining thousands of individuals.

Similar to the CCP's emphasis on economic reform following Tiananmen, the third policy response was to promote frontier economic development. Xinjiang's party bosses believed that raising the standard of living would ameliorate growing tensions between Han and non-Han peoples.[139] In 1992, Xinjiang was part of a national campaign to open minority border areas to increased trade with neighboring states. In 1999, the government launched its "Great Western Development" (*xibu da kaifa*) campaign and increased state subsidies to Xinjiang. Government reports on enhancing stability and promoting national unity in Xinjiang all stressed this theme. In the words of Jiang Zemin, the campaign represented a "long-term development strategy" to "maintain the unity of ethnic groups, national unification and social stability."[140]

All these internal measures, however, required cooperative relations with Xinjiang's neighbors. Paradoxically, the need to quash internal unrest required external peace, forming the basis for China's diplomatic en-

---

[135] "Tomur Dawamat Reports"; *Xinjiang tongzhi: gongan zhi.*

[136] Lillian Craig Harris, "Xinjiang, Central Asia and the Implications for China's Policy in the Islamic World," *The China Quarterly*, no. 133 (1993): 121.

[137] The campaign itself led to an increase in unrest, bombings, and the like, especially in 1997 and 1998.

[138] McNeal, *China's Relations*, 10.

[139] For official documents, see "Tomur Dawamat Reports"; Central Committee, "Document (1996) No. 7." For scholarly accounts, see Xing, "China and Central Asia," 164–165; Yin Zhuguang and Mao Yongfu, *Xinjiang minzu guanxi yanjiu* [Research on Nationality Relations in Xinjiang] (Wulumuqi: Xinjiang renmin chubanshe, 1996), 181–182, 261; Zhonggong zhongyang zuzhibu, ed., *Zhongguo diaocha baogao: xin xingshi xia renmin neibu maodun yanjiu* [China Investigative Report: Research on Internal Contradictions of the People under New Circumstances] (Beijing: Zhongyang bianyi chubanshe, 2001), 243–281.

[140] *RMRB*, 16 September 2000, 1.

gagement of the region. The 1996 Central Committee document linked China's regional diplomacy with the internal situation in Xinjiang, instructing the government to

> Limit the activities of outside ethnic separatist activities [coming] from many sides. Bear in mind the fact that Turkey, Kazakhstan and Kyrgyzstan are the home-bases for the activities of outside separatist forces. Through diplomacy, urge these countries to limit and weaken the activities of separatist forces inside their border. Take full advantage of our political superiority to further develop the bilateral friendly cooperation with these countries. At the same time, always maintain pressure on them.[141]

The Central Committee document also called for strengthened border security to block the entry of separatists, again demonstrating the internal-external linkage identified by China's leaders:

> Tighten measures for controlling the border and border defense posts. Prevent the entry of outside ethnic separatists, weapons, and propaganda materials. Prevent internal and external ethnic separatists from coming together and joining hands.[142]

Finally, the document also stressed the importance of promoting economic development.

Attempts to compromise in territorial disputes formed the basis of China's diplomatic engagement with its Central Asian neighbors. With renewed instability in Xinjiang, China's territorial disputes became much more costly to pursue because they blocked cooperation that would be essential for maintaining internal security. As new states with fragile institutions, the Central Asian republics were naturally quite wary of China and vulnerable to Chinese pressure. Nevertheless, China did not use its relative power after the Cold War to bargain hard for disputed territory. Instead, it chose to improve ties with these states by dropping expansive territorial claims to territory once part of the Qing empire, compromising over disputed areas and accepting the territorial status quo. In return, China hoped to gain cooperation to support stability within Xinjiang.

As the Soviet Union collapsed, China moved quickly to establish formal diplomatic relations with all the former Soviet republics, including those in Central Asia. Although China sought to preempt these states from recognizing Taiwan, territorial disputes and terrorism were also key issues from the start. In the joint communiqués issued after the establishment of diplomatic ties, China and its new neighbors "highly evaluated" the

---

[141] Central Committee, "Document no. 7 (1996)."
[142] Central Committee, "Document no. 7 (1996)."

progress achieved in past Chinese-Soviet talks. By stating that negotiations should be "on the basis of existing treat[ies]," China signaled early on that it would not press new claims against these states. In return, China and its neighbors agreed to "cooperate in the struggle against international terrorist activities."[143]

With respect to territorial disputes, negotiations between China and its Central Asian neighbors were conducted through two separate channels. The first was bilateral, usually at the vice–foreign ministerial level and above, where most of the major decisions were made. At the working level, a joint delegation structure was used, whereby China negotiated with a delegation composed of representatives from Russia and the three Central Asian states. The reason was practical: Russian troops still guarded the Central Asian borders of the new Commonwealth of Independent States, and Russian diplomats possessed the technical expertise and historical knowledge needed for boundary negotiations. This structure ensured the smooth resumption of negotiations at the working level, without each of the republics having to prepare extensively. Moreover, the use of joint delegations ensured that China could not profit from information asymmetries it might have possessed if it conducted only bilateral negotiations. China agreed to resume talks on the basis of the Chinese-Soviet negotiating record knowing that its opening position would not be as strong as it might otherwise have been.

The creation and development of the "Shanghai Five" and later the Shanghai Cooperation Organization reflect these same diplomatic goals. This regional grouping had its origins in border demilitarization talks that continued after the collapse of the Soviet Union. The same joint negotiating structure that was used in the territorial discussions was used in the demilitarization talks initiated with the Soviet Union in 1990, reaching important demilitarization and confidence-building agreements in 1996 and 1997 that helped to reassure China's new Central Asian neighbors.[144] In 1996, heads of the five states agreed to institutionalize their annual gatherings as the Shanghai Five, which, with the addition of Uzbekistan in 2001, formed the Shanghai Cooperation Organization (SCO).[145] At their inaugural gathering in April 1996, the heads of state pledged a shared opposition to "separatism," again linking external cooperation with internal threats.[146] The SCO's goals matched China's objectives in

[143] Xinhua, 28 February 1992; Xinhua, 16 May 1992 (Lexis-Nexis).

[144] Genrikh Kireyev, "The Serpentine Path to the Shanghai G-5," *International Affairs*, vol. 49, no. 3 (2003): 85–92.

[145] Xu Tao and Ji Zhiye, eds., *Shanghai hezuo zuzhi: xin anquan guan yu xin jizhi* [Shanghai Cooperation Organization: New Security Concept and New Mechanism] (Beijing: Shishi chubanshe, 2002).

[146] Xinhua, 26 April 1996 (Lexis-Nexis).

the region: to secure a long border through demilitarization, cooperate to oppose ethno-nationalist movements, and increase regional trade. These last two goals resulted from a shared desire to counter internal threats from pan-Islamic forces that threatened governments throughout the region. In 1999, for example, the five states agreed to establish a counterterrorism center in Kyrgyzstan and, in 2001, when founding the SCO, the leaders signed a convention on "combating terrorism, separatism and extremism."[147]

China Compromises

In October 1992, China and the new states held their first meeting at the joint delegation level. The month before, the foreign ministers had agreed to resume talks at the point where the Chinese-Soviet negotiations had stopped. Importantly, all sides agreed to use the same principles that had been applied earlier, namely that existing agreements and the territorial status quo would form the basis for a comprehensive settlement. Moreover, because the Central Asian republics occupied most of the land under dispute, this indicated that China was prepared to compromise from the start. After the October meeting held to resume talks, the first round of negotiations under the new structure began in April 1993 and addressed China's border with Kazakhstan.

KAZAKHSTAN

Kazakhstan inherited fifteen disputed sectors from the Chinese-Soviet territorial disputes. These sectors comprised approximately 2,240 square kilometers and were mostly held by Kazakhstan.[148] The disputes had emerged from ambiguities surrounding earlier agreements between China and Russia signed in the nineteenth century and included several areas that had not been previously demarcated.

Improved ties with Kazakhstan, China's largest Central Asian neighbor, were key to China's overall engagement of the region. Kazakhstan had the largest Uighur population outside China and was home to many Uighur-based organizations and political groups. Kazakhstan's border with Xinjiang, more than 1,740 kilometers long, provided numerous points of entry for insurgents and smugglers.[149] One of Xinjiang's most restive areas, the Yili Prefecture, abuts Kazakhstan. Chinese support of Kazakhstan's secular state would help to prevent the spread of Islamic radicalism in the region, which might further destabilize Xinjiang. Al-

---

[147] http://www.sectsco.org/html/00093.html.

[148] Zhang Zhouxiang, *Xinjiang bianfang gaiyao* [Overview of Xinjiang's Frontier Defense] (Wulumuqi: Xinjiang renmin chubanshe, 1999), 135.

[149] See, for example, AFP, 13 October 1995 (Lexis-Nexis).

though China might have been able to realize all its territorial claims in Central Asia through a more aggressive posture, it would not have achieved its other goals. Instead, a more aggressive approach in these territorial disputes may very well have increased support for the Islamic movements in these countries and weakened China's ability to maintain stability inside Xinjiang.

After two rounds of talks in April and July 1993, China and Kazakhstan reached a provisional agreement over most disputed sectors. In early October, Kazakh president Nursultan Nazarbayev stated during an interview that consensus had been reached in eight of the eleven disputed sectors.[150] After two additional rounds of talks, the two sides initialed a boundary agreement, which Premier Li Peng and Nazarbayev signed in April 1994.[151] In this document, China and Kazakhstan agreed to divide several areas, including the Ala Pass (*ala shankou*). China received the area around the source of the Korgas River but appears to have dropped claims to many other disputed sectors held by Kazakhstan (see map 2.5). In return, Kazakhstan agreed to help China maintain stability within Xinjiang. Following the signing of the agreement, Nazarbayev stated that Kazakhstan "opposes national splittism . . . and will never allow factions of 'East Turkestan' to involve themselves in activities here against China that will hurt Sino-Kazakhstan relations." In response, Li "voiced appreciation for Nazarbayev's remarks on not allowing national separatists to engage in activities against China in Kazakhstan and for his stance on Taiwan and Tibet."[152] To support these goals, China's Public Security Ministry signed a cooperation agreement with Kazakhstan's Home Affairs Ministry in June 1993.[153]

The remaining three disputed sectors were resolved in two separate agreements. In September 1997, Li and Nazarbayev signed the first of two supplemental boundary agreements, which addressed the last 11 kilometers of the southern section of the border and the sacred Khan-Tengri Mountain at the tripoint with Kyrgyzstan.[154] In July 1998, Jiang Zemin and Nazarbayev signed a second supplemental agreement resolving the last two disputed sectors, which were divided evenly.[155] China received 70

---

[150] *ZGWJ*, 1994, 601. Also, Xu and Ji, *Shanghai hezuo zuzhi*, 128. This total number of sectors is smaller than the fifteen reported by Zhang above (see n. 148). Most likely, the fifteen sectors were condensed into eleven, as no additional sectors of dispute were reported.

[151] *TYJ*, 1994, 288–308.

[152] Xinhua, 26 April 1994 (Lexis-Nexis).

[153] Xinhua, 29 June 1993 (Lexis-Nexis).

[154] *ZGWJ*, 1998, 344; *TYJ*, 1997, 90–94; Dow Jones Energy Service, 23 September 1997 (Factiva).

[155] Waijiao bu, ed., *Zhonghua renmin gongheguo bianjie shiwu tiaoyue ji: ZhongHa juan* [Collection of Treaties on the PRC's Boundary Affairs: China-Kazakhstan] (Beijing: Shijie zhishi chubanshe [internal circulation], 2005), 487–493.

percent of the 315 square kilometers in the Sary-Childy River area but only 30 percent of the 629 square kilometers of Chogan-Obo and Bay-Murza Pass (map 2.5).[156]

The timing of these supplemental agreements, which addressed the most difficult sectors under dispute, was linked to increased Chinese concerns about ethnic unrest within Xinjiang. After the February 1997 Yining uprising, Jiang and Nazarbayev held an emergency meeting to discuss stability in the region.[157] At the same time, Kazakh leaders continued to express their support for China's efforts to maintain stability in Xinjiang. Visiting China one month after the conclusion of the first supplemental agreement, Defense Minister Muhtar Alteinbaev stated that Kazakhstan steadfastly opposed separatism and would prevent the conduct of separatist activities aimed at China.[158] After signing the second supplemental agreement, Nazarbayev again reiterated Kazakhstan's commitment to opposing separatist activities.[159] During a 1999 summit, Jiang and Nazarbayev agreed to "coordinate efforts to effectively combat national splittism, religious extremism, terrorism, illegal arms trafficking, drug smuggling, illegal immigration and other types of crimes."[160] In addition to public statements, Kazakhstan has helped China by restricting Uighur activities on its own territory. In 1999, for example, Kazakhstan repatriated three Uighur separatists demanded by China.[161] The Kazakhstan government has also dissolved political parties, closed newspapers, and arrested suspected militants.[162]

In these three boundary agreements, China offered considerable concessions. China received approximately 34 percent of the 2,420 square kilometers under dispute. Based on the statements of Kazakh officials, all three agreements closely mirrored the territorial status quo. As Kazakhstan's foreign minister stated, "The border runs along the line along which it has always run, i.e. along the guarded line. In other words, Kazakhstan did not gain or lose anything."[163] Demarcation work began soon after the signing of the first agreement. The joint demarcation commission held its first

---

[156] "Kazakh Parliament Ratifies 'Advantageous' Border Agreement with China," Interfax-Kazakhstan News Agency (Alma-Ata), 3 February 1999, BBC Monitoring Central Asia, 4 February 1999 (Factiva).

[157] *South China Morning Post*, 20 February 1997 (Lexis-Nexis).

[158] AFP, 5 October 1997 (Lexis-Nexis).

[159] Xinhua, 4 July 1998, BBC Worldwide Monitoring (Lexis-Nexis).

[160] Reuters, 23 November 1999 (Factiva).

[161] Human Rights Watch, *China: Human Rights Concerns in Xinjiang* (New York: Human Rights Watch, 2001).

[162] See, for example, Interfax-Kazhakstan, 24 February 1999 (Lexis-Nexis); Jean-Christophe Peuch, "Central Asia: Uighurs Say States Yield to Chinese," RFERL, http://www.rferl.org/nca/features/2001/03/29032001104726.asp.

[163] WPS Russian Media Monitoring Agency, 18 June 1999 (Factiva).

meeting in July 1996 and began to erect boundary markers in 1997. By the end of 2001, more than 548 boundary markers had been placed along the border. A protocol specifying the delineation of the border along the associated maps was signed by the foreign ministers in May 2002. In the words of Nazarbayev, "we have fully resolved the border problems."[164]

KYRGYZSTAN

Kyrgyzstan inherited seven disputed sectors from the Chinese-Soviet territorial disputes, which comprised approximately 3,656 square kilometers.[165] The majority of these sectors, including parts of the Uzengi-Kush river basin, were under Kyrgyz control. As in China's disputes with Kazakhstan, conflicting claims had originated from ambiguities surrounding earlier agreements signed between China and Russia in the nineteenth century.

Along with Kazakhstan, Kyrgyzstan was the other Central Asian state mentioned in the 1996 Central Committee document on stability in Xinjiang. In addition to possessing a very small Uighur population, Kyrgyzstan was home territory for around 100,000 Kyrgyzs living in Xinjiang, mostly in the restive southwestern areas. As with Kazakhstan, China pursued cooperation in this territorial dispute in order to improve relations with Kyrgyzstan, gain its assistance against separatists, and increase cross-border trade.

China and Kyrgyzstan first began to address their dispute as part of the joint negotiating structure established after the collapse of the Soviet Union. During Li Peng's April 1994 trip to Central Asia, China and Kyrgyzstan agreed to accelerate settlement of the dispute. In July 1995, Kyrgyzstan's foreign minister traveled to China for high-level consultations.[166] In September 1995, the joint delegation began the process of drafting a boundary agreement.[167] In July 1996, Presidents Jiang Zemin and Askar Akayev signed a boundary agreement that covered six of the seven disputed sectors, most of which were held by Kygyzstan. The only sector left unresolved was the Uzengi-Kush river basin (see map 2.5).[168]

As in China's negotiations with Kazakhstan, the two sides appear to have addressed the simplest issues first. In general, China dropped most of its claims to sectors held by Kyrgyzstan, while Kyrgyzstan recognized the areas held by China. In return for these concessions, China gained assistance in its efforts to squash separatist groups. Even before the agreement was signed, Prime Minister Apas Jumagulov pledged that Kyr-

---

[164] "Border Problems with China 'Fully Resolved,' Kazakh President," BBC Monitoring Central Asia, 25 November 1999 (Factiva).

[165] Zhang, *Xinjiang*, 135.

[166] *ZGWJ*, 1996, 297.

[167] *ZGWJ*, 1996, 695.

[168] Zhang, *Xinjiang*, 135. For a copy of the agreement, see *TYJ*, 1996, 100–110.

gyzstan would not shelter "separatists."[169] In a joint communiqué issued after signing the agreement, Akayev stated that Kyrgyzstan was "firmly opposed to national separatism and will not allow any anti-China activities on its territory."[170] Kyrgyzstani leaders have issued such commitments in every high-level meeting with Chinese officials since 1994.[171]

The dispute over the Uzengi-Kush river basin was settled in 1999. After several years of intermittent negotiations, an agreement was drafted in November 1998.[172] In August 1999, Presidents Jiang and Akayev signed a supplemental boundary agreement.[173] Here again, China chose to compromise. China initially demanded somewhere between 50 and 96 percent of this area but in the end agreed to accept only 30 percent.[174] Moreover, the conclusion of this agreement and the final settlement of the territorial dispute occurred after increased unrest in Xinjiang following the 1997 Yining incident. In a joint statement, Akayev again repeated Kyrgyzstan's support for China's crackdown against separatism. He stated that Kyrgyzstan would "stick to its stand of opposing separatism, religious extremism and terrorism, and would not allow any force to make use of its soil to conduct activities against China."[175]

To settle its dispute with Kyrgyzstan, China offered considerable concessions. In both the 1996 and 1999 agreements, China received approximately 1,208 square kilometers, or 32 percent of disputed territory.[176] Although precise data are unavailable, China may have gained control over some of the Uzengi-Kush that it did not control before. Demarcation work began in June 2001, leading to the placement of 105 boundary markers and the signing of a boundary protocol in September 2004.[177]

TAJIKISTAN

Tajikistan inherited three disputed sectors from the Chinese-Soviet territorial disputes. The largest disputed area concerned the Pamir Mountains, which had plagued China's relations with Russia since the nineteenth century and comprised approximately 28,000 square kilometers. China

---

[169] AFP, 24 October 1995 (Lexis-Nexis).

[170] Xinhua, 4 July 1996 (Lexis-Nexis).

[171] See ZGWJ, various years.

[172] ZGWJ, 1999, 285, 688.

[173] Waijiao bu, ed., *Zhonghua renmin gongheguo bianjie shiwu tiaoyue ji: ZhongJi juan* [Collection of Treaties on the PRC's Boundary Affairs: China-Kyrgyzstan] (Beijing: Shijie zhishi chubanshe [internal circulation], 2005), 415–421.

[174] ITAR-TASS, 17 May 2002 (Lexis-Nexis).

[175] Xinhua, 26 August 1999 (Lexis-Nexis).

[176] AP, 20 February 2003 (Lexis-Nexis).

[177] "Kyrgyz-Chinese Border Talks Reopen in Western China," Bishkek AKIpress, 27 October 2003, FBIS-CEP20031027000251; ZGWJ, 2005, 336.

claimed that the region had been illegally annexed by Russia in an 1895 agreement with Britain to which China was not a party.[178] The other two disputed areas comprised 430 square kilometers.[179]

China's attempts to settle its territorial dispute with Tajikistan were quite protracted, lasting until May 2002. The first reason was the ongoing civil war in Tajikistan between old-guard communists and several opposition parties, the largest of which was Islamic.[180] China and the Tajik government were unable to hold talks under such conditions, and China surely did not want to strengthen the oppositions' hand by raising the territorial dispute. A peace agreement was not reached until 1997, the same year in which China and Tajikistan started negotiations. The second reason was the Pamir dispute itself. One of China's largest claims, this area had formed the crux of the Chinese-Soviet dispute. For historical reasons, China's leaders were reluctant to compromise over this area even though in the end China relinquished almost its entire claim.

After the resolution of the Tajik civil war, China and Tajikistan began to hold talks over disputed sectors. In October 1997, a week of talks at the vice–foreign ministerial level over the territorial dispute achieved "tangible progress" and reached an agreement over the two smaller disputes. The Markansu Valley was divided evenly while China dropped its claim to the Uzbel Pass (map 2.5).[181] Continuing differences over how to divide the Pamir area prevented the two sides from signing a formal agreement at the time. China had offered to compromise, but the two sides could not agree on an appropriate division. Nevertheless, the timing of the informal agreement reached in 1997 corresponds with China's renewed efforts to quash unrest after the Yining uprising, reflecting the role of ethnic instability in shaping China's willingness to compromise.

Because of continuing disagreement over the Pamirs, China and Tajikistan did not sign an agreement until 1999. In August 1999, presidents Jiang Zemin and Emomali Rahmonov signed a boundary agreement, which delimited the entire border except for the Pamir section and codified the earlier consensus regarding the division of the two disputed passes.[182] Again echoing China's other attempts to settle disputes with

---

[178] See John W. Garver, "The Sino-Soviet Territorial Dispute in the Pamir Mountains Region," *The China Quarterly*, no. 85 (1981): 107–118; Zhang, *Xinjiang*, 137–142.

[179] Zhang, *Xinjiang*, 136.

[180] On the civil war, see *Accord*, no. 10, March 2001.

[181] AFP, 31 October 1997 (Factiva); *ZGWJ*, 1998, 360–361; Interfax, 21 May 2002 (Lexis-Nexis).

[182] *Leninabadskaya Pravda* (Khujand), 27 July 2002, BBC Monitoring Central Asia, 3 August 2002 (Factiva). For a copy of the agreement, see Waijiao bu, ed., *Zhonghua renmin gongheguo bianjie shiwu tiaoyue ji: ZhongTa juan* [Collection of Treaties on the PRC's Boundary Affairs: China-Tajikistan] (Beijing: Shijie zhishi chubanshe [internal circulation], 2005), 197–204.

Xinjiang's neighbors, joint statements issued after the signing ceremony provided clear support for China's internal goals. The two sides stressed "their opposition to any form of national splittism, religious extremism, or international terrorism and pledged to prohibit any organization and force from carrying out separatist activities within their boundaries against the other."[183] Tajikistan has offered similar support in other joint statements since 1996.[184]

Nevertheless, the Pamirs remained a sticking point. In previous rounds of negotiations, China had agreed to compromise and drop most of its claims.[185] Although Tajikistan clearly wanted an agreement, China's original claim against the Soviet Union now constituted approximately 20 percent of the country. In 2000, the two sides reached an informal agreement, which a joint delegation then codified over the next year into a formal document.[186] In May 2002, presidents Jiang and Rahmonov signed a supplemental boundary agreement, which contained dramatic but realistic concessions by China.[187] In the end, China received only 1,000 square kilometers of the 28,000 square kilometers it claimed.[188] Moreover, this agreement consolidated the existing territorial status quo and required little or no exchange of territory. According to the Russian head of the joint delegation negotiating with China, "the border line, which has been fixed by China and Tajikistan, practically reiterates what has been existing before, with slight changes . . . there have been no revolutionary shifts of the historically established border."[189] In the 1999 and 2002 agreements, China received only 4 percent of the 28,430 square kilometers under dispute. Demarcation of the border began in 2006 and has yet to be completed.[190]

External Threats?

China's numerous compromises in territorial disputes with its Central Asian neighbors provide little support for the mechanism of external threats as the reason for China's decisions to compromise. Given the dramatic shift in the global balance of power following the Cold War, this

[183] Xinhua, 13 August 1999 (Lexis-Nexis).

[184] See, for example, AFP, 20 September 1996 (Lexis-Nexis).

[185] Interview, Beijing, June 2002.

[186] Interview, Beijing, June 2002; "Tajikistan, China Settle Border Issue in Principle," ITAR-TASS, 26 December 2001, BBC Monitoring Former Soviet Union, 26 December 2001 (Factiva).

[187] Waijiao bu, *Zhonghua renmin gongheguo bianjie shiwu tiaoyue ji: ZhongTa juan*, 260–266.

[188] Reuters, 20 May 2002 (Factiva).

[189] Quoted in "Tajikistan, China Settle Border Issue in Principle."

[190] *ZGWJ*, 2006, 325.

explanation would point to a desire to counter U.S. influence as the source of China's willingness to compromise. The timing of China's concessions, however, fails to support this explanation. China had already committed to compromise in disputes with Kazakhstan and Kyrgyzstan well before the upsurge of U.S. interest in Caspian oil in the mid- to late 1990s. More-over, the U.S. military presence in the region before the terrorists attacks of September 11, 2001, and Operation Enduring Freedom in Afghanistan was sporadic, suggesting a limited threat to China's western border. Al-though NATO and regional forces held two joint exercises in 1997 and 2000, respectively, they focused only on training for peacekeeping mis-sions, not combat operations, which would have been much more alarming from China's perspective.

The increased U.S. presence in the region after September 11 did worry China's leaders, but when this occurred China had already signed six of seven boundary agreements resolving disputes in the area. Little evidence exists to suggest that China's leaders anticipated the U.S. presence in Af-ghanistan before this time. Likewise, the joint statements issued at various summit meetings and through the SCO included few direct references to the United States. Instead, they stressed problems associated with the "three forces" of terrorism, separatism, and extremism; bilateral trade; and other shared regional issues linked with internal security and stabil-ity.[191] The most vocal opposition to the U.S. presence in Central Asia oc-curred several years after China had settled all its disputes in the region and the SCO had been established. At its 2005 July summit, the SCO heads of state called on "members of the antiterrorist coalition [to] set a final timeline for . . . [the] stay of their military contingents on the territor-ies of the SCO member states."[192] Such a statement, however, cannot be invoked to explain compromises initiated more than a decade earlier.

Norm Internalization?

The agreements that China reached during this period largely confirmed the existing territorial status quo on its Central Asian border. Although China has not released precise information on the amount of land over which control was transferred, the agreements with its Central Asian neighbors were based on prior boundary agreements, including the un-equal treaties in which the Qing government had ceded large tracts of land. Again, however, this provides weak support for a norms-based ex-planation of decisions to compromise. The norm against conquest itself cannot explain why and when China chose to compromise in these dis-

---

[191] *ZGWJ*, various years.
[192] http://www.sectsco.org/html/00500.html.

putes. The timing of China's decisions to compromise tracks closely with the 1990 Baren uprising and 1997 Yining riots. Moreover, internal government documents clearly link diplomatic engagement with these internal threats, not external ones or a norm against conquest.

Democracy or Economic Interdependence?

Other potential alternative explanations also cannot account for China's willingness to compromise in these disputes. Arguments based on the democratic peace and norms of pacific conflict resolution are again clearly not relevant to China's efforts to compromise in Central Asia, as the state remained authoritarian. Likewise, while China did seek to increase trade during this period, and the settlement of disputed land borders facilitated the expansion of cross-border trade, it also falls short of explaining China's behavior. In the 1996 Central Committee document and other sources, China's leaders clearly posited economic development in Xinjiang as a factor that would decrease ethnic unrest and increase political stability, thereby improving the regime's security in this troubled frontier. Trade, in other words, was a means for increasing political stability and thus the regime's security.

BORDER STABILIZATION WITH INDIA AND BHUTAN

China's regime insecurity helps explain the limited progress that was achieved in stabilizing disputes with both India and Bhutan in the 1990s, the only two countries with which China still contests territory on its land border. Attempts to settle these disputes have necessarily been linked, as India "guides" Bhutan's foreign and defense policy through a 1949 treaty.

In addition to the internal sources of insecurity created by the Tiananmen upheaval and Xinjiang unrest, China's leaders faced the prospect of increased instability returning to Tibet. Protests in 1987, 1988, and early 1989 led to the imposition of martial law for one year. Unrest continued throughout the region afterward, especially in monasteries. In response, China adopted many of the same measures used in Xinjiang: a reassertion of central control, increased regulation of religious activity, and public campaigns against separatism.[193] Improved ties with India were part of this effort, as a rigid pursuit of territorial claims in the Himalayas had become much more costly for China's leaders. By improving ties, China hoped to preempt Indian support for "separatist" activities within Tibet,

---

[193] Karmel, "Ethnic Tension," 485–508.

even though India had far less influence in the region than it had enjoyed in the 1950s.

Before 1989, China had little reason to compromise with India. In February 1979, when India's foreign minister visited Beijing, Deng repeated Zhou Enlai's offer to settle the border dispute through a package deal.[194] Although this offer did not present any new concessions to India, it likely reflected an effort to counter the Soviet Union, which had just invaded Afghanistan. The two sides began negotiations in 1981 at the vice–foreign ministerial level, but the talks failed to achieve any progress. India preferred to discuss each sector separately, and then a crisis erupted over Sumdurong Chu near the McMahon Line in 1986, as discussed in the next chapter.[195] To prevent further confrontation, the two sides agreed during Indira Gandhi's 1988 visit to China to establish a Joint Working Group (JWG). This lack of progress provides strong evidence against an external explanation for China's behavior. With close ties to the Soviet Union, India might have been an attractive target for Chinese efforts to compromise if China's primary motive had been to balance against the Soviets and reduce Soviet pressure on China's tense northern border, especially during the early 1980s.

After 1989, however, China and India began to make progress. In 1991, Li Peng visited India, marking the first time a Chinese premier had traveled to New Delhi in more than thirty years. After his trip, Li instructed the Chinese delegation "to expedite the settlement" of the dispute.[196] In 1992, the fourth meeting of the JWG included military representatives, marking the first time that military officers held direct talks on reducing tensions along the border. In this session, the two sides began to discuss potential confidence-building measures, such as fixed meetings by border defense forces.[197] At the JWG's fifth meeting in June 1993, the two sides initialed a draft agreement for maintaining the status quo along the disputed frontier. India also reaffirmed that Tibet was a part of China.[198] In September 1993, Tang Jiaxuan and R. L. Bhatia signed an agreement "to maintain peace and tranquility" along the line of actual control

[194] Deng repeated his offer again to an Indian journalist in 1980. Mira Sinha Bhattacharjea, "India-China: The Year of Two Possibilities," in Satish Kumar, ed., *Yearbook on India's Foreign Policy, 1985–86* (New Delhi: Sage Publications, 1988), 150.

[195] On these talks, see Bhattacharjea, "India-China," 150–161; Sumit Ganguly, "The Sino-Indian Border Talks, 1981–1989: A View from New Delhi," *Asian Survey*, vol. 29, no. 12 (1989): 1123–1135.

[196] Press Trust of India, 13 June 1992, BBC Summary of World Broadcasts, 15 June 1992, FE/1407/A2/1 (Lexis-Nexis).

[197] ZGWJ, 1993, 510.

[198] Reuters, 28 June 1993 (Factiva).

(LAC).[199] Further negotiations of the JWG, as well as a new group of defense and military experts, produced a 1996 agreement on confidence-building measures, which included limiting the number of forces near the LAC, avoiding large-scale exercises, and limiting the flight of combat aircraft, among other measures.[200] Importantly, China and India also agreed to a mutual withdrawal of forces around Sumdurong Chu.[201] Finally, these agreements affirmed that China would accept the boundary depicted by the McMahon Line in the eastern sector, as this line corresponded with the LAC.

During this period, however, the two sides achieved no breakthrough in actually solving the territorial dispute. Moreover, because no agreement has been reached, it is quite difficult to determine whether compromise offers were made by either side. In 1997, for example, an Indian newspaper reported that China had again offered in September 1996 to settle the dispute based on a revival of Zhou Enlai's 1960 "package deal," which required mutual concessions in the eastern and western sectors. According to the report, the Chinese apparently sought to link this compromise to Jiang Zemin's November 1996 trip to New Delhi.[202] Although such a compromise is consistent with the effects of regime insecurity, it has not been verified and, like Deng's 1979 offer, it does not appear to represent any further concessions. As in China's negotiations with Vietnam, the legacy of war between China and India and internal opposition to compromise have continued to pose significant obstacles to a final settlement.

Nevertheless, the 1993 and 1996 agreements have increased stability on the border and improved relations between the two countries. In the absence of any settlement, these agreements have established an effective boundary, which in turn has facilitated the reopening of trade routes and a gradual reduction of tensions. Moreover, these agreements appear to give China most of what it wanted—improved ties with an important neighbor at a time of isolation and regime insecurity, demilitarization of an important stretch of China's border, and increased border trade to stimulate economic development in a key frontier area. Efforts to settle the dispute progressed somewhat in July 2003, when the two sides nominated high-level special representatives to outline the parameters of a po-

[199] Refers to the line of actual control at the end of the 1962, which was largely consistent with the line of control in 1959.

[200] On their implementation, see Waheguru Pal Singh Sidhu and Jing-dong Yuan, "Resolving the Sino-Indian Border Dispute," *Asian Survey*, vol. 41, no. 2 (March/April 2001): 351–376.

[201] ZGWJ, 1997, 510.

[202] "Chance to Resolve Dispute Missed?" *The Telegraph* (Calcutta), 15 May 1997, FBIS# 19970515001285.

litical settlement to the dispute. Although a declaration of guiding principles was signed in April 2005, a final settlement remains elusive.[203]

During this period, China also made progress in its border dispute with the kingdom of Bhutan. This dispute has been particularly challenging to study because of a dearth of information from both sides. In general, however, the dispute itself cannot be separated from China's conflict with India, given New Delhi's prominent role in the kingdom's foreign policy. China and Bhutan have held annual talks on their border dispute since 1984, but China's primary goal has been to pressure India by supporting Bhutan's desire for enhanced autonomy. In 1990, after China and India held the first round of the JWG, Beijing apparently dropped its claims to 76 percent of the 1,128 square kilometers of land disputed along Bhutan's western border.[204] As this region abuts a key communication route to Tibet, it is possible that China sought increased cooperation from Bhutan in light of the Tibetan protests in the late 1980s. In 1996, this compromise offer was repeated, though Bhutan has yet to agree to China's demand for the remaining 269 square kilometers over three areas.[205] In 1998, the two sides signed an agreement to maintain peace and tranquility along the border, also in line with the 1993 and 1996 confidence-building agreements that China signed with India.[206]

The absence of settlement with Bhutan, as with India, provides strong evidence against explanations based on external threats—although in this case China would have been balancing against the United States rather than the Soviet Union. In 2001, the Bush administration established a new emphasis on strengthening ties with India, implicitly to counter China's growing influence in the region. After the EP-3 incident in April 2001, in which a Chinese fighter airplane collided with a U.S. surveillance plane, China might have been even more alarmed about growing U.S. influence in the region, which in turn might have made settlement with India more attractive. While September 11 dramatically altered U.S. foreign policy priorities, there is no evidence that growing U.S. ties with India made settlement of the dispute more attractive to China. Moreover, in the early to mid-1990s, when the two confidence-building agreements were signed,

[203] "Agreement between the Government of the Republic of India and the Government of the People's Republic of China on the Political Parameters and Guiding Principles for the Settlement of the India-China Boundary Question," http://www.mea.gov.in/treatiesagreement/2005/11ta1104200501.htm.

[204] Rajesh S. Kharat, *Foreign Policy of Bhutan* (New Delhi: Manak, 2005), 138.

[205] "Bhutan, China Near Border Deal: Diplomat," AFP, 14 July 1997.

[206] Waijiao bu, ed., *Zhonghua renmin gongheguo bianjie shiwu tiaoyue ji: ZhongYin ZhongBu juan* [Collection of Treaties on the PRC's Boundary Affairs: China-India, China-Bhutan] (Beijing: Shijie zhishi chubanshe [internal circulation], 2004), 124–126.

U.S. ties with India were quite poor and thus cannot explain China's willingness to pursue those agreements.

CONCLUSION

In the 1990s, renewed regime insecurity created strong incentives for China's leaders to compromise in their country's remaining frontier disputes. The upheaval of Tiananmen and the collapse of socialism led China to settle disputes with the Soviet Union, Laos, and Vietnam to increase external support for its own socialist system of government. Renewed unrest in Xinjiang from 1990 aggravated overall regime instability after Tiananmen. In response, China pursued compromise in disputes with Kazakhstan, Kyrgyzstan, and Tajikistan to limit external support for separatist groups. The internal threats to regime security increased the cost of pursuing territorial claims because China's leaders needed external cooperation to support its internal goals of regime consolidation. The timing of China's agreements, public statements by Chinese officials, and scholarly analysis explain why and when China pursued compromise.

Looking forward, only two of China's sixteen frontier disputes remain unresolved: those with India and Bhutan. Although factors that provoke regime insecurity, especially internal threats to territorial integrity associated with ethnic rebellion, have played a central role in China's past efforts to compromise, they may paradoxically be less relevant in the settlement of these last disputes in the future. In stark contrast to the 1950s, the central government has greatly strengthened its position in Tibet with a network of highways, primary, and secondary roads as well as military bases.[207] Years of embargo by India have deepened economic links between Tibet and China proper. At the same time, national leaders on both sides, especially India, face high domestic costs for pursuing territorial compromise. External threats now offer the most likely source of settlement. To date, however, such threats have not been strong enough to produce further compromises from China.

[207] Dawa Norbu, *China's Tibet Policy* (London: Curzon Press, 2001).

CHAPTER FOUR

Escalation in Frontier Disputes

BOTH in the early 1960s and throughout the 1990s, China pursued compromise in its frontier disputes. In settling these conflicts, China has sought to consolidate the continental boundaries of the late Qing dynasty and gain external recognition of its sovereignty over large ethnic minority frontiers. Although China has been willing to settle its frontier disputes through compromise, it has nevertheless used force in three of these conflicts. Declining claim strength best explains the variation in the use of force across frontier disputes and over time in conflicts with India, the Soviet Union, and Vietnam.

Overall, China's claims in its frontier disputes have been strong. In most of these conflicts, it occupied some of the land that it was contesting. With one of the largest standing armies after World War II, China has also been able to project power over disputed areas on land much more readily than across the Taiwan Strait or over offshore islands. With such strong claims, China could be confident about the final outcome of these disputes and negotiate from a position of strength. As a result, China has never used force in the majority of its frontier disputes, because it never faced conditions in which its otherwise strong claims would weaken at the expense of its bargaining power in these conflicts.

By contrast, China has used force in frontier disputes with its militarily most powerful neighbors, the very states that could mount a challenge to China in the local balance of forces. In its conflicts with India and the Soviet Union, China used force when these states sought to strengthen their claims at China's expense by seeking to shift the local military balance to their advantage through increased troop deployments, by adopting forward and aggressive postures in disputed areas, and, at times, by increasing the amount of contested land under their control. In 1962, 1967, and 1969, military pressure from India and the Soviet Union coincided with internal political instability associated with economic fallout from the Great Leap Forward and the upheaval of the Cultural Revolution. China's leaders viewed the rise of such military pressure on its claims at times of domestic unrest as deliberate, a conclusion that underscored the importance of using force to prevent any further deterioration in the local balance and strengthen China's relative position in these disputes.

Repeated clashes with Vietnam, discussed briefly at the end of this chapter, reflect the dynamics of rivalry, not negative shifts in claim strength.

1962: THE CHINA-INDIA BORDER WAR

In April 1960, Zhou Enlai traveled to New Delhi to negotiate a settlement to China's territorial dispute with India. During his visit, Zhou proposed a "package deal" in which each side would recognize the disputed land held by the other. China would keep the Aksai Chin and other areas in the west, and India would retain the North Eastern Frontier Agency (NEFA) in the east (that is, the territory south of the McMahon Line). Two years later, however, on October 20, Chinese forces assaulted Indian positions all along the contested frontier. By the time China ended a second offensive in late November, 722 Chinese and 4,885 Indian soldiers had been killed.[1] On November 21, China announced a unilateral ceasefire and its intention to withdraw from all territory that it had seized during the fighting and even from territory it previously occupied, pulling back 20 kilometers behind the November 7, 1959, line of control.[2]

---

[1] *ZYBJ*, 435–437.

[2] Key English-language sources on Chinese decision making include Cheng Feng and Larry M. Wortzel, "PLA Operational Principles and Limited War: The Sino-Indian War of 1962," in Mark A. Ryan, David M. Finkelstein, and Michael A. McDevitt, eds., *Chinese Warfighting: The PLA Experience since 1949* (Armonk, N.Y.: M. E. Sharpe, 2003), 173–197; John W. Garver, "China's Decision for War with India in 1962," in Alastair Iain Johnston and Robert S. Ross, eds., *New Directions in the Study of China's Foreign Policy* (Stanford, Calif.: Stanford University Press, 2006), 86–130; Melvin Gurtov and Byong-Moo Hwang, *China under Threat: The Politics of Strategy and Diplomacy* (Baltimore: Johns Hopkins University Press, 1980), 99–154; Roderick MacFarquhar, *The Origins of the Cultural Revolution*, vol. 3 (New York: Columbia University Press, 1997), 297–318; Neville Maxwell, *India's China War* (New York: Pantheon Books, 1970); Allen S. Whiting, *The Chinese Calculus of Deterrence: India and Indochina* (Ann Arbor: University of Michigan Press, 1975).

Important Chinese sources include *ZYBJ*; Wang Hongwei, *Ximalaya shan qingjie: ZhongYin guanxi yanjiu* [Himalayan Sentiments: A Study of Chinese-Indian Relations] (Beijing: Zhongguo zangxue chubanshe, 1998); Wang Zhongxing, "60 niandai ZhongYin bianjing chongtu yu Zhongguo bianfang budui de ziwei fanji zuozhan" [The 1960s Chinese-Indian Border Conflict and the Counterattack in Self-defense of China's Frontier Defense Troops], *Dangdai Zhongguo yanjiu*, no. 5 (1997): 13–23; Xu Yan, *ZhongYin bianjie zhizhan lishi zhenxiang* [The True History of the Chinese-Indian Border War] (Hong Kong: Cosmos Books, 1993).

Two Chinese sources with extensive quotations from Mao and other leaders were not used in this research, as their reliability is unclear: Shi Bo, *1962: ZhongYin dazhan jishi* [1962: Record of China-India War] (Beijing: Dadi chubanshe, 1993); Sun Xiao and Chen Zhibin, *Ximalaya shan de xue: ZhongYin zhanzheng shilu* [Himalayan Snow: Record of the China-India War] (Taiyuan: Beiyue wenyi chubanshe, 1991). For a surprisingly candid critique of

Newly available Chinese sources largely confirm Allen Whiting's and Neville Maxwell's seminal accounts of the Chinese decision to launch the October 20 offensive.[3] These sources demonstrate how assessments of growing vulnerability and declining claim strength created incentives to use force when diplomacy failed. In late 1961, India sought to strengthen its position in what became termed the "forward policy" of increasing its military presence in disputed territory. At the same time, India maintained a diplomatic stance of refusing to negotiate unless China withdrew from territory that India claimed in the western sector. As Whiting notes, heightened concerns about the Chinese state's territorial integrity and the economic crisis of the Great Leap magnified its leaders' assessment of the consequences of Indian actions along the disputed border.[4] Reflecting China's goal of deterrence, a Chinese diplomat recalls that Mao Zedong believed that attacking India would "create 10 years of border stability."[5]

As demonstrated below, China's willingness to use force in this dispute has varied with perceptions of decline in its claim strength and bargaining power in the dispute. Decline in claim strength corresponds with decisions to use force in 1962, 1967, and 1986. By contrast, during periods of stable claim strength in the 1970s and since the 1990s, China has refrained from using force.

Declining Claim Strength

The core factor in the Chinese decision to use force was the growing Indian military presence after February 1962 under the thrust of the

---

the Sun and Chen book by a noted PLA historian, see Xu Yan, *"Neimu" da baoguang* [Revealing the Secrets of "Inside Stories"] (Beijing: Tuanjie chubanshe, 1994), 144–197.

For the Indian Ministry of Defence's official history, see *HCC*. Key memoirs include J. P. Dalvi, *Himalayan Blunder: The Curtain-Raiser to the Sino-Indian War of 1962* (Bombay: Thacker and Company, 1969); B. M. Kaul, *The Untold Story* (Bombay: Allied Publishers, 1967); B. N. Mullik, *My Years with Nehru: The Chinese Betrayal* (Bombay: Allied Publishers, 1971); D. K. Palit, *War in High Himalaya: The Indian Army in Crisis, 1962* (New Delhi: Lancer International, 1991).

[3] This section focuses mostly on Chinese decision making. The most detailed account of Indian decision making is Steven A. Hoffman, *India and the China Crisis* (Berkeley: University of California Press, 1990).

[4] Whiting, *Calculus*. For similar arguments, Gurtov and Hwang, *China under Threat*; Gerald Segal, *Defending China* (Oxford: Oxford University Press, 1985).

[5] Zhang Tong, "DuiYin ziwei fanji zhan qianhou de huiyi" [Recollections of the Counterattack in Self-defense against India], in Pei Jianzhang, ed., *Xin Zhongguo waijiao fengyun* [New China's Diplomatic Storms] (Beijing: Shiji zhishi chubanshe, 1990), 75. At the time of the war, Zhang was a diplomat in the MFA's Asia Department. Another scholar reports that Mao mentioned "thirty years." See Xiao Xinli, ed., *Mao Zedong yu gongheguo zhongda lishi shijian* [Mao Zedong and Major Historical Events of the Republic] (Beijing: Renmin chubanshe, 2001), 338.

forward policy. Focused primarily on the western sector, the increased Indian presence weakened China's claim strength in several ways. First, by August India had occupied an additional 3,000 square kilometers of land in this sector claimed by China. Second, Chinese tactical counter-measures, threats, and diplomacy all failed to arrest the pace of Indian troop deployments throughout the summer of 1962. Third, India's deployments indicated that it would likely occupy any territory from which it demanded a Chinese withdrawal as a precondition for negotiations. Overall, China's leaders believed that the forward policy reflected an Indian desire to use military means, not diplomacy, to settle the dispute on India's terms.

The forward policy itself, however, must be viewed within the broader context of how Indian leaders perceived their position in the dispute with China. In particular, when the policy was launched in late 1961, Nehru had concluded that India's position had declined precipitously in the previous two years. Although this book focuses on China's management of its territorial disputes, India's decision to pursue the forward policy provides further support for the role of negative shifts in claim strength in decisions to use force, and it illustrates the pernicious effects of the security dilemma when each side in a territorial dispute views its actions as defensive.

Prior to the outbreak of widespread revolt in Tibet in 1959, the local balance of forces in the border dispute between China and India was relatively stable. In the central sector, a number of nonviolent confrontations occurred in the mid-1950s, especially around Shipki Pass (see maps 2.1 and 4.1), but each side mainly consolidated control of territory that it already held. In the much larger and more important eastern and western sectors, however, each side moved to strengthen its position in areas that were inaccessible to its adversary. India steadily consolidated its control of the North East Frontier Agency (NEFA) south of the McMahon Line, especially the Tawang (Dawang) tract, while China started to build the Xinjiang-Tibet highway through the Aksai Chin plateau in March 1956.[6] Nevertheless, apart from the central sector, both sides had few troops deployed in close proximity to each other.

After the Tibetan revolt, however, the local military balance shifted as China deployed troops to suppress the rebellion. In the eastern sector, China's forces moved quickly to seal the Tibetan border along the McMahon Line, which resulted in repeated confrontations with Indian troops that China believed to be aiding and protecting Tibetan rebels. As described in chapter 2, China occupied the village of Longju on the McMahon Line in August 1959 after a brief clash with Indian forces. In the

[6] For areas in the west occupied by China before 1956, see ZYBJ, 46–47.

summer and fall of 1959, China began to expand its military presence in the western sector to secure the Xinjiang-Tibet highway. The October 1959 clash at Kongka Pass reflected the expansion of the Chinese presence, as according to Indian sources China had no post there in 1958.[7]

Over the next two years, competition to control unoccupied disputed territory occurred primarily in the west. For China, consolidation of control over the western sector was key to the security of the Xinjiang-Tibet highway, especially after India disputed China's claim to Aksai Chin in 1958 and dispatched a patrol to survey the new road.[8] Unlike in the eastern sector, where its position was strong, India had no forces permanently stationed on the land that it claimed in the west. On May 5, 1960, Zhou Enlai sent a telegram to Mao regarding China's troop deployments. Zhou noted that because the joint statement issued after his talks with Nehru lacked an agreement to suspend patrolling in disputed areas, Indian "nibbling" had started. He suggested that the Tibetan and Southern Xinjiang MDs should seize the opportunity and favorable weather to establish more sentry posts in the western sector inside China's claim line. Once the posts were added, Chinese troops should continue to suspend patrols, but if they encountered Indian troops, "they should persuade them to leave and avoid armed conflict." The following day, Mao approved Zhou's suggestion. Deng Xiaoping then implemented the plan for the expansion of China's presence in the western sector.[9]

In September 1961, an Intelligence Bureau (IB) report concluded that China had gained an advantage in the dispute. According to the report, China since June 1959 had established as many as twenty-one new posts in the western sector, most of which were connected to each other and the Xinjiang-Tibet highway through a comprehensive road network. Through these efforts, India believed that China had occupied an additional 4,600 square kilometers of disputed land.[10] The total number of Chinese positions in this sector, however, is unknown. India had a total of twenty-seven positions, though many were not located in disputed territory but on the Indian side of the Chinese claim line.[11] The IB also noted that China had established twenty-five new positions along the McMahon Line in the eastern sector in this same time period.[12]

---

[7] Mullik, *My Years*, 242.

[8] *WP*, I, 26.

[9] Liu Wusheng and Du Hongqi, eds., *Zhou Enlai junshi huodong jishi, 1918–1975 (xia)* [Chronicle of Zhou Enlai's Military Activities, vol. 2] (Beijing: Zhongyang wenxian chubanshe, 2000), 525.

[10] Palit, *War*, 97.

[11] *HCC*, 67–68.

[12] Mullik, *My Years*, 313. India's inability to keep pace with China after 1959 resulted from geographical challenges, fragmented responsibility for border control, economic con-

Perceiving its own decline, India redoubled efforts to strengthen its position in the western sector. The IB report concluded that China would continue to occupy disputed land in the west and that only an increased Indian military presence would prevent further incursions.[13] Moreover, approximately 9,000 square kilometers in the west remained vacant and vulnerable to Chinese occupation.[14] On November 2, 1961, Prime Minister Jawaharlal Nehru chaired a meeting with national security advisers to discuss the situation on the border. The result of the meeting was a series of instructions, which became known as the "forward policy," for strengthening India's claim in the dispute. In the western sector, Indian forces were instructed to patrol as far as possible from India's present positions toward its claim line inside Chinese-held territory and to establish "additional posts to prevent the Chinese from advancing and also to dominate any Chinese posts already established in our territory."[15] In the central and eastern sectors, Indian forces were instructed to "be in effective occupation of the entire frontier," as most of the disputed areas here were already occupied by India.[16]

In the western sector, winter weather hampered the initial implementation of the plan. As the snow melted, however, India began to deploy additional troops. From March to May 1962, Indian units focused their efforts in the Chip Chap Valley (map 4.1). In July, Indian troops targeted the Galwan Valley.[17] By September, India had established thirty-six new posts in the west, many of them near and sometimes behind Chinese positions.[18] Moreover, according to the official internal history of the conflict from the PLA's Academy of Military Science (AMS), India had occupied a total of 3,000 square kilometers.[19] In the eastern sector, implementation of the forward policy began in February 1962 when the Assam Rifles, a paramilitary force, established four new posts near Tawang. Two of these positions, at Bum La and Khinzemane, were located north of the McMahon Line according to the 1914 map (see map 4.2).[20] In April, an Indian reconnaissance patrol returned to Longju, which China had vacated in

---

straits, and logistical difficulties. See Dalvi, *Himalayan Blunder*, 55–106; Hoffman, *India*, 92–97; Maxwell, *India's China War*, 199–205; Palit, *War*, 246–110.

[13] Hoffman, *India*, 95–96; HCC, 59–68. China had established these positions before 1961, but they had not been discovered by Indian patrols.

[14] Mullik, *My Years*, 309.

[15] Quoted in HCC, 68.

[16] For a detailed account, see Hoffman, *India*, 96–100. Also see Maxwell, *India's China War*, 221–223; HCC, 68–69.

[17] ZYBJ, 138–170.

[18] Maxwell, *India's China War*, 235; HCC, 70.

[19] ZYBJ, 154.

[20] HCC, 69.

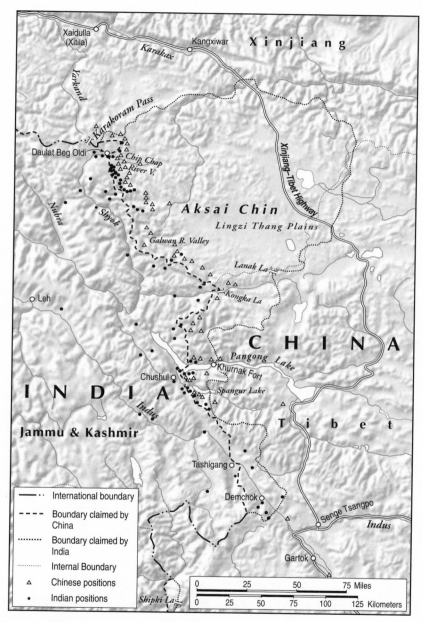

Map 4.1 China-India Border (Western Sector)

June 1960.[21] By July 20, India had built a total of thirty-four new posts in the eastern sector, bringing its total in that sector to fifty-six, including several such as Khinzemane located north of the McMahon Line.[22]

From China's perspective, the initiation and implementation of the forward policy represented a threat to the local military balance. In the two years since the Zhou-Nehru talks, the border had remained relatively calm. Although both sides continued to consolidate control over disputed territory under their effective occupation, they had limited the extent of military patrols and maintained a large distance between their positions, often tens of kilometers. Although diplomacy had yet to yield results, China's leaders may have believed that India had come close to accepting its position in the western sector, thereby "creating conditions" for an eventual settlement. Stability and an absence of armed clashes on the border were the next best alternative to an agreement, as a stable border supported China's internal goal of eliminating potential Indian influence within Tibet and along China's southwestern frontier.

India's forward policy shattered this calm. The Indian Army's operations directly challenged PLA positions in areas China believed that it had controlled throughout the 1950s. Although the outposts erected by both sides were in contested territory, China had established a presence in most areas of the western sector for many years, including the construction of the Xinjiang-Tibet highway in 1956, and had strengthened its position after 1959. As indicated on map 4.1, many of the Indian posts in the western sector, by contrast, were not only erected in areas on China's side of the claim line but also located to dominate Chinese positions. Moreover, in all sectors India placed troops within the 20-kilometer buffer zone where China had suspended patrolling at the end of 1959. The launch of the forward policy challenged the efficacy of what China viewed as its policy of restraint in the dispute, which aimed to reduce the potential for conflict and increase stability on the border. By early summer, Indian officials started declaring that more than 6,000 square kilometers of territory had been occupied in the western sector even though the actual amount was smaller.[23] For China's leaders, such reports only increased the sense of threat on the border.

Regime Insecurity and Perceptions of Decline

India's military pressure coincided with other challenges to territorial integrity and political stability that China's leaders faced in the spring of

---

[21] *ZYBJ*, 96.

[22] Mullik, *My Years*, 136; *HCC*, 71.

[23] *Washington Post*, 6 July 1962, A7. Also see Maxwell, *India's China War*, 328–329.

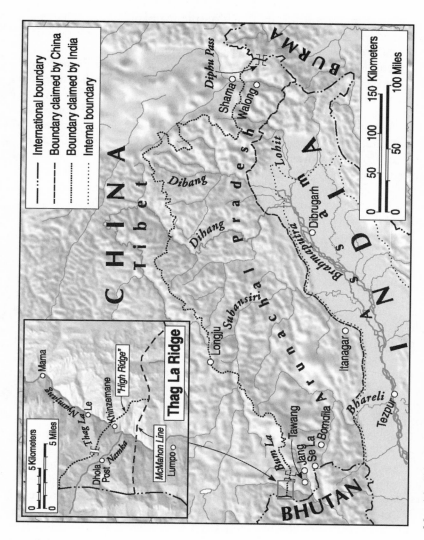

Map 4.2 China-India Border (Eastern Sector)

1962. As chapter 2 details, those challenges included the economic crisis and famine after the Great Leap Forward, ethnic unrest in Xinjiang, and Taiwan's mobilization for an attack on the mainland. These challenges magnified the sense of vulnerability and long-term threat that India posed to China's territorial integrity in several different ways.

First, amid other challenges to territorial integrity, Indian pressure was seen as especially dangerous, threatening not just the control of disputed areas on the border but also stability within Tibet. In February 1962, before China's leaders appreciated the extent of the forward policy, the CMC ordered all PLA units in Tibet to shift their efforts from pacification to economic development, similar to the role of Xinjiang's Production and Construction Corps.[24] This shift reflected a belief that control over the region had been consolidated and that the central government had few resources to spare because of the need to address the economic crisis throughout China proper. The pacification campaigns had successfully crushed the Tibetan revolt and thus closed channels through which external influence could operate within this part of China.

In this context, China's leaders viewed the intensification of the territorial dispute in 1962 as an effort by India to maintain influence within Tibet and challenge Chinese authority. India's claims in the western sector threatened the PLA's most secure communication route connecting Tibet with China proper.[25] India's position in the eastern and central sectors allowed it to control access to the traditional trade routes into Tibet. At the same time, India's support of the Dalai Lama created the potential for a second government-in-exile challenging the CCP's legitimacy in addition to the Nationalist (KMT) on Taiwan. Moreover, India's economic sanctions on essential foodstuffs exacerbated China's economic crisis in the wake of the Great Leap, thereby increasing internal challenges for the CCP regime.[26]

China's regime insecurity, however, did not create incentives to use force to divert attention from the economic crisis. Instead, the 1962 crisis increased the sensitivity of China's leaders to external threats to the frontiers. With the instability created by the Great Leap's failure, China's leaders placed a premium on stability in the vast frontiers in order to manage more pressing threats at the core. India not only targeted China's most vulnerable frontier region but did so at a time when China's leaders felt weak at home. External pressure challenged China's ability to rebuild,

---

[24] *ZYBJ*, 463.

[25] Zhang Zhirong, "ZhongYin guanxi de huigu yu fansi: Yang Gongsu dashi fangtan lu" [Review and Reflections on Chinese-Indian Relations: Record of an Interview with Ambassador Yang Gongsu], *Dangdai yatai*, no. 8 (2000): 17–25.

[26] See chapter 2, 79–83.

and instability in the frontiers would only complicate the consolidation of authority in China proper. Unrest in Xinjiang and Indian pressure against Tibet's frontier raised the issue of territorial integrity precisely when political stability was paramount.

Second, again amid other internal threats to regime security, India's forward policy was seen as part of a broader effort by external actors to benefit from China's political instability. As chapter 2 describes, these varied challenges to territorial integrity were seen as neither isolated events nor coincidental. Instead, Indian military deployments, unrest in Xinjiang, and the threat from Taiwan were viewed as efforts by outsiders to profit when China's leaders were focused on domestic problems. As Zhou Enlai noted in a speech in early June, "Now the Americans and Chiang exploit [*liyong*] our dire straits to carry out provocations, while the Soviet leadership group also exploits our difficulties to create difficulties."[27] Moreover, military strategists shared this assessment. The CMC's strategy research small group, convened in May 1962, had concluded that China's economic troubles provided an "extremely rare opportunity" (*qian zai nan feng*) for other states to pressure China.[28]

Third, Indian pressure came at a time of declining military strength within China. The Great Leap had had a dramatic impact on the PLA, as it had had on other parts of the Chinese government. It was no coincidence that PLA units in Tibet were instructed to focus on economic development efforts in early 1962. Internal documents captured by Tibetan guerrillas in 1961 highlighted the impact of China's food shortages and declining industrial production on the readiness and morale of Chinese soldiers.[29]

Diplomacy and Deterrence

Facing this decline in its dispute with India, China moved to bring stability to its southwestern frontier through a combination of diplomacy and deterrence. China's short-term goal was the elimination of Indian military pressure on the frontier, thereby strengthening its claim in the dispute and its control over Tibet. China's long-term goal remained a settlement of the dispute based on the package deal that Zhou had proposed in 1960. The forward policy represented a clear challenge to both: India sought to

[27] *Zhou Enlai junshi wenxuan* [Zhou Enlai's Selected Works on Military Affairs] (Beijing: Renmin chubanshe, 1997), 435.

[28] Wang Shangrong, "Xin Zhongguo dansheng hou jici zhongda zhanzheng" [Several Major Wars after the Emergence of New China], in Zhu Yuanshi, ed., *Gongheguo yaoshi koushushi* [An Oral History of the Republic's Important Events] (Changsha: Henan renmin chubanshe, 1999), 277–278.

[29] Whiting, *Calculus*. See the documents in J. Chester Cheng, ed., *Politics of the Chinese Red Army* (Stanford, Calif.: Hoover Institution Publications, 1966).

use military means to compel China to abandon its position in the western sector, including the Xinjiang-Tibet highway, while strengthening Indian control over the eastern sector.

Allen Whiting has covered the broad outlines of China's response to Indian pressure and the road to the 1962 war, detailing the mix of diplomatic demarches, deterrent threats, and military maneuvers.[30] Newly available sources, including the AMS history mentioned above, underscore the depth of vulnerability that Chinese leaders perceived and illuminate the timing and content of specific decisions. China's inability to arrest India's forward policy through diplomacy and deterrence ultimately led to the decision to launch a large-scale offensive in October.

China's first response was to establish blocking positions to thwart any further expansion of Indian troops in the western sector. Initially, the PLA focused its efforts in the Chip Chap Valley, countering the initial thrust of India's forward policy.[31] As the intensity of the forward policy increased in late April 1962, China announced that it would resume patrolling in most of the western sector. In mid-May, after a number of Indian patrols had crossed the McMahon Line, the General Staff Department (GSD) further instructed the Tibetan Military District (MD) to prepare to resume patrols in the eastern sector, a move not publicly announced by China at the time.[32] Throughout this tit-for-tat period, GSD instructions stressed the importance of avoiding armed clashes with Indian forces and controlling escalation.

As the forward policy continued, China's second response was to prepare for a possible war with India. On May 14, Zhou Enlai held a meeting with China's senior military commanders, Luo Ruiqing and Yang Chengwu, to discuss the security of China's entire border, one of the very few times Zhou ever convened such a meeting.[33] Zhou stated that China must prepare for possible armed conflicts on the border with India and must complete these preparations by the end of June.[34] Contrary to arguments that the war resulted from divisions within the Chinese leadership, this meeting demonstrates leadership unity on issues of national security. On May 29, the GSD issued a report on war preparations, which concluded that units in the eastern sector should prepare to attack to support

---

[30] Whiting, *Calculus*. Also see Gurtov and Hwang, *China under Threat*; Maxwell, *India's China War*.

[31] *ZYBJ*, map 2.

[32] *ZYBJ*, 158.

[33] As early as February, PLA units on the Chinese-Indian border had been ordered to prepare for possible conflict. At the time, orders focused on studying operational plans, stockpiling supplies, furthering road-building efforts, and completing communications work. *ZYBJ*, 462–463.

[34] Liu and Du, *Zhou Enlai junshi huodong jishi (xia)*, 564.

the conflict in the western sector. The report also contained instructions concerning troop deployments, the establishment of a command post in the western sector, operational plans and supply services.[35] In early June, the Tibetan 419 Unit (*Zangzi* 419 *budui*) was established as the frontline headquarters (*qianxian zhihui bu*) for the eastern sector to command the 154th, 155th, and 157th regiments, formerly part of the Eighteenth Army.[36] In the west, the Xinjiang MD established its own frontline headquarters at Kangxiwar. Soon thereafter, frontline units began combat training.[37]

The timing of these instructions underscores the Chinese leaders' sense of vulnerability on the southwestern frontier. Most scholars have speculated that they turned their attention to the Chinese-Indian border only after the situation across the Taiwan Strait stabilized, at the end of June.[38] In fact, Zhou's meeting with Luo and Yang, as well as the May GSD report, occurred before similar orders were issued to counter a possible attack from the KMT. At the time, China's leaders could not foresee the extent of the forward policy or Nationalist plans. The imperatives of territorial security produced a roughly simultaneous response to both threats. Nevertheless, Zhou specifically instructed that China should prepare to fight only if India attacked first, a move designed to prepare for conflict but avoid fighting on two fronts if possible.[39]

China's third response to the forward policy was to shift from blocking tactics and patrolling to a policy of "armed coexistence" (*wuzhuang gong-chu*). A deliberate pun on the 1950s Bandung-era slogan of the "Five Principles of Peaceful Coexistence," this policy involved maneuvering so as to dominate any Indian post located near a Chinese one. The objective was to compel Indian forces to retreat through a firm display of force. The GSD specifically instructed frontline units not to encircle Indian positions, fire on them, or pursue them if they withdrew. Rather, Chinese troops were ordered to "give a wrongdoer a way out" (*wangkai yimian*) and permit Indian troops to withdraw.[40] Mao issued a 20-character slogan regarding the new policy direction: "resolutely do not yield, but strive to avoid bloodshed; create interlocking positions for long-term armed coexistence" (*juebu tuirang, lizheng bimian liuxue; quanya jiaocuo, changqi wuzhuang gongchu*).[41]

---

[35] "Concrete Arrangements for the China-India Border Military Struggle" (*guanyu Zhong-Yin bianjing junshi douzheng de juti anpai*), in ZYBJ, 465.

[36] ZYBJ, 158.

[37] ZYBJ, 466.

[38] Whiting, *Calculus*, 79–80.

[39] Liu and Du, *Zhou Enlai junshi huodong jishi (xia)*, 564.

[40] ZYBJ, 142.

[41] ZYBJ, 143.

The spark for this policy shift occurred in early July, when India began to move forces into the Galwan Valley on July 5. Within days, India established a post behind a PLA position, interdicting its supply and communication lines. Previously, most of the Indian posts had been placed opposite Chinese positions, not behind them. China responded first with a diplomatic protest and the deployment of two companies to occupy the high ground on either side of the new Indian post. China then reinforced these positions with approximately one battalion, while India inserted more troops via helicopter. A tense standoff ensued, with the Indian position blocked on three sides.[42]

The events in the Galwan Valley marked the apogee of tension for China's leaders. Once the situation erupted, Zhou requested to receive updates every two hours and personally supervised the disposition of units in the valley. In one instance, he ordered the re-siting of a Chinese post to facilitate an Indian withdrawal. Moreover, if attacked, the PLA troops at Galwan were permitted to report directly to the GSD, not through the normal chain of command via the Kangxiwar headquarters and Xinjiang MD. On July 14, senior officers from the GSD's Operations Department arrived in Xinjiang to command the Chinese troops directly.[43]

China's leaders hoped that the policy of armed coexistence would compel an Indian retreat or at least arrest the momentum of the forward policy. PLA forces maintained better lines of supply in both sectors and especially in the east, where Indian troops had to be resupplied by air. Nevertheless, the Galwan Valley incident increased tensions all along the border. The close proximity of troops created more opportunities for tactical miscalculation and escalation. Moreover, after the incident, the rules of engagement for Indian forces changed from "fire only if fired upon" to "fire in self-defence."[44] Likewise, PLA soldiers were ordered to fire if Indian troops advanced on Chinese positions. Unsurprisingly, the first armed clash since October 1959 occurred on July 21, 1962, in the Chip Chap Valley.

China's final response to Indian pressure was to seek a negotiated settlement of the dispute in order to maintain the status quo on the border. In late February 1962, as the pace of the forward policy increased, China reminded India of its willingness to hold talks and negotiate. According to a diplomatic note, "as far as the Chinese side is concerned, the door for negotiations is always open."[45] To support this objective, the PLA took specific steps to avoid armed conflicts with Indian forces that might

---

[42] *ZYBJ*, 138–145.
[43] *ZYBJ*, 140–142.
[44] *HCC*, 78.
[45] *WP*, VI, 16.

inadvertently escalate. All the key GSD instructions issued from February to July underscored the importance of avoiding armed conflict. For example, the May 1962 guidelines for the resumption of patrolling outlined how to deal with Indian provocations without shedding blood or creating an incident.[46] Chinese troops were even forbidden to hunt for game within five kilometers of an Indian post.[47]

A settlement acceptable to China would involve all sectors of the border and would require compromise by both sides as envisioned in Zhou's 1960 proposal. India viewed this demand as unreasonable, as it did not recognize a dispute in the eastern sector.[48] Each Chinese effort to open talks encountered the same obstacle concerning the scope of negotiations. China sought to hold talks without preconditions and pursue a "package deal" for all sectors. India insisted that talks could begin only after Chinese forces withdrew from the western sector and sought to discuss only this sector, not the entire border. Nehru had first proposed this condition in November 1959, and then he repeated it in a May 14, 1962, note to China.[49] As Nehru himself acknowledged, India's proposal required that China vacate approximately 33,000 square kilometers of territory claimed by India without a corresponding Indian withdrawal from Chinese-claimed land south of the McMahon Line.[50]

In July, China linked the policy of armed coexistence with a new diplomatic initiative. During the height of the Galwan Valley confrontation, the Chinese ambassador in New Delhi, Pan Zili, informed Nehru on July 13 that China would be willing to hold talks on the basis of a report written by Chinese and Indian officials in late 1960.[51] On July 23, two days after the armed clash in the Chip Chap Valley, Foreign Minister Chen Yi and Defense Minister Krishna Menon held three rounds of informal talks in Geneva on the sidelines of the Laos conference. According to one Indian participant, Chen reaffirmed China's willingness to acknowledge the boundary contained in the McMahon Line and arrange a deal for the western sector. Moreover, Chen reportedly suggested that China would be willing to accept a division of the Aksai Chin, proposing

---

[46] "Concrete Steps for the Resumption of Border Patrols and Principles for the Handling of Situations by Frontier Defense Sentry Posts" (*guanyu huifu bianjing xunluo de juti cuoshi he bianfang shaoka chuzhi qingkuang de yuanze*), in ZYBJ, 127.

[47] "Several Rules for the Implementation of the Center's Guiding Principles for the China-India Border Struggle in the Western Sector" (*guanche zhongyang guanyu ZhongYin bianjing xiduan douzheng fangzhen de ruogan guiding*), in ZYBJ, 152–153.

[48] Zhou contributed to this misperception in his conversations with Nehru.

[49] WP, VI, 43.

[50] The Indian negotiating strategy has always been predicated on the assumption that the only dispute exists in the west, not the east.

[51] Whiting, *Calculus*, 80.

even more than what Zhou offered in April 1960. Chen finally suggested issuing a joint statement, but delayed instructions from Nehru prevented its release.[52]

India replied to China's overtures on July 26. A diplomatic note stated that it would be willing to hold talks on the basis of the 1961 officials' report "as soon as the current tensions have eased and the appropriate climate is created."[53] China probed the ambiguity in India's response in early August, noting that that it would be willing to hold talks without preconditions.[54] Facing strong opposition from Parliament, however, Nehru stated that India would hold talks with China only when the 1957 status quo had been restored, requiring a Chinese withdrawal from the western sector and exposing the Xinjiang-Tibet highway.[55]

By the end of August, China's leaders had concluded that only military force could stop the deterioration of the situation on the China-India border. In mid-August, General Lei Yingfu, then deputy director of the GSD's Operations Department, toured the western sector. In his trip report, General Lei judged that the situation had already reached the point where "not fighting was not enough to prevent the Indian intrusions."[56] Throughout August and early September, the number of small-scale clashes began to increase, given the close proximity of troops.[57] The resumption of patrolling, the policy of armed coexistence, the general military buildup, and diplomatic initiatives had all failed to halt the decline in China's claim strength. From China's perspective, the combination of military deterrence and diplomatic warnings had been unable to arrest Indian pressure, much less start negotiations that would affirm the territorial status quo and secure the Tibetan frontier.

Dohla and the Decision for War

Against this backdrop of diplomatic stalemate and troop deployments in the western sector, a new confrontation emerged in early September around the Namka Chu area in the eastern sector. Amid the failure of

---

[52] Arthur Lall, *The Emergence of Modern India* (New York: Columbia University Press, 1981), 156. Chinese sources contain no information on these meetings.

[53] *WP*, VII, 4.

[54] *WP*, VII, 17–18.

[55] *WP*, VII, 36–37. On Parliament's role, see Nancy Jetly, *India China Relations, 1947–1977: A Study of Parliament's Role in the Making of Foreign Policy* (New Delhi: Radiant Publishers, 1979); Maxwell, *India's China War*, 253. Whiting argues that China's reference to holding talks "without conditions" needlessly provoked an Indian rejection of its offer. Whiting, *Calculus*, 88.

[56] Xu, *ZhongYin*, 91–92.

[57] *WP*, various volumes.

deterrence, this confrontation hardened China's leaders' perceptions of India's commitment to a military solution. As the confrontation over Namka Chu escalated, China's leaders concluded that only war would allow them to achieve their territorial objectives.

The Namka Chu region was an area at the western tip of the McMahon Line, near the China-India-Bhutan trijunction. As map 4.2 shows, the Namka Chu itself is a river that flows from west to east, parallel to the Thag La ridge of the Himalayan range. In this area, a discrepancy existed between the depiction of the McMahon Line on the 1914 map from the Simla Conference and the topographical features that might serve as an effective boundary.[58] For roughly its last 15 kilometers, the McMahon Line did not follow a watershed or a high ridge but was depicted as a straight line south of the highest ridge in the area. India claimed that McMahon had intended his line to follow the high ridge in the area, which contained a pass called Thag La. China had acknowledged the McMahon Line as the de facto boundary in the area but adopted a strict interpretation based on the 1914 map. In 1959, the Khinzemane confrontation and Longju clash both occurred in areas between the line and the natural features claimed by India as representing the boundary. During the expert meetings in 1960 after the Zhou-Nehru talks, China had stressed its opposition to India's interpretation of the McMahon Line.[59]

On June 4, 1962, India established a post on the south bank of the Namka Chu as part of the extension of the forward policy in the eastern sector. This position became known as the Dhola post, though in fact it was several kilometers north of a pass called Dhola.[60] In July and August, PLA units began to occupy positions along the Thag La ridge north of the Dhola post, which the Chinese called *chedong*.[61] Acting on GSD instructions, the Tibetan MD dispatched a patrol on September 6 to the Namka Chu to determine the status of India's post and, if necessary, establish a blocking position.[62]

On September 8, a reconnaissance company of approximately forty soldiers reached the Indian post at Dhola.[63] The company established a position on the north side of the Namka Chu, destroyed one of the log

---

[58] For a description, see Dalvi, *Himalayan Blunder*, 133–139; Maxwell, *India's China War*, 292–298; Palit, *War*, 190–191; Whiting, *Calculus*, 96–97.

[59] Hoffman, *India*, 110–111.

[60] The Indian officer in charge misnamed the post because of misgivings about its location north of the McMahon Line as depicted on the 1914 map. See Maxwell, *India's China War*, 295; Niranjan Prasad, *The Fall of Towang, 1962* (New Delhi: Palit & Palit, 1981), 23.

[61] *HCC*, 76, 94.

[62] *ZYBJ*, 158.

[63] *ZYBJ*, 158; *HCC*, 77.

bridges across the river, and threatened the Indian water supply.[64] The initial Indian reports flashed to headquarters stated that Dhola had been surrounded by more than six hundred Chinese soldiers, a deliberate exaggeration designed to speed the dispatch of reinforcements to what was otherwise an indefensible position located in a remote river valley. This misinformation, however, was not corrected for more than a week and certainly enhanced Indian fears of China's intentions. Viewing the Chinese move as an assault and not a blocking measure, India rapidly deployed reinforcements. Over the next week, Defense Minister Krishna Menon formulated a plan called "Operation Leghorn" to destroy China's new post, clear the PLA from south of the Thag La ridge, and establish posts on the Thag La ridge itself, all by force if necessary. On September 15, the Indian Army headquarters issued the implementing orders for this operation.[65]

Why China did not challenge the Indian position at Dhola earlier remains unclear. Whiting speculates that the Chinese challenge to Dhola was a final and carefully calculated probe of India's intentions, a decision that occurred after India's August 22 note that attached the precondition of a Chinese withdrawal for the opening of negotiations.[66] Historian Xu Yan states that China was not immediately aware of the post because the area south of Thag La was infrequently patrolled by Chinese forces and that local residents had informed the PLA of India's new position.[67] Indian sources indicate that China was aware of the post by the middle of July and had developed defensive positions on the southern slope of the ridge for roughly a brigade of troops.[68] In any case, the establishment of the Chinese post appeared to be an extension of China's armed coexistence policy from the western sector to the eastern sector in order to block any further Indian advances, especially in this contested area.[69]

In the following weeks, both sides began to reinforce their positions on either side of the Namka Chu. For India, China's move across Thag La represented a clear violation of the McMahon Line and an assault on Indian territory. News of the Chinese move fanned the flames of Indian public opinion, which pressed for a swift and forceful response. For

---

[64] Whiting, *Calculus*, 98.

[65] On Indian decision making, see Hoffman, *India*, 130–142; Maxwell, *India's China War*, 291–325; HCC, 95–96. Also Dalvi, *Himalayan Blunder*, 211; Kaul, *Untold Story*, 358–359.

[66] Whiting, *Calculus*, 96–98.

[67] Xu, *ZhongYin*, 96.

[68] Prasad, *Fall of Towang*, 22–24.

[69] Whiting further speculates that China's establishment of the Namka Chu post was linked to the September 13 offer to hold talks. In all available sources, however, there is no indication that the September 8 patrol was linked with this proposal.

China, India's rapid response represented an escalation beyond the tense stalemate in the western sector and affirmed General Lei's conclusion that only fighting could arrest Indian pressure. Both sides began to strengthen their positions along the river, though the Chinese held the advantage because of their proximity to a PLA base at Le, only a few kilometers north of the ridge along the Nyamjang Chu (see map 4.2). Moreover, the area was located along the edge of the Tibetan Plateau, which facilitated the movement of Chinese troops. By contrast, Indian forces had to march uphill to reach Thag La.

Similar to the sequence of events in the western sector, a diplomatic initiative accompanied China's extension of the armed coexistence policy to Thag La. On September 13, China proposed that both sides institute a 20-kilometer withdrawal to create a demilitarized area and hold talks in Beijing on October 15. The delivery of the Chinese note five days before India's public announcement of its intention to evict Chinese forces strengthens Whiting's conjecture that China's move into Namka Chu was linked to one last attempt to seek a negotiated settlement. By extending the policy of armed coexistence to disputed areas in the eastern sector such as Namka Chu, China sought not only to test India's commitment to using military pressure in the dispute but also to create leverage for its proposal to trade its claim in the east for its occupation of the western sector. Referring to the July attempt to open talks, the Chinese note stated that talks should be held without preconditions for the purpose of reducing tensions.[70] Another Chinese note issued on the same day included the warning that "he who plays with fire will eventually be consumed by fire."[71]

On September 19, India rejected China's offer. India repeated its position that it would hold talks only if China first agreed to withdraw from disputed areas in the western sector. Moreover, India's rejection of China's offer to hold talks was issued four days after Indian Army headquarters issued its implementing orders for Operation Leghorn and only one day after an Indian government spokesman announced publicly that the army had been instructed to remove the Chinese from Thag La, indicating that India was unlikely to negotiate.[72] After the Indian note, tensions increased further in both sectors, especially around Namka Chu.[73] On September 29, Indian forces attempted to outflank PLA positions by patrolling across the river.[74] Newly available sources indicate that clashes were initiated by both sides as they probed each other's positions.[75] Meanwhile,

[70] WP, VII, 73.

[71] WP, VII, 67–68.

[72] Kaul, Untold Story, 360; HCC, 95.

[73] ZYBJ, 160–161.

[74] Kaul, Untold Story, 363.

[75] ZYBJ, 160–162; HCC, 99–102.

India's public stance became more strident as a variety of Indian leaders issued pledges to evict the Chinese. These statements only strengthened the perception of China's leaders that India intended to persist with the forward policy, especially because India's rejection of unconditional talks was linked to its statements that Chinese troops would be removed from the disputed areas by force.

In early October, China again moved to open talks. On October 3, a Chinese diplomatic note called again for talks without preconditions on October 15. In the intervening period, however, two events convinced China's leaders that war with India would be necessary. On October 4, the Indian Army established a new unit, IV Corps, to implement Operation Leghorn and evict the PLA from Thag La. The establishment of IV Corps one day after China's third effort to open talks no doubt strengthened China's leaders' belief that India was dedicated to a military solution. Drawing on foreign press reports, a GSD report concluded on October 5 that "India had already decided to drive the Chinese back" and that India might soon launch an attack.[76] On October 6, India rejected China's third offer to open talks in a blunt diplomatic note. India stated that it would not negotiate under duress and demanded that China vacate the Namka Chu area as well as the western sector before any talks could be held.[77]

As India rejected China's third offer to negotiate, Mao and China's senior leaders decided that war was necessary. On October 5, Zhou Enlai ordered Luo Ruiqing, chief of the General Staff, to accelerate troop deployments along the border.[78] On October 6, the GSD transmitted instructions from Mao Zedong and the Central Committee, which stated "if the Indian army attacks, hit back ruthlessly. If they attack do not just repulse them, hit back ruthlessly so that it hurts."[79] According to the AMS history, these instructions outlined the general policy direction for a military campaign against India and stressed that operations would focus in the eastern sector around the Namka Chu.[80] The Indian plans to evict Chinese forces from south of Thag La, the creation of IV Corps, and the rejection of unconditional talks convinced China's leaders that only an offensive against India's troops along the disputed border would blunt Indian military pressure in the region.[81]

---

[76] *ZELNP2*, 500.

[77] *WP*, VII, 100–102.

[78] *ZELNP2*, 500.

[79] *ZYBJ*, 179.

[80] *ZYBJ*, 179. By demonstrating its resolve in the east, China hoped to create more bargaining flexibility over the west.

[81] Xu, *ZhongYin*, 106, 108.

Sometime between October 6 and 8, the CMC met to order the attack.[82] At this meeting, Foreign Minister Chen Yi, deputy chief of the GSD Yang Chengwu, and deputy director of the GSD's Operations Department Lei Yingfu all delivered reports.[83] On October 8, the GSD issued an advanced order (*yuxian haoling*) that formalized the decision to launch an attack in the eastern sector.[84] The order stated that the CMC had decided to attack Indian forces in the Namka Chu area with a diversionary operation at the eastern end of the McMahon Line and a complementary assault in the western sector. The timing of this meeting demonstrates that China chose war two full days before Indian forces sought to outflank PLA positions at Thag La on the evening of October 9, which sparked a large clash the following morning.[85]

Following the advanced order, the PLA began to prepare for battle. On October 8, Zhou Enlai met with the Soviet ambassador while the Chinese ambassador in Moscow, Liu Xiao, met with Khrushchev.[86] Both sought to inform Moscow of China's plans. On October 9, the CMC ordered the 130th Division based in Sichuan to enter Tibet immediately to support the upcoming operation, and the General Political Department issued instructions for political work the following day. The Tibetan MD established a frontline headquarters at Mama on October 14, and the construction of POW detention centers began on October 15. Meanwhile, frontline forces prepared for the final order to strike. On October 17, the CMC issued the "Operational Order to Destroy the Invading Indian Army" (*jianmie ruqin Yinjun de zuozhan mingling*). During an enlarged

---

[82] There are four separate descriptions of this meeting, but none of them state the date, only that it occurred in the middle of October. One of the outcomes of the meeting, however, was the transfer of the 130th Division from Sichuan to Tibet, which the CMC ordered on October 9, indicating that the meeting was held sometime between October 6 and 8. See Wang Hongwei, *Ximalaya*, 228–230; Xiao Xinli, *Mao Zedong*, 336–338. For additional details, see Lei Yingfu, *Zai zuigao tongshuaibu dang canmou: Lei Yingfu huiyilu* [Staff Officer at the Supreme Command: General Lei Yingfu's Recollections] (Nanchang: Baihuazhou wenyi chubanshe, 1997), 206–209; Wang Shangrong, "Xin Zhongguo," 281–285. For the decision to transfer the 130th Division, see *ZYBJ*, 472; Xiao, *Mao Zedong*, 338.

[83] Other attendees included Zhou Enlai (premier), Lin Biao (defense minister), Ye Jianying (retired marshal), Liu Bocheng (retired marshal), Luo Ruiqing (chief of the General Staff), Xiao Hua (General Political Warfare Department director), Zhang Guohua (Tibetan MD commander), and He Jiachan (Xinjiang MD commander).

[84] "Advanced Order to Destroy India's Invasion of Kejielang [Namka Chu]" (*jianmie ruqin kejielang Yinjun yuxian haoling*), in *ZYBJ*, 472.

[85] K. C. Praval, *The Red Eagles: A History of the Fourth Division of India* (New Delhi: Vision Books, 1982), 229–233.

[86] *ZELNP2*, 502; Liu Xiao, *Chushi Sulian ba nian* [Eight Years as Ambassador to the Soviet Union] (Beijing: Zhonggong dangshi ziliao chubanshe, 1986), 121.

meeting of the Politburo on October 18, the final order was given to launch the offensive on October 20.[87]

China's military objectives in its Himalayan campaign were clearly linked to the ongoing concerns about territorial integrity that had emerged in 1962, especially concerns regarding Indian pressure on China's southwestern frontier. According to the CMC's operational order, China's objectives were threefold: to protect the stability of the homeland's frontiers (*baowei zuguo bianjiang anning*), to create conditions for a negotiated settlement of the dispute, and to attack "reactionaries."[88] The immediate objective was to destroy Indian positions in disputed areas along the line of actual control, thereby eliminating India's instruments of military pressure. By destroying the military assets of the forward policy, China further hoped to create conditions for a package-deal settlement by demonstrating that only negotiations based on the territorial status quo could resolve the dispute.

China's military objectives sought to counter China's declining claim strength in the dispute. Since the spring and summer of 1962, India had been increasing the amount of contested territory it held and strengthening its position in the local military balance. The economic crisis of the Great Leap, instability in Xinjiang, and tensions across the Taiwan Strait all enhanced the threat that India posed to China's vulnerable Tibetan region. As Mao observed in July, "they want to use the opportunity of our temporary difficulties to push us into battle."[89] China's mix of diplomacy and deterrence had failed. In the eastern sector, India's preparations to attack Chinese positions on Thag La and its third refusal to hold talks provided the final nails in a coffin that had been built throughout the summer of 1962.[90] China's senior civilian and military leaders concluded that there was no option short of war that could halt India's efforts to change the local balance of forces and strengthen its claim in the dispute.

China's leaders identified three reasons for fighting, which reflect concerns with declining claim strength. First, they believed that India continued to harbor territorial ambitions in Tibet. In an oral report to Mao during the October CMC meeting, General Lei Yingfu described Nehru as continuing the British policy of northern expansion into Tibet, seeking to transform Tibet into an Indian colony (*zhimin di*) or protectorate (*baohu guo*).[91] In Chinese eyes, Nehru first opposed China's occupation of Tibet in 1950, later supported Tibetan rebels, and then provided refuge

---

[87] *ZYBJ*, 471–474.
[88] *ZYBJ*, 473–474. Also see *ZYBJ*, 178.
[89] *ZYBJ*, 142.
[90] Xu, *ZhongYin*, 106–108.
[91] Lei, *Zai zuigao tongshuaibu*, 207. Also, see Garver, "China's Decision."

to the Dalai Lama. After China's suppression of the Tibetan rebellion, Indian policy shifted from supporting groups inside China to intensifying the territorial dispute. Nehru's formal claim to the Aksai Chin on March 22, 1959, two days after the outbreak of the rebellion in Lhasa, was no coincidence for China's leaders. The territorial dispute was not just about contested territory but also about India's broader goals in China's vulnerable frontier. According to the October 17 order, war was necessary because India otherwise would continue to press north and expand inside Tibet and Aksai Chin.[92] Without war, China's claim would continue to weaken, potentially threatening stability within Tibet.

Second, China's leaders concluded that India was deliberately taking advantage of China's current domestic weakness. General Lei stated that Nehru believed China was facing threats on multiple fronts, especially from the USSR and the United States, during a period of economic upheaval and as a result would not be willing to fight with India.[93] As Zhou stated in an internal speech after the attack, "they reckoned that our famine was very serious, Tibet was empty, the rebellion unsettled."[94] He also noted, "when you have no room for retreat and you do not counterattack, that is really showing weakness and they will believe that you are easily cowed."[95] The implication for Chinese leaders was that outsiders were seeking to profit from China's internal difficulties and believed that China lacked the resolve to defend its territorial interests. Moreover, given this belief, China's leaders viewed fighting with India as not only securing its frontier in the southwest but also deterring other territorial challenges during a period of continued domestic instability.

Third and most importantly, China's leaders themselves had concluded that the policy of restraint and diplomacy had failed to bring stability to the Chinese-Indian border. As Zhou stated, "They wouldn't talk with us! What should I do! We tried several times, but it wouldn't work."[96] In his report, General Lei stated that, since 1950, China had tolerated and made concessions to India's "expansionist" policy by not sending troops or using force when India occupied areas claimed by China.[97] Even the shift to patrolling and armed coexistence had failed to halt Indian efforts to dominate Chinese positions. Lei concluded that Nehru believed China was "weak and easily bullied." Proof for China was the continuation of the forward policy and India's intention to evict Chinese forces from Thag La. Chinese military historian Xu Yan also notes the importance of the

[92] *ZYBJ*, 473–474.
[93] Lei, *Zai zuigao tongshuaibu*, 207.
[94] *Zhou Enlai junshi wenxuan*, 472.
[95] *Zhou Enlai junshi wenxuan*, 472.
[96] *Zhou Enlai junshi wenxuan*, 471.
[97] Lei, *Zai zuigao tongshuaibu*, 208.

inability of armed coexistence to arrest Indian pressure on the border. After each small engagement, Indian forces returned. Unless Indian forces were destroyed, the border would "not be peaceful for a very long time."[98] According to Xu, China's leaders believed that stability on the border could be secured only by fighting fiercely, thereby teaching "the invaders" that they would not be able to conduct similar "nibbling" in the future.[99]

On October 18, the Politburo held an enlarged meeting to discuss the attack against India. During this meeting, Mao summarized China's reasons for going to war with India, which underscored the long-term vulnerability that would exist if China failed to act. According to General Lei, Mao said:

> For many years we have adopted many different methods to seek a peaceful resolution of the border problem, but India refuses to do so. Deliberately provoking armed conflicts, which are more progressive and more fierce, is definitely going too far [*qi ren tai shen*]. A colloquial saying goes conflict creates communication [*buda bu chengjiao*]. If we counterattack one time, then the border will become stable and the boundary problem can be peacefully resolved. Only then can our hopes be realized. But our counterattack is only to warn and punish, only to tell Nehru and the Indian government that they cannot use military means to resolve the border problem.[100]

Two days later, the PLA launched an offensive and started the 1962 Chinese-Indian War.

Military and diplomatic operations during the first phase of the war provide further support for the role of growing weakness in the dispute. In the first phase of the campaign, from October 20 to 25, PLA units concentrated their offensive on India's frontline positions that had been established under the forward policy. After the PLA destroyed these units and paused on the battlefield, Zhou sent a note to Nehru proposing that China would withdraw to the north of the McMahon Line if the two sides established a demilitarized zone along the line of actual control and held talks at the prime ministerial level.[101] The launching of the second phase, in mid-November, occurred after India refused Zhou's offer. After the PLA routed Indian forces throughout the NEFA region, Zhou announced that China would institute a unilateral withdrawal to the November 1959 line of control, again a clear signal that China did not pursue expansionist aims in its war with India.

[98] Xu, *ZhongYin*, 110.
[99] Xu, *ZhongYin*, 110.
[100] Quoted in Lei, *Zai zuigao tongshuaibu*, 210.
[101] *RMRB*, 24 October 1962, 1; *RMRB*, 27 October 1962, 1.

In both phases, China limited its advance to those areas that it claimed but did not occupy. At the end of the withdrawal, the line of actual control (LAC) separating Indian and Chinese forces was similar to that which existed before the start of the forward policy. China claimed officially that its forces had withdrawn to the November 1959 line of control. China may have gained some additional territory even after its withdrawal. With its victory on the battlefield, China was clearly able to occupy whatever areas it wanted.

Conflict and Stability after 1962

Following the 1962 war, the China-India border witnessed three main periods of tension. As discussed in chapter 1, in September 1965 China mobilized forces along the western sector to support Pakistan in its war with India by threatening to open a second front in the Himalayas. Even though China's actions increased tensions on the border and resulted in several armed clashes, the objective was extended deterrence, not territorial claims. China's uses-of force in 1967 at Nathu La and in 1986 over Sumdurong Chu, however, further reflect the effects of negative shifts in claim strength and bargaining power in decisions to escalate territorial disputes. These events also illustrate the effects of regime insecurity on the use of force, as this factor was much more prominent in 1967 than during the 1986 crisis over Sumdurong Chu.

1967—CENTRAL SECTOR

On September 11, 1967, Chinese forces at Nathu La in the central sector unleashed a punishing attack on Indian forces (see map 2.1). When the clash ended two days later, thirty-two Chinese and sixty-five Indian soldiers had been killed.[102] On October 1, a similar clash erupted between border guards at Cho La in which thirty-six Indian soldiers and an unknown number of Chinese were killed.[103] Both clashes were limited to the central sector along the China-Sikkim border.

Although sources on these events are limited, three factors highlight the role of declining claim strength in China's decision to initiate the use of force. First, following its defeat in the 1962 war, the Indian Army doubled in size. As part of this expansion, a total of ten mountain divisions were

---

[102] *HCC*, xxiv; Wang Chenghan, *Wang Chenghan huiyilu* [Wang Chenghan's Memoirs] (Beijing: Jiefangjun chubanshe, 2004), 482. Also see "1962 nian yihou ZhongYin bianjing de liangci jiaoda chongtu" [Two Relatively Large Conflicts on the Chinese-Indian Border after 1962], from http://bwl.top81.com.cn/war_cn/india/202.htm.

[103] "1962 nian yihou."

raised to guard India's northern borders.[104] Although three of these divisions faced Pakistan, the others were deployed to defend against any Chinese attack. Most of these forces were not based near the border, with the exception of the Chumbi Valley, where troops from both sides were deployed in close proximity to each other, often just a few meters apart at certain key passes such as Nathu La. As a result, as the number of Indian troops increased in this area, small-scale clashes were reported frequently in the press starting in 1963.

Second, India appeared to become more aggressive in asserting its claims near the border. At Nathu La, under the shadow of India's military expansion, efforts by both sides to strengthen their control of the pass resulted in a Chinese attack on September 11, 1967. Confrontations between the two sides had become frequent and, as the LAC was undemarcated, even fistfights among border guards were not uncommon.[105] In August 1967, India began to erect barbed wire fencing to form a barrier between the two sides and reduce tensions. The PLA commander, however, viewed this as seizure of Chinese territory, resulting in verbal protests and shoving matches into early September. On September 11, Indian Army engineers began to erect a new stretch of fencing. According to an Indian memoir, after issuing a protest, the PLA soldiers returned to their positions and then opened fire with machine guns and artillery. Indian artillery soon responded, sparking a three-day duel in which many PLA fortifications at Nathu La were destroyed because India controlled the high ground near the pass.[106]

Third, the turmoil associated with China's Cultural Revolution was likely a contributing factor in Chinese perceptions of Indian actions. The Chinese attack in September 1967 followed perhaps the most unstable period of the Cultural Revolution, as events began to spin beyond the control of the central government over the summer of 1967.[107] Given the tensions on the border and perceived pressure from India to enforce its claims, Chinese leaders likely magnified the potential threat from India and concluded that a forceful response was required.

Although the competition to control disputed land in the Chumbi Valley played a key role in the escalating tensions, the actual Chinese attack

[104] Lorne J. Kavic, *India's Quest for Security: Defence Policies, 1947–1965* (Berkeley: University of California Press, 1967), 192–196.

[105] G. S. Bajpai, *China's Shadow over Sikkim: The Politics of Intimidation* (New Delhi: Lancer Publishers, 1999), 156–181.

[106] Bajpai, *China's Shadow*, 183–195. Also, Sheru Thapliyal, "Nathula Skirmish of 1967," *Force* (January 2006), OSC#SAP20060228016001.

[107] Roderick MacFarquhar and Michael Schoenhals, *Mao's Last Revolution* (Cambridge, Mass.: Belknap Press of Harvard University Press, 2006); Andrew G. Walder and Yang Su,

may not have been authorized by the CMC. According to General Wang Chenghan's memoir, the Tibetan MD did not establish a frontline headquarters at Yadong, near Nathu La, until after the initial exchange of fire on September 11. When General Wang arrived at Yadong on September 12, he organized a mobile reserve force and dispatched heavy artillery pieces to Nathu La, as the frontline PLA troops were initially outgunned.[108] The only record of Zhou Enlai's involvement in the clash is instructions that appear to have been issued after the attack stating that Chinese forces should return fire only if fired upon.[109] For the PLA, the establishment of a frontline headquarters and rules of engagement usually precedes the initiation of any authorized operation.

1986—EASTERN SECTOR

Following the 1967 clashes in the central sector, the Chinese-Indian border witnessed almost twenty years of stability. China focused instead on countering a potential Soviet attack from the north, especially in the 1970s. Areas along the Chinese-Indian border that Chinese troops had vacated after 1962 in the eastern and western sectors remained neutral zones unoccupied by either side. In 1981, the two sides began their first formal talks over the territorial dispute.

In July 1986, reports from New Delhi that China had seized a seasonal Indian observation post near the Thag La ridge in the eastern sector shattered this stability. Over the next twelve months, both sides deployed significant forces to the area, sparking fears of a second China-India war. At the height of the crisis, India deployed two mountain divisions near Sumdurong Chu along with a third elsewhere in the eastern sector while China mobilized units from the Chengdu and Lanzhou MRs.[110]

Three factors likely account for the Chinese occupation of the Indian post, which was located in an area south of Thag La along the Sumdurong Chu River. First, India had established this post in 1984 by seizing land in the neutral zone between the McMahon Line and the high ridge line (see map 4.2). After the 1962 war, neither side maintained a presence here until India's IB moved into the area.[111] From China's perspective, India's own action represented a clear challenge to the status quo in this sensitive

"The Cultural Revolution in the Countryside: Scope, Timing and Human Impact," *The China Quarterly*, no. 173 (March 2003): 85.

[108] Wang, *Wang Chenghan*, 481–482.

[109] Liu and Du, *Zhou Enlai junshi huodong jishi (xia)*, 667.

[110] Pravin Sawhney, *The Defence Makeover: 10 Myths That Shape India's Image* (New Delhi: Sage Publications, 2002), 30. For a detailed account, see John W. Garver, "Sino-Indian Rapprochement and the Sino-Pakistan Entente," *Political Science Quarterly*, vol. 111, no. 2 (Summer 1996): 337–343.

[111] Garver, "Sino-Indian Rapprochement," 338.

sector. As the post was seasonal, China occupied it in May or June before the Indian soldiers returned after vacating the post for the winter.[112]

Second, India's move toward Thag La occurred amid a much broader effort to strengthen its military position in the eastern sector. Code-named "Operation Falcon," army chief Khrisna Rao's plan envisioned the occupation of strategic heights on the Indian side of the line of actual control "as close to the McMahon [Line] as possible."[113] The goal was to ensure defense of the Tawang tract, which Chinese troops had overrun in 1962, and consolidate control of this sector to limit any potential concessions to China in the ongoing negotiations. This was the first such effort to strengthen defenses along the McMahon Line since 1967. Third, the boundary talks started in 1981 had stalled. Although China had agreed to India's request for a sector-by-sector approach, each side adopted irreconcilable negotiating positions over the eastern sector at the sixth round of talks in November 1985 based on divergent interpretations of the location of the McMahon Line. Thus, as India strengthened its military position in the eastern sector, both sides adopted more rigid negotiating positions.[114]

Following the report of the Chinese occupation, the situation escalated quickly. By October, India had airlifted a brigade to Zimithang, a ridge overlooking Sumdurong Chu. The brigade reportedly prepared to attack the Chinese contingent, which had not fortified its position and was exposed to Indian forces dominating the high ground.[115] The following spring, both sides deployed large formations of troops to the area under the pretext of military exercises. By May, troop levels around Sumdurong Chu exceeded those at the start of the 1962 war, reaching as high as 50,000.[116]

Although the Chinese-Indian border appeared primed for conflict, the situation did not escalate further. Tensions subsided in June 1987 when the Indian foreign minister visited Beijing and the two sides agreed to resume border talks. In August, Indian and Chinese forces withdrew some troops from the area.[117] China did not further escalate the dispute in 1987

---

[112] Mira Sinha Bhattacharjea, "India-China: The Year of Two Possibilities," in Satish Kumar, ed., *Yearbook on India's Foreign Policy, 1985–86* (New Delhi: Sage Publications, 1988), 152, 156; T. Karki Hussain, "India's China Policy: Putting Politics in Command," in Satish Kumar, ed., *Yearbook on India's Foreign Policy, 1989* (New Delhi: Sage Publications, 1990), 121; Sawhney, *Defence Makeover*, 29.

[113] "Red Heat," *Force* (December 2004), OSC# SAP20041209000096.

[114] Bhattacharjea, "India-China," 152–155.

[115] Hussain, "India's China Policy," 122.

[116] On Indian forces, see Sawhney, *Defence Makeover*, 30. On Chinese forces, see *FEER*, 4 June 1987, 42.

[117] AP, 15 June 1987; Reuters, 14 August 1987 (Factiva).

for several reasons. The Indian effort to occupy vacant territory was limited to one small area in the eastern sector. By contrast, India's forward policy in 1962 had extended along the entire frontage of the western sector. Although both sides responded vigorously in 1987, the scope of the mobilization was limited to the Thag La area. China was able to match India's deployments, thereby maintaining its position in the local military balance. Finally, the Chinese state was much more stable in 1987 than in 1962. The central government maintained firm control over Tibet. The CCP's legitimacy improved steadily under Deng's opening and reform program. China had begun to normalize relations with the Soviet Union and maintained warm ties with the United States.

One might argue that China's occupation of the post at Sumdurong Chu and mobilization against India was intended to signal resolve to its other rivals, especially the Soviet Union. Several factors, however, weigh against this argument. China did not publicize its 1986 occupation of the Indian post, yet such publicity would have been a key part of any effort to signal resolve to other countries. Instead, the occupation surfaced only when it was reported by the Indian press a month later. Although China did mobilize large-scale forces in 1987, ties with the Soviet Union had begun to improve following Gorbachev's speech at Vladivostok in July 1986.

After the Sumdurong Chu incident, China's position in its dispute with India stabilized. Neither country erected new outposts in other neutral zones. In 1993 and 1996, agreements to observe the line of actual control and limit the number of troops along the disputed border greatly reduced the potential for shifts in the local military balance or for the occupation of vacant territory by either side that might create incentives to use force. Although a final settlement of this dispute remains elusive, stability has prevailed in the region since 1987.

1969: Zhenbao Island Ambush

On the morning of March 2, 1969, two Chinese patrols on Zhenbao Island in the Ussuri (Wusuli) River ambushed Soviet border guards, sparking perhaps the most tense period of China's own Cold War with the Soviet Union. This use of force represented a stark departure from Beijing's delaying strategy in the dispute with Moscow following the effort to compromise during the 1964 talks discussed in chapter 2. A second clash occurred less than two weeks later, on March 15. In these engagements, China suffered 91 casualties (30 killed, 61 wounded) while the

Soviet Union suffered more than 200 casualties (approximately 91 killed and 109 wounded).[118]

The Chinese ambush sparked a summer of tension and hostility all along the Chinese-Soviet border as well as a sustained Soviet effort to bolster its defenses in the Far East. To deter further Chinese attacks, Moscow used a combination of diplomacy and military threats to bring Beijing to the negotiating table. These actions culminated in a series of nuclear threats against China in August 1969, including hints that the USSR might launch a preemptive strike against China's nuclear facilities in Xinjiang.[119] Tensions began to ease after Zhou Enlai met with Premier Alexey Kosygin at the Beijing airport on September 11. Formal talks between the sides followed in October and lasted until 1978. Nevertheless, although the Soviets succeed in opening talks with China, these sessions achieved little progress toward resolving conflicting claims in the dispute, stressing instead conflict prevention and crisis management.[120]

The analysis below examines the Chinese decision to initiate the March 2 ambush, the event that defined Chinese-Soviet relations throughout the

---

[118] Xu Yan, "1969 nian ZhongSu bianjie de wuzhuang chongtu" [The 1969 Armed Conflict on the Chinese-Soviet Border], *Dangshi yanjiu ziliao*, no. 5 (1994): 7–8.

[119] Thomas W. Robinson, "The Sino-Soviet Border Conflict," in Stephen S. Kaplan, ed., *Diplomacy of Power: Soviet Armed Forces as a Political Instrument* (Washington, D. C.: The Brookings Institution, 1981); Yang Kuisong, *Mao Zedong yu Mosike de enen yuanyuan* [Personal Feelings between Mao Zedong and Moscow] (Nanchang: Jiangxi renmin chubanshe, 1999), 494–509.

[120] For overviews of the clash, see Gurtov and Hwang, *China under Threat*, 187–241; Thomas W. Robinson, *The Sino-Soviet Border Dispute: Background, Development and the March 1969 Clashes* (Santa Monica, Calif.: RAND Corp., 1970); Robinson, "Sino-Soviet Border," 265–313; Segal, *Defending China*, 176–196; Richard Wich, *Sino-Soviet Crisis Politics: A Study of Political Change and Communication* (Cambridge, Mass.: Harvard University Press, 1980).

For Chinese sources, see *DDZGJD*, 635–645; Li Ke and Hao Shengzhang, *Wenhua dageming zhong de renmin jiefangjun* [The People's Liberation Army during the Cultural Revolution] (Beijing: Zhonggong dangshi ziliao chubanshe, 1989), 312–326; Xu, "1969," 2–13; Yang, *Mao Zedong*, 485–513. Of these, the chapter by Li and Hao is foundational because it has served as the empirical basis for almost every subsequent scholarly Chinese article on the subject.

Other important Chinese sources include Li Danhui, "1969 nian ZhongSu bianjie chongtu: yuanqi he jieguo" [The 1969 Chinese-Soviet Border Conflict: Origins and Outcome], *Dangdai Zhongguo shi yanjiu*, no. 3 (1996): 39–50; Li Lianqing, *Lengnuan suiyue: yibo sanzhe de ZhongSu guanxi* [Hot and Cold Times: The Twists and Turns of Chinese-Soviet Relations] (Beijing: Shijie zhishi chubanshe, 1999), 346–383; Niu Jun, "1969 nian ZhongSu bianjie chongtu yu Zhongguo waijiao zhanlue de tiaozheng" [The 1969 Chinese-Soviet Border Conflict and the Restructuring of China's Diplomatic Strategy], *Dangdai Zhongguo shi yanjiu*, no. 1 (1999): 66–77; Xiao Xinli, *Mao Zedong*, 388–397; Yu Yan, *Wushi nian guoshi jiyao: junshi juan* [Summary of 50 Years of State Affairs: Military Affairs] (Changsha: Hunan remin chubanshe, 1999), 528–551.

1970s. By using force, China's leaders sought to counter a steep decline in their bargaining power in the varied territorial disputes with the Soviet Union. In the years preceding the clash, China's claim strength had declined considerably as the Soviets doubled their number of troops in the Far East in less than four years and adopted an assertive, forward-patrolling posture in disputed areas, especially on the islands in the eastern sector. The enunciation in September 1968 of the Brezhnev doctrine to interfere in the affairs of socialist states only increased China's perception of decline, especially given the domestic instability of the Cultural Revolution. Newly available documents support earlier interpretations of China's motives, demonstrating a clear link between the Soviet military posture and China's willingness to use force.[121]

Rivalry?

At one level, China's decision to use force in 1969 cannot be separated from its broader rivalry with the Soviet Union. The rivalry centered on leadership of the socialist bloc, and it was one that China was losing in the late 1960s, especially after the start of the Cultural Revolution. The Soviet troops deployed to the Far East during this period exceeded those required to defend the Soviets' own territorial claims or to deter a Chinese attack and thus clearly had a coercive purpose given the hostile relations between the two sides. The Brezhnev doctrine implied that the Soviets might coerce regime change in China to strengthen the socialist bloc against the West, and the troops on the border were an instrument of such change. When China launched its ambush on Zhenbao, it signaled not only its resolve to defend its territorial claims that the Soviet Union had threatened but also its commitment to resist Soviet coercion more broadly.

By the late 1960s, however, the territorial disputes had come to play a central role in the rivalry. Communication between the two communist parties had ceased, and China was isolated from almost every other socialist state along with most Western countries. After 1966, the Soviet Union used pressure in the territorial dispute to intimidate China, which further increased the prominence of the dispute in the rivalry. As a result, it is difficult in this period to separate competition in the dispute from competition in the rivalry. Once the rivalry was hitched to the territorial dispute, my theory of escalation explains the Chinese decision to use force. Although China's actions in the territorial conflict had broader implications, it is consistent with the logic of declining claim strength.

[121] Gurtov and Hwang, *China under Threat*, 187–241; Robinson, *Sino-Soviet Border*; Robinson, "Sino-Soviet Border," 265–313; Segal, *Defending China*, 176–196; Wich, *Sino-Soviet Crisis*.

Declining Claim Strength

China's declining claim strength in 1969 stemmed from three factors. First and most importantly, Soviet troop deployments in the Far East threatened China's position in the local military balance. Following the hard break in relations between the communist parties of the two countries in 1964, the Soviet Union began to shift its military policy toward China in early 1965 by increasing the number of troops stationed along the Chinese-Soviet border.[122] In 1966, as the split deepened, the Soviet Union signed a defense treaty with Mongolia, which allowed it to deploy troops along an additional 2,000 kilometers of China's northern frontier.[123] By 1969, the total number of Soviet divisions facing China had doubled from fourteen in 1965 to as many as thirty-four.[124] Moreover, as illustrated in figure 4.1, these deployments represented a dramatic shift in the number of Soviet troops facing China since the late 1950s. Although complete data going back to 1949 are unavailable, the increased deployments after 1965 constituted a stark and dramatic shift in the local balance of forces on the border.

Assessing the precise balance of forces is tricky. China enjoyed a purely numerical superiority, with approximately fifty-nine divisions in its three northern military regions (MR) compared with thirty-four Soviet divisions.[125] Declassified CIA estimates, however, reveal several aspects of the Soviet deployments that likely weakened China's position in the local balance. First, as discussed above, the number of Soviet troops deployed on the border with China had doubled in a roughly four-year period before the ambush. China had not matched these deployments, so the Soviets had strengthened their position relative to the previous balance. Second, Soviet troops adopted an offensive posture along the border. Approximately 70 percent of the USSR's troops in the Far East were based along the border with Manchuria, China's industrial heartland, threatening not just disputed territory but China's territorial integrity more broadly. In addition, these troops were deployed near the border. Although this was dictated by the need to defend the Trans-Siberian Railway, which ran along the Chinese-Soviet border, it was nevertheless threatening (see map 3.1). By contrast, China deployed only nine divi-

---

[122] On the Chinese-Soviet relations, see Lorenz Luthi, *The Sino-Soviet Split* (Princeton, N.J: Princeton University Press, 2008).

[123] Office of National Estimates, *The Soviet Military Buildup along the Chinese Border*, SM-7–68 [Top Secret] (Washington, D.C.: Central Intelligence Agency, 1968).

[124] Directorate of Intelligence, *Military Forces along the Sino-Soviet Border*, SR-IM-70–5 [Top Secret] (Washington, D.C.: Central Intelligence Agency, 1970).

[125] National Intelligence Board, *The USSR and China*, NIE 11–13–69 [Top Secret] (Washington, D.C.: Central Intelligence Agency, 1969), 5.

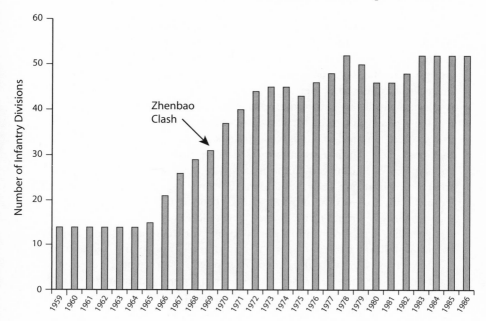

Figure 4.1 Soviet Troops Deployed along China's Land Border (1959–1986)

Source: Central Intelligence Agency, *Military Forces along the Sino-Soviet Border*, SM-70-5 (Washington, D.C.: Central Intelligence Agency, 1970); Office of National Estimates, *Soviet Military Buildup*; Robinson, "China Confronts the Soviet Union," 299; Gerald Segal, *Sino-Soviet Relations after Mao*, Adelphi Paper No. 202 (London: International Institute for Strategic Studies, 1994).

sions near the border, placing the rest in reserve 500 or more kilometers away.[126] Third, the Soviet troops possessed superior equipment. Most Soviet divisions were mechanized, while China possessed only light infantry. Even two years after the clash, China's best divisions in the north possessed only one-third of the artillery and wheeled vehicles of the Soviet units and only one-sixth of the tracked vehicles.[127] In addition, the Soviets had about 600 tactical aircraft in the region, while China had only 294.[128]

Lyle Goldstein argues that the Soviet buildup after the March 1969 clash demonstrates that the Soviets were far more worried about the local balance than the Chinese. Between 1969 and 1976, the number of Soviet

[126] National Intelligence Board, *The USSR and China*, 5.

[127] National Intelligence Board, *Warsaw Pact Forces for Operations in Eurasia*, NIE 11–14–71 [Top Secret] (Washington, D.C.: Central Intelligence Agency, 1971), 27.

[128] Directorate of Intelligence, *Military Forces along the Sino-Soviet Border*, 5.

divisions in the region increased from thirty-four to forty-three.[129] Nevertheless, the post-1969 buildup is a poor indicator of how leaders assessed the local balance and the threat it posed before the March clash. Indeed, even though the PLA maintained numerical superiority, China's leaders viewed the increased Soviet deployments as representing a sharp decline in China's ability to secure the border and project power over disputed areas, especially given the forward posture of Soviet troops. In December 1966, Chen Yi noted to foreign journalists that the Soviet Union "has 13 divisions on the Chinese frontier moved there from Eastern Europe."[130] In January 1967, Mao urged Chinese troops to increase their preparedness: "there are more air activities along the Sinkiang border, and [Soviet] ground forces are on the move."[131] In October 1968, the *People's Daily* began openly referring to the Soviet troop increases.[132] The increased Soviet presence was worrying in part because it threatened to add a third potential military front for China in addition to Taiwan and Vietnam. In relative terms, China's ability to project power over disputed areas and resist Soviet coercion decreased with the Soviet deployments even though China may have maintained an advantageous position in terms of total troop numbers and, in the northeast, shorter supply lines.

The second source of decline was the assertive pattern of patrolling that Soviet forces adopted in the Far East. This pattern of patrolling signaled how the Soviets might use the troops that they were deploying along the border.[133] Before the 1962 Yita incident, neither side aggressively patrolled the border, though violations by civilians were quite common. After the failed 1964 talks, China continued to assert its claims by using disputed areas, especially islands in the Amur and Ussuri rivers that were allocated to China in the talks. Nevertheless, in 1966, Soviet border guards were ordered to adopt a new approach. According to one Soviet diplomat's recollection, Soviet border guards were instructed to "rebuff all attempts by the Chinese to land on the islands" but to "exercise restraint" by not using small arms.[134]

[129] Thomas W. Robinson, "China Confronts the Soviet Union: Warfare and Diplomacy on China's Inner Asian Frontiers," in Roderick MacFarquhar and John K. Fairbank, eds., *The Cambridge History of China*, vol. 15, part 2 (Cambridge: Cambridge University Press, 1991), 299. On Goldstein, see note 139.

[130] *NYT*, 11 December 1966, 3.

[131] Quoted in *Current Background*, no. 892 (21 October 1969): 50.

[132] *RMRB*, 1 October 1968, 6.

[133] For a detailed discussion, see Gurtov and Hwang, *China under Threat*, 208–216; Wich, *Sino-Soviet Crisis*, 97–99.

[134] Sergei Goncharov and Victor Usov, "Kosygin-Zhou Talks at Beijing Airport," *Far Eastern Affairs*, no. 4–6 (1992): 98.

The Soviet shift to a more assertive patrolling posture was particularly alarming for China because it signaled a rejection of the consensus reached in 1964 for the eastern sector. As discussed in chapter 2, roughly half of the disputed river islands were allocated to China. Even before the 1964 agreement, many of these islands had been used by Chinese peasants, as they were located close to the Chinese bank of the river. It was precisely these islands that became nodes of confrontation after 1967. Whenever Chinese civilians or patrols approached them, especially in the winter months, Soviet border guards would move to evict them. As the number of incidents increased, China began to increase the number of armed patrols. In most cases, Soviet forces used clubs and armored vehicles to compel the Chinese to leave, occasionally injuring or killing Chinese personnel. On these occasions, Chinese forces responded by using the same level of force but not firing small arms.[135]

In the years preceding the 1969 clash on Zhenbao Island, the number and scope of Soviet patrols increased. In 1966, the Soviet Union began to blockade Chinese navigation to the north and east of the disputed Heixiazi Island at the confluence of the Amur and Ussuri rivers.[136] In 1967, the first confrontations on river islands occurred on Wubalao Island in the Amur (Heilongjiang) River (see map 3.1).[137] By the end of 1968, river island confrontations had spread to Qiliqin and Zhenbao islands, both in the Ussuri River. On January 5, 1968, five Chinese were killed in a confrontation with Soviet border guards. In the preceding two months, a total of eighteen confrontations had occurred over Qiliqin Island.[138] In all these instances, which usually resulted in severe beatings and eviction from disputed areas, Soviet border guards vastly outnumbered the Chinese patrols.

The August 1968 Soviet military intervention in Czechoslovakia presented a third source of pressure, as it altered the context of the growing troop deployments and violent confrontations over the river islands. The September 1968 announcement of the Brezhnev doctrine, which asserted Moscow's right to intervene in the affairs of other socialist states, created fears that the Soviets might seek to use military pressure against China. Goldstein argues the role of the Brezhnev doctrine in Chinese thinking is overstated. It was a "minor event" because it did not block NATO from pursuing détente and Soviet intervention in Eastern Europe affirmed the

---

[135] After January 1968, Chinese frontier defense forces were specifically instructed to "counterattack" with a corresponding level of force and not to escalate the dispute. Li and Hao, *Wenhua dageming*, 317; Xu, "1969," 5.

[136] Xu, "1969," 4.

[137] Meng Zhaobi, ed., *Xinjiang tongzhi: junshi zhi* [Xinjiang Gazetteer: Military Affairs] (Wulumuqi: Xinjiang renmin chubanshe, 1997), 179; Xu, "1969," 4.

[138] Li and Hao, *Wenhua dageming*, 317; Li, *Lengnuan suiyue*, 346–347; Xu, "1969," 5.

status quo.[139] China's leaders, however, seemed to have a different view.[140] Only a few weeks after the Soviet action in Czechoslovakia, the Chinese Foreign Ministry protested publicly against repeated violations of China's airspace. The statement noted that the occurrence of these violations after the intervention in Czechoslovakia was "absolutely not coincidental."[141] In remarks to an Albanian delegation on China's national day, Zhou Enlai linked Soviet actions in Eastern Europe with further "provocations" against China, including "deploying large numbers of troops on the Chinese-Soviet and Chinese-Mongolian border."[142] At the same time, Zhou gave a speech that tied Soviet revisionism with a possible invasion, while PLA chief of the General Staff Huang Yongsheng stressed concerns about Soviet troops on the border.[143] In late December 1968, China tested a three-megaton nuclear device, which was not announced publicly but would have been detected by the Soviet Union.[144]

Once the ice began to harden on the Amur and Ussuri rivers, the number of armed confrontations between the two sides increased. In the winter of 1969, the focus of confrontation shifted south from Qiliqin to Zhenbao. Every time that China sought to assert its claims to islands on the Chinese side of the main channel of navigation, Soviet border guards would respond by forcibly evicting Chinese patrols. As listed in table 4.1, nine violent confrontations over Zhenbao Island occurred between December 27, 1968, and February 25, 1969. On January 23, 1969, Soviet border guards beat twenty-eight Chinese soldiers, thirteen seriously.[145] During a confrontation on February 6, live ammunition was used for the first time when the Soviets fired warning shots at a Chinese patrol.[146] As the situation deteriorated in the eastern sector, Soviet pressure also increased on disputed areas in the western sector. From December 1968 to March 1969, Soviet forces repeatedly challenged Chinese herders in the Bie'erkewu region, a move that no doubt enhanced the sense of threat for China's leaders, given China's strategic vulnerability in the west.[147]

---

[139] Lyle Goldstein, "Return to Zhenbao Island: Who Started Shooting and Why It Matters," *The China Quarterly*, no. 168 (December 2001): 990–991.

[140] For a detailed discussion, see Wich, *Sino-Soviet Crisis*, 41–74.

[141] *RMRB*, 17 September 1968, 5.

[142] *RMRB*, 1 October 1968, 6.

[143] Whiting, *Calculus*, 238–239.

[144] John Wilson Lewis and Litai Xue, *China Builds the Bomb* (Stanford, Calif.: Stanford University Press, 1988), 244.

[145] Li and Hao, *Wenhua dageming*, 317; Li, *Lengnuan suiyue*, 347; Xu, "1969," 5.

[146] Xu, "1969," 5.

[147] Meng, *Xinjiang tongzhi: junshi zhi*, 339.

TABLE 4.1
Armed Confrontations over Zhenbao Island (December 1968–March 1969)

Date	Action
27 Dec. 1968	Soviet armored vehicles land on Zhenbao Island and beat Chinese soldiers
4 Jan. 1969	30 Soviet soldiers enter Zhenbao Island and evict the Chinese soldiers, seriously injuring 4
6 Jan. 1969	Soviet troops capture and club two Chinese fishermen on the island
23 Jan. 1969	28 Chinese wounded in violent clash with a Soviet patrol on the island
6 Feb. 1969	50 Soviet troops land on Zhenbao Island, challenging a Chinese patrol
7 Feb. 1969	Reports that shots were fired for the first time by Soviet troops
16 Feb. 1969	Tense standoff between Chinese and Soviet patrols
22 Feb. 1969	Armed confrontation on the island, including the Soviet use of a helicopter
25 Feb. 1969	Armed confrontation on the island

Sources: Li and Hao, *Wenhua dageming*, 317–318; Li, *Lengnuan suiyue*, 347–348; Xu, "1969," 5–6.

Regime Insecurity and Perceptions of Decline

All these varied forms of external military pressure coincided with the political instability created by the Cultural Revolution. Especially after the enunciation of the Brezhnev doctrine, China's internal unrest offered an additional source of vulnerability and sense of declining claim strength. For China's leaders, it was likely not a coincidence that Soviet military pressure increased as China's domestic situation deteriorated. This suggested both a Soviet effort to profit from China's unrest and perception of a weakened Chinese ability to respond.

Although the Cultural Revolution defies simple categorization as a social phenomenon, it created severe and often violent divisions within the Chinese Communist Party (CCP) and society. Mao originally launched the mass movement in 1966 to rectify what he believed to be growing "revisionist" tendencies within all levels of the CCP and government bureaucracy.[148] One of the tools that Mao chose was the mobilization of

---

[148] On the Cultural Revolution, see MacFarquhar and Schoenhals, *Mao's Last Revolution*.

students and later other segments of society to criticize party leaders and implement rectification. By allowing and even encouraging criticism of the CCP, the mass mobilization quickly escalated out of control. Instead of rectifying the party, the movement became a tool of factional politics and sparked three years of instability at all levels of government. From 1966 to 1969, 60 to 80 percent of central and provincial leaders were purged. At the local level, militant Red Guard groups started in January 1967 to seize power from party committees across the country. Deadly conflicts occurred in the provinces between rival groups and with military units seeking to maintain order. In this radical phase, an estimated 500,000 people died in struggle sessions, violent power seizures, intra–Red Guard competition, and other conflicts.[149]

With respect to China's territorial disputes, the Cultural Revolution constituted a dramatic decline in China's ability to project power over territory disputed with the Soviet Union. During this period, China's senior leaders were consumed by factional politics and a desire to maintain stability, both of which prevented China from taking many diplomatic initiatives. More specifically, as the instability of the Cultural Revolution deepened, the PLA became the bulwark of internal stability and was involved in most attempts to restore social order throughout the country, including frontier provinces.[150] In 1967 and 1968, PLA units assumed administrative control of many provincial governments and deployed troops around the country to maintain critical infrastructure. More than two million soldiers and officers reportedly participated in civilian affairs during this period.[151] On the borders, the PLA maintained only a minimal force because so many troops became involved in domestic affairs in the provinces.[152] During the radical phase of the Cultural Revolution, PLA units were removed from Manchuria to help maintain domestic stability elsewhere. At the same time, China's leaders viewed the growing Soviet military pressure during the chaos of the Cultural Revolution as being designed to profit from China's weakness and compel a change in China's domestic and foreign policies.[153] Mao apparently believed that the Soviets might intervene in China to support the "revisionist" faction in the Cultural Revolution.[154]

[149] Harry Harding, "The Chinese State in Crisis," in Roderick MacFarquhar and John K. Fairbank, eds., *The Cambridge History of China*, vol. 15, part 2 (Cambridge: Cambridge University Press, 1991), 212–214.

[150] On the role of the PLA during the Cultural Revolution, see Li and Hao, *Wenhua dageming*; Harding, "Chinese State in Crisis," 169–170; MacFarquhar and Schoenhals, *Mao's Last Revolution*; Andrew Scobell, *China's Use of Military Force: Beyond the Great Wall and the Long March* (New York: Cambridge University Press, 2003), 94–11.

[151] Harding, "Chinese State in Crisis," 169.

[152] Xu, "1969," 4–6.

[153] Xu, "1969," 5.

[154] Interviews, Beijing, July 2002; Beijing, February 2004.

Signaling Resolve

As China's position in the dispute declined during a period of internal political instability, China's leaders chose to respond with force. After the USSR's intervention in Czechoslovakia and announcement of the Brezhnev doctrine, China's leaders believed that Moscow was seeking to profit from China's weakness—not only to make gains in the territorial dispute but also to bring about policy changes within China. The growing intensity of Soviet patrolling as China's position in the local balance weakened could be stopped only by changing the rules of engagement on the islands and using force. As tensions increased over Qiliqin and Zhenbao, China's leaders, most likely Mao, decided to change its approach for dealing with Soviet patrols, from clubs to combined arms.

China first began to consider the use of force one year earlier, in January 1968. After the clash on Qiliqin Island that left five Chinese dead, the CMC instructed the Shenyang and Beijing MRs to increase their alert status and strengthen border defense preparations. The instructions also described clear rules of engagement for future clashes: Chinese forces should respond to Soviet actions only with same level of force. The firing of small arms was prohibited unless Chinese units were first fired upon and then fired two sets of warning shots. Finally, the CMC directed the relevant MRs to develop contingency plans for launching strikes against Soviet "provocations."[155] In response, the Shenyang MR ordered the transfer of elite troops to the Qiliqin area to prepare for an attack. The melting of the river ice and a decrease in the number of Soviet patrols, perhaps as a result of Moscow's own problems in Eastern Europe, led to fewer confrontations on the border in the spring and summer of 1968 and thus no further Chinese action.[156]

Following the Czechoslovakian intervention, confrontations on Zhenbao Island began to escalate. After the large confrontation on January 23 that injured twenty-eight Chinese soldiers, the Heilongjiang MD proposed a plan for attacking Soviet patrols that envisioned using three companies, with one company hidden from view to surprise the Soviets.[157] Most likely, the planners intended to use the hidden company to compel the Soviet forces to accept Chinese control of the island. The senior leadership in Beijing approved the plan only after a further deterioration of the situation in February when Soviet border guards fired warning shots, the

[155] The first Chinese source to discuss these instructions is Li and Hao, *Wenhua dageming*, 318–319.

[156] Xu, "1969," 5. Yang Kuisong states that China was prepared to attack Soviet patrols at this time. See Yang Kuisong, "The Sino-Soviet Border Clash of 1969: From Zhenbao Island to Sino-American Rapprochement," *Cold War History*, vol. 1, no. 1 (August 2000): 28.

[157] Li and Hao, *Wenhua dageming*, 319; Xu, "1969," 6.

first time that live ammunition had been used over the island. On February 19, the Central Committee, GSD, and MFA approved the Heilongjiang MD plan, which determined Zhenbao Island as the location for a Chinese attack but instructed that only one strengthened platoon should be used.[158] Afterward, the Shenyang MR transferred roughly six hundred elite troops to the Zhenbao area to begin preparations for the ambush.[159] Senior commanders from the CMC and Shenyang MR supervised the preparations.[160]

Unfortunately, it is not known precisely if or when a final order was issued instructing Chinese forces to spring their trap. One Chinese informant speculates that no specific date was set, because the Heilongjiang MD plan would be enacted only if Soviet border guards challenged a Chinese patrol on the island.[161] Nevertheless, local PLA commanders knew from past experience that Soviet guards would contest any Chinese presence on the island and relied on the usual Soviet reaction to launch the ambush. On March 2, after preparations were complete, the local command post ordered two groups to patrol the island, one in plain view and the other hidden from the Soviets. Approximately ten minutes after the Chinese patrol arrived on the island, a Soviet patrol moved across the ice to challenge the move. When the Soviets discovered the second Chinese squad, shots were fired and the first clash erupted.[162]

China's immediate objective was to deter future armed provocations along the Chinese-Soviet border, especially over islands on the Chinese side of the main channel of navigation. Similar to its strategy in the 1962 Chinese-Indian war, China sought to counter what it believed to be increasing military pressure created by a sharp decline in the local military balance and assertive Soviet behavior during a period of domestic unrest. The goal of the Heilongjiang MD's initial plan was to teach the Soviets a "bitter lesson" about the dangers of armed confrontations over disputed areas.[163] This lesson was linked quite specifically to China's claim in the dispute, which was that China intended to assert control of areas over which a consensus had been reached in 1964. Given the extent of disunity and chaos within China during the Cultural Revolution, China's leaders

---

[158] Li and Hao, *Wenhua dageming*, 319; Xu, "1969," 6.

[159] Yang, "Sino-Soviet," 28–29.

[160] Xu, "1969," 6.

[161] Interview, Beijing, February 2004.

[162] For Chinese scholarly descriptions of events, see Li and Hao, *Wenhua dageming*, 320–324; Xu, "1969," 6–9; Yang, *Mao Zedong*, 488–494. For an official Chinese account, see *Peking Review*, no. 11 and no. 12 (March 1969). For a Soviet description, see "Soviet Report to GDR Leadership on 2 March 1969 China-Soviet Border Clashes," Cold War International History Project Virtual Archive.

[163] Quoted in Yang, "Sino-Soviet," 28, 30.

also likely sought to teach the Soviets a lesson about the efficacy of military pressure on China, both to prevent a larger Soviet attack or intervention along the lines of the Brezhnev doctrine and to prevent meddling in China's internal politics.

Several aspects of the March 2 operation reflect concern with decline in China's claim strength. The selection of Zhenbao for the clash was deliberate, as it was one of the islands allocated to China during the 1964 talks. The February 1969 CMC and Shenyang MR instructions specifically prohibited Chinese troops from crossing the median line in any armed confrontation with Soviet forces.[164] In addition, Zhenbao was the only such island in the Ussuri River that was situated near a hilltop on the Chinese side, which created a substantial tactical advantage for the ambush, as the Soviets lacked any high ground on their side of the river. The selection of a disputed island in the Far East, as opposed to territory in the western sector of the border adjacent to Xinjiang, was also significant. By challenging the Soviets where their position was relatively weaker, especially when compared with their strength in Mongolia and Central Asia, China sought to underscore the strength of its own position with regard to these islands and the Soviet risks of using military pressure in the dispute.

The results of the clash were mixed. From a tactical perspective, China achieved its territorial goal. By 1970, the Soviet Union had ceased challenging Chinese patrols on islands located on the Chinese side of the main channel of navigation. Thus, China successfully defended the territory that it claimed.[165] From a strategic perspective, however, the clash was costly. In the short run, the ambush increased Soviet military pressure on China, with raids during the spring and summer of 1969 in both the eastern and western sectors that Moscow used to coerce China to the negotiating table. Soviet overall military pressure peaked in August 1969, which as discussed below created real fears of an all-out invasion. On August 13, a Soviet force of three hundred soldiers including ten tanks and armored vehicles penetrated two kilometers within China near Tielieketi (Zhalanshkol) in Xinjiang's Yumin County, killing approximately twenty border guards and garrison troops.[166] Only days later, Moscow began to issue nuclear threats. In early September China relented, and Alexey Kosygin flew to Beijing to meet with Zhou Enlai, a visit that paved the way for formal talks in October. Nevertheless, the Zhou-Kosygin

---

[164] Xu, "1969," 6.

[165] Directorate of Intelligence, *Sino-Soviet Exchanges, 1969–84: A Reference Aid*, EA 84–10069 [Top Secret] (Washington, D.C.: Central Intelligence Agency, 1984), 5; Neville Maxwell, "The Chinese Account of the 1969 Fighting at Chenpao," *The China Quarterly*, no. 56 (December 1973): 731.

[166] Meng, *Xinjiang tongzhi: junshi zhi*, 340.

talks focused on crisis management and conflict prevention, not the sovereignty of disputed areas.[167]

Diversion?

In recent years, scholars have argued that diversionary incentives, not decline in the dispute, explain China's decision to ambush Soviet forces in March 1969. According to this argument, Mao ordered the raid to create an external crisis that he could use to rally society and end the radical phase of the Cultural Revolution at the Ninth Party Congress scheduled for April 1969.[168] During the height of the clash, Mao stated that "we should let them come in, which will help us in our mobilization."[169]

Although the lack of archival documents makes a definitive judgment difficult to render, the evidence from newly available sources fails to support the diversionary hypothesis. First, if "rallying" best explains China's use of force, then the onset of domestic conflict should be linked with foreign policy assertiveness and escalation. Political instability and unrest were almost a constant feature of Chinese politics during Cultural Revolution, yet only once did China seek to escalate a dispute with its main ideological ally, the Soviet Union. Moreover, if diversion explains China's decision to ambush the Soviets in 1969, it is surprising that Mao did not seek to use such a tactic earlier, when he feared losing control of the Cultural Revolution. Instead, the ambush occurred when it was arguably least needed from the perspective of social stability. Relatively speaking, the first few months of 1969 were calm, especially when compared with the violence, disorder, and collapse of authority that had occurred in the preceding two years, especially the summer of 1967 and the spring of 1968, when military units were ordered to assume control of many provincial-level governments. These moments would have been ripe for creating an external crisis to enhance internal unity and justify the military's intervention in politics, but escalation was not pursued at that time.

Second, if Mao believed that China needed an external threat to unite society and bring the Cultural Revolution to an end, it is unclear why he chose to attack the Soviets. According to the Ninth Party Congress' political report, China's main enemy remained the United States. In the immediate aftermath of the Zhenbao Island clash, China's propaganda apparatus

---

[167] Sergei Goncharov, "Kosygin-Zhou Talks at Beijing Airport," *Far Eastern Affairs*, nos. 1–2 (1993), 52–65; Goncharov and Usov, "Kosygin-Zhou Talks." Both articles include the recollections of Alexei Elizavetin, a Soviet diplomat.

[168] Goldstein, "Return," 997; Li, "1969," 39–50.

[169] Quoted in Yang, "Sino-Soviet," 30, citing archival documents.

emphasized U.S. imperialism, not Soviet revisionism or a potential Soviet invasion, as China's main adversary.[170] If Mao did seek to rally the public, it might have been easier and certainly much less risky to target the United States, which China was fighting in Vietnam and had previously confronted on the Korean Peninsula and across the Taiwan Strait. Instead, Mao chose to attack one superpower while already engaged in competition with the other superpower, an extremely risky action, as the USSR and China shared one of the longest land borders in the world. It is difficult (though not impossible) to conclude that Mao would have shouldered such risk simply for the purpose of rallying the masses.

Third, the "war scare" that swept China in the summer of 1969 stemmed from genuine concerns about an invasion, one that Mao had hoped to deter. In the immediate aftermath of the Zhenbao clash, no military mobilization was ordered. April and May remained relatively calm. In June, after a series of Soviet-sparked clashes in both the eastern and western sectors, the CMC began to reconsider the likelihood of an invasion and ordered war preparations in the three northern MRs. Following the August raid in Xinjiang and Soviet nuclear threats, PLA troops including nuclear forces on the northern border were placed on high alert. At the same time, Zhou agreed to talks with Kosygin to ease tensions and reduce the threat of invasion, action inconsistent with diversion. These actions were not taken to capitalize on an upsurge in patriotism following the March 1969 clash but in response to specific Soviet military actions that increased fears of a general war. Mobilization did occur, but as a result of Mao's miscalculations about the Soviet response, not as a strategy for addressing domestic instability.[171]

Averted Crises in the 1970s

Soviet troop deployments continued after the March 1969 ambush, reaching fifty-four divisions in the early 1980s. Yet China never again used force in its disputes with the Soviet Union. Moreover, this absence of escalation is remarkable given several small clashes that occurred in the 1970s on the Chinese-Mongolian border and additional clashes in the rivers of the eastern sector. Although the border appeared primed for escalation, it remained relatively peaceful despite the potential challenge to China's claim strength that the Soviet forces presented.

---

[170] John W. Garver, "Chinese Foreign Policy in 1970: The Tilt Towards the Soviet Union," *The China Quarterly*, no. 82 (June 1980): 214–249.

[171] On China's mobilization and response to perceived Soviet threats in the summer and fall of 1969, see Liu Zhinan, "1969 nian, Zhongguo zhanbei yu dui MeiSu guanxi de yanjiu he tiaozheng" [China's War Preparations and the Story of the Readjustment of Relations

Several factors, both external and internal, most likely account for China's return to a delaying, or do nothing, strategy in the dispute. One was that, in part, China learned its own lesson. The "war scare" in the summer and fall of 1969 demonstrates the degree to which a harsh Soviet reaction to the March ambush was unanticipated in Beijing. As one Chinese scholar observers, "the tensions of the Sino-Soviet border conflict had begun to go beyond Mao's expectations."[172] The Soviets amply communicated their capabilities and resolve to escalate in response to further Chinese provocations.

In addition, three other factors account for the stability in the dispute after 1969. First, following the October 1969 Zhou-Kosygin talks, both sides agreed to adopt measures to reduce the risk of escalation. In late 1969, the Soviet Union proposed a number of conflict prevention measures, including limits on forward patrolling by each side beyond the line of actual control, which China reciprocated.[173] Through the 1970s, Chinese-Soviet talks focused only on conflict prevention, not sovereignty, reflecting the shared goal of crisis management, not dispute settlement. Nevertheless, these conflict management procedures successful limited the potential for escalation.

Second, China's ambush had achieved its narrow territorial goal, namely Soviet acceptance of China's control of islands on its side of the main channel of navigation. With this de facto concession by the Soviets, combined with the conflict prevention and crisis management measures, China's claim strength in the dispute improved significantly. By early February 1970, the Soviets had withdrawn from many disputed islands, including Zhenbao, and refrained from forward patrolling that would threaten China's claim strength.[174]

Third, although the increased Soviet deployments to the Far East still threatened to shift the local balance of forces, China was able to some degree to match Soviet deployments. In 1969 and 1970, China moved five armies from the south to the three northern MRs. Although these units were stationed far from the border, at distances ranging from 700 to 1,500 kilometers, they strengthened China's reserve force that could be used in the event of an invasion.[175] China's ability to focus its military assets on a potential Soviet threat only increased through rapprochement with the United States and the end of the U.S. war in Vietnam, which both

---

with the U.S. and Soviet Union in 1969], *Dangdai Zhongguo shi yanjiu*, no. 3 (1999): 41–50; Yang, *Mao Zedong*, 494–509.

[172] Yang, "Sino-Soviet," 49.

[173] Directorate of Intelligence, *Sino-Soviet Exchanges*, 5.

[174] Directorate of Intelligence, *Sino-Soviet Exchanges*, 5.

[175] Directorate for Research, *Luring Deep: China's Land Defense Strategy*, DDB-2610–31–80 [Top Secret] (Defense Intelligence Agency, 1980), 13.

allowed China to station more troops in the north and increased global military pressure on Moscow.

Fourth, the growing stability in China's domestic politics also played a role in dampening perceptions of decline. Especially by the later half of the 1970s when Soviet deployments began to increase again, China's domestic politics were much more stable than in the late 1960s during the radical phase of the Cultural Revolution.

1980s: CHINA-VIETNAM BORDER CLASHES

As discussed in chapter 1, deterrence of Soviet influence on China's southern flank, not territorial objectives, motivated China's 1979 attack against Vietnam. In the early 1980s, the Chinese-Vietnamese border remained heavily militarized and the site of numerous small-scale clashes and artillery duels, reflecting an ongoing desire to maintain military pressure on the Soviet Union's key client in the region.[176]

Amid this hostility, China launched three assaults on Vietnamese-held hills along the land border, occupying disputed territory after each attack. In October 1980, China assaulted Luojiapingda Mountain along Yunnan's border with Vietnam. In May 1981, China attacked Faka and Koulin mountains along the Guangxi and Yunnan provincial borders, respectively. Finally, in April 1984, China attacked Lao and Zheyin mountains near the town of Malipo along Yunnan's border with Vietnam.[177] These assaults were bloody, protracted seizures of disputed land. After China's April 1984 occupation of Lao and Zheyin mountains, this portion of the border witnessed five Vietnamese counterattacks over the next eighteen months.[178] Reportedly, control of the mountains changed repeatedly, and the two sides also engaged in artillery duels along the border that lasted until 1989.[179]

Owing to a reported 1993 agreement between the Chinese and Vietnamese communist parties to suppress discussion of past disputes, little information on Chinese decision making in these conflicts is available. Moreover, the origin of the disputes that involved these hilltops is vague. Chinese sources indicate that Vietnam occupied them when the PLA with-

---

[176] For a detailed account of some of these conflicts, see "Bianfang 15 tuan duiYue zuozhan jianshi" [A Short History of the 15th Frontier Defense Regiment's Operations against Vietnam], http://xzc.2000y.net/mb/1/ReadNews.asp?NewsID=93421.

[177] Sun Cuibing, ed., *Yunnan shengzhi: junshi zhi* [Yunnan Provincial Gazetteer: Military Affairs] (Kunming: Yunnan renmin chubanshe, 1997), 424–435.

[178] Sun, *Yunnan shengzhi: junshi zhi*, 424–435.

[179] Edward C. O'Dowd, *Chinese Military Strategy in the Third Indochina War: The Last Maoist War* (New York: Routledge, 2007), 89–107.

drew after its February 1979 offensive.[180] Maps of the border indicate that all these mountains lie close to if not on the boundary line contained in the Qing dynasty's nineteenth-century agreements with France.

Although data remain thin, these clashes along the Chinese-Vietnamese border appear to be a continuation of the conflict started in 1979 and Chinese coercive diplomacy, not responses to a decline in China's claim strength in its land border dispute with Vietnam. The maintenance of military pressure on Vietnam through the clashes underscored China's "three obstacles" for improved ties with Moscow, one of which was Soviet support for Vietnam's occupation of Cambodia.

In the context of Chinese-Soviet and Chinese-Vietnamese rivalry, however, the 1980 and 1981 attacks are consistent with the effects of declining claim strength and unfavorable shifts in the local military balance. The broader rivalries best explain the larger and more violent assault on Lao and Zheyin mountains. According to Chinese sources, Vietnam had seized and fortified areas along the border including Luojiapingda, Faka, and Koulin mountains in early 1980.[181] Most likely, Vietnam sought to strengthen its own border defenses against another Chinese invasion. As tensions increased over these areas, local Chinese commanders decided to destroy the Vietnamese positions, launching attacks in October 1980 against Luojiapingda and in May 1981 against Faka and Koulin. By contrast, the January 1984 decision to attack Lao and Zheyin was not preceded by increased tension along this part of the border.

Several factors support this interpretation. PLA forces in the 1980 and 1981 attacks were limited to those under the Yunnan MD responsible for the defense of this part of the border. Moreover, local frontier defense regiments (*bianfang tuan*) and not main force PLA units played a key role in these operations, indicating that the attacks were linked to a localized struggle for control of the border, not part of a broader effort to signal resolve in the rivalry. China's April 1984 assault on Lao and Zheyin mountains, however, involved substantially more troops, including units from several divisions of the Kunming MR. After the attack, units from each of China's seven MRs were rotated through the Laoshan front, where low-level fighting continued for the rest of the 1980s.[182] In addition to maintaining pressure on Vietnam and the Soviet Union, these rotations gave key PLA units and officers combat experience in line with China's new doctrine to fight local, limited wars.

[180] *DDZGJD*, 679.

[181] Sun, *Yunnan shengzhi: junshi zhi*, 424.

[182] "Ge dajunqu Laoshan canzhan jianjie" [Brief Introduction to Each Military Region's Participation in the Laoshan War]," http://bwl.top81.com.cn/war79/file1/270–1.htm.

CONCLUSION

Although China has pursued compromise in all its frontier disputes, it has used force in three of these conflicts. In particular, China has used force to arrest or reverse declines in claim strength when its militarily most powerful neighbors have sought to shift the local balance of forces in their favor. Although China could have perhaps more easily used force in other frontier disputes, it engaged in combat only with its strongest neighbors—India, the Soviet Union, and Vietnam—the only states that possessed the means to limit China's ability to consolidate the land boundaries of the late Qing empire.

The timing of decline in China's relative position in disputes with India and the Soviet Union, government documents, and leadership statements explain why and when China has used force in its frontier disputes. In most of these uses of force, the combination of negative shifts in bargaining power in the disputes and political instability within China was deadly. In 1962, 1967, and 1969, internal political instability increased China's sense of vulnerability to external threats. The combination of declining claim strength and internal unrest led China's leaders to conclude that its neighbors sought to profit from their domestic difficulties. Political instability is thus linked to the use force, but not along the pathway of diversionary war as commonly assumed. Instead, regime insecurity magnified the perceived nature and severity of external threats, further increasing the utility of using force to signal resolve to China's adversaries.

CHAPTER FIVE

Homeland Disputes

IN ITS HOMELAND DISPUTES, China has pursued ambitious territorial objectives: the unification of Han Chinese territories that were not under PRC control in 1949, namely Hong Kong, Macao, and Taiwan. National unification has been a long-standing political goal for contemporary Chinese leaders, communist and nationalist alike, linked to the vision of establishing a strong, secure, and modern state. Indeed, these disputes are so important that they are often described as "domestic affairs" (*nei-zheng*), not interstate conflicts. Because of their importance, compromise over the sovereignty of homeland areas is inconceivable for China's leaders. Perhaps unsurprisingly, since 1949 China has never offered any territorial concessions in these disputes or moderated its long-term goal of unification.

Instead, what has varied is China's willingness to use force in these conflicts. China has never used force in disputes over Hong Kong and Macao, but it initiated several military crises over Taiwan, most recently in 1995–96. Declining claim strength best explains this variation in escalation across homeland disputes and over time in the Taiwan conflict. Although China controlled none of the disputed homeland areas in 1949, it could have conquered Hong Kong and Macao at any time. Military superiority gave China's leaders great confidence about the eventual unification of these territories. By contrast, China has for many decades been unable to project power across the Strait, a military weakness in the Taiwan dispute that generates an acute sensitivity to actions that might weaken its claim even more and further reduce the prospects for unification. When faced with decline in its already weak claim in the 1950s and the 1990s, China has used force to signal its determination to achieve national unification.

By examining China's behavior in its most important conflicts, this chapter provides a clear illustration of the effects of declining claim strength on decisions to escalate territorial disputes. Although the stakes in these disputes for China have been constant since 1949, what has changed is its bargaining power. Since higher stakes in a conflict increase the utility of using force, the effects of decline in claim strength should be easily and readily observed in China's homeland disputes.

UNIFICATION THROUGH DELAY: HONG KONG AND MACAO

In its disputes over Hong Kong and Macao, China adopted a delaying strategy of postponing settlement. In the end, this strategy resulted in the resolution of these two disputes without any compromise in Chinese sovereignty over contested land. A key factor in the success of this delaying strategy was China's dominant position over Britain and Portugal in the local military balances. With the ability to seize both territories with ease, China's leaders were much more confident about their eventual unification with the mainland and, paradoxically, much more willing to wait to achieve this goal.

This section examines in detail China's dispute with Great Britain over Hong Kong. Of the two conflicts, it was more prominent given Hong Kong's size, population, and economic role as a trade and financial center in East Asia. In addition, Portugal first unilaterally agreed to return Macao to China and then largely followed Britain's lead in negotiating its transfer to China.[1]

Implementation of the Delaying Strategy

China's adoption of a delaying strategy toward Hong Kong and Macao began in the early 1950s soon after the establishment of the PRC. The strategy involved a combination of firm sovereignty claims over the disputed homeland territories and a conscious decision that no action would be taken to unify these areas in the short to medium term. Sovereignty over Hong Kong and Macao was nonnegotiable, but regaining actual occupation and control was not a pressing matter for China's leaders.

During the final days of the Chinese civil war, China did not seize Hong Kong. Despite possessing the military capability to occupy the colony, the PLA was ordered not to move within 25 miles of the territory after it captured the city of Guangzhou. In the following months, the PRC made no explicit demands for the return of Hong Kong even though it was a clear referent in Article 55 of the 1949 Common Program as one of the unequal treaties that China might revisit when the CCP took power. Indeed, China

---

[1] Chinese sources on Hong Kong include Chen Xueying, *Deng Xiaoping yu xianggang* [Deng Xiaoping and Hong Kong] (Beijing: Dangdai shijie chubanshe, 1997); *DDZGWJ*, 379–383; Qi Pengfei, *Deng Xiaoping yu Xianggang huigui* [Deng Xiaoping and the Return of Hong Kong] (Beijing: Huaxia chubanshe, 2004); Li Hou, *Bainian quru shi de zhongjie: Xianggang wenti shimo* [The End of 100 Years of Humiliation: The Story of the Hong Kong Issue] (Beijing: Zhongyang wenxian chubanshe [internal circulation], 1997). An excellent account in English is Robert Cottrell, *The End of Hong Kong: The Secret Diplomacy of Imperial Retreat* (London: John Murray, 1993).

made few official references to Hong Kong during this period.[2] Although China had made clear that the treaties ceding Hong Kong to Britain were "unequal," it did not say when these areas would be recovered.

China's strategy of delaying became official policy in the mid-1950s. In October 1955, Zhou Enlai met with Sir Alexander Grantham, then the governor of Hong Kong, who paid a private visit to Beijing. In the meeting, Zhou apparently identified rules of conduct for the territory as the quid pro quo for China's willingness to delay settlement and not abrogate the treaties ceding Hong Kong Island and the Kowloon Peninsula. Britain was not to foster democracy, allow third parties to use the territory as a military base, permit subversive Nationalist (KMT) activities, or obstruct China's economic interests.[3] All these actions, of course, would have adversely affected the prospects for the unification of Hong Kong with the mainland. In 1956, Mao described the delaying strategy when he stated: "it is better if we temporarily do not take back Hong Kong. We are in no hurry. At present, Hong Kong is still of use to us."[4] In 1960, after summarizing the first ten years of experience in dealing with Hong Kong, Mao described China's policy as "long-term planning, full utilization" (*changqi dasuan, chongfen liyong*), which reflected a continuation of the delaying strategy and stressed Hong Kong's role as a base for trade with the outside world.[5] Moreover, Mao had suggested in private conversations that China would wait until the expiration, in 1997, of Britain's ninety-nine-year lease for the New Territories (a part of Hong Kong that the Qing had leased, not ceded).[6]

Most remarkably, the delaying strategy continued even after China and Britain normalized diplomatic relations in 1972. According to British diplomats, the question of Hong Kong's status was not raised in the normalization negotiations. Although China insisted in the UN that Hong Kong and Macao were Chinese territories and not colonies that might achieve their independence from China, Zhou Enlai stated that China would not "embark on such matters [as negotiations over Hong Kong] with undue haste. . . . In a changing world this matter would have to be settled, but it does not have to be considered now."[7]

[2] According the *People's Daily* historical database, only seven articles with "xianggang" in the title and "yige Zhongguo" in the text were published before 1979.

[3] Cottrell, *End*, 27.

[4] Li, *Bainian*, 40.

[5] Ye Zhangyu, "Zhonggong diyidai lingdao jiti jiejue Xianggang wenti zhanlue jueci de lishi kaocha" [Historical Examination of the CCP's First-Generation Leaders' Strategic Decisions for Resolving the Hong Kong Problem], *Dangdai Zhongguo shi yanjiu*, vol. 14, no. 3 (2007): 48.

[6] *Mao Zedong wenji* [Mao Zedong's Collected Works], vol. 8 (Beijing: Xinhua chubanshe, 1999), 337; Li, *Bainian*, 41.

[7] Quoted in Cottrell, *End*, 33. Zhou did note that "a state must negotiate when a treaty expires," referring to the 99-year lease.

China adopted a delaying strategy over Hong Kong for four reasons. The first was China's local military superiority. Similar to Goa, a Portuguese enclave on the west coast of India, Hong Kong was extremely vulnerable to any military pressure from the mainland, and Britain could mount no meaningful defense against a PLA attack. Moreover, Chinese leverage further increased when Guangdong became the territory's principal source of water and food in the mid-1950s. As Mao stated in 1963, "as for Hong Kong, Britain does not have much military power. We could occupy it if we want to."[8] China's military dominance gave its leaders a great deal of confidence about the eventual unification of Hong Kong with the mainland. China could, in essence, determine when to push for unification because its relative military position would not significantly change. In short, barring British efforts to nationalize the colony, no perceptions of decline or vulnerability might arise to make the use of force necessary for China to achieve its territorial goals.

Taiwan was a second factor behind China's delaying strategy. Early on, China's leaders identified Taiwan as their most important homeland dispute and the area that should be "unified" with the mainland first. Taiwan was key because it symbolized the continuation of the Chinese civil war, as the KMT's claim to the mainland challenged the CCP's legitimacy. Unification with Taiwan, more than Hong Kong or Macao, was necessary to consolidate China's territorial integrity. As Chen Yi stated in 1966, "we must first resolve the most important problem, Taiwan . . . and then, at the opportune moment, we will claim Macao and Hong Kong."[9]

The third factor supporting a delaying strategy was the economic benefit that the mainland derived from access to Hong Kong. As early as 1950, the territory was a source of goods and services necessary first for China's war effort in Korea and later, even before 1979, for China's economic development as well as foreign intelligence.[10] By not pressing the issue of Hong Kong's return to the mainland, China ensured its access to foreign markets, technology, and capital. After the United States and UN placed sanctions on China in the early 1950s, Hong Kong became China's principal channel for circumventing the embargo.[11]

Great-power politics was a fourth factor behind the delaying strategy. In the early 1950s, China sought to drive a wedge between Britain, which maintained diplomatic representation in Beijing at the chargé d'affaires level, and the United States, which recognized the KMT on Taiwan

[8] *Mao Zedong wenji*, vol. 8, 337.

[9] *NYT*, 11 December 1966, 3.

[10] Qi, *Deng Xiaoping*, 26–28; Zhang Shu Guang, *Economic Cold War: America's Embargo against China and the Sino-Soviet Alliance, 1949–1963* (Stanford, Calif.: Stanford University Press, 2001), 36–38.

[11] Cottrell, *End*, 27.

as the legitimate government of China.[12] China's leaders feared that an aggressive policy toward Hong Kong might result in U.S. military intervention, given Britain's inability to defend the colony militarily. Thus, according to Zhou Enlai, "It is better [now] to leave Hong Kong in Britain's hands."[13]

Unification through Delay

Britain, however, lacked China's patience. Toward the end of the 1970s, Britain became increasingly concerned about Hong Kong's future. The immediate issue was the expiration in 1997 of the ninety-nine-year lease for the New Territories, which created uncertainty about the legality of contracts and loan agreements in the colony after this date. When Foreign Trade Minister Li Qiang invited the Hong Kong governor, Sir Crawford Murray MacLehose, to visit Beijing in March 1979, Britain saw an opportunity to discuss Hong Kong's future. Deng, however, surprised the British delegation, informing MacLehose that "Hong Kong is a part of China, this question itself is nonnegotiable. . . . Even in 1997 when this question is settled, we will respect Hong Kong's special status."[14] MacLehose then raised the lease issue, proposing that contracts include the phrase "for so long as the Crown administers the territory,"[15] implying British administration of the territory after 1997. Deng replied that "even when there is a political settlement, it will not harm the interests of those continuing to invest. Investors can have confidence, this is a long-term policy."[16] Deng also noted that there should be no reference to "British administration" for land leases after 1997, indicating that China would seek to exercise sovereignty by that date.[17]

Surprised by Deng's candor with MacLehose, Britain continued to probe China's position on Hong Kong's future. In July 1979, Britain sent China a formal memorandum on the lease issue. Although China was focused on Taiwan at this time, Deng instructed the government in early 1981 to develop a policy for Hong Kong's return. In April, the State Council's Hong Kong and Macao Affairs Office under the leadership of Liao Chengzhi drafted a report for the CCP leadership that outlined how to resume sovereignty while maintaining the territory's prosperity. In April and December 1981, the CCP secretariat held two meetings to dis-

---

[12] Qi, *Deng Xiaoping*, 26–28; Qiang Zhai, *The Dragon, the Lion, and the Eagle: Chinese-British-American Relations, 1949–1958* (Kent, Ohio: Kent State University Press, 1994).

[13] Li, *Bainian*, 40.

[14] Leng Rong and Wang Zuoling, eds., *Deng Xiaoping nianpu, 1975–1997* [Chronicle of Deng Xiaoping's Life, 1975–1997] (Beijing: Zhongyang wenxian chubanshe, 2004), 500.

[15] Quoted in Cottrell, *End*, 55.

[16] Leng and Wang, *Deng Xiaoping nianpu*, 501.

[17] Quoted in Cottrell, *End*, 55–56.

cuss the twelve points highlighted in Liao's report. The CCP decided at these meetings that China should resume sovereignty in 1997 but that the territory should be governed by the people of Hong Kong and its political and economic system should remain unchanged.[18]

When Britain announced in January 1982 that Prime Minister Margaret Thatcher would visit China, Beijing was prepared to begin negotiations over Hong Kong. Thatcher's goal for her September trip was to open unconditional talks over Hong Kong's status. Privately, Thatcher hoped to continue British sovereignty over the territory or at least continue British administration.[19] Deng, however, had a different plan. He stated that "the question of sovereignty is not one that can be discussed. China on this question has no room for maneuver." Moreover, Deng emphasized that "on this question in 1997 when China takes back Hong Kong, this will include not only the New Territories, but also Hong Kong Island and Kowloon," areas that the Qing had ceded to Britain in the nineteenth century.[20] According to Thatcher, "the Chinese refused to budge an inch."[21]

The conflict between China and Britain soon became clear. Thatcher told Deng that because the existing treaties had ceded Hong Kong Island and Kowloon, China could resume sovereignty only through a mutual agreement with Britain. Moreover, she stated that, regardless of sovereignty, only continued British administration could ensure the territory's future prosperity. At the end of their talks, the only agreement reached was that the two sides would enter into formal negotiations. Deng also issued a veiled ultimatum, stating that "within one or two years, China will formally announce its decision to recover Hong Kong."[22]

From October 1982 to March 1983, Vice–Foreign Minister Zhang Wenjin and Ambassador Percy Cradock held five rounds of consultations. Britain sought first to negotiate arrangements to maintain the region's prosperity, while China consistently linked administration with sovereignty.[23] To break the impasse, Thatcher wrote a letter to Premier Zhao Ziyang in March 1983 stating the she would recommend to Parliament the territory's transfer to China if "arrangements acceptable to the people Hong Kong" would be made.[24] Based on this letter, China agreed to hold formal talks even though the British position remained unchanged.

When the negotiations began in July 1983, they immediately reached an impasse. Britain started the talks with the aim of continuing its admin-

---

[18] Li, *Bainian*, 66–70.
[19] Cottrell, *End*, 71, 84.
[20] *DXPWX3*, 12.
[21] Margaret Thatcher, *The Downing Street Years* (London: HaperCollins, 1993), 261.
[22] *DXPWX3*, 12.
[23] Li, *Bainian*, 96–97.
[24] Cottrell, *End*, 102.

istration of the territory after 1997, while China remained committed to the resumption of full sovereignty. In the first few rounds, British diplomats presented briefing papers highlighting the challenges of governing the territory, but the Chinese negotiators remained adamant. In October 1983, Britain stopped insisting on continued administration after 1997 and agreed to consider China's own proposals based on Liao Chengzhi's report. In November, Cradock used the sixth round of talks to state that Britain would seek no authority over the territory if other arrangements could be made.[25]

In less than one year, Britain had conceded the two key issues, sovereignty over Hong Kong and continued British administration. Moreover, Britain made these concessions while China stood firm. Subsequent negotiations focused on arrangements for the transfer of sovereignty based on a more detailed version of Liao Chengzhi's twelve points for the preservation of Hong Kong's economic and political system.[26] In April 1984, China agreed to include an annex detailing the territory's governance after the handover. In June 1984, the two sides established a joint working group to draft an agreement. On December 19, 1984, Thatcher and Zhao signed a joint declaration for the transfer of Hong Kong with an annex describing how China would govern the territory.[27]

In the joint declaration, China received almost everything that it had originally wanted. Contrary to Thatcher's initial position, China regained sovereignty over all of Hong Kong, including those areas ceded by the Qing. Contrary to Britain's fallback position of continued administration, China insisted on the resumption of full sovereignty. Some might argue that China's guarantees to preserve Hong Kong's political and financial system for fifty years constituted a large concession, but Deng had outlined such an approach in his meeting with MacLehose as early as 1979, which became policy at the December 1981 CCP secretariat meeting. China's only real concessions were the acceptance of a watered-down joint commission to oversee Hong Kong in the final years before 1997 and the inclusion of an annex in the joint declaration. China resumed sovereignty over Hong Kong on July 1, 1997, 155 years after the island was ceded in the Treaty of Peking.

Macao

The resolution of the dispute over Macao was relatively simple in comparison to Hong Kong. Following a leftist coup in Portugal in 1974, the

---

[25] Cottrell, *End*, 132; Li, *Bainian*, 115–117.

[26] Cottrell, *End*, 112–113.

[27] Cottrell, *End*, 205–223.

Portuguese government decided to relinquish all colonial possessions. As a result, it recognized Chinese sovereignty over Macao, thereby negating the 1887 treaty in which China had ceded the territory.[28] Nevertheless, at the time, Beijing asked Lisbon to continue to administer the territory. During normalization talks in 1979, Macao was recognized as a Chinese territory under Portuguese administration, and both sides agreed that the handover of Macao should be solved through bilateral negotiations at some unspecified point in the future.

The 1984 Chinese-British joint declaration provided a road map for Portugal to follow. In 1985, Portugal and China agreed to hold formal talks on Macao's future. Using the joint declaration as a guide, four rounds of talks were held from June 1986 to March 1987. On April 13, 1987, the two sides signed a joint declaration in Beijing. The document was quite similar to the 1984 agreement between China and Britain and outlined a similar governance structure for Macao as a special administrative region. China resumed sovereignty over Macao in 1999.

THE TAIWAN DISPUTE UNDER MAO

China's most important territorial dispute, the one over Taiwan, began as a continuation of the civil war between the KMT and CCP. Despite establishing the People's Republic in 1949, China's new communist leaders were never able to defeat all the KMT forces and claim final victory. After 1949, the Chinese civil war continued as the PLA prepared to conquer the remaining areas under KMT control, including Taiwan and islands off the coast of Zhejiang and Fujian called the "coastal islands."[29] Reflecting the intensity of the conflict, China described its policy in this period as "liberation by force" (*wuli jiefang*). Negotiation much less compromise was not viewed as a policy option, as the stakes were zero-sum. Likewise, the KMT under Chiang Kai-shek remained committed to retaking the mainland by force and defeating the CCP. For both sides, the fundamental issue was acquiring sufficient military capability to defeat the other and govern all of China.

---

[28] On the Chinese-Portuguese talks, *DDZGWJ*, 379–383; Qi Pengfei and Zhang Xiaojing, *Aomen de shiluo yu huigui* [Macao's Loss and Return] (Beijing: Xinhua chubanshe, 1999), 173–217; Steve Shipp, *Macau, China: A Political History of the Portuguese Colony's Transition to Chinese Rule* (Jefferson, N.C.: McFarland & Company, 1997).

[29] Although many English-language publications describe these islands as "offshore islands," coastal islands is a more accurate translation of the Chinese term (*yanhai daoyu*) and distinguishes them from the offshore islands discussed in chapter 6 as a separate category of territorial disputes.

In the context of liberation by force, China under Mao Zedong adopted a mix of delaying and escalation strategies over Taiwan. These strategies were designed to increase the prospects for unification by raising the overall likelihood of successful military operations against KMT-held territory. The operational obstacles created by the physical barrier of the Taiwan Strait and then U.S. security guarantees dictated that any such liberation was impossible in the short term. To seize Taiwan, China needed to strengthen its own military capabilities, occupy the coastal islands, and eliminate U.S. support for the KMT. As a result, a strategy of delaying settlement prevailed as China sought to improve its otherwise inferior position in the Taiwan dispute.

In 1954 and 1958, China's uses of force in the Taiwan Strait created two of the most tense crises of the Cold War. In both cases, U.S. military and diplomatic support for the KMT created perceptions of deep vulnerability for China's leaders in a vital dispute where their state's claim was already inferior. As its bargaining power declined, China used force to signal its determination to pursue unification. Declining claim strength was most acute in the 1954 crisis amid negotiations over an alliance treaty between Taiwan and the United States. In the 1958 crisis, China's leaders pursued mixed objectives, seeking to reverse deepening ties between the United States and Taiwan while also mobilizing domestic support for the Great Leap. The degree of U.S. support for the KMT, and the impact of this support on the overall prospects for ending the Chinese civil war, played a central role in weakening China's relative position in the dispute. After 1958, China's claim strength in the dispute stabilized, even though it remained weak. The United States, hoping to avoid a direct conflict with China as it increased its involvement in Vietnam, stopped increasing its support for Taiwan. When Chiang Kai-shek mobilized to attack the mainland in the spring of 1962, for example, the United States indicated clearly to China that if Chiang did launch an attack, he would do so without American support. By 1971, in the secret diplomacy resulting in National Security Adviser Henry Kissinger's visit to China, the United States agreed to reduce its military support for Taiwan.

Ongoing conflict between the PRC and the KMT over the coastal islands, however, establishes an important context for the crises in 1954 and 1958. Only five miles from the mainland, Jinmen Island was the KMT's most important base along the Chinese coast, supporting harassment operations against the mainland and serving as a first line of defense against any PLA operations. At the same time, the troops on Jinmen reflected the KMT's own determination to challenge CCP authority and retake the mainland. PLA attacks against the coastal islands were an integral part of the CCP's struggle with the KMT. By attacking and seizing coastal islands, the CCP would decrease the amount of territory that the KMT controlled, further weakening its claim to govern China.[30]

The Civil War along the Coast

Despite the establishment of the People's Republic in October 1949, final military victory in the civil war remained elusive for the CCP. The KMT still controlled Taiwan, Hainan Island, portions of Yunnan and Guangxi, and numerous coastal islands adjacent to Fujian and Zhejiang provinces. Other areas, including Tibet, parts of Xinjiang, and regions in the southwest, were controlled by autonomous ethnic groups, sometimes with loose ties to the KMT. When Chiang Kai-shek and his forces retreated to Taiwan, the CCP sought to extend its control over all other areas, seizing Hainan Island in 1950 and occupying Tibet proper in 1951. By the end of 1953, with the conclusion of the bandit suppression campaigns (*jiaofei zhanyi*) in the west and southwest, the CCP had vanquished all potential challengers to its authority on the mainland.[31]

Nevertheless, the PLA remained unable to defeat the KMT. Instead, the civil war continued along the coastal islands near Fujian and Zhejiang. The KMT used these islands for guerrilla operations against the mainland and to harass coastal shipping. More importantly, these islands, especially Jinmen (Kinmen) and Mazu (Matzu), constituted the first line of defense against any PLA assault on Taiwan. In October 1949, PLA General Ye Fei led a failed assault on Jinmen, losing more than 9,000 soldiers.[32] In early 1950, China prepared to assault Taiwan to defeat the KMT and end the civil war. After the outbreak of the Korean War and deployment of the U.S. Seventh Fleet to the Strait, the Central Military Commission (CMC) postponed the campaign to conquer Taiwan until 1952. Perhaps reflecting optimism about the situation in Korea, plans to attack the coastal islands were delayed only until 1951.[33] When China entered the war in October 1950, however, all operations in the Taiwan Strait were shelved.[34]

[30] Niu Jun also stresses the importance of the coastal island battles in the 1954 and 1958 crises. See Niu Jun, "Sanci Taiwan haixia junshi douzheng juece yanjiu" [A Study of Decision Making in Three Military Battles in the Taiwan Strait], *Zhongguo shehui kexue*, no. 5 (2004): 37–50.

[31] See, for example, *DDZGJD*, 276–320.

[32] For a description of this campaign, Cong Letian, ed., *Huigu Jinmen denglu zhan* [Reflections on the Battle to Land on Jinmen] (Beijing: Renmin chubanshe, 1994); He Di, "The Last Campaign to Unify China: The CCP's Unrealized Plan to Liberate Taiwan, 1949–1950," in Mark A. Ryan, David M. Finkelstein, and Michael A. McDevitt, eds., *Chinese Warfighting: The PLA Experience since 1949* (Armonk, N.Y.: M. E. Sharpe, 2003), 44–146.

[33] He, "Last Campaign."

[34] On China's decision to enter the Korean War, see Chen Jian, *China's Road to the Korean War: The Making of the Sino-American Confrontation* (New York: Columbia Uni-

In the early 1950s, the coastal islands remained the front line of the civil war. As a Central Committee report stated, "the civil war against Chiang Kai-shek never ended in the coastal regions."[35] According to one PLA history, from late 1949 to July 1953, the KMT conducted more than seventy large-scale raids from these islands against the mainland.[36] As table 5.1 demonstrates, the KMT launched seven assaults against islands it did not control in a bid to strengthen its position along the front line. The largest such attack occurred in July 1953, when 10,000 KMT troops and irregulars assaulted Dongshan Island near Fujian (map 5.1). China responded by attacking KMT-held islands and establishing air superiority in selected areas. The PLA launched eight major assaults from 1950 to early 1955, gaining control of twenty islands. In these exchanges, more than 9,000 KMT soldiers and irregulars were killed, wounded, or captured, along with a similar number of PLA troops.[37]

As a continuation of the civil war, the battles over these islands are unsurprising. Control of the mainland coast reflected each side's strength in the dispute and was linked more broadly to the defense of Taiwan itself. As early as 1949, China's senior military commanders concluded that any assault on Taiwan would require control of Jinmen and Mazu.[38] In the early 1950s, PLA commanders debated China's posture in the area as part of a long-term drive to defeat the KMT. In June 1952, the PLA began preparations to seize the Dachens off the Zhejiang coast, which Mao postponed until the end of the Korean War.[39] In September 1953, the East China Military Region (MR) submitted a plan for assaulting Jinmen. Mao

---

versity Press, 1994); Thomas J. Christensen, *Useful Adversaries: Grand Strategy, Domestic Mobilization, and Sino-American Conflict, 1947–1958* (Princeton, N.J.: Princeton University Press, 1996), 138–193; Allen S. Whiting, *China Crosses the Yalu: The Decision to Enter the Korean War* (New York: Macmillan, 1960).

[35] *Zhonggong zhongyang wenjian huibian* [Collection of Documents of the Central Committee of the Chinese Communist Party], quoted in Gordon H. Chang and He Di, "The Absence of War in the U.S.-China Confrontation over Quemoy and Matsu in 1954–1955: Contingency, Luck, Deterrence?" *American Historical Review*, vol. 98, no. 1 (December 1993): 1054.

[36] Deng Lifeng, ed., *Zhonghua renmin gongheguo junshi shiyao* [A Brief History of the PRC's Military Affairs] (Beijing: Junshi kexue chubanshe, 2005), 448.

[37] Cui Zhiqing, ed., *Haixia liang'an guanxi rizhi (1949–1998)* [Daily Record of Cross-straits Relations] (Beijing: Jiuzhou tushu chubanshe, 1999), 44. For descriptions of the many coastal island battles, see *DDZGJD*, 134–161, 221–253, 321–353; Huang Zheng-miao, ed., *Zhejiang sheng junshi zhi* [Zhejiang Province Military Affairs Gazetteer] (Beijing: Difangzhi chubanshe, 1999), 682–698; Wang Ziwen, ed., *Fujian shengzhi: junshi zhi* [Fujian Provincial Gazetteer: Military Affairs] (Beijing: Xinhua chubanshe, 1995), 267–278.

[38] He, "Last Campaign."

[39] He Dongfang, *Zhang Aiping zhuan* [Zhang Aiping's Biography] (Beijing: Renmin chubanshe, 2000), 656; Xu Yan, *Jinmen zhi zhan* [Battle for Jinmen] (Beijing: Zhongguo guangbo dianshi chubanshe, 1992), 147–196.

TABLE 5.1
Coastal Island Engagements (1950–1955)

Date	Island	Defender	Outcome	Casualties	
				KMT	CCP
6 July 1950	Dongtou Islands (Zhejiang)	CCP	Attacked and seized by 2,000 KMT troops	N/A	N/A
7–8 July 1950	Shengsi Island (Zhejiang)	KMT	Attacked and seized by PLA	300	N/A
11–12 July 1950	Pishan Island (Zhejiang)	KMT	Attacked and seized by PLA	120	N/A
7 Dec. 1951	Nanri Island (Fujian)	CCP	Attacked by 500 KMT irregulars	150	N/A
6 June and 12 Dec. 1951	Dongtou Islands (Zhejiang)	KMT	Attacked twice by PLA	N/A	N/A
11 Jan. 1952	Dongtou Islands (Zhejiang)	KMT	Attacked and seized by PLA	N/A	N/A
28 Jan. and 13 Feb. 1952	Meizhou Island (Fujian)	CCP	Attacked by 3,000 KMT troops	N/A	N/A
28 Mar. 1952	Baishashan Island (Zhejiang)	CCP	Attacked by KMT irregulars	200	N/A
10 June 1952	Huangjiao Island (Zhejiang)	CCP	Attacked by 1,200 KMT troops	310	N/A
11 Oct. 1952	Nanri Island (Fujian)	CCP	Attacked by more than 9,000 KMT troops and irregulars	800	1,300
29 May to 24 June 1953	Yangyu Islands (Zhejiang)	KMT	Attacked and seized by PLA	730	326
24 June 1953	Jigushan Island (Zhejiang)	KMT	Seized by PLA after a one-day battle	96	214
15 July 1953	Dongshan Island (Fujian)	CCP	Attacked by more than 10,000 KMT troops	3,379	1,250
15 May 1954	Dongji Islands (Zhejiang)	KMT	Attacked and seized by PLA	73	N/A
18 Jan. 1955	Yijiangshan Island (Zhejiang)	KMT	Attacked and seized by PLA	567	1,420

Sources: DDZGJD, 320–339; Huang, Zhejiang shengzhi: junshi zhi, 682–698; Lu, Sanjun; Wang, Fujian shengzhi: junshi zhi, 267–277; Xu, Jinmen, 147–166.

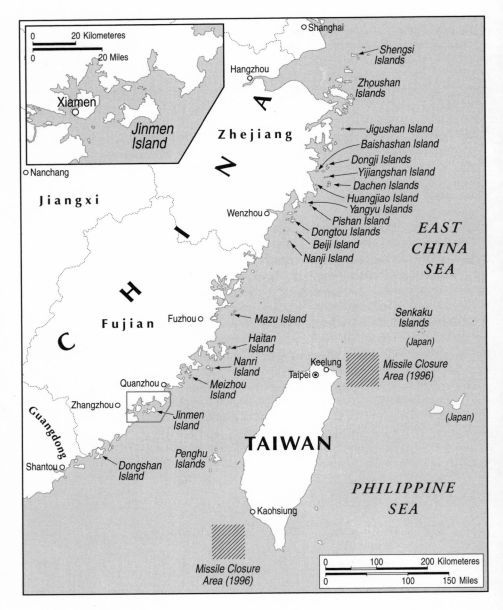

Map 5.1 Taiwan Strait

approved the plan, noting that preparations for the attack should be completed by January 1955. In December 1953, however, Mao ordered the East China MR to halt preparations after his advisers concluded that insufficient troops were available and the material cost (in terms of equipment) was too high.[40] In short, China's position in the dispute was too weak to take the military action it desired.

THE 1954 TAIWAN STRAIT CRISIS

On September 3, 1954, PLA artillery batteries in Fujian began a punishing shelling of Jinmen Island. Over a two-month period, the PLA shelled the island approximately seventy times, linking its strikes to the arrival of supply ships in the island's harbor.[41] When the smoke cleared, approximately one thousand KMT soldiers had been killed or wounded along with an unknown number of PLA troops.[42] A month after the shelling, the United States and Taiwan began formal negotiations over a mutual defense treaty, which was signed in December 1954.

[40] Wang Yan, ed., *Peng Dehuai nianpu* [Chronicle of Peng Dehuai's Life] (Beijing: Renmin chubanshe, 1998), 563–565.

[41] For an overview of the crisis, see John Wilson Lewis and Litai Xue, *China Builds the Bomb* (Stanford, Calif.: Stanford University Press, 1988), 11–34; Thomas E. Stolper, *China, Taiwan, and the Offshore Islands: Together with Some Implications for Outer Mongolia and Sino-Soviet Relations* (Armonk, N.Y.: M.E. Sharpe, 1985).

For Chinese accounts of the crisis, see *DDZGJD*, 254–275; Lu Hui, *Sanjun shouzhan Yijiangshan* [Three Armed Services First Battle Yijiangshan] (Beijing: Jiefangjun chubanshe, 1988); Nie Fengzhi et al., eds., *Sanjun huige zhan donghai* [The Three Armed Services March into Battle in the East China Sea] (Beijing: Jiefangjun chubanshe, 1985); Wang Yan, *Mubiao, Yijiangshan—Wojun shouci luhaikong lianhe duhai denglu zuozhan jishi* [Target, Yijiangshan: Record of Our Army's First Land, Sea, and Air Joint Amphibious Landing Operation] (Beijing: Haichao chubanshe, 1990); Xu, *Jinmen*.

For English-language accounts based on some of these Chinese materials, see Chang and He Di, "Absence of War"; Gong Li, "Tension across the Strait in the 1950s: Chinese Strategy and Tactics," in Robert S. Ross and Jiang Changbin, eds., *Re-examining the Cold War: U.S.-China Diplomacy, 1954–1973* (Cambridge, Mass.: Harvard University Press, 2001), 141–172; He Di, "Evolution of the People's Republic of China's Policy toward the Offshore Islands," in Warren I. Cohen and Akira Iriye, eds., *The Great Powers in East Asia: 1953–1960* (New York: Columbia University Press, 1990), 222–245; Li Xiaobing, "Making of Mao's Cold War: The Taiwan Straits Crisis Revised," in Li Xiaobing and Li Hongshan, eds., *China and the United States: A New Cold War History* (Lanham, Md.: University Press of America, 1998), 49–72; Li Xiaobing, "PLA Attacks and Amphibious Operations during the Taiwan Straits Crisis of 1954–55 and 1958," in Mark A. Ryan, David M. Finkelstein, and Michael A. McDevitt, eds., *Chinese Warfighting: The PLA Experience since 1949* (Armonk, N.Y.: M. E. Sharpe, 2003); Zhang Shu Guang, *Deterrence and Strategic Culture: Chinese-American Confrontations, 1949–1958* (Ithaca, N.Y.: Cornell University Press, 1992).

[42] Wang, *Fujian shengzhi: junshi zhi*, 280.

The crisis continued with a PLA campaign to seize the Dachen Islands off the Zhejiang coast approximately two hundred nautical miles north of Taiwan. Although the attack was the first step in a larger plan to seize the remaining coastal islands under KMT control, it was also linked directly to negotiations over the U.S.-ROC Mutual Defense Treaty. On January 18, 1955, the PLA seized Yijiangshan Island near the Dachens. In the one-day battle, 567 Nationalists were killed and another 519 were captured. The PLA lost 393 soldiers with 1,027 wounded.[43] In late January, President Eisenhower requested congressional authorization to use U.S. forces to defend Taiwan and the Penghu Islands. Congress responded by passing the Formosa Resolution, which only further strengthened security ties between the United States and Taiwan. In mid-February, escorted by the U.S. Navy, the KMT evacuated more than 32,000 troops and civilians from the Dachens.[44] By end of February, the PLA controlled all the Dachens as well as Beiji, Nanji, and other islands along the Zhejiang coast.

Declining claim strength best explains China's willingness to initiate this crisis, seize Yijiangshan, and compel the Dachens' evacuation. The analysis of this crisis below supports the prevailing interpretation that has emerged in the new Cold War history, which demonstrates that China used force to signal opposition to Taiwan's growing ties with the United States.[45] After the end of the Korean War, negotiations to form an alliance between the United States and Taiwan placed increased pressure on China's already weak claim in the dispute. From the perspective of achieving unification, the U.S.-ROC treaty threatened to create a permanently divided China secured by U.S. military power. In response to this growing vulnerability, China sought to deter the two sides from signing such a treaty and demonstrate its resolve to "liberate" Taiwan by force. Once the treaty was signed, China assaulted Yijiangshan Island to probe whether the KMT-held coastal islands, which China still planned to conquer, were covered by the agreement.

DECLINING CLAIM STRENGTH

Following the July 1953 armistice in the Korean War, China's leaders became more pessimistic about the prospects for occupying Taiwan. Although China did not envision a rapid conquest of the island, the notion of permanent U.S. involvement in its civil war with the KMT threatened to reduce even further the odds of unification. Three factors account for this perception of a decline in claim strength. First, in the final months of the Korean War, the United States began to strengthen its security relation-

---

[43] Xu, *Jinmen*, 184.
[44] Deng, *Zhonghua renmin gongheguo junshi shiyao*, 451.
[45] See the sources in note 41 above.

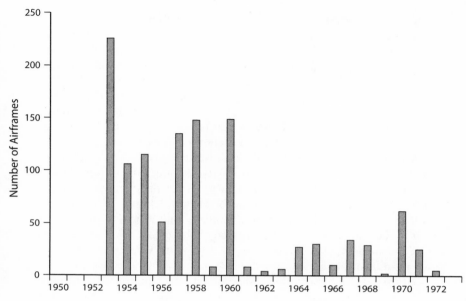

Figure 5.1 U.S. Deliveries of Fighter Aircraft to Taiwan (1950–1973)
Source: Adapted from John W. Garver, *The Sino-American Alliance: Nationalist China and American Cold War Strategy in Asia* (Armonk, N.Y.: M. E. Sharpe, 1997), 67.
Note: No data for 1950–52.

ship with Taiwan. China's leaders had originally hoped that a relaxation of hostilities on the Korean Peninsula might extend to the Taiwan Strait, perhaps moderating U.S. support for the KMT. In early 1953, however, Eisenhower "unleashed Chiang" by stating that the U.S. Seventh Fleet would not longer restrain KMT forces from conducting attacks on the Chinese mainland. In August, U.S. and KMT naval and air forces conducted joint military maneuvers. In September, the United States and Taiwan signed an Agreement on Mutual Military Understanding, which included the coastal islands.[46] From 1950 to 1954, Washington provided Taiwan with more than (U.S.)$1 billion in military aid, while the White House received congressional approval to deliver twenty-five warships to the KMT navy.[47] As depicted in figure 5.1, the delivery of fighter aircraft to the KMT, including F-84 and F-86 jets, began to increase substantially after 1953. All this military aid increased China's weakness in the dispute.

[46] Gong, "Tension," 145.
[47] Zhang, *Deterrence*, 193.

The second source of decline was the prospect of a formal military alliance between the United States and Taiwan. Such a treaty would further strengthen Taiwan's ability to counter any mainland assault. Wellington Koo, Taiwan's ambassador in Washington, first broached the idea in March 1953. During Vice President Richard Nixon's November 1953 trip to Taiwan, Chiang Kai-shek also raised the subject. The next month, the Ministry of Foreign Affairs in Taipei submitted a draft text to the U.S. ambassador. In early 1954, discussions continued, while high-level U.S. officials, such as Defense Secretary Charles Wilson and General James Van Fleet, visited Taiwan. China's leaders mistakenly believed that Van Fleet's three trips were linked to treaty negotiations. In June, erroneous U.S. press reports stated that Taiwan and the United States had agreed to a treaty.[48] According to the memoir of a senior Chinese diplomat, China's leaders believed that such an alliance would not only increase the threat to the mainland through increased deployments of U.S. forces near China but also legalize Taiwan's separation from China—all at the expense of unification.[49]

The third source of declining claim strength was the emerging U.S. alliance system in East Asia. From China's perspective, the deepening of U.S. relations with Taiwan was part of America's overall strategy in the region to contain China.[50] In the early 1950s, the United States concluded security or defense treaties with Australia (1951), New Zealand (1951), the Philippines (1951), Japan (1951), and Korea (1953). In the spring of 1954, the United States initiated talks to create a regional alliance, the Southeast Asia Treaty Organization (SEATO).[51] The U.S.-ROC Mutual Defense Treaty would incorporate Taiwan into this network, further increasing the KMT's international support and legitimacy while reducing the odds of Taiwan's unification with China.

By the summer of 1954, the situation had deteriorated quite dramatically for China. In May and June, U.S. and KMT officials publicly discussed signing a defense treaty, which would integrate Taiwan into the U.S. alliance system. The division of Vietnam at the 1954 Geneva Conference affirmed a Cold War trend of partitioning nations such as Korea and Germany.[52] In the context of treaty negotiations, the United States

---

[48] Stolper, *China, Taiwan*, 21–26.

[49] Wang Bingnan, *ZhongMei huitan jiunian huigu* [Reflections on Nine Years of Chinese-American Talks] (Beijing: Shijie zhishi chubanshe, 1985), 41.

[50] Xu, *Jinmen*, 176; Zhang, *Deterrence*, 191.

[51] Xu, *Jinmen*, 176.

[52] The Geneva Conference was especially worrisome for China's leaders because Zhou had hoped to hold high-level talks with Dulles and to raise the Taiwan issue with the other great powers. See Gong, "Tension," 145; Xu, *Jinmen*, 175.

appeared poised to "split" China permanently by institutionalizing its commitment to defend Taiwan, which would further weaken China's already poor relative position in the dispute.

ARTILLERY DIPLOMACY AND YIJIANGSHAN ASSAULT

In response to this growing vulnerability, China used force to signal its commitment to unify Taiwan with the mainland and deter the United States from forming an alliance with Taiwan. On July 7, 1954, Mao convened an enlarged meeting of the Politburo to discuss Taiwan. Mao stated that "the Taiwan issue is a long-term problem, [but] we must think of some measures to destroy the possibility of the U.S. and Taiwan signing a [defense] treaty. . . . In the diplomatic arena, [we] need an appropriate expression (*biaoshi*)."[53] The Politburo's assessment was outlined in a telegram sent on July 27 to Zhou Enlai, who was attending the Geneva Conference on Vietnam:

> After the end of the Korean War, we did not promptly raise [the liberation of Taiwan] to all of the people in the country (we are now about six months behind). We did not in a timely manner adopt the necessary measures or conduct effective work in the military, diplomatic and propaganda areas. This is not proper. *If we now still do not put forward this task and still do not work toward it, then we will have made a serious political mistake* [emphasis added].[54]

The Politburo made two key policy decisions at this meeting. The first was to launch a propaganda campaign around the theme of "liberating Taiwan." The opening salvo was fired in a July 23 *People's Daily* editorial titled "We Must Liberate Taiwan."[55] On August 1, in a speech commemorating the founding of the PLA, Zhu De repeated this line, which was echoed throughout the Chinese media. Similar speeches by other Chinese officials, including Zhou Enlai's work report on foreign affairs, stressed this theme. All this became part of China's first international propaganda campaign since 1949 focused on Taiwan.[56]

---

[53] "Mao Zedong zai zhonggong zhongyang zhengzhiju kuoda huiyi de jianghua" [Mao Zedong's Speech at an Enlarged Meeting of the Politburo], 7 July 1954, quoted in Gong Li, "Liangci Taiwan haixia weiji de chengyin yu ZhongMei zhijian de jiaoliang" [The Causes of the Two Taiwan Strait Crises and Chinese-U.S. Disputes], in Jiang Changbin and Robert S. Ross, eds., *Cong duizhi zouxiang huanhe: lengzhan shiqi ZhongMei guanxi zai tantao* [From Confrontation to Rapprochement: Reexamining China-U.S. Relations during the Cold War] (Beijing: Shijie zhishi chubanshe, 2000), 42.

[54] Pang Xianzhi and Jin Chongji, eds., *Mao Zedong zhuan* [Mao Zedong's Biography] (Beijing: Zhongyang wenxian chubanshe, 2003), 585.

[55] RMRB, 23 July 1954, 1.

[56] Stolper, *China, Taiwan*; Zhang, *Deterrence*, 191–192.

The second decision was to use force. On July 11, the CMC instructed the East China MR "to use the navy and air force to bomb the Dachens and use the army to capture Yijiangshan Island."[57] The Dachens, home to more than 18,000 troops, were the Nationalists' third most important forward operating base after Jinmen and Mazu. In issuing the instructions, Defense Minister Peng Dehuai linked the military action with the deteriorating situation across the Strait, stating that the goal of this offensive was to "attack the American-Chiang mutual defense plot" and ascertain the likely U.S. military response to Chinese action against KMT-held islands.[58]

In addition, the Politburo agreed to "start the fight for liberating Taiwan" (*kaizhan jiefang Taiwan douzheng*), and the CMC tasked General Zhang Zhen to develop a military plan and implementing measures.[59] Mao's overall policy was "fighting while building" (*bianda bianjian*), that is, attacking the KMT while strengthening China's navy and air force and improving infrastructure in Fujian to support the large numbers of troops and equipment that would be required for a frontal assault on Jinmen.[60] As General Zhang recalls in his memoir, his document marked the first time since 1949 that a strategic plan had been formulated regarding Taiwan.[61] The plan, which the CMC approved on August 15, outlined a scheme to seize all the coastal islands, starting with the KMT's weakest positions and then seizing Jinmen and Mazu by the end of 1957.[62]

The decision to seize Yijiangshan was part of a broader effort to attack the remaining KMT-held coastal islands, starting with those where the KMT was most vulnerable. General Zhang's plan also included shelling Jinmen around August 10, 1954. On August 2, however, Peng decided with Mao's approval to postpone the shelling until early September. Preparations had not yet been completed, as they had been hampered by flooding during the rainy season in Fujian.[63] The decision to shell Jinmen, and not seize it, reflected China's continued weakness in the dispute, which Taiwan's improved ties with the United States threatened to aggra-

---

[57] Wang, *Peng Dehuai nianpu*, 571. The initial plan called for establishing air superiority over the Dachens by September or October and then occupying Yijiangshan Island. See Xu, *Jinmen*, 172, 310.

[58] Wang, *Peng Dehuai nianpu*, 571.

[59] Wang, *Peng Dehuai nianpu*, 573.

[60] Pang and Jin, *Mao Zedong zhuan*, 585.

[61] Zhang Zhen, *Zhang Zhen huiyilu* [Zhang Zhen's Memoirs] (Beijing: Jiefangjun chubanshe, 2003), 499.

[62] *Su Yu wenxuan* [Su Yu's Selected Works], vol. 3 (Beijing: Junshi kexue chubanshe, 2004), 155; Yin Qiming and Cheng Yaguang, *Diyi ren guofang buzhang* [First Minister of Defense] (Guangzhou: Guangdong jiaoyu chubanshe, 1997), 194.

[63] Zhang, *Zhang Zhen*, 574.

vate. Even though the shelling did not begin for almost another month, the original August date for the operation underscores the sense of urgency among China's leaders in the summer of 1954 as the treaty was being discussed.

As PLA units prepared for operations against Jinmen and the Dachens, the situation across the Strait continued to deteriorate. In light of the "liberate Taiwan" propaganda drive, the United States stiffened its rhetorical support for Taiwan, and the two countries appeared to move even closer toward a formal defense treaty, precisely the outcome that Mao had hoped to "destroy." At the time, China's leaders believed incorrectly that such a treaty would be signed in September. On August 24, Secretary of State John Foster Dulles had stated that he might visit Taiwan after his trip to Manila to sign the SEATO treaty.[64] As an August 29 *People's Daily* editorial stated, "Recently, the U.S. and Chiang even threaten to conclude a 'mutual defense treaty' in September, intensifying military deployments for plans to attack the PRC."[65]

On August 25, the CMC ordered Ye Fei, the commander of the East China MR, to shell Jinmen. The shelling started on September 3, a date chosen by Ye for maximum effect because KMT supply ships were scheduled to arrive in Jinmen harbor.[66] As others have argued, the primary purpose of the shelling was political: it was a military demonstration of China's resolve to liberate Taiwan, a supplement to the propaganda campaign.[67] Chinese sources also link the purpose of the shelling to attempts to signal China's opposition to the U.S.-ROC treaty. Ye Fei recollects that the goal of the operation was to attack the U.S. policy of "aggression," stop Chiang's coastal harassment, and unleash a punishing attack before the signing of the treaty.[68] China had no intention to seize Jinmen, and PLA ground forces in Fujian Province had undertaken no preparations to do so.[69]

Little evidence exists to suggest that China's leaders, especially Mao, sought to use the shelling of Jinmen or the attack on Yijiangshan to mobilize support for domestic objectives. One telegram does state that the propaganda campaign could be used to "raise the political consciousness and political alertness of the whole country, arousing people's enthusiasm to promote national development," but even in this document, domestic mo-

---

[64] *NYT*, 25 August 1954, 1.

[65] *RMRB*, 29 August 1954, 1.

[66] Ye Fei, *Ye Fei huiyilu* [Ye Fei's Memoirs] (Beijing: Jiefangjun chubanshe, 1988), 645–646.

[67] Gong, "Tension," 148; He, "Evolution," 226; Li, "Making of Mao's Cold War," 54–55.

[68] Ye, *Ye Fei*, 644.

[69] For an assessment of China's military weakness, see Zhang, *Zhang Zhen*, 491–492.

bilization does not appear to be the main goal.[70] On the other hand, the question of how to deal with the KMT-held coastal islands had occupied the attention of Chinese military commanders since the end of the civil war on the mainland.

The shelling backfired. Instead of deterring, it expedited U.S. and Nationalist treaty negotiations, which began in October.[71] China now feared that defense of the KMT-held coastal islands would be covered by the treaty, which might not only embolden Chiang to conduct more raids against the mainland but also weaken greatly China's ability to seize Jinmen and Mazu as steps toward an attack on Taiwan. Although the planned September bombing of the Dachens had been postponed in late August, Mao approved a plan to assault Yijiangshan in late October.[72] On November 1, the PLA Air Force (PLAAF) began four days of air raids against islands off the Zhejiang coast. On November 30, the chief of the General Staff, Su Yu, issued an operational order that linked the Yijiangshan campaign to the U.S.-ROC Mutual Defense Treaty, which had just been initialed but not yet signed. According to Su's order, "The East China Military Region should attack and seize Yijiangshan Island on or around December 20 to force the scope of the so-called 'defense treaty' that America and Chiang are about to sign to exclude our coastal islands that the enemy occupies."[73]

The Mutual Defense Treaty was signed on December 2, 1954. Due mostly to a desire to avoid combat with U.S. forces who were conducted exercises in adjacent waters in December, the assault on Yijiangshan began on January 18, 1955, more than a month after the treaty was signed. The treaty, however, did not specify whether the coastal islands were covered. Instead, it referred explicitly only to Taiwan and the Penghu Islands, stating elliptically that it "will be applicable to such other territories as may be determined by mutual agreement."[74] In addition to achieving a long-standing goal of securing the Zhejiang coast, the Yijiangshan campaign also probed the treaty's scope. When the attack occurred, the United States did not intervene to defend the coastal islands.

In sum, China's leaders faced two different types of decline in the dispute: first that a security treaty would be signed and then that the coastal islands would be included in the scope of the treaty. Although the shelling of Jinmen certainly brought international attention to China's Taiwan problem, it failed to deter the United States from pursuing the treaty and

---

[70] Li Ping and Ma Zhisun, eds., *Zhou Enlai nianpu, 1949–1976* [Chronicle of Zhou Enlai's Life], vol. 1 (Beijing: Zhongyang wenxian chubanshe, 1997), 405.

[71] Stolper, *China, Taiwan*, 49–52.

[72] Li, "PLA Attacks," 151.

[73] Quoted in Wang, *Mubiao*, 53. Also, *Su Yu wenxuan*, 132.

[74] Article VI of the 1954 treaty.

only increased U.S. support for the KMT. The attack on Yijiangshan demonstrated that not all the coastal islands would be covered by the new treaty, but it also elevated U.S. concerns about China's intentions, producing the Formosa Resolution and veiled nuclear threats—both of which deepened American ties with Taiwan and further weakened China's ability to liberate the island and end the civil war.

1958 TAIWAN CRISIS

On August 23, 1958, PLA forces began a second punishing shelling of Jinmen along with Mazu Island. The military objective was to blockade the islands, most likely to compel a KMT retreat similar to the evacuation of the Dachens in February 1955.[75] In addition to artillery strikes, a limited number of naval forces, especially torpedo boats, attacked KMT ships in Jinmen's harbor, and a significant number of aircraft had been deployed to Fujian. On September 4, Secretary of State John Foster Dulles stated that the United States would use force if necessary to prevent the PRC from capturing Jinmen, a clear display of U.S. commitment to defend and support Taiwan.[76] U.S. warships began to escort Nationalist supply convoys on September 7, which further clarified U.S. intentions as six aircraft carriers deployed to the region.[77]

In September, the crisis began to abate. On September 6, Zhou Enlai agreed to resume ambassadorial-level talks in Warsaw, which began a week later. Toward the end of the month, the Nationalist supply effort began to bolster Jinmen's defenses, alleviating the sense of urgency. Like-

---

[75] For Chinese sources on the 1958 crisis in addition to those in note 41, see *DDZGJD*, 381–422; Lei Yingfu, *Zai zuigao tongshuaibu dang canmou: Lei Yingfu huiyilu* [Staff Officer at the Supreme Command: General Lei Yingfu's Recollections] (Nanchang: Baihuazhou wenyi chubanshe, 1997), 187–216; Liao Xinwen, "1958 nian Mao Zedong juece paoji Jinmen de lishi kaocha" [A Historical Investigation of Mao Zedong's 1958 Decision to Shell Jinmen], *Dang de wenxian*, no. 1 (1994): 31–36; Shen Weiping, *8.23 paoji Jinmen* [August 23 Shelling of Jinmen] (Beijing: Huayi chubanshe, 1998); Yang Qiliang, *Wang Shangrong jiangjun* [General Wang Shangrong] (Beijing: Dangdai Zhongguo chubanshe, 2000), 418–441; Zhai Zhirui and Li Yuzhuang, *Jinmen jishi: wushi niandai Taihai weiji shimo* [Jinmen Record: The Whole Story of the 1950s Taiwan Strait Crisis] (Beijing: Zhonggong zhongyang dangxiao chubanshe, 1994).

For English-language sources, see note 41 as well as Chen Jian, *Mao's China and the Cold War* (Chapel Hill: University of North Carolina Press, 2001), 163–204; Christensen, *Useful Adversaries*, 194–241.

[76] On U.S. decision making, see Robert Accinelli, " 'A Thorn in the Side of Peace': The Eisenhower Administration and the 1958 Offshore Islands Crisis," in Robert S. Ross and Jiang Changbin, eds., *Re-examining the Cold War: U.S.-China Diplomacy, 1954–1973* (Cambridge, Mass.: Harvard University Press, 2001), 106–140.

[77] *NYT*, 17 September 1958, 17.

wise, it became clear that the shelling was not the prelude to a broader Chinese offensive against KMT coastal positions, much less Taiwan. On October 6, China proposed a cease-fire linked to the withdrawal of U.S. escorts, though large-scale bombardments occurred in November and December. China effectively ended the crisis on October 25 by announcing that it would shell Jinmen only on odd-numbered days, a practice that would continue until 1979.[78] Approximately 2,428 Nationalists were killed or wounded in the attacks over the next two months, while the PLA suffered more than 460 casualties.[79]

The prevailing explanation of these events is that Mao initiated the crisis to mobilize domestic support for the Great Leap Forward. The Great Leap started as an effort to skip stages of economic development and pull China rapidly into the industrial age. Mao famously claimed that China would match Britain's steel production within fifteen years. Thomas Christensen argues that the Taiwan crisis was necessary to create domestic support for these ambitious economic goals, which were part of a much larger change in grand strategy designed to improve China's position in the international system.[80] Rapid economic change could be achieved only through the widespread mobilization of society, which Mao believed would be facilitated by an external crisis that could galvanize the population. The documentary record of Mao's speeches and the absence of a direct threat to China's security from U.S. forces stationed on Taiwan support the mobilization explanation. Chen Jian's variant of this argument examines more specifically Mao's personality. Chen stresses Mao's "postrevolution anxiety," describing the 1958 decision to shell Jinmen as a "revolutionary outburst."[81] The Great Leap was one of Mao's many efforts to continue revolution, as he used the crisis "to create an enemy" and increase support for his economic policy.[82]

Nevertheless, more than what Chen Jian describes as a "singular logic" explains China's use of force in 1958. The analysis below demonstrates that China pursued multiple motives by shelling the islands.[83] Domestic

---

[78] In December 1961, the CMC instructed frontline units in Fujian to stop using live ammunition and instead to shell the island with propaganda leaflets. Wang, *Fujian shengzhi: junshi zhi*, 291.

[79] Wang, *Fujian shengzhi: junshi zhi*, 290; Guofangbu shizheng bianju, *Guomin geming jianjun shi, di si bu, di san ce* [History of Building an Army in the Nationalist Revolution: Part 4, Volume 3] (Taibei: Guofangbu, 1987), 1673–1674. According to Wang, the number of Nationalist causalities was much higher, around 7,000.

[80] Christensen, *Useful Adversaries.*

[81] Chen Jian, *Mao's China*, 171.

[82] Chen Jian, *Mao's China*, 180.

[83] On mixed motives, see Christensen, *Useful Adversaries*, 201. For Christensen, domestic mobilization was primary and the other motives were secondary. For a Chinese perspective on mixed motives, see Xu, *Jinmen*, 203–204.

mobilization concerns account for the timing of the attack, but China's public and private diplomacy also sought to counter the decline of China's claim strength that had occurred since 1955 in the Taiwan dispute. Assessments of a growing deterioration of China's position in the dispute and increasing fears of the permanent separation of Taiwan as part of "two Chinas" prompted the initial considerations to blockade the islands and signal China's commitment to defeating the KMT and ending the civil war. Mao's desire to mobilize the Chinese people in support of the Great Leap then shaped the timing of the shelling.

DECLINING CLAIM STRENGTH

In the months preceding the crisis, China's leaders faced continued vulnerability in their country's most important territorial dispute. The first source of decline in claim strength was the failure of China's "peaceful reunification" initiative. In the spring and summer of 1955, Zhou Enlai proposed a shift in China's Taiwan policy from "liberation by force" (*wuli jiefang*) to "peaceful liberation" (*heping jiefang*), suggesting a negotiated end to the civil war.[84] In 1956, Zhou further refined this proposal, outlining the "one principle, four goals" (*yi wang si mu*) that would serve as the basis for unification without armed conquest.[85] Chiang Kai-shek did dispatch emissaries from Hong Kong to probe Beijing's intentions, but no progress was made toward opening talks between the two sides. By late 1957, it was clear to China's leaders that this short-lived peace offensive had failed.[86] These initiatives were not attempts to compromise over Taiwan but rather attempts to pursue unification through diplomatic means.

The second source of declining claim strength was an inability to make progress in talks with the United States. As the 1954 Taiwan Strait crisis abated in the spring of 1955, the United States and China agreed to hold talks at the ambassadorial level in Geneva, which constituted the first and only official communication channel between the two sides. In the talks, China hoped to prepare for higher-level negotiations and decrease U.S.

[84] On China's Taiwan policy during this period, see Yang Qinhua, "Zhongguo gongchandang he Zhongguo zhengfu jiejue Taiwan wenti zhengce de youlai ji fazhan" [Origins and Development of the CCP and Chinese Government's Policy for Resolving the Taiwan Problem], *Zhonggong dangshi ziliao*, no. 53 (1994): 65–80; Yu Manfei and Lin Xiaoguang, "50 nian lai Zhongguo gongchandang duiTai zhengce de fazhan bianhua" [Development and Transformation of the CCP's Policy to Taiwan over the Past 50 Years], *Zhonggong dangshi ziliao*, no. 69 (1996): 137–153; Zhang Tongxin and He Zhongshan, 'Yiguo liangzhi' yu haixia liang'an guanxi ["One Country Two Systems" and Cross-straits Relations] (Beijing: Zhongguo renmin daxue chubanshe, 1998), 91–151.

[85] These programs included guarantees for the island's autonomy that presaged Deng Xiaoping's notion of "One Country, Two Systems."

[86] On Chinese frustration, see *DDZGJD*, 385; Lei, *Zai zuigao tongshuaibu*, 174–175.

support for Taiwan.[87] The United States, however, insisted that as a pre-condition for discussing any other subject, China should renounce the use of force against the island. China stated it would consider a cease-fire only with the United States and not with Taiwan. China's goal was a U.S. withdrawal, which would greatly strengthen its military position in the dispute. In December 1957, the talks stalled after Ambassador U. Alexis Johnson was replaced with a lower-ranking official, which Beijing viewed as downgrading the talks. For China's leaders, the talks' failure under-scored the depth of the U.S. commitment to defend Taiwan and remain involved in China's civil war.

The third source of decline was the deepening of the U.S.-Taiwan secu-rity relationship, which was the most immediate obstacle to the armed or peaceful liberation of Taiwan. In March 1957, China learned that the United States planned to base nuclear-tipped Matador missiles on the is-land, compounding fears of potential nuclear war initially raised during the 1954 crisis.[88] The United States also constructed a large air base capable of supporting B-52 bombers that could be used in strikes against the main-land. In November 1957, the United States and Taiwan held military exer-cises and maneuvers on the island and in the Strait. In January 1958, re-ports surfaced that the United States was considering revising the alliance to clarify its commitment to defend Jinmen and other coastal islands.[89] In February 1958, an American commander said that the United States would retaliate with missiles if China launched offensive operations in the Strait.[90] In March 1958, the United States consolidated the seventeen military aid agencies that had been established to provide assistance to Taiwan into the U.S.-Taiwan Defense Command.[91] As demonstrated in figures 5.1 and 5.2, troop deployments and weapons deliveries reflected this increased U.S. sup-port for the island, support that weakened China's position.

Observing these events, China's leaders had become more pessimistic about the likelihood of unifying Taiwan with the mainland. One histo-rian, for example, notes that China's leaders in early 1958 "perceived that any further deterioration of the situation in the Taiwan Strait could be

---

[87] Steven M. Goldstein, "Dialogue of the Deaf? The Sino-American Ambassadorial-Level Talks, 1955–1970," in Robert S. Ross and Changbin Jiang, eds., *Re-examining the Cold War: U.S.-China Diplomacy, 1954–1973* (Cambridge, Mass.: Harvard University Press, 2001), 209–213; Gong, "Tension," 152–154.

[88] Zhang, *Deterrence*, 226. On the nuclear threats, see Richard K. Betts, *Nuclear Black-mail and Nuclear Balance* (Washington, D.C.: The Brookings Institution, 1987), 48–61, 66–78; Lewis and Xue, *China Builds the Bomb*, 32–41.

[89] *NYT*, 10 January 1958, 3.

[90] Chen Chonglong and Xie Jun, eds., *Haixia liang'an guanxi dashiji* [Chronicle of Events in Cross-strait Relations] (Beijing: Zhonggong dangshi chubanshe, 1993), 129.

[91] Gong, "Tension," 156; Zhang, *Deterrence*, 227.

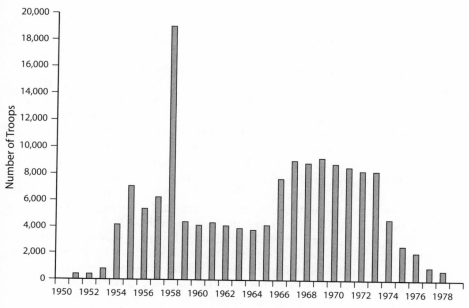

Figure 5.2 U.S. Troops Stationed in Taiwan (1950–1979)
Source: Global U.S. Troop Deployment Dataset, Heritage Foundation, October 2004.

dangerous."[92] According to General Lei Yingfu, deputy director of the Operations Department in the GSD and Zhou Enlai's military secretary, Mao believed that China's restraint, symbolized by not pursuing Nationalist troops retreating from the Dachens in 1955, had led the United States and Chiang to believe that China was "weak and easily bullied" (*ruan ruo ke qi*) over Taiwan.[93] Reflecting these concerns, in November 1957 the *People's Daily* published an editorial titled "Oppose America's Plot to Create 'Two Chinas.' "[94] In February 1958, Zhou Enlai's foreign policy report to the State Council stated that America wanted China to accept its "occupation" of Taiwan and that the United States intended to create "two Chinas" divided by the Strait.[95] A *People's Daily* commentary around the same time concluded that "Washington has no sincere intention to seek a peaceful solution to the conflict in the Taiwan area."[96]

[92] For a detailed discussion of these perceptions, see Zhang, *Deterrence*, 227–230.

[93] Lei, *Zai zuigao tongshuaibu*, 188.

[94] *RMRB*, 2 November 1957, 1.

[95] "Zhou Enlai zongli guanyu muqian guoji xingshi he woguo waijiao zhengce de baogao" [Premier Zhou Enlai's Report on Current International Trends and Our Country's Foreign Policy], 10 February 1958, in 1958 *Waijiao huibian*, 20–21. Also see Chen and Xie, *Haixia liang'an*, 129.

[96] Quoted in Zhang, *Deterrence*, 228.

ARTILLERY DIPLOMACY

China's growing weakness in the dispute occurred as China's leaders began to contemplate sweeping economic reforms. Facing the "dangerous" situation across the Strait, China began preparations for military action against Taiwan. After the shelling started, China's public and private diplomacy was linked to efforts to weaken U.S. influence over Taiwan and increase the likelihood of unification. Although domestic mobilization concerns and the euphoria of the Great Leap account for the timing and attractiveness of artillery diplomacy in late August, the vulnerability that China's leaders perceived over Taiwan explains the original plans for the operation and the diplomatic conduct of the crisis itself.

As the situation deteriorated across the Taiwan Strait in late 1957, China's leaders began to contemplate military action. Following Mao's instructions, the PLA Air Force submitted a plan to the CMC in January 1958 to deploy aircraft to airfields in Fujian Province that were constructed after the 1954 crisis. On April 27, acting on CMC instructions, Fujian MD commanders Ye Fei and Han Xianchu submitted operational plans for a large-scale artillery blockade of Jinmen and began preparations for a strike at the appropriate moment.[97]

Mao and China's other leaders did not immediately act on these plans. At the time, they were preoccupied with preparations to launch the Great Leap. Moreover, trends across the Strait were not as acute or urgent as they had been in the summer of 1954. In July, however, the deployment of U.S. and British troops to Lebanon to support its pro-Western government provided an opportunity to strike.

In response, Mao instructed Peng Dehuai on July 17 to transfer air force units to Fujian and prepare artillery batteries to shell Jinmen.[98] The following evening, Mao gathered senior members of the CMC and armed services to discuss the shelling operation, which was planned to last for two months. In the meeting, the bombardment of Jinmen was scheduled to begin on or around July 25, and units were to be transferred during the following weeks.[99] General Lei Yingfu described the purpose of the shelling as to "blockade Jinmen to create momentum (*shengshi*) for liberating Jinmen."[100] Based on high-level interviews, He Di concludes that the military objective of the operation was "recovering" Jinmen and Mazu, presumably by compelling an evacuation of Nationalist forces.[101] According to General Lei, the political goal of the operation was to probe

---

[97] *DDZGJD*, 386.
[98] On the July planning of the operation, see *DDZGJD*, 386–387; Xu, *Jinmen*, 319.
[99] Li, "Making of Mao's Cold War," 61.
[100] Lei, *Zai zuigao tongshuai bu*, 191.
[101] He, "Evolution," 234.

the scope of the U.S.-ROC Mutual Defense Treaty and determine whether the United States had offensive or defensive aims.[102]

Despite making these preparations to shell Jinmen, Mao was apparently not convinced that it was appropriate to use force. During the night of July 26, Mao postponed the operation, which was to start the following morning.[103] One reason is that the frontline units needed more time to prepare for combat, as many of the aircraft necessary for defending coastal batteries from KMT air strikes could not deploy to Fujian until mid-August.[104] Additionally, Mao and China's other top leaders were consumed with the launching of the Great Leap, whose planning peaked in the spring and summer of 1958. The final decision to shell Jinmen was not taken until mid-August, during a series of Politburo meetings at the Beidaihe retreat convened to discuss economic policy. In this meeting, Mao clearly linked the external tension that the crisis would create with domestic mobilization and the goals of the Great Leap Forward, stating that "to have an enemy in front of us, to have tension, is to our advantage."[105]

After being delayed for almost a month, the shelling of Jinmen began on August 23. This timing supports the domestic mobilization explanation: the shelling began after the UN had already resolved the crisis in the Middle East, and thus China could not have been acting in support of the struggle against "imperialism," as some suggest. China's conduct during the crisis, however, demonstrates that its leaders pursued more than domestic mobilization. By shelling the islands, Mao clearly hoped to reduce U.S. support for Taiwan. Ideally, the KMT would withdraw from the coastal islands, weakening Taiwan's first line of defense, while the United States would be forced to reconsider the depth of its support for Taiwan—two outcomes that would strengthen China's position in the dispute.

Three kinds of evidence support this interpretation. First, public and private statements by China's leaders emphasize that one goal was to improve the prospects for unification. The specific military objective was to compel the Nationalists to evacuate Jinmen and Mazu, thereby weakening Taiwan's first line of defense. In July 1958, when Mao initially ordered preparations to shell the islands, he stated that "Jinmen and Mazu

---

[102] Lei, *Zai zuigao tongshuai bu*, 191.

[103] *Jianguo yilai Mao Zedong wengao* [Manuscripts of Mao Zedong since the Founding of the Nation], vol. 7 (Beijing: Zhongyang wenxian chubanshe [internal circulation], 1992), 326.

[104] Xu, *Jinmen*, 209–215.

[105] "Talks at the Beidaihe Conference (Draft Transcript)," in Roderick MacFarquhar, Timothy Cheek, and Eugene Wu, eds., *The Secret Speeches of Chairman Mao: From the Hundred Flowers to the Great Leap Forward* (Cambridge, Mass.: Harvard University, Council on East Asian Studies, 1989), 403. See Christensen, *Useful Adversaries*, 219–220.

are Chinese territory. By striking Jinmen and Mazu, we will punish the KMT army."[106] But there was also a further, indirect objective. Mao instructed Peng Dehuai that the shelling should be targeted so as to "deal with Chiang directly and the Americans indirectly,"[107] that is, hit the KMT hard enough to pressure the United States to decrease its support. Wu Lengxi, then the editor of the *People's Daily* and later deputy director of the Central Committee's Propaganda Department, recalls that Mao stated that the shelling was "intended to punish the Americans" for their involvement in Taiwan.[108] Moreover, Mao linked the attack to China's long-standing demand that the United States leave Taiwan and the Nationalists relinquish the coastal islands.[109] In early September, Mao had stated, "in order to avoid a war with us, America has to find a way out. How? The only way is to withdraw the 110,000 [Nationalist] troops from Jinmen and Mazu as they did for the Dachens in 1955."[110] Likewise, Zhou Enlai explained to the Soviet ambassador that the shelling was designed to punish the Nationalist troops and prevent the United States from creating two Chinas on either side of the Strait.[111]

Second, throughout the crisis, China's leaders, especially Mao, stressed the importance of testing the U.S. commitment to defend Taiwan. Such behavior is consistent with a perception of declining claim strength. According to Wu Lengxi, Mao repeatedly stated that the purpose of the shelling was to probe U.S. intentions. On August 25, Mao stated that "the main goal of the shelling was . . . to reconnoiter and test the American resolve."[112] Similarly, China's declaration of sovereignty over territorial waters issued on September 4 was designed to prevent U.S. warships from resupplying Nationalist troops stationed on the coastal islands. As Mao stated on September 8, "firing artillery is a probe through force. . . . Holding talks is a reconnaissance through diplomacy."[113]

Finally, during specific moments in the crisis, Mao managed events to increase the likelihood for unification. In this respect, China's use of force in 1958 was quite similar to that of 1954. When the crisis started, the

---

[106] Mao paraphrased in *DDZGJD*, 387.

[107] Liu Wusheng and Du Hongqi, eds., *Zhou Enlai junshi huodong jishi, 1918–1975 (xia)* [Chronicle of Zhou Enlai's Military Activities, vol. 2] (Beijing: Zhongyang wenxian chubanshe, 2000), 458.

[108] Wu Lengxi, *Yi Mao zhuxi: wo qinshen jingli de ruogan zhongda lishi shijian pianduan* [Remembering Chairman Mao: Fragments of Certain Major Historical Events Which I Personally Experienced] (Beijing: Xinhua chubanshe, 1995), 75. In this recollection, Wu Lengxi paraphrases Mao's comments during the crisis and does not quote them verbatim.

[109] Wu, *Yi Mao zhuxi*, 80.

[110] Quoted in Zhang, *Deterrence*, 235.

[111] Liu and Du, *Zhou Enlai*, 460.

[112] Wu, *Yi Mao zhuxi*, 76.

[113] Wu, *Yi Mao zhuxi*, 80.

objective of the artillery bombardment was to blockade Jinmen and compel a KMT evacuation, thereby demonstrating China's commitment to achieving unification, by force if necessary. On September 9, Zhou Enlai instructed Wang Bingnan, China's representative to the ambassadorial talks in Warsaw, to inform the United States that China would not pursue Nationalist troops if they withdrew from Jinmen and Mazu. Moreover, Zhou's instructions directed Wang to inform the United States that China would strive to use peaceful means to liberate Taiwan and the Penghu Islands after it recovered all the other coastal islands.[114] In short, these instructions linked U.S. support for Taiwan with China's ability to achieve unification.

China began to defuse the crisis when events developed in an unexpected manner that had even more negative implications for its position in the dispute. On September 30, Secretary of State Dulles suggested that the KMT troops might be withdrawn from the coastal islands if a ceasefire could be reached between China and Taiwan. China's leaders believed that the United States was seeking to institutionalize a "two China" division across the Strait, whereby the Nationalists would withdraw from the coastal islands and renounce plans to retake the mainland in return for China's agreement not to use force, "exchanging Jinmen and Mazu for Taiwan and the Penghu Islands."[115] Mao's solution was the "noose" (*jiao-suo*) strategy of leaving the coastal islands under Nationalist control in order to maintain a physical link between Taiwan and the mainland. Although official histories hail this strategy as the "success" of 1958, it was a reaction to events during the crisis and not the original political goal of the shelling. The noose strategy itself was a response to Mao's miscalculation that the United States would not maintain Taiwan's link to the mainland through Jinmen and Mazu.

THE 1962 AVERTED CRISIS AND BEYOND

After 1958, China's position in the dispute across the Strait began to stabilize. China no longer challenged KMT control of the coastal islands, which were now viewed as supporting unification through the noose strategy by maintaining a link between Taiwan and the mainland. Although the KMT's claim to the mainland created some measure of stability in terms of avoiding a permanent separation, China's leaders acknowledged

---

[114] For a copy of Zhou's letter, see Shen, *8.23 paoji Jinmen*, 752–753. For Wang Bingnan's statement in the negotiations, see *DDZGWJ*, 107–108; Wang, *ZhongMei huitan*, 70–74.

[115] *ZELNP2*, 177. For a fuller account of this change, see Chen Jian, *Mao's China*, 197–201.

that unification would occur only when the United States decreased its support for Taiwan. As Deng told Soviet ambassador Pavel Iudin in 1959, China must "wait a bit." Nevertheless, Deng observed that circumstances for unification would become more favorable as China became stronger and supporting Taiwan became too costly for the United States to continue.[116] Recognizing the role of U.S. support for Taiwan, China's leaders adopted a delaying strategy for the rest of the Mao era. Jinmen was shelled briefly in 1960 during Eisenhower's visit to Taiwan, but otherwise the Strait was largely peaceful apart from small-scale Nationalist harassment operations.[117] The shelling of Jinmen on odd-numbered days continued until 1979, but frontline units stopped using live ammunition in December 1961 and switched to shells with propaganda leaflets. As Mao described the delaying strategy to Kissinger in 1973, "I say that we can do without Taiwan for the time being, and let it come after one hundred years. . . . Why is there need to be in such great haste?"[118]

In 1962, however, the United States and China faced a potential crisis across the Strait, which Harold Hinton described as the "Taiwan Straits Crisis III."[119] Although not linked directly to the prospects for unification, it demonstrated the central role of the United States in China's leaders' assessments of their state's position in the Taiwan dispute. Violence was avoided in 1962 because the United States used diplomatic channels to reassure China's leaders that Washington did not support Chiang's adventurism and dissuaded him from attacking the mainland.

As discussed in chapter 2, tensions across the Strait were part of China's larger territorial crisis, including its frontier dispute with India, in the spring of 1962. Sensing weakness in the aftermath of the Great Leap, Chiang saw a window of opportunity to strike against the mainland and moved to take action. In late 1961, Chiang began to offer bellicose statements about an imminent Nationalist return to the mainland, increasing his rhetoric in March.[120] From early March to May, the Nationalist government issued a conscription mobilization decree in order to increase

---

[116] P. F. Iudin, "Report of Conversation with the General Secretary of the CC CCP, Deng Xiaoping," 27 May 1959, Cold War International History Project Virtual Archive.

[117] Low-level violence did continue through the end of the 1960s, focused on KMT infiltration efforts along the coast.

[118] "Memorandum of Conversation, 12 November 1973, Chairmen Mao's Residence, Beijing" in William Burr, ed., *The Kissinger Transcripts: The Top Secret Talks with Beijing and Moscow* (New York: The New Press, 1998), 186. While Kissinger and many others attribute this statement to Mao's 1972 meeting with Nixon, it in fact was made by Mao in 1973, during a separate meeting with Kissinger. See Burr, *The Kissinger Transcripts*, 59–68; Henry Kissinger, *White House Years* (Boston: Little, Brown & Co., 1979), 1062.

[119] Harold C. Hinton, *Communist China in World Politics* (New York: Houghton Mifflin, 1966), 270.

[120] *NYT*, 30 March 1962, 2.

military manpower, adopted a special budget to fund wartime mobilization efforts, and imposed a "return to the mainland" tax to help fund the effort.[121]

By late May, China's leaders had concluded that the threat from Taiwan was real. In a series of meetings, the CMC and GSD developed plans to repel the attack.[122] In early June, the CMC instructed Shandong, Zhejiang, Fujian, Jiangxi, and Guangdong provinces to undertake war preparations, while five first-grade divisions of approximately 100,000 troops were deployed to the frontline and existing units were placed on high alert (*jinji zhanbei zhuangtai*).[123] On June 10, 1962, the CMC issued "Instructions for Smashing Nationalist Raids in the Southeast Coastal Area," which implemented a widespread mobilization in coastal provinces.[124]

By the end of June, however, it was apparent that the potential invasion across the Strait would not materialize. Although Chiang faced his own operational challenges in mounting any assault, the lack of U.S. support played a key role in the avoidance of conflict. At the time, Beijing viewed the slew of high-level U.S. officials who visited Taiwan as demonstrating U.S. support for an attack.[125] Importantly, China's leaders had previously concluded that the situation across the Strait was quite stable and that time was on their side because Taiwan would simply become too costly for the United States to protect.[126] To probe U.S. intentions, the Chinese delegation in Warsaw sought a meeting with their U.S. counterparts.[127] At the June 23 meeting, U.S. ambassador John Cabot stated that the "US government had no intention of supporting any [ROC] attack on the Mainland under existing circumstances." He further stressed that if Chiang did attack, it would be "without the support of the US."[128] U.S. reassurances played an important role in preventing a crisis from occurring.

Following this crisis, the situation across the Strait remained stable. Although Chiang still harbored hopes of returning to the mainland, U.S.

---

[121] Melvin Gurtov and Byong-Moo Hwang, *China under Threat: The Politics of Strategy and Diplomacy* (Baltimore: Johns Hopkins University Press, 1980), 127–128; Hinton, *Communist China*, 280–272; Allen S. Whiting, *The Chinese Calculus of Deterrence: India and Indochina* (Ann Arbor: University of Michigan Press, 1975), 62–72.

[122] On Chinese decision making, see Yang, *Wang Shangrong*, 484–492.

[123] Wang Shangrong, "Xin Zhongguo dansheng hou jici zhongda zhanzheng" [Several Major Wars after the Emergence of New China], in Zhu Yuanshi, ed., *Gongheguo yaoshi koushushi* [An Oral History of the Republic's Important Events] (Changsha: Henan renmin chubanshe, 1999), 278.

[124] Yang, *Wang Shangrong*, 486.

[125] In fact, these officials were dispatched to dissuade Chiang from taking such action.

[126] Iudin, "Report of Conversation."

[127] For a detailed recollection of the talks, see Wang, *ZhongMei huitan*, 85–90.

[128] Quoted in Goldstein, "Dialogue of the Deaf?" 228.

military support did not increase appreciably. Instead, if measured in terms of both weapons deliveries and troop deployments, U.S. support declined slightly. As demonstrated in figure 5.1, the last major delivery of fighter aircraft occurred in 1960. Moreover, as figure 5.2 shows, the number of U.S. troops based on Taiwan declined slightly until the escalation of the war in Vietnam in 1965, when the island served as an important base for the United States. This increase, however, was not directed against China, nor was the United States seeking to enhance the KMT's ability to resist unification with the mainland.

At the same time, successive U.S. administrations explored improving ties with China, resulting in Kissinger's 1971 secret trip to China and rapprochement between the two rivals. Moreover, U.S. policy toward Taiwan played a central role in this process. In the Shanghai communiqué released during President Nixon's 1972 trip to Beijing, the United States acknowledged the Chinese position that "there is but one China" and agreed not to "challenge that position." Although emphasizing an interest in a peaceful settlement, the United States also pledged to withdraw "all U.S. forces and military installations from Taiwan."[129] Reduced support for Taiwan was a key Chinese demand, a demand clearly linked to strengthening China's position in the dispute.[130]

THE TAIWAN DISPUTE AFTER MAO

When Deng assumed power after Mao's death, he maintained a delaying strategy in the dispute. Overall, the situation increasingly favored China. Following Nixon's visit to China in 1972, the United States began withdrawing troops from the island, and the last combat forces left in 1976. In 1979, the United States established diplomatic relations with the PRC, breaking ties with Taiwan. The United States also abrogated the 1954 U.S.-ROC Mutual Defense Treaty, though in the absence of a Chinese renunciation to use force it pledged to continue to provide Taiwan with military hardware.

The reduction in U.S. support for Taiwan greatly strengthened China's position in the dispute. Under Mao, China had pursued a policy of liberation, achieving unification by force if necessary. Once the United States intervened in the conflict in the summer of 1950, China's leaders viewed liberation as a long-term process that required strengthening China's military power and eliminating U.S. backing of the KMT. When U.S. support

---

[129] http://usinfo.state.gov/eap/Archive_Index/joint_communique_1972.html.
[130] Robert S. Ross, *Negotiating Cooperation: The United States and China, 1969–1989* (Stanford, Calif.: Stanford University Press, 1995), 17–54.

was greatly reduced after normalization, China shifted its strategy to "peaceful unification" (*heping tongyi*). Marshall Ye Jianying announced this shift in a September 1981 speech, which advanced nine principles for Taiwan's peaceful unification with the mainland. In practical terms, it embodied the concept of "one country, two systems," indicating that any political relationship was possible so long as both the mainland and Taiwan were part of the same China.[131]

Peaceful unification, however, did not signal a shift in China's unwillingness to compromise over sovereignty. Instead of waiting to achieve the military superiority necessary to conquer the island, China's leaders now sought to achieve unification through Taiwan's increased economic dependence on the mainland. In addition, peaceful unification excluded a renunciation of the use of force despite its emphasis on a negotiated outcome.[132] Deng and other senior leaders believed that time was on their side and that eventual unification was likely. Similar to the return of Hong Kong and Macao, "one country, two systems" contained no compromise over the sovereign status of these homeland areas. Rather, it was a carrot to facilitate unification through guarantees of autonomy within the framework of "one China."

Under Deng, China remained acutely sensitive to any increase in U.S. support for Taiwan after normalization in 1979. Even before Marshall Ye's speech on peaceful unification, events threatened to weaken China's recently enhanced position in the dispute. In June 1980, President Carter permitted two U.S. defense contractors to begin discussions with Taiwan over the sale of an advanced fighter known as the FX to replace Taiwan's aging fleet of F-5Es. The situation worsened with the election of President Ronald Reagan, who had condemned Carter's abandonment of Taiwan on the campaign trail. In the meantime, the U.S. delivery of weapons to the island continued. In short, it appeared as if China had gained less from normalization than it had anticipated.[133]

China took action. Even before Reagan's election, China protested against the continued arms sales. When Secretary of State Alexander Haig visited China in June, Deng indicated that he wanted the United States to terminate arms sales to the island, an issue that Premier Zhao Ziyang raised with Reagan in October 1981. When negotiations began in Decem-

[131] For a detailed discussion of the meaning of "one China," see Alan D. Romberg, *Rein in at the Brink of the Precipice: American Policy toward Taiwan and U.S.-PRC Relations* (Washington, D.C.: Henry Stimson Center, 2003).

[132] Cheng Guangzhong, "Congwei chengnuo fangqi duiTai shiyong wuli: sandai lingdao jiti jiejue Taiwan wenti fangzhen de lishi kaocha" [Never Promising to Renounce the Use of Force: A Historical Examination of the Third-Generation Leaders' Policy for Resolving the Taiwan Problem], *Junshi lishi*, no. 5 (1999): 37–39.

[133] This paragraph and the next draw on Ross, *Negotiating Cooperation*, 163–200.

ber 1981, China demanded a clear timetable for the reduction of arms sales, while the United States linked any reduction with a renunciation of force, harking back to the ambassadorial talks in the 1950s. In the 1982 August communiqué, the United States agreed that future sales would not exceed those in recent years and stated that it intended a gradual reduction without a specified timetable. China noted that peaceful unification was its "guiding principle" (fangzhen).

Although a diplomatic compromise was found, this episode demonstrates China's continued sensitivity to U.S. actions that strengthened Taiwan's ability to resist Chinese pressure. In the end, force was not used, as the U.S. did not authorize the sale of any new systems and both sides needed each other in their shared struggle against the Soviet Union. Following the 1982 communiqué, China's relative power in the Taiwan dispute improved slightly as the pace of U.S. arms sales decreased gradually through the 1980s and Taiwan removed restrictions on travel to the mainland in the late 1980s.

When Jiang Zemin became CCP general secretary in 1989, China continued its delaying strategy keyed to peaceful unification, in part because Deng was still a dominant figure in Chinese foreign policy-making. At the same time, China faced no long-term challenges to its position in the dispute. Trade continued to deepen between China and Taiwan, especially after 1989, while the United States avoided any dramatic increases in support for Taiwan. For China's leaders, the status quo in place since the early 1980s, whereby trade increased between the two sides under a broad, if ambiguous, acceptance of the "one China" principle, was a stable equilibrium. China could continue to be patient because growing economic interdependence supported unification.

THE 1995–96 TAIWAN STRAIT CRISIS

In the summer of 1995, China initiated a series of large-scale military exercises culminating with provocative missile tests just before Taiwan's March 1996 presidential election. The story behind China's missile diplomacy is now a familiar one, as Taiwan's drift toward formal independence and more visible U.S. support for the island created new perceptions of decline in the dispute. The turning point was the U.S. decision to grant President Lee Teng-hui a visa to receive an honorary doctorate from his alma mater, Cornell University. China used military exercises and missile diplomacy to signal its commitment to unification, by force if necessary, thereby arresting the island's drift toward independence and limiting further U.S. support.

Other scholars have noted how domestic politics in Taiwan and U.S. policy in the dispute created increased insecurity for China's leaders. Nevertheless, the consistency with which China's leaders have used force when faced with long-term vulnerability in the Taiwan dispute supports the broader theoretical argument advanced in this book.[134] Despite more than a decade of military modernization, China's position in the local military balance remained weak. At the same time, growing support within Taiwan for independence threatened to undermine the basis for unification under the one-China principle by increasing international support for Taiwan. Moreover, the United States appeared to Chinese leaders to be facilitating or supporting this drift. When Lee visited the United States in 1995, China's leaders concluded that they must take action to signal their resolve to strengthen China's weakening claim in the dispute.

DECLINING CLAIM STRENGTH

The spark for China's shift from delay to escalation was President Bill Clinton's 1995 decision to grant Taiwan president Lee Teng-hui a visa to visit the United States. Although the trip's purpose was a private visit to speak at Cornell University, China's leaders were alarmed nonetheless. This single event embodied two important sources of political pressure on China's weak claim in the Taiwan dispute: the island's drift toward formal independence and a perception of enhanced U.S. support for this change. Both types of pressure contributed to China's leaders' assessment of declining claim strength, as China's military position, while improving steadily since the late 1950s, remained weak, as China could not conquer the island.

Three different changes convinced China's leaders that Lee harbored "separatist" aims to increase Taiwan's international recognition and, ultimately, establish juridical independence from China. The first change was the island's democratization, which gave increasing internal and interna-

---

[134] Key works include John W. Garver, *Face Off: China, the United States, and Taiwan's Democratization* (Seattle: University of Washington Press, 1997); Robert S. Ross, "The 1995–1996 Taiwan Strait Confrontation: Coercion, Credibility, and the Use of Force," *International Security*, vol. 25, no. 2 (Fall 2000): 87–123; Andrew Scobell, *China's Use of Military Force: Beyond the Great Wall and the Long March* (New York: Cambridge University Press, 2003), 171–191; Michael D. Swaine, "Chinese Decision-Making Regarding Taiwan, 1979–2000," in David M. Lampton, ed., *The Making of Chinese Foreign and Security Policy in the Era of Reform* (Stanford, Calif.: Stanford University Press, 2001), 289–336; Zhao Suisheng, ed., *Across the Taiwan Strait: Mainland China, Taiwan and the 1995–1996 Crisis* (New York: Routledge, 1999). For an important alternative interpretation of Lee Teng-hui's motives and policy toward the mainland, see Richard C. Bush, *Untying the Knot: Making Peace in the Taiwan Strait* (Washington, D.C.: Brookings Institution Press, 2005).

tional legitimacy to domestic groups favoring independence.[135] Moreover, democratization shattered the long-standing acceptance of the one-China principle on both sides of the Strait that forty years of authoritarian KMT rule had sustained. In 1987, President Chiang Ching-kuo initiated the island's transition to democracy by lifting martial law. One key element of this transition was the legalization of opposition parties, the so-called "dang-wai" movement, especially the Democratic Progressive Party (DPP), which featured the independence of Taiwan as part of its party platform. The liberalization of the media and the broadening of elections at all levels gave a louder voice to those elements of Taiwanese society favoring independence.[136] Reflecting these changes, public support for independence increased from 8 percent in 1989 to 27 percent in April 1994.[137]

The KMT responded to new electoral pressures by decreasing its own support for unification, in order to co-opt the emerging DPP. From Beijing's perspective, Taiwan's 1991 adoption of "Guidelines for National Unification" (*guojia tongyi gangling*) and termination of the "Mobilization Period for the Suppression of the Communist Rebellion" were the first steps in the erosion of the one-China principle previously shared by the KMT and CCP. The "Guidelines" acknowledged that each side of the Strait was ruled separately and that Taiwan no longer sought to "retake" the mainland but instead would seek a peaceful union if and when beneficial to both sides.[138] The 1993 resignation of Premier Hao Bocun provided another indication of declining support for the one-China principle on Taiwan. As a retired chief of the General Staff, Hao was a KMT hard-liner dedicated to unification with the mainland. Hao's departure, which President Lee engineered to consolidate his own position, symbolized the decreasing influence of mainland-born officials within the ruling Nationalist party.[139]

A second shift that worried China's leaders was Taiwan's efforts to increase its recognition and legitimacy in the international community. In the early 1990s, Taiwan sought to increase the quality and quantity of its official and unofficial diplomatic relations. Most generally, Taiwan

[135] More generally, democratization increased Taiwan's support from advanced industrialized democracies. Under the KMT's authoritarian rule, many countries had found it much harder to embrace the island.

[136] Zhao Suisheng, "Changing Leadership Perceptions: The Adoption of a Coercive Strategy," in Zhao Suisheng, ed., *Across the Taiwan Strait: Mainland China, Taiwan and the 1995–1996 Crisis* (New York: Routledge, 1999), 108.

[137] Zhao, "Changing Leadership Perceptions," 108.

[138] Jean-Pierre Cabestan, "Taiwan's Mainland Policy: Normalization, Yes; Reunification, Later," *The China Quarterly*, no. 148 (December 1996): 1261–1262.

[139] M. Taylor Fravel, "Towards Civilian Supremacy: Civil-Military Relations in Taiwan's Democratization," *Armed Forces & Society*, vol. 29, no. 1 (Fall 2002): 76.

adopted a "pragmatic diplomacy" designed to increase its international standing, which included acceptance of dual diplomatic recognition along the German and Korean models. For China, dual recognition portended the creation of "two Chinas," which Mao and Zhou had tried so hard to prevent in the 1950s. In 1993, seeking to co-opt a DPP platform plank, Lee launched a campaign for Taiwan to enter the UN while also continuing efforts to join other intergovernmental organizations for which sovereignty was a condition of membership. Although this bid was unsuccessful, it did demonstrate Taiwan's future intentions to Beijing. Lee and Premier Lien Chan also embarked on "vacation diplomacy" to Southeast Asian countries, using private visits to conduct official diplomacy and expand Taiwan's base of diplomatic support.[140] By early 1995, it was clear that Taiwan sought to increase its support and legitimacy in the international community.

Lee's May 1994 interview with a Japanese journalist, Ryotaro Shiba, reflected the culmination of these negative shifts. From Beijing's perspective, the interview was full of inflammatory statements, such as "Taiwan . . . must be [a country] for Taiwanese. This is the fundamental idea." Lee likened himself to Moses, with the clear implication that he was leading his people, the Taiwanese, away from their oppressor, the PRC. Lee also stated that Taiwan always had been governed by foreign powers and that the Nationalists were "nothing more than a political party that came to rule the Taiwanese." Finally, Lee even challenged the territorial integrity of the mainland itself, stating that "if Taiwan declares independence, Beijing should be scared because Tibet or Xinjiang might then act for independence as well."[141] As a Xinhua commentary noted, Lee had "become more and more ineffective in concealing his true colors."[142]

A final change that alarmed China's leaders was the growing stalemate in attempts to negotiate closer relations across the Strait. In April 1993, Wang Daohan and Koo Chen-fu, chairmen of semiofficial institutions from both sides responsible for cross-Strait relations, held talks in Singapore. China's leaders viewed the meeting as a first step toward negotiating

---

[140] For Chinese sources on Taiwan's diplomatic efforts, see Zhou Zhihuai, "Guanyu 1995–1996 nian Taihai weiji de sikao" [Reflections on the 1995–1996 Taiwan Straits Crisis], *Taiwan yanjiu jikan*, no. 2 (1998): 4.

[141] "The Grief of Being Born a Taiwanese," *Asahi Weekly*, 6–13 May 1994. Translated version available from http://www.fas.org/news/taiwan/1994/s940721-taiwan2.htm. On the Chinese reaction to the interview, see Song Liansheng and Gong Xiaohua, *Duizhi wushi nian* [Fifty Years of Confrontation] (Beijing: Taihai chubanshe, 2000), 302–306; Zhou, "Guanyu 1995–1996 nian Taihai weiji," 3–4.

[142] "Two-Faced Tactic Cannot Conceal His True Intentions—A Commentary on Li Denghui's Statements at His News Conference," Xinhua, 13 June 1995, FBIS# FTS19950613000282.

unification, albeit only through semiofficial organizations. In January 1995, Jiang Zemin offered his own proposal in his Chinese New Year speech, which included eight points designed to start talks between the two sides.[143] The document suggested that the two sides discuss officially ending hostilities and indicated that, under the "one China" principle, everything else was negotiable. Taiwan's reply came in April, when Lee Teng-hui used an official speech to state that talks could be held only after the mainland renounced the use of force and accepted divided rule.[144]

In addition to Taiwan's own actions, a second source of China's declining claim strength was the assessment that U.S. policy was supporting Taiwan's moves toward independence. From China's perspective, the United States began to increase its support for the island when President George H. W. Bush authorized the sale of 150 F-16 fighter aircraft during the 1992 presidential election campaign.[145] Although motivated largely by domestic political concerns, the sale was viewed by China as symbolically dangerous. As the largest arms-sales package in more than a decade, China maintained that it violated the 1982 communiqué in which the United States had pledged to reduce military sales to Taiwan and, indirectly, decrease its military support for the island. After taking office in 1993, President Clinton authorized a review of the U.S. relationship with Taiwan, which led to a September 1994 official protocol upgrade for the island.[146] In December 1994, during an official visit to the island, Secretary of Transportation Federico Pena entered the Office of the President and held an official meeting with Lee.[147] From China's perspective, these actions signaled a growing closeness in relations between Washington and Taipei that furthered the goals of Taiwan's pragmatic diplomacy.

In the context of growing support for Taiwan's independence, Lee's June 1995 trip to the United States added fuel to a smoldering fire. Clinton decided to permit Lee to visit after the U.S. House and Senate voted overwhelming in a "sense of Congress" to grant Lee a visa. Only the month before, Secretary of State Warren Christopher had assured Chinese foreign minister Qian Qichen that the granting of a visa to President Lee would "not conform with the unofficial relationship between the

---

[143] *Jiang Zemin wenxuan* [Jiang Zemin's Selected Works], vol. 3 (Beijing: Renmin chubanshe, 2006), 418–424.

[144] Cabestan, "Taiwan's Mainland Policy," 1265.

[145] For Chinese sources on the role of U.S. policy toward Taiwan leading up to the crisis, see Zhou, "Guanyu 1995–1996 nian Taihai weiji," 3–5.

[146] Reuters, 7 September 1994 (Factiva).

[147] Zhao, "Changing Leadership Perceptions," 115.

United States and Taiwan," which was based on the one-China policy.[148] Moreover, in the days before Clinton's decision, the State Department had continued to assure China's Foreign Ministry that Lee would not be permitted to visit. From Beijing's perspective, the granting of the visa not only directly supported Lee's strategy to increase Taiwan's international standing but was also a clear reversal of U.S. policy. Since 1979, the U.S. had not allowed senior officials from Taiwan to enter the country for any reason other than transit, usually when flying from Taiwan to Latin America.

Clinton's decision occurred, moreover, during a period of increased tension in the U.S.-China relationship. After Tiananmen, U.S.-China ties continued to be marred by mutual suspicion and mistrust, which only seemed to grow in the years before Lee's visit. In September 1993, U.S. Navy personnel boarded a Chinese freighter, *Yinhe*, that the United States claimed was transporting chemical weapons to Iran. In October 1994, Congress passed a resolution vigorously opposing China's bid to host the Olympics in 2000, while the United States continued to oppose China's admission as a charter member of the World Trade Organization. In early 1995, the United States threatened economic sanctions over market access issues and intellectual property rights violations. In May 1995, just before Lee's visit, the United States issued a public commitment to maintain freedom of navigation in the South China Sea after the Mischief Reef incident.[149]

Lee's visit to the United States confirmed China's leaders' worst fears: that he sought to achieve de facto independence for Taiwan. By visiting the United States and speaking publicly at Cornell University as president of the ROC, Lee was able to increase his own stature worldwide and his popularity at home. In his speech, Lee constantly referred to "the Republic of China on Taiwan,"[150] which only further angered Beijing. By authorizing the trip, President Clinton directly supported—and in China's eyes, encouraged—Taiwan's move toward independence. Reflecting China's sense of growing vulnerability, a Xinhua commentary characterized Lee's visit as "an elaborately planned major step designed to boost Taiwan's status with the help of foreigners and to achieve a 'domino effect' leading to the international community's recognition of Taiwan's 'political status.'"[151]

---

[148] Qian Qichen, *Waijiao shiji* [Ten Stories of a Diplomat] (Beijing: Shijie zhishi chubanshe, 2003), 305.

[149] U.S. Department of State, *United States Policy on the Spratlys and the South China Sea*, 10 May 1995.

[150] Lee Teng-hui, "Always in My Heart," 9 June 1995, http://www.news.cornell.edu/campus/Lee/ Lee_Speech.html.

[151] "The Protective Umbrella and Chief behind the Scenes Backer of 'Taiwan Independence,'" Xinhua, 2 August 1995, FBIS# FTS19950802000235.

MILITARY EXERCISES AND MISSILE DIPLOMACY

After Lee's visit to the United States, China's leaders moved quickly to strengthen China's weakening claim. In the propaganda arena, Beijing launched a barrage of attacks on Lee personally and on the idea of Taiwanese independence. By mid-August, more than four hundred articles and commentaries had been written.[152] Beijing also canceled the second round of Wang-Koo talks, which had been scheduled for July 1995. The most serious response, however, was the decision to undertake a series of ballistic missile tests and live ammunition military exercises designed to demonstrate China's opposition to Taiwanese independence and its commitment to unification by force if necessary. In the words of a Xinhua commentary, "We will definitely not sit around doing nothing about any act of separation which obstructs or damages the great cause of China's reunification."[153] According to a Hong Kong paper, "Beijing could no longer show tolerance towards Li's overt visit to the U.S. to create two Chinas. Hence, with Lee going further step by step in his move to create two Chinas, the [CCP] has made stronger and stronger responses."[154]

China's senior leaders concluded that Lee's provocation demanded a tough response. Contrary to reports of a division between civilian and military elites, Jiang and China's other senior leaders, including Premier Li Peng and Admiral Liu Huaqing, were all convinced of the need to take a tough stand.[155] They all acknowledged, in short, that China faced growing vulnerability in the dispute that needed to be arrested. In the short term, other countries needed to be deterred from following the U.S. lead of supporting Taiwan's efforts to enhance its international standing. In the longer run, China also sought to deter Taiwan from pursuing formal independence and the United States from supporting such efforts.[156] Chinese diplomats led by Qian Qichen argued for a tough diplomatic and political response, while generals argued for a military demonstration in the form of "tests."[157]

[152] Zhao, "Changing Leadership Perceptions," 113.

[153] "Li Teng-hui Is Guilty of Damaging Relations between the Two Sides of Taiwan Straits," Xinhua, 26 July 1995, FBIS# FTS19950726000130.

[154] "Gradual Escalation of China's Strategy against United States, Taiwan," *Hsin Pao*, 28 June 1995, FBIS# FTS19950630000091.

[155] Swaine, "Chinese Decision-Making," 322. You Ji also explains how this decision was based on a consensus among Jiang Zemin and Li Peng along with the senior military leaders. You Ji, "Changing Leadership Consensus: The Domestic Context of the War Games," in Zhao Suisheng, ed., *Across the Taiwan Strait: Mainland China, Taiwan and the 1995–1996 Crisis* (New York: Routledge, 1999), 77–98.

[156] On China's deterrent goals, see Ross, "1995–1996 Taiwan Strait Confrontation."

[157] Swaine, "Chinese Decision-Making."

In early July 1995, Jiang instructed the PLA to develop plans for a show of force against Taiwan. In mid-July, the PLA proposed a series of military exercises and missile tests before Taiwan's December 1995 legislative elections and the March 1996 presidential election. On July 18, China announced that missile tests along with air and naval exercises would be held off the Fujian coast near Taiwan the following week. In seven days, four M-9 and two DF-21 ballistic missiles were launched at target zones approximately one hundred miles north of Taiwan. On August 10, Xinhua announced that additional missile tests would be held from August 15 to August 25. These were probably regularly scheduled exercises for the Second Artillery, the PLA's missile force, but the public announcement was clearly linked to the Taiwan crisis.[158]

In the months that followed, additional military exercises and missile tests were linked to political developments across the Strait. In the fall, this intimidation effort began when Jiang observed a series of military exercises held in October. China's leaders were increasingly worried that the outcome of Taiwan's upcoming legislative and presidential elections might be seen as furthering Taiwan's drift toward political independence from the mainland, a possibility that required a strong response, namely sustained displays of force. In November, the Nanjing MR held joint-service exercises, which included the establishment of a war zone (*zhanqu*) command structure that would be formed for an actual attack. These November exercises coincided with the official two-week campaign period before Taiwan's December elections for the Legislative Yuan. The largest and most dangerous exercises were held from March 8 to March 25, 1996, before the presidential election. These exercises included missile tests and joint-service live ammunition exercises designed to simulate an amphibious assault of Taiwan. Most ominously, the target zones for the missile tests were two areas near Kaohsiung and Keelung harbors, Taiwan's largest ports, demonstrating a willingness to blockade the island (see map 5.1).

The purpose of these exercises was clear. China's leaders sought to arrest Taiwan's continued drift toward independence and increased international legitimacy, while deterring the United States from encouraging and supporting Taiwan.[159] One Chinese scholar stated that the goal was to "show to the world China's resolve" to safeguard national reunification and protect territorial integrity.[160] Public statements by Chinese officials clearly support this interpretation. According to the Chinese Foreign Min-

---

[158] UPI, 10 August 1995 (Lexis-Nexis).

[159] For a detailed discussion of China's coercive objectives, see Ross, "1995–1996 Taiwan Strait Confrontation."

[160] Zhou, "Guanyu 1995–1996 nian Taihai weiji," 2.

istry spokesman Shen Guofang, "The U.S. must take actions to stop further damage . . . it's up to the U.S. to correct its mistakes. . . . What we are going to do is to make the U.S. realise the importance of Sino-U.S. relations to prompt them to take the right track."[161] According to a Xinhua commentary, "If there are some who dare to split Taiwan from the map of the motherland, the Chinese people will surely use their blood and lives to defend the integrity of the territory and sovereignty of the state."[162] China's March 1996 missiles tests and military exercises, however, failed to prevent Lee Teng-hui's election as president or, as discussed in the next section, efforts by Taiwan's leaders to move toward independence.

AVERTED CRISES IN THE LATE 1990s

A brief examination of averted crises across the Strait illustrates the central role of U.S. policy in shaping Chinese assessments of claim strength in the dispute. In the two episodes discussed below, crises were avoided when, despite Taiwanese provocations, the United States indicated that it did not support Taiwan's efforts to move toward formal independence or enhanced international legitimacy.

In 1999, President Lee Teng-hui threatened to spark another crisis. During a July interview on German television, his comments appeared to claim Taiwan's independence. Lee stated that the ROC "has been a sovereign state since it was founded in 1912." As a result of the 1991 amendments to the ROC Constitution, he described "cross-strait relations [as] a special state-to-state relationship. Consequently, there is no need to declare independence." In 1991, Article 10 of the Additional Articles stated that the area covered by the Constitution was limited to Taiwan. Lee stated that this amendment had "placed cross-strait relations as a state-to-state relationship or at least a special state-to-state relationship, rather than an internal relationship between a legitimate government and a renegade group, or between a central government and a local government."[163] In short, Lee implied that Taiwan did not need to declare formal independence because it already was independent. For China's leaders, Lee's formulation of a state-to-state relationship, soon dubbed the "two-state theory" (*liangguo lun*), was alarming, representing a renewed effort to move toward independence.

---

[161] "Qian Urges U.S. 'To Correct Its Mistakes,' " *South China Morning Post*, 1 August 1995, 1, FBIS# FTS19950801000169.

[162] "Artificially Escalating Hostility and Sabotaging Cross-strait Relations," Xinhua, 27 June 1995, FBIS# FTS19950627000167 (Lexis-Nexis).

[163] "President Lee's Deutsche Welle Interview (July 9, 1999)," available on http://taiwansecurity.org/ts/ss-990709-Deutsche-Welle-Interview.htm.

Beijing responded with harsh statements designed to discredit Lee and express its opposition to his potential change in policy. The tenor of these remarks implied that China might again consider using force. On July 13, Foreign Ministry spokesman Zhu Bangguo warned Taiwan not to underestimate the PRC's resolve. Lee was urged to "rein in at the brink of the precipice and immediately cease all separatist activities."[164] More alarmingly, in the first of five commentaries, on July 15 a *Liberation Army Daily* article warned "don't play with fire." The commentary stated that China "will absolutely not sit by and watch even an inch of territory split off from the motherland."[165] Likewise, Defense Minister Chi Haotian stated that the PLA was "ready at any time to safeguard the territorial integrity of China and smash any attempts to separate the country."[166]

In response to what appeared to be a growing crisis, the United States quickly signaled its opposition to Lee's initiative. By clearly not supporting the two-state theory, Washington hoped to reassure Beijing about the prospects for unification. On July 13, State Department spokesman James Rubin reiterated the U.S. commitment to its one-China policy. He also repeated the "three no's" that Clinton had stated publicly for the first time during his 1998 trip to China.[167] In addition, the United States arranged a series of meetings with both sides to communicate the same message of restraint. On July 14, the chief U.S. representative in Taiwan, Darryl Johnson, met with Lee and restated the U.S. commitment to the one-China policy.[168] Deputy Secretary of State Strobe Talbott likewise met with the Chinese chargé d'affaires in Washington. Most importantly, on July 18, Clinton placed a thirty-minute phone call to Jiang Zemin in which he repeated the U.S. commitment to the one-China policy and the desire for talks between Beijing and Taipei.[169] At the end of the month, Clinton dispatched two advisers to the region to affirm this message, with Assistant Secretary of State Stanley Roth visiting Beijing and American Institute in Taiwan director Richard Bush traveling to Taipei.[170]

Toward the end of the summer, tensions between China and Taiwan decreased somewhat. Unlike the events precipitating the 1995–96 crisis,

---

[164] *RMRB*, 13 July 1999, 1.

[165] "Li Denghui buyao wanhuo" [Li Teng-Hui Don't Play with Fire], *Jiefangjun Bao*, 15 July 1999, 1. Four more commentaries were published from 18 to 21 August 1999.

[166] *RMRB*, 15 July 1999, 4.

[167] U.S. Department of State, Daily Press Briefing, 13 July 1999, available on http://secretary.state.gov/www/briefings/9907/990713db.html. The "three no's" are: "We do not support Taiwan independence; we do not support Taiwanese membership in organizations where statehood is required; we do not support a two-China policy or a one-China/one-Taiwan policy."

[168] Kyodo News Service, 14 July 1999 (Lexis-Nexis).

[169] *Christian Science Monitor*, 23 July 1999 (Lexis-Nexis).

[170] *The Straits Times*, 25 July 1999 (Lexis-Nexis).

the United States quickly used public and private channels to indicate that it did not support Lee's efforts to increase the island's international legitimacy. As a result, Taiwan began to backtrack, emphasizing how Lee's remarks did not reflect a change in policy.[171] This counterfactual analysis cannot control for all factors, but it is quite likely that a different U.S. response, especially one that appeared to support or encourage Lee, might have led China's leaders to conclude that their position was further weakening. In the summer of 1999, U.S.-China relations were especially tense. When Premier Zhu Rongji visited the United States in February, he was embarrassed by Clinton's refusal to finalize negotiations over China's entry into the World Trade Organization. In May, during the NATO intervention in Kosovo, U.S. aircraft had mistakenly bombed the Chinese embassy in Belgrade, an event that sparked dramatic protests in front of the U.S. embassy in Beijing and threatened to send U.S.-China ties into a tailspin. In this context, strong U.S. support for Lee might have increased China's sense of vulnerability in the Taiwan dispute. Given the general level of suspicion and mutual distrust at the time, China's leaders might have viewed such support for Lee as part of an anti-China shift in U.S. policy.

In 2002, President Chen Shui-bian, taking a page from Lee Teng-hui's playbook, used a public speech to float another change in Taiwan's status. On August 3, President Chen addressed the Twenty-ninth Annual Meeting of the World Federation of Taiwanese Associations via videoconference in Tokyo. Offering a forceful statement of Taiwan's sovereignty, which Beijing heard as a declaration of independence, he stated that "Taiwan is our country . . . [and] not a part of any other country, nor is it a local government or province of another country. . . . Taiwan has always been a sovereign state." He issued his own formula for describing Taiwan's international status, coining the phrase "one country on each side" (*yibian yiguo*). Specifically, he stated that with "Taiwan and China standing on opposite sides of the Strait, there is one country on each side. This should be clear."[172] Chen then floated the idea of holding a referendum to determine Taiwan's status with the mainland—a move that alarmed China's leaders.

China again reacted with a series of harsh statements, condemning Chen's remarks and their implications for unification. Again, in order to prevent an escalation of the situation across the Strait, the United States

---

[171] On the importance of these public statements, see Song and Gong, *Duizhi wushi nian*, 392–394.

[172] "President Chen's Opening Address of the 29th Annual Meeting of the World Federation of Taiwanese Associations," http://www.gio.gov.tw/taiwan-website/4-oa/20020803/2002080301.html.

acted quickly to demonstrate that it did not support Chen's apparent change in policy. On August 5, a State Department spokesperson upheld the one-China policy, stating that "our policy has not changed at all." On August 7, a National Security Council spokesperson repeated this message, stating that the United States had "a one-China policy and we do not support Taiwan independence."[173] The spokesman also stated that the White House had been assured that Chen's August 3 statement was not a call for independence. At the end of the month, Deputy Secretary of State Richard Armitage, who was in Beijing on a previously scheduled trip, clearly stated that "the U.S. does not support Taiwan independence."[174]

Unlike its suspicious stance in the 1999 episode, China immediately recognized the intended role of U.S. statements. The *People's Daily*, for example, noted that the "U.S. Reiterates It Does Not Support Taiwan Independence."[175] In 2002, many factors militated against a violent response from Beijing. U.S.-China relations were on a much firmer footing than they had been in 1995 or even 1999, as both sides were preparing for an October meeting in Texas between Bush and Jiang. More generally, U.S.-China relations in the aftermath of September 11, 2001 had improved from the nadir of the April 2001 EP-3 airplane collision incident. In addition, given the economic downturn in Taiwan, China's leaders were much more confident about the long-term prospects for unification. Nevertheless, if the U.S. government had not quickly and clearly shown its lack of support for Chen, China's leaders might have drawn a different assessment of the situation and most likely would have considered a more violent response.

CONCLUSION

No set of territorial disputes are more significant for China's leaders than homeland disputes. Because of their importance, compromise over these areas is not viewed as a viable policy option. Moreover, China's leaders are especially sensitive to factors that threaten to decrease or block the prospects for achieving unification. In disputes over Hong Kong and Macao, China enjoyed extremely strong claims underpinned by the small size of these territories and their shared border with the mainland. Mili-

---

[173] Wendy S. Ross, "U.S. One-China Policy Remains Unchanged, Official Says," Washington File, Office of Information Programs, U.S. Department of State, 8 August 2002.

[174] U.S. Department of State, "Transcript: Armitage Says U.S. Does Not Support Taiwan Independence," Washington File, Office of Information Programs, U.S. Department of State, 26 August 2002.

[175] *RMRB*, 7 August 2002, 3.

tarily, China could have occupied these territories at any time since 1949, which paradoxically lessened the urgency for settling these conflicts.

By contrast, China's relative position in its dispute over Taiwan has been quite weak. This weakness has increased greatly the sensitivity of China's leaders to any further decline in an already inferior claim and a willingness to use force to signal resolve in the dispute. When China sought to liberate the island by force during the Mao era, increased U.S. military support for the KMT threatened to weaken China's relative position and further reduce the odds of unification. A decrease in U.S. support for the island in the 1960s and 1970s was linked with a period of stability across the Strait. Although China's claim strength remained poor, its relative position began to improve, especially after the United States recognized the PRC in 1979. After China pursued unification through diplomacy under Deng and Jiang, Taiwan's democratization created a new type of external pressure on China's claim in the dispute because it decreased support on the island for "one China" and eventual unification. Perceived U.S. support for Taiwan's push for enhanced autonomy created renewed decline in the dispute, which China's leaders sought to counter through missile diplomacy in 1995 and 1996.

CHAPTER SIX

Offshore Island Disputes

IN ITS OFFSHORE ISLAND DISPUTES, China has sought to secure a maritime frontier. Achievement of this goal has proved to be challenging, as China controlled little offshore territory when the PRC was established and lacked the ability to project military power beyond its coastline. The value of the Paracel (Xisha), Spratly (Nansha), and Senkaku (Diaoyu) islands for China and other littoral states lies in their economic and strategic importance. Control of the islands is key to the assertion of maritime rights, the security of sea lines of communication, and regional naval power projection. According to Admiral Liu Huaqing, the commander of the People's Liberation Army Navy (PLAN) in the 1980s, "whoever controls the Spratlys will reap huge economic and military benefits."[1]

Given the importance of sovereignty over offshore islands, China has bargained hard in these disputes and generally preferred delay to cooperation. With just one exception, China has never entered into talks with any of its adversaries concerning the sovereignty of these areas, nor has it indicated a willingness to drop its claims to even just some of the land that it contests. The consistency with which China has pursued delay in these disputes, even when its claims strengthened through its occupation of additional territory in 1974 and 1988, is noteworthy.

In two of its offshore island disputes, China occupied contested territory by force. In 1974, China seized the Crescent Group in the western Paracels held by South Vietnam, and in 1988 it occupied six features in the Spratlys claimed by Vietnam and the Philippines. In both instances, China's efforts to strengthen its weak or inferior claims resulted in violent clashes. Given the value of offshore islands, China has been sensitive to the long-term implications of decline in its weak claims, weakness exacerbated by its lack of a physical presence before 1988 in the largest group of offshore islands, the Spratlys. China used force when the rising value of offshore island territory after the 1970s and the occupation of contested islands and reefs by other states in these conflicts posed a threat to China's relative position in these disputes.

[1] Liu Huaqing, *Liu Huaqing huiyilu* [Liu Huaqing's Memoirs] (Beijing: Jiefangjun chubanshe, 2004), 538.

THE DOMINANCE OF DELAY

Since 1949, China has compromised in only one offshore island dispute, the one over White Dragon Tail (Bailongwei) Island, while either delaying or using force in disputes over the Paracel, Spratly, and Senkaku islands.[2] Several factors underpin the appeal of delaying the settlement of these disputes. Since 1949, the economic importance of offshore islands has continued to grow, especially after the increasing worldwide interest in maritime resources in the 1970s. Many states view offshore islands as one tool for asserting an exclusive economic zone (EEZ) under the 1982 UN Convention on the Law of the Sea (UNCLOS), through which they may claim rights to natural resources in the water column and seabed. As a result, littoral states including China have been more willing to bargain hard over offshore island claims and wait for an optimal settlement, as the islands can be used as baselines for determining maritime rights.

At the same time, offshore islands are cheap for states to dispute. Maintaining a claim requires only the symbolic presence of a few troops. These forces serve as a trip wire, as any individual island is largely indefensible without the capability to control the surrounding waters and air space, which all claimants including China lack. Claims to these islands also often fail to harm bilateral ties, which might otherwise increase the cost of disputing such land and create incentives for compromise. As desolate and unpopulated areas, these islands are not linked to vital security interests, such as homeland territorial integrity or the security of key population centers, which limits the negative impact of these disputes on how states view each other's intentions.

Finally, the politics of the Chinese civil war have limited the PRC's willingness to consider compromise. As the Nationalists also claim the Paracels, Senkakus, and Spratlys in the name of the Republic of China, the mainland's position in these disputes is linked with its claims to rule "one China." Compromise by either side would be seen as weakening its claim to be the legitimate government of China.

In contrast to frontier disputes, external threats explain China's one attempt to compromise in an offshore island conflict. In 1957, China agreed to transfer White Dragon Tail Island, which lies in the middle of the Tonkin Gulf, to North Vietnam. Unfortunately, very little is known about this dispute and its settlement.[3] According one internally circulated

---

[2] For a detailed review of these disputes, see Greg Austin, *China's Ocean Frontier: International Law, Military Force, and National Development* (Canberra: Allen & Unwin, 1998).

[3] See Li Dechao, "Bailongwei dao zhengming" [Rectification of White Dragon Tail Island's Name], *Zhongguo bianjiang shidi yanjiu baogao*, vols. 1–2, no. 3 (1988): 21–23;

source, Mao ordered the island's transfer to support North Vietnam in its conflict with the United States.[4] At the time, the United States was increasing its support for Ngo Dinh Diem's government in South Vietnam and strengthening its presence along China's southern flank through the establishment of SEATO, a multilateral security pact designed to contain communism. Along with America's bilateral alliances in the region, the deepening U.S. involvement in South Vietnam compounded China's sense of threat and encirclement from the south. Under these circumstances, strengthening an ally through a territorial concession was more important than holding out for whatever value the island might have in the future.

This concession itself, however, was extraordinary for several reasons. At the time, the island was seen as having little economic value, as China and other East Asian states did not yet fully appreciate the importance of offshore islands for securing maritime resources. No petroleum had been discovered in the region, and the maritime legal regime remained in its infancy. During subsequent attempts to demarcate the Tonkin Gulf, the island became a point of contention, as Vietnam sought to use it as a baseline for claiming two-thirds of the Gulf.[5] In addition, Mao's own personality may have played a role. Some Chinese scholars believe that for Mao, who was influenced by socialist idealism, territorial sovereignty was less important than defending an ideological ally.[6] Finally, control of White Dragon Tail may have been exchanged for North Vietnam's 1958 decision to recognize China's claims to the Paracels and Spratlys, which South Vietnam also claimed. No sources exist to support the notion of such a swap, but the timing of Hanoi's decision in 1958 suggests that this remains an intriguing possibility.[7]

After the White Dragon Tail concession, China has never again offered to compromise over the sovereignty of an offshore island. Instead, apart from the episodes of escalation, China has chosen to delay settlement in all its other offshore island disputes, a strategy that reflects Deng Xiao-

---

Mao Zhenfa, ed., *Bianfang lun* [On Frontier Defense] (Beijing: Junshi kexue chubanshe [internal circulation], 1996), 137.

[4] Mao, *Bianfang lun*, 137. Interviews, Beijing, June–July 2001.

[5] Zou Keyuan, "Maritime Boundary Delimitation in the Gulf of Tonkin," *Ocean Development & International Law*, vol. 30, no. 3 (1999): 10.

[6] Interviews, Beijing, July 2001.

[7] This includes a letter from Prime Minister Pham Van Dong supporting China's 1958 territorial waters declaration that claimed sovereignty over the Paracels and the Spratlys. For Chinese copies of this and other letters, see Guo Ming, ed., *ZhongYue guanxi yanbian sishi nian* [Evolution of Chinese-Vietnamese Relations over 40 Years] (Naning: Guangxi renmin chubanshe [internal circulation], 1992), 146–148; Guo Ming, Luo Fangming, and Li Baiyin, eds., *Xiandai ZhongYue guanxi ziliao xuanbian* [Selected Materials on Contemporary Chinese-Vietnamese Relations] (Beijing: Shishi chubanshe [internal circulation], 1986), 340–349.

ping's maxim for these conflicts to "set aside conflict [and] pursue joint development" (*gezhi zhengyi, gongtong kaifa*).[8] In the Paracels, delay has given China time to strengthen its claim. Before the 1974 clash, China focused on consolidating its control of the Amphitrite Group, which it had occupied in 1950. After seizing the Crescent Group, China has continued to delay settlement to persuade Hanoi to accept China's control over the entire archipelago. The time that delaying buys further entrenches this status quo and also has allowed China to upgrade infrastructure on the islands, including building a runway on Woody Island in 1991. Moreover, China has refused to hold any talks with Vietnam over the islands' sovereignty despite Hanoi's repeated requests.

In the Spratlys, China has held talks with other claimants, but it has never participated in negotiations over sovereignty. Instead, these discussions have focused on crisis management or joint development, not sovereignty. During land boundary negotiations in the 1990s, China and Vietnam established a maritime issues expert group (*haishang wenti zhuanjia xiaozu*) to discuss only the Spratly Islands in July 1995.[9] This group has met almost every year, but talks have focused on deepening cooperation in maritime affairs in the South China Sea, not sovereignty.[10] In the future, however, this forum could address sovereignty questions.

Likewise, following its 1994 occupation of Mischief Reef, China held several rounds of talks with the Philippines over the Spratlys. Similar to the talks with Vietnam, however, these dealt with crisis management, not sovereignty, and reflect a continuation of China's delaying strategy in the dispute. In August 1995, the two sides signed a bilateral code of conduct in which they agreed to settle the dispute "in a peaceful and friendly manner."[11] In June 1997, after an additional round of talks, China and the Philippines agreed to advance notification of activities in contested areas.[12] Although these talks reflect efforts to defuse tension, they did not address each side's sovereignty claim. Moreover, these agreements consolidated China's position and its control of Mischief Reef, as the Philippines repeatedly acknowledged.

[8] *DXPWX3*, 87–88. Also see Wang Taiping, ed., *Deng Xiaoping waijiao sixiang yanjiu lunwenji* [Collected Papers on the Study of Deng Xiaoping's Diplomatic Thought] (Beijing: Shijie zhishi chubanshe, 1996), 350–359.

[9] Tang Jiaxuan, ed., *Zhongguo waijiao cidian* [Dictionary of China's Diplomacy] (Beijing: Shijie zhishi chubanshe, 2000), 751. An expert group (*zhuanjia xiaozu*) is one of the lowest levels of diplomatic exchange China uses in such talks, below vice-ministerial-level negotiations and working group talks typically headed by assistant foreign ministers.

[10] *ZGWJ*, various years.

[11] Xinhua, 11 August 1995 (Lexis-Nexis).

[12] Lee Lai To, *China and the South China Sea Dialogues* (Westport, Conn.: Praeger, 1999), 115.

Finally, after the 1994 Mischief Reef occupation, China held bilateral talks with the Association of Southeast Asian States (ASEAN) over a code of conduct for the Spratlys dispute. After three years, these talks resulted in the 2002 "Declaration on a Code of Conduct" between China and ASEAN.[13] Negotiations for such a code began in 1999, but Chinese and ASEAN drafts disagreed over key language, including a prohibition on occupying or erecting structures on uninhabited reefs.[14] Although neither the draft versions nor the final declaration addressed sovereignty or maritime rights, China did make a small concession in the 2002 declaration, as its text includes most of the language proposed by ASEAN in 1999 and almost none of China's. This concession was probably linked to China's broader efforts to engage ASEAN and minimize the impact of the dispute on its diplomatic engagement with the region.[15]

Delay has also dominated China's approach to the Senkakus. China and Japan have never held talks over the sovereignty of these islets and rocks. The two sides did discuss the islands in negotiations leading up to the 1978 peace treaty, but only to ensure that the dispute would be excluded from the agreement.[16] China's leaders have consistently pursued a delaying strategy, both to bide time and to avoid damaging China's relations with Japan. In 1978, for example, Deng described the delaying strategy, stating: "It doesn't matter if this question is shelved for some time, say, ten years. Our generation is not wise enough to find common language on this question. Our next generation will certainly be wiser. They will certainly find a solution acceptable to all."[17] Moreover, China has been remarkably consistent in pursuit of this strategy even when nationalist activists from Taiwan and Hong Kong sought to plant flags on the islands in the mid-1990s. Although China's leaders reiterated their territo-

---

[13] http://www.aseansec.org/13163.htm.

[14] The Chinese draft only urged the parties to refrain from the use of force. See Scott Snyder, Brad Glosserman, and Ralph A. Cossa, *Confidence Building Measures in the South China Sea* (Honolulu: Pacific Forum CSIS, 2001), E-1.

[15] Leszek Buszynski, "ASEAN, the Declaration on Conduct, and the South China Sea," *Contemporary Southeast Asia*, vol. 25, no. 3 (December 2003): 343–362.

[16] Austin, *China's Ocean Frontier*, 777–779. The only exception to this delaying strategy was a display of force by China in April 1978. In March 1978, a group of LDP members of the Japanese Diet opposed the Sino-Japanese Treaty of Peace and Friendship and publicly pressured the Japanese government to link the treaty with China's recognition of Japan's claims to the Senkakus. In April, a flotilla of Chinese fishing boats, some of them armed, appeared in the surrounding waters and lingered for a week, underscoring China's commitment to its claim while Chinese officials urged Japan not to raise the issue. See Daniel Tretiak, "The Sino-Japanese Treaty of 1978: The Senkaku Incident Prelude," *Asian Survey*, vol. 18, no. 12 (December 1978): 1235–1249.

[17] *Peking Review*, no. 44 (3 November 1978), 16.

rial claims to the Senkakus, they did not support these groups and severely limited any demonstrations in Beijing against Japan over the islands.[18]

Since issuing its first claim in 1970, several factors have deterred China from challenging Japan's control of these islands. The first is Japan's alliance with the United States, which includes the defense of areas under the administration of Japan, including the Senkakus. The second is Japan's importance as a source of foreign investment and technology, inputs key to China's reforms. The third is most likely an awareness that any harsh statements by the government could spark anti-Japan sentiments in China that may be hard to control and could turn easily against the CCP. China's leaders also acknowledge that raising the issue would complicate already tense relations without producing any tangible results.

Although China has pursued a strategy of delay in its offshore island disputes, it has used force in two of these conflicts. The remainder of this chapter will examine these two disputes, demonstrating in both instances that China sought to counter efforts by opposing states to occupy contested land and assert maritime rights, actions that weakened China's long-term position in these conflicts. In both cases, China's enhanced naval capabilities gave it the means to use force that it had previously lacked. At the same time, China was not tempted by military opportunity. Instead, it employed its enhanced naval power when its claim strength was challenged. In the absence of such challenges, China has generally refrained from using force.

Consolidation of the Paracels

On January 19, 1974, Chinese and South Vietnamese forces clashed over the Paracel Islands. When the fighting was over, China had seized the Crescent Group in the western part of the archipelago from Republic of Vietnam (RVN) forces, thereby consolidating its control of all contested features. Casualties were heavy on both sides. RVN forces suffered 18 killed, 43 wounded, and over 165 missing, some of whom had surrendered to China and others of whom were subsequently rescued on the high sea. Among PLAN forces, eighteen sailors were killed and sixty-seven wounded.[19]

The clash resulted from China's decision to increase its physical presence in the Paracels and surrounding waters. Soon thereafter, subsequent

[18] Erica Strecker Downs and Phillip C. Saunders, "Legitimacy and the Limits of Nationalism: China and the Diaoyu Islands," *International Security*, vol. 23, no. 3 (Winter 1998/1999): 114–146.

[19] Xu Ge, *Tiemao gu haijiang: gongheguo haizhan shiji* [Steel Anchors Consolidating Maritime Frontiers: Record of the Republic's Naval Battles] (Beijing: Haichao chubanshe, 1999), 300–301.

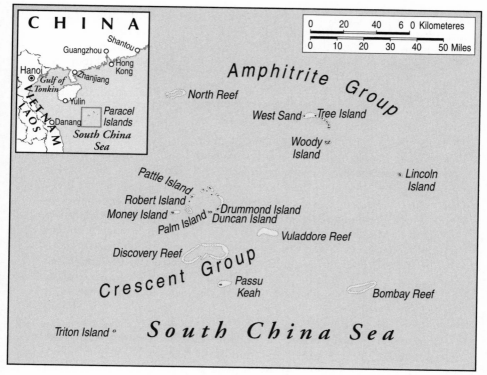

Map 6.1 Paracel Islands

actions quickly escalated to high levels of violence. In the early 1970s, the growing importance of maritime rights increased the value of controlling offshore islands, such as the Paracels, that could be used to assert these rights to exploit petroleum resources. Given China's inferior position in the Senkakus and the Spratlys (the largest group of offshore islands that China claims), efforts by other states to assert their claims through the occupation of features in the Spratlys only further weakened China's bargaining power in all these conflicts. Because of the limited reach of the PLAN, the Paracels were the only disputed offshore islands where China could strengthen its territorial claims.

Prelude to the 1974 Clash

The Paracels consist of two separate island groups, the Crescent (Yongle) Group in the southwest and the Amphitrite (Xuande) Group in the northeast (map 6.1). In 1950, PLA troops occupied Woody (Yongxing) Island, the single largest feature in the Paracels, located in the Amphitrite Group, after it was evacuated by Nationalist troops.[20] At around the same time, French forces occupied Pattle (Shanhu) Island in the Crescent Group, thus dividing control of the archipelago. In 1956, France transferred its positions to RVN forces.[21]

Through the 1950s, control of the disputed islands was fluid. Chinese fishermen from Hainan operated in the Paracels' surrounding waters, using many of the islands in the Crescent Group as shelters. In June 1956, for example, a Nationalist surveillance flight reported observing roughly seventy-five people on Robert (Ganquan) Island, approximately 3 nautical miles from the RVN position on Pattle.[22] In early 1959, RVN naval forces began to challenge the Chinese presence. In February 1959, RVN forces arrested eighty-two Chinese fishermen on Duncan (Chenghang) Island, which sparked a sharp protest from Beijing. Another confrontation occurred in March when RVN ships evicted Chinese fishermen who had returned to Duncan.[23] After this second confrontation, Saigon gained control of Robert, Duncan, Drummond (Puqing), and Palm (Guangjin) islands, thereby consolidating its hold of the Crescent Group at China's expense. Although China's claim strength declined during this period, it lacked the naval power to respond with force, especially if the United States chose to intervene.

Despite facing clear pressure on its claim, China was too weak to take action and had to accept the status quo of divided control. China's navy remained small, and almost all its ships were deployed in areas around the Taiwan Strait. In its order of battle, the South Sea Fleet responsible for the defense of the Paracels had no destroyers and only ninety-six patrol craft, mostly small torpedo boats. In 1960, the largest vessel in the fleet was a single patrol escort ship, displacing only one thousand tons.[24] As a result, China moved to consolidate its position in the Amphitrite Group. Following the second eviction of Chinese fishermen from the Crescent Group in March 1959, Premier Zhou Enlai instructed Defense Minister Peng Dehuai to establish a "military stronghold" (*junshi judian*) in the

---

[20] Dieter Heinzig, *Disputed Islands in the South China Sea: Paracels, Spratlys, Pratas, Macclesfield Bank* (Wiesbaden: Otto Harrassowitz, 1976), 32.

[21] Marwyn S. Samuels, *Contest for the South China Sea* (New York: Methuen, 1982), 86–87; Xu, *Tiemao*, 287.

[22] "Paracel Islands," Memorandum, Office of the Chief of Naval Operations, 11 June 1956.

[23] Samuels, *Contest*, 87; Xu, *Tiemao*, 287.

[24] National Intelligence Board, *Chinese Communist Capabilities and Intentions in the Far East*, SNIE 13–3–61 [Top Secret] (Washington, D.C.: Central Intelligence Agency, 1961), 29.

Amphitrite Group.[25] In 1960, the British navy reported the construction of four radio masts and one observation tower on Woody Island. On March 17, 1960, China's Central Military Commission (CMC) ordered the PLAN to patrol the area regularly.[26] Over the next nine months, the PLAN conducted sixteen patrols around the Paracels, including trips to the Crescent Group, to protect Chinese fishing vessels.[27] By the end of 1973, the PLAN had conducted a total of seventy-six long-range patrols to the islands, averaging five per year, mostly to the Amphitrite Group but also around the Crescent Group.[28]

For most of the 1960s, China's relative position in the dispute remained stable, as it faced no new challenges from South Vietnam. The last reported clash occurred in March 1961, when the RVN navy seized one Chinese fishing boat near Palm Island.[29] The stability of China's claim strength in the dispute stemmed from two sources. First, the PLAN remained weak, especially the South Sea Fleet responsible for defending China's claims to the Paracels and Spratlys in addition to the Guangzhou, Guangxi, and Hainan coasts. By 1970, the fleet still lacked the destroyers and submarines allocated to the East and North Sea fleets.[30] Although the RVN navy was not strong, its support from the United States further limited China's military options. During one of the first patrols in 1959, a PLAN commander reported seeing an American communications station on Robert Island.[31] Throughout the 1960s, U.S. aircraft regularly patrolled the archipelago, prompting swift Chinese protests.[32] Given the PLAN's limited capabilities, the U.S. presence surely deterred China from taking any action beyond patrols even when challenged by Saigon in 1959.

---

[25] Zhao Qimin, "Yuanhang qianli, shoujin Xisha" [Ocean Voyage for a Thousand Miles, First Advance to the Paracels], in *Haijun: huiyi shiliao* [Navy: Recollections and Historical Materials] (Beijing: Jiefangjun chubanshe [military circulation], 1999), 425. Zhao was the commander of the first naval patrol of the Paracels in 1959.

[26] Xu, *Tiemao*, 288.

[27] Zhao, "Yuanhang qianli," 429.

[28] Xu, *Tiemao*, 291.

[29] *NYT*, 5 April 1961, 2.

[30] National Intelligence Board, *Communist China's General Purpose and Air Defense Forces*, NIE 13–3–70 [Top Secret] (Washington, D.C.: Central Intelligence Agency, 1970), 26.

[31] Zhao, "Yuanhang qianli," 428.

[32] From 1958 to 1971, China issued 497 protests and warnings over U.S. violations of China's territorial waters and airspace around the Paracels. Han Zhenhua, ed., *Woguo nanhai zhudao shiliao huibian* [Collection of Historical Materials on Our Country's South China Sea Islands] (Beijing: Dongfang chubanshe [internal circulation], 1988), 484; Samuels, *Contest*, 88.

The second source of stability was the war in Vietnam, which kept Saigon's attention focused domestically. In 1966, RVN forces withdrew from Duncan, Drummond, and Palm islands, which they had occupied in 1959, leaving only Pattle under RVN control in the Crescent Group.[33] Until the 1974 clash, South Vietnam's sole presence was a civilian-operated weather station on that island. Although China continuously strengthened its base in the Amphitrite Group, it did not exploit the advantage that the South Vietnamese force reduction presented, which provides evidence against any windows of opportunity explanation for China's use of force in 1974.

Growing Importance and Declining Claim Strength

In East Asia, the 1970s began with an upsurge of interest in exploiting maritime resources, especially petroleum. The growing prominence of maritime rights increased the importance of controlling contested offshore islands such as the Paracels, which could now provide a legal basis for developing maritime resources. As all contestants in the region sought to strengthen their claims and even occupied disputed features, China's long-term vulnerability in its offshore island conflicts increased, as it did not occupy any of the Senkaku or Spratly islands that it claimed.

The race for maritime resources, however, began in the East China Sea near the disputed Senkaku Islands, not in the South China Sea. Following the publication of a seismological survey in 1969, Taiwan's China Petroleum Company signed agreements to develop resources in waters around the Senkakus, which were followed by a formal ROC claim to the islands. Japan replied by asserting its own claim, as the islands were about to be transferred from the United States to Japan through the 1971 Okinawa Reversion Agreement. In December 1970, China joined the fray by issuing its own claim.[34] At around this same time, the PRC media began to discuss maritime rights. As figure 6.1 indicates, the number of articles in the *People's Daily* on maritime resources increased dramatically in the early 1970s, demonstrating by implication the growing importance of securing contested offshore islands. China's previous claims to other offshore islands issued in 1951 and 1958 did not stress maritime rights, only the sovereignty of the contested features and adjacent territorial waters.[35]

[33] Han, *Woguo nanhai*, 675. For the recollection of the deputy chief of staff for operations in the RVN navy, see Kiem Do and Julie Kane, *Counterpart: A South Vietnamese Naval Officer's War* (Annapolis: Naval Institute Press, 1998), 172–173.

[34] *RMRB*, 29 December 1970, 1. China maintains that the islands reverted to Taiwan after the end of World War II, which abrogated the 1895 Treaty of Shimonoseki that had transferred the islands to Japan. See Austin, *China's Ocean Frontier*, 162–176.

[35] For copies of these documents, see Han, *Woguo nanhai*, 444–456.

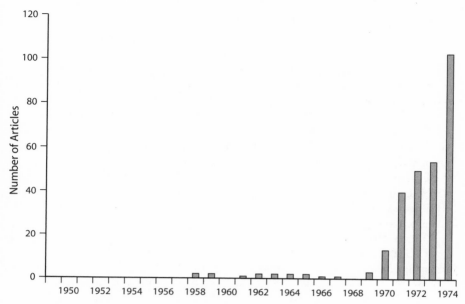

Figure 6.1 *People's Daily* Articles on Maritime Resources (1949–1974)
Source: *Renmin Ribao* [People's Daily] historical database.

Interest in offshore petroleum—which increased the importance of as-serting maritime rights—soon spread to the South China Sea. In 1970, the Philippines completed a seismic survey of these waters and began drilling test wells in 1971.[36] Likewise, South Vietnam initiated a program to exploit offshore petroleum resources, announcing in 1971 that it would offer oil concessions to foreign companies for exploration blocks in the South China Sea.[37] In July 1973, Saigon awarded eight offshore exploration con-tracts to Western oil companies, and initial drilling that fall revealed the presence of oil.[38] In January and August 1973, RVN ships conducted seis-mic surveys around Triton (Zhongjian) and Duncan islands, indicating that South Vietnam intended to explore for oil in the waters surrounding the Paracels.[39] Finally, in December 1973, Hanoi announced its intention to prospect for oil in the Tonkin Gulf northwest of the Paracel Islands.[40]

As regional interest in maritime resources increased, China strengthened its position in the one area where it already occupied some disputed islands

[36] Samuels, *Contest*, 90.
[37] *NYT*, 10 June 1971, 9.
[38] Samuels, *Contest*, 98–99.
[39] Han, *Woguo nanhai*, 676.
[40] Zou, "Maritime Boundary Delimitation," 236.

in the South China Sea, the Paracels. In 1970, the PLAN conducted geological, meteorological, and topographical surveys of the area, a prelude to a major effort launched in 1971 to upgrade the infrastructure on Woody Island that included the construction of a 350-meter reinforced concrete wharf for medium-sized ships.[41] China also began to link territorial claims to offshore islands with the assertion of maritime rights to adjacent waters. In July 1971, the MFA issued a note protesting the Philippines' presence in the South China Sea, while *People's Daily* articles described how other countries were stealing China's maritime resources.[42] In 1971, China also launched its own effort to develop offshore petroleum, drilling several wells in the Bohai Gulf and purchasing rigs from Japan.[43] Finally, in March 1973, China issued its first formal claim to maritime resources beyond its territorial waters when the MFA stated that "the undersea resources in the sea areas along China's coast all belong to China."[44]

China's offshore claims grew increasingly vulnerable, however, as other states began to occupy contested features in the Spratlys, the largest and most important of China's offshore island conflicts. To bolster its own claims, the Philippine government occupied five islands and reefs in 1970 and 1971, its first seizure of territory in this dispute.[45] Through a display of force, the Philippines challenged Taiwan's garrison on the largest island in the Spratlys, Itu Aba, which prompted protests from China and South Vietnam.[46] In August 1973, South Vietnam occupied six islands and reefs in the Spratlys, also its first seizure of land in this dispute.[47] On September 6, South Vietnam announced the incorporation of eleven Spratly islands into Phuoc Thuy Province, a political move intended to bolster its claim and secure exploration rights for its foreign investors. As demonstrated in figure 6.2, the occupation of eleven disputed features in less than three years reflected a dramatic change in the territorial status quo, weakening China's bargaining power, as it occupied none of the land that it claimed.[48]

---

[41] Yang Guoyu, ed., *Dangdai Zhongguo haijun* [Contemporary China's Navy] (Beijing: Zhongguo shehui chubanshe, 1987), 581–582, 547–548.

[42] Han, *Woguo nanhai*, 448–450.

[43] Selig S. Harrison, *China, Oil and Asia: Conflict Ahead?* (New York: Columbia University Press, 1977), 57–88.

[44] *RMRB*, 16 March 1971, 1. Also see Austin, *China's Ocean Frontier*, 50.

[45] Lei Ming, ed., *Nansha zigu shu Zhonghua* [The Spratlys Are China's since Ancient Times] (Guangzhou: Guangzhou junqu silingbu bangongshi [internal circulation], 1988), 206.

[46] Taiwan has occupied this island since 1956.

[47] Heinzig, *Disputed Islands*, 36. One Chinese source states that Vietnam did not move until November. See Wu Shicun, *Nasha zhengduan de youlai yu fazhan* [Origin and Development of the Nansha Disputes] (Beijing: Haiyang Chubanshe [internal circulation], 1999), 47.

[48] Before, only Taiwan had controlled any of the disputed features. China did not view this as threatening, because Taiwan's claims were made in the name of the Republic of China and thus affirmed Chinese sovereignty.

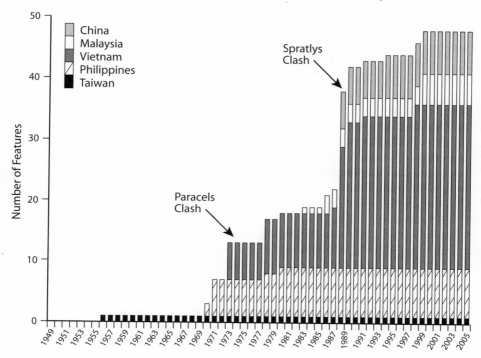

Figure 6.2 Occupation of Contested Features in the Spratly Islands (1949–2005)
Source: News reports from Lexis-Nexis, Factiva, and ProQuest; Lei, *Nansha*.

As the increasing value of controlling offshore islands created growing vulnerability in the dispute, the U.S. withdrawal from South Vietnam removed an important obstacle that might have restrained China from taking military action. With the January 1973 Paris Peace Accords, the United States completed "Vietnamization" of the war and no longer participated in combat missions. Reflecting this change, China issued its 497th and last diplomatic protest over U.S. violations of its airspace around the Paracels on December 25, 1971.[49] Although China's relative position in its offshore island disputes remained weak, it now possessed the option to use force. By contrast, the United States maintained a strong presence in northeast Asia that prevented China from taking action in the Senkakus, as did China's desire to normalize ties with Japan.[50] China's

---

[49] Han, *Woguo nanhai*, 492.

[50] In 1972, Zhou Enlai and Kakuei Tanaka agreed to shelve the dispute. Zhou reportedly said, "let's talk about it later . . some problems should be discussed after time has passed." Quoted in Zhang Zhirong, ed., *ZhongRi guanxi yu diaoyutai wenti yanjiu lunji* [Collection

improved ties with the United States suggested that it would face little opposition to any use of force against South Vietnam. Nevertheless, China still waited more than two years before seeking to strengthen its claim, in part because its navy remained weak even in the absence of an engagement with the United States.

1974 Clash over the Crescent Group

As South Vietnam increased the tempo of its activities in the South China Sea, China adopted an assertive posture to defend its claim to the Paracels. China's first response was to increase its physical presence, which occurred sometime in the fall of 1973, especially around Duncan Island in the eastern part of the Crescent Group.[51] In November, an RVN patrol ship rammed a Chinese fishing vessel near the Paracels, detaining the crew for interrogation in Danang.[52] In mid-December, the crews from two Chinese fishing boats established a camp on Duncan, which had not been occupied by either side since the early 1960s. On January 9, 1974, they moved to Robert Island, close to the RVN position on Pattle in the western part of the Crescent Group, and planted flags on Money Island.[53] As these crews were armed, their presence was not strictly commercial.[54]

In addition, China reiterated through diplomatic channels its claims to the islands. On January 11, 1974, the Foreign Ministry issued a statement challenging Vietnam's September 1973 declaration on the administration of the Spratlys. China's first official statement in more than two years not only reiterated sovereignty over the Paracels and the Spratlys but also marked the first time that China linked territorial claims to offshore islands with maritime rights, which reflected the growing importance of these contested features. The statement declared that "the resources of these islands and their adjacent seas . . belong entirely to China."[55]

---

of Studies on Chinese-Japanese Relations and the Diaoyutai Problem] (Xianggang: Lizhi chubanshe, 1999), 433.

[51] China may have occupied these islands even earlier. Heinzig notes that Chinese activity around Duncan Island increased in the fall of 1973. See Heinzig, *Disputed Islands*, 34.

[52] Li Ke and Hao Shengzhang, *Wenhua dageming zhong de renmin jiefangjun* [The People's Liberation Army during the Cultural Revolution] (Beijing: Zhonggong dangshi ziliao chubanshe, 1989), 329.

[53] Xu, *Tiemao*, 289–290.

[54] Wei Mingsen, "Xisha ziwei fanji zhan" [Paracels Counterattack in Self-defense], in *Haijun: huiyi shiliao* [Navy: Recollections and Historical Materials] (Beijing: Jiefangjun chubanshe [military circulation], 1997), 615. Wei Mingsen was the commander of the PLAN forces during the clash.

[55] Han, *Woguo nanhai*, 451–452.

The Saigon government responded quickly. On January 15, it announced the incorporation of the Paracels into Danang and dispatched a destroyer escort ship (HQ-16) to the islands. When the ship arrived that day, it briefly shelled the Chinese fishing vessels near Robert and briefly shelled the island.[56] On January 17, the situation escalated when a second RVN ship (HQ-4) arrived, deploying troops on Robert and Money islands and thereby securing control of the western part of the Crescent Group.[57] Previously, China was able to expand its presence precisely because there were no RVN forces or patrols to stop it. South Vietnam had greatly reduced its position on these islands as its own civil war intensified, keeping only a token presence on Pattle.[58]

China's assertiveness set the stage for conflict between the two sides. Although China did adopt a more aggressive posture, it had apparently not prepared to seize Pattle from South Vietnam.[59] Most likely, China's long-term strategy was simply to wait for Saigon to abandon its only position or to occupy that position when the Saigon government collapsed. When the first RVN ship arrived, no PLAN vessels were operating in the area, not even in the Amphitrite Group. After several confrontations between the RVN cutter and Chinese fishing boats on January 15 and 16, the CMC ordered a naval patrol to the islands. China hoped to persuade Vietnam to accept the new status quo in the Crescent Group and perhaps even abandon its sole position on Pattle Island. The CMC instructed Chinese forces to engage in a "struggle of persuasion" (*shuoli douzheng*) to convince South Vietnam to accept China's claims. The CMC also instructed units not to fire first or engage in provocative activity but to return fire if attacked.[60] The initial Chinese deployment consisted of two sub chasers (*lieqian ting*) and two minesweepers (*saolei ting*) along with two platoons of militia.

As both sides dispatched reinforcements, the tactical situation escalated. When the first two Chinese sub chasers arrived from Hainan's Yulin

---

[56] According to one Chinese source, the fishermen were harvesting sea cucumbers, which were being dried on Robert and Duncan islands. See Xu, *Tiemao*, 289.

[57] Do and Kane, *Counterpart*, 175.

[58] This, however, is questionable, because the weather station crew apparently did not notify the RVN government of the Chinese presence. Either the presence of Chinese fishing vessels was not new, or there was no permanent RVN presence on Pattle.

[59] See Wei, "Xisha." Other important accounts include *DDZGJD*, 646–657; Xu, *Tiemao*, 286–307; Yang, *Dangdai Zhongguo haijun*, 392–399. The best account in English, which draws on many of these sources, is Lu Ning, *Flashpoint Spratlys!* (Singapore: Dolphin Press, 1995).

[60] On the CMC's orders, see Li and Hao, *Wenhua dageming*, 329–330; Li Li, "Nanwang de shishi, shenke de qishi: wo suo jingli de Xisha ziwei fanji zuozhan" [Memorable Facts, Profound Inspirations: My Personal Experience in the Paracels Self-defensive Counterattack

naval base on the afternoon of January 17, they issued warnings to the RVN ships, moved to protect the fishing boats, and landed troops on Duncan, Drummond, and Palm islands. On the morning of January 18, President Nguyen Van Thieu ordered RVN units to evict the Chinese.[61] That afternoon, RVN ships probed China's positions around these islands, while two PLAN minesweepers arrived from Shantou in Guangdong.

By the night of January 18, both sides had reinforced their positions, and a clash was imminent. South Vietnam had four ships, including two high-endurance cutters, one destroyer escort, and one minesweeper, displacing in total more than 8,000 tons. With two additional sub chasers that arrived on the morning of January 19, China had a total of six naval vessels in addition to the two fishing boats, displacing roughly 2,400 tons.[62] China had more ships, but they were smaller in size and total firepower. Although this gave them tactical advantages of speed and maneuverability around the disputed islands, the Chinese would be outgunned in any force-on-force encounter.

On the morning of January 19, the first armed clash occurred. RVN ships approached China's positions on Duncan, Drummond, and Palm islands from two sides, squaring off against the four PLAN boats. Unable to approach the islands directly, dinghies were used to land approximately forty RVN troops on Duncan and Palm. The RVN troops on Duncan retreated, but the two sides clashed on Palm before the RVN force suffered three casualties and withdrew. In response, the RVN ships were ordered to attack. When the smoke cleared, one Chinese minesweeper was badly damaged and beached on Duncan.[63] The RVN cutters sustained light damage, while the RVN minesweeper was badly damaged. Throughout the engagement, China held two of its four sub chasers in reserve, which were then ordered to sink the RVN minesweeper as it withdrew. Following the battle, RVN ships were ordered to retreat.[64] In retrospect, the South Vietnamese forces were hardly prepared to fight. The minesweeper was operating with only one engine, while the destroyer escort's

---

Operation], in *Zongcan moubu: huiyi shiliao* [General Staff Department: Recollections and Historical Materials] (Beijing: Jiefangjun chubanshe [military circulation], 1997), 599.

[61] Do and Kane, *Counterpart*, 173–179. Also see Austin, *China's Ocean Frontier*, 73; Lo Chi-kin, *China's Policy Towards Territorial Disputes: The Case of the South China Sea Islands* (New York: Routledge, 1989), 56, 59.

[62] Xu, *Tiemao*, 291, 293, 300.

[63] The memoirs of Chinese and Vietnamese participants agree on almost every point, including the RVN's attempt to land commandos on the Chinese-held islands and the attack on PLAN ships. The only differences concern the number of commandos, only twenty according to Do Kiem, and the number of Chinese ships damaged. Do states that two were sunk, while Chinese sources refer only to one. Contrary to contemporary press reports, Do confirms that only four PLAN ships were initially involved.

[64] Do and Kane, *Counterpart*, 178.

forward three-inch gun was inoperable, requiring it to shoot "like a skunk," facing backward.[65] Moreover, one of the cutters had been damaged by friendly fire, not PLAN ships.[66]

After the clash, China's objectives in the dispute changed. The Politburo's leading small group (*lingdao xiaozu*) overseeing the Paracel operation instructed the PLAN units to seize the opportunity created by the clash to capture the three islands in the western part of the Crescent Group held by Vietnam.[67] For the operation, fifteen ships were dispatched from the Yulin naval base on Hainan on the afternoon of January 19, including five torpedo boats, eight gunboats, one sub chaser, and one medium escort along with 508 soldiers, a task force that represented a significant proportion of the vessels in the South Sea Fleet.[68] The assault began the following morning, but PLA forces faced little resistance. The RVN troops on Robert and Money islands had been evacuated on January 19. The forty-eight RVN soldiers and one American observer on Pattle surrendered.[69] By noon, China had occupied all three islands, consolidating its control of the entire archipelago.

Strategic Setup?

One alternative explanation for China's decision to escalate this dispute is that it intended from the outset to lure the South Vietnamese into striking first in order to justify its seizure of the Crescent Group. According to this argument, Saigon's September 1973 administrative declaration did not threaten China sufficiently to warrant any forceful response and was "nothing new" in terms of South Vietnam's sovereignty claims or its ability to defend the Paracels.[70] China's January 1974 declaration was thus timed cleverly to pick a fight with Saigon, providing diplomatic cover for a military operation to seize the islands. As in the 1969 Zhenbao Island ambush of the Soviets, China's actions were designed to "lure the Vietnamese into initiating military action in the islands. . . . Strategically, the Vietnamese were set-up."[71]

[65] Do and Kane, *Counterpart*, 177.

[66] Do and Kane, *Counterpart*, 178. Also see the account of commander Vu Huu San, "The Paracel Islands (Hoang-Sa) Sea Battle," reprinted from *Doan Ket* magazine (Austin, Texas), http://www.xuquang.com/dialinhnk/hsrinh.html.

[67] Fan Shuo, *Ye Jianying zhuan* [Biography of Ye Jianying] (Beijing: Dangdai Zhongguo chubanshe, 1995), 617; Li, "Nanwang de shishi," 602–603; Xu, *Tiemao*, 301.

[68] Xu, *Tiemao*, 301.

[69] Xu, *Tiemao*, 301.

[70] Lo, *China's Policy*; David G. Muller, *China's Emergence as a Maritime Power* (Boulder, Colo.: Westview Press, 1983).

[71] Muller, *China's Emergence*, 154.

To be sure, China's more aggressive posture and increased activity in the Crescent Group precipitated the clash. Nevertheless, newly available sources fail to sustain the strategic setup hypothesis. If China's initial goal was to evict the remaining South Vietnamese from the Paracels, then luring Saigon into a fight carried unnecessary risks. In January 1974, South Vietnam maintained a presence on only one of six islands in the Crescent Group, apparently with only civilian personnel.[72] Tactically, China would have been able to capture this island without firing a shot, presenting the embattled Saigon government with a fait accompli. Although this would not have allowed China to seize the moral high ground of "counterattacking in self-defense," it would have ensured the highest probability of success with the least cost or potential for escalation.

Instead, China's weakening claims in increasingly important offshore island disputes, and the reduced constraints on China's use of force that the U.S. drawdown in Southeast Asia created, best explain the decision to escalate. In the three years preceding the clash, China asserted its maritime rights with growing frequency. The January 11 Foreign Ministry statement continued the trend, linking China's territorial claims with maritime rights. Li Li, then deputy director of the Operations Department in the GSD, recalled that Saigon's goals were "to use its military presence in the Paracels area .. to pressure us to make concessions to realize its illegal territorial demands and further plunder our South China Sea's abundant maritime resources and seabed petroleum and mineral resources."[73] From Beijing's perspective, South Vietnam challenged China's position elsewhere by occupying disputed features in the Spratlys, prospecting for oil, and conducting seismic surveys in the Paracels.

At the tactical level, China's behavior is inconsistent with strategic setup hypothesis. When China issued the January 11 statement, no PLAN vessels were on patrol in the Crescent or Amphitrite groups. China's initial response was to increase its military presence to defend the fishing crews and the islands that they had apparently occupied earlier in the western part of the Crescent Group. The force deployed consisted mostly of coastal vessels that were ill equipped to defend these islands against larger RVN ships. Moreover, none of the six PLAN vessels involved in the January 19 clash had been prepositioned at China's base on Woody Island in the Amphitrite Group, a move necessary if the goal had been to concentrate forces around the Paracels. Instead, the initial deployment of troops consisted of placing two platoons of militia troops on two islands that were already under China's control, not challenging Vietnam elsewhere.

---

[72] Lu, *Flashpoint*, 77.
[73] Li, "Nanwang de shishi," 598.

More generally, China's naval forces at the time did not seem prepared to launch an ambush on the high seas. On January 16, most of the senior commanders from the Yulin naval base on Hainan were attending a training meeting at the South Sea Fleet headquarters in Guangdong Province, not preparing to strike in the Paracels. The initial reserve force organized in Yulin consisted of only several gunboats (*huwei ting*) and torpedo boats (*yulei kuaiting*), a minimal force compared with the RVN vessels.[74] One of the minesweepers had emerged from dry dock only days before and, equipped as a supply ship, was ill prepared for combat.[75] After China decided to seize the remaining islands in the Crescent Group, most of the regular army troops sent from Hainan suffered from seasickness during the twelve-hour voyage, which suggests that they had not received training for amphibious operations.[76]

Finally, the timing of the CMC's decisions is inconsistent with the logic of a strategic lure. The decision to deploy a patrol to the islands was made on the afternoon of January 16, five days after the January 11 statement. Either China did not expect South Vietnam to respond to its statement (and thus no patrol had been planned) or China thought Vietnam would respond at a later date. Four of the six ships ordered to the region were not from the Yulin naval base on Hainan's east coast but from Shantou in Guangdong, more than 850 nautical miles away.[77] The Politburo's small group formed to oversee the situation was not established until the morning of January 19, after South Vietnam's probe of China's position around Duncan, Drummond, and Pattle islands.[78] Until that point, China was not prepared to launch an attack and, given the forces it had deployed, apparently did not expect one.

Soviet Rivalry?

Another explanation for China's decision to escalate the dispute is that China sought to counter decline in its rivalry with the Soviet Union. Seizing the Paracels before the fall of Saigon would minimize objections from the Soviets and prevent any further deterioration of ties with North Viet-

[74] Wei, "Xisha," 610–611.
[75] Lu, *Flashpoint*, 85.
[76] Li and Hao, *Wenhua dageming*, 336.
[77] *DDZGJD*, 648–649. Had these boats not arrived by January 18, Vietnam may well have captured Duncan, Drummond, and Palm islands during its attack on the morning of January 19.
[78] On the leading small group, see Li, "Nanwang de shishi," 600. The group was composed of Ye Jianying, Deng Xiaoping, Wang Hongwen, Zhang Chunqiao, Chen Xilian, and Su Zhenhua. Ye and Deng led the group. Also on decision making during this period, see Fan, *Ye Jianying zhuan*, 614–617.

nam.[79] A variant of this argument stresses Chinese concerns about the long-term threat posed by Soviet naval power, which increased the urgency of consolidating control over the islands.[80] China's leaders likely considered both factors, especially the potential threat of the Soviet navy. Nevertheless, available documents fail to indicate that they were central to China's decision to adopt a more aggressive approach in late 1973.

The assertion that China acted to gain control of the entire archipelago before the collapse of South Vietnam is problematic on two counts. The first is that China did not necessarily believe that the Paracels would be a point of friction with North Vietnam. Since the mid-1950s, Hanoi acknowledged China's claims to all the South China Sea islands and renounced its own. Although the North might have been supporting China's position out of expedience, the two sides nevertheless acknowledged disputes on their land border, which indicates that Hanoi was not simply accepting all of China's territorial claims. As a result, China's leaders probably did not greatly fear North Vietnam's entry into the Paracels dispute, as Hanoi had not reversed its earlier position.

The second problem concerns the impact of China's clash on ties with North Vietnam. If in late 1973 China's leaders were concerned about relations with Hanoi, it is unclear why seizing the islands from South Vietnam would assuage the North's fears about China's territorial ambitions or improve relations with Hanoi more generally. Seizing the islands at all would have been counterproductive, which likely explains why China increased its activity in the Crescent Group through fishing boats, not naval vessels. To maintain ties with the North and achieve its territorial objectives, China's best option would have been to wait for South Vietnam to be defeated.[81] At that point it would not need to use force, because the only other claimant would no longer exist. Given its earlier statements, North Vietnam would have been hard-pressed to oppose China's actions. Forcibly seizing the islands, even from South Vietnam, ran the risk of increasing suspicion and worsening ties. And if China did not care about improving ties with the North, then there was less pressure to settle the dispute before the collapse of the South.

The other potential source of decline concerns the long-term naval threat from the Soviet Union. According to this view, China's main interest in these islands was strategic because they are situated near the main

[79] Gerald Segal, *Defending China* (Oxford: Oxford University Press, 1985), 197–210.

[80] Thomas J. Christensen, "Windows and War: Trend Analysis and Beijing's Use of Force," in Alastair Iain Johnston and Robert S. Ross, eds., *New Directions in the Study of China's Foreign Policy* (Stanford, Calif.: Stanford University Press, 2006), 72; Lo, *China's Policy*.

[81] Indeed, this appears to have been China's strategy, namely to increase civilian presence in the area as the war in Vietnam drew to a close.

shipping lanes in the region.[82] The USSR had gradually increased its naval presence in the area as reflected in its 1971 treaty with India and its objections to Indonesian and Malaysian positions on the sovereignty of the Strait of Malacca, which connects the Indian Ocean with northeast Asia. By 1974, China's leaders must have concluded that if they did not act, they would be increasingly vulnerable in the South China Sea, especially if the Soviet Union assumed control over the Paracels as a forward base for operations against China.

The logic of this argument is compelling. Nevertheless, Chinese sources provide no evidence of such a motivation among China's leaders. Neither official histories nor internal military sources refer to the Soviet Union, a striking absence given the state of Chinese-Soviet relations at the time and the militarization of China's northern border. The only possible exception comes from Li Li, who writes that China's action in the Paracels would "contain . . the hegemonism and expansionism of South Vietnam and our country's peripheral nations."[83] This may be a veiled reference to the USSR, but, given the context of that statement, it may also refer to the Philippines. Although China's propaganda apparatus began to publish articles on the Soviet navy in the late 1960s, they were usually quite general and linked to the overall anti-Soviet line. More specifically, despite an awareness of a potential threat, the PLA did not allocate resources to meet this growing challenge. Following the death of Lin Biao in 1971, the navy's budget was cut because rapprochement with the United States removed the immediate naval threat to China. Disagreements over the navy's budget continued after the Paracels operation, which Jiang Qing's political faction claimed demonstrated that China's naval power was sufficient. Only after the Soviets' worldwide "OKEAN 75" exercise in April 1975 did Mao instruct the CMC to focus attention on naval force development.[84] If China was reacting to the Soviet threat, the Paracels operation appears to have been an outlier with respect to China's naval policy at the time.[85]

ENTRY INTO THE SPRATLYS

On March 14, 1988, Chinese and Vietnamese forces clashed on Johnson (Chigua) Reef in the Spratly Islands. In the fighting, three Vietnamese ships were sunk, resulting in seventy-four casualties. This clash was Chi-

---

[82] Lo, *China's Policy.*
[83] Li, "Nanwang de shishi," 598.
[84] This draws on Muller, *China's Emergence*, 168–173.
[85] Muller, *China's Emergence*, 168–173.

na's first use of force in the Spratlys and occurred following China's estab-lishment of a base and meteorological observation station on Fiery Cross (Yongshu) Reef in February 1988. By the end of March, China had seized a total of six coral reefs. Although these features had been unoccupied, China's actions reflected a new willingness and capability to defend its claims to the Spratlys much more assertively than in previous decades.

The critical decision, which occurred sometime in 1987, was to estab-lish a permanent physical presence in the disputed area. Several important changes in the dynamics of the dispute over the Spratlys account for this decision. The first was a growing long-term vulnerability in the South China Sea. The PRC had been claiming these islands since 1951, but it still lacked a physical presence with which to support its claims. By the early 1980s, the other disputants had occupied all the islands permanently above the high-tide line, leaving only some semisubmerged reefs and shoals vacant. As other states continued to occupy contested features in the 1980s, China's relative position continued to deteriorate. The second change was China's gradual development of its long-range naval capabili-ties, which China had previously lacked but that could now be used to sustain a presence in the Spratlys. In addition, a third factor likely helped shape this decision. As John Garver has argued, it was in the PLAN's own bureaucratic interests to impress on the civilian leadership the importance of defending China's weak claim, as this mission provided a rationale for increased budgetary resources and doctrinal change.[86]

China's more assertive posture created the conditions for the March clash to occur. Nevertheless, available evidence indicates that it was a by-product of China's decision to occupy Fiery Cross and adjacent features, not part of a larger policy to use force to seize disputed territory held by other claimants. Indeed, what is striking about the events of March 1988 is that China did not use its tactical victory to evict Vietnamese forces from other features, especially prime Spratlys real estate such as Nam Yit, Spratly, or Sin Cowe islands.

Growing Importance and Continued Decline in Claim Strength

The tactical or operational decision to establish a presence in the Spratlys occurred in early 1987. The strategic decision to occupy territory, however, was most likely made much earlier. In November 1980, the CMC ordered two Hong-6 bombers from the PLAN's air wing to con-duct an aerial reconnaissance of the islands. The navy's deputy commander personally delivered these orders, which were designed explicitly to exercise China's sovereignty over the area and marked the beginning of China's "push" south.[87] Over the next six years, two factors combined to create a perception among China's leaders of growing vulnerability in the Spratlys and increase incentives to occupy contested features: the continued importance of the islands for claiming maritime rights and the ongoing deterioration of China's position relative to other claimants.

The first factor was the continued interest in maritime rights for exploiting petroleum resources, which increased the importance of controlling disputed features. With Deng's economic reform, China's economic center of gravity shifted from the interior provinces back to the coastal regions. In addition to increasing the importance of coastal defense, economic reform also increased the value of securing access to maritime resources, especially petroleum, to sustain high levels of economic growth. It is no coincidence that, in early 1979, offshore petroleum was the first industry that China opened to foreign investment. After four years of preparation, the first round of bidding for exploration blocks was held in 1982 and included many concessions in the waters south of Hong Kong and Hainan and north of the Spratlys. To further develop this industry, China held a second round of bidding in 1984, again focusing on concessions in these waters.[88]

Although first piqued in the 1970s, the interest of littoral states in the petroleum potential of the seabed around the Spratlys continued to grow. In 1980, Vietnam and the Soviet Union signed an agreement to explore for petroleum on Vietnam's continental shelf, which drew sharp protests from Beijing. In 1982, the drafting of the UNCLOS codified an international regime for the assertion of maritime rights. Chinese scientists began to examine the area for petroleum in the mid-1980s, when the Chinese Academy of Sciences and the State Oceanographic Administration (SOA) conducted a series of surveys. In 1987, Vietnam followed China in opening its offshore oil industry to foreign investment, further increasing interest in the area. Also in 1987, Chinese researchers announced that there were large deposits of petroleum in the region.[89]

The second factor was that China saw its claim in this increasingly important area as weakening as other states continued to occupy disputed islands and reefs. Although the Philippines had already occupied seven

---

[87] Yang, *Dangdai Zhongguo haijun*, 482.

[88] On China's offshore oil industry, see Kenneth Lieberthal and Michel Oksenberg, *Policy Making in China: Leaders, Structures, and Processes* (Princeton, N.J.: Princeton University Press, 1988); Qin Wencai, *Shiyou shiren: zai haiyang shiyou zhanxian jishi* [Oil Brigade: The Record of the Battle for Offshore Oil] (Beijing: Shiyou gongye chubanshe, 1997).

[89] Xinhua, 16 November 1987; Xinhua, 24 July 1987 (Lexis-Nexis).

features in the 1970s, it seized Commodore Reef in 1980 (map 6.2).[90] In 1982, the Philippine prime minister toured islands in the area while President Ferdinand Marcos ordered the Defense Ministry to increase the Philippine presence.[91] In 1980, Malaysia joined the fray when it claimed a 200-nautical-mile EEZ, which included claims to twelve features in the Spratlys. In August 1983, Malaysia announced that its commandos had occupied Swallow (Danwan) Reef. Three years later, in October 1986, Malaysia seized Ardasier (Guangxingzai) and Mariveles (Nanhai) reefs.[92] In 1987, Vietnam began to occupy additional features, seizing Barque Canada (Bai) Reef in February and West (Xi) Reef in December.[93] China responded to almost all these changes to the control of disputed territory, not only reiterating its own claims but also demonstrating an awareness of the increasing weakness of its own position. As Admiral Liu Huaqing recalled in his memoir, "since the 1970s, they had continued to seize the islands and reefs of our Spratly Islands. . . almost all above-water islands and reefs had been occupied by Vietnam, the Philippines, and Malaysia . . . their seizures increased steadily."[94]

As the strength of China's claim in the Spratlys continued to weaken while the competition for maritime resources increased, bureaucratic interests played an indirect role in shaping incentives for China's leaders to use force. Newly available sources confirm John Garver's analysis of the role of the navy and in particular its commander for most of the 1980s, Admiral Liu Huaqing. Liu emphasized establishing a presence in the Spratlys as a key mission for China's navy in part because that would require a shift from coastal defense to long-range and ultimately blue-water capabilities.[95] He used public speeches and interviews to link expanding the capabilities of the PLAN with ensuring access to maritime resources necessary for Deng's economic reform policies. In a lengthy 1984 *Liberation Army Daily* article, Liu wrote, "We must arm the navy with modern science and technology so that it can . . defend our vast territorial waters and our legal maritime rights and interests."[96]

As the importance of asserting China's claims to these islands increased, so did its long-range naval capabilities. In May and June 1980, the PLAN successfully recovered an ICBM test-fired in the South Pacific.[97] In 1984

---

[90] Han, *Woguo nanhai*, 686.

[91] *FEER*, 28 April 1983, 38.

[92] Lei, *Nansha*, 207; Lu, *Flashpoint*, 56.

[93] Lei, *Nansha*, 204.

[94] Liu, *Liu Huaqing*, 534–535.

[95] Garver, "China's Push."

[96] "Naval Commander Stresses Navy's Role in National Construction," Xinhua, 23 November 1984, BBC Summary of World Broadcasts, 27 November 1984, FE/7811/BII/1.

[97] *Haijun shi* [History of the Navy] (Beijing: Jiefangjun chubanshe, 1989), 304–309.

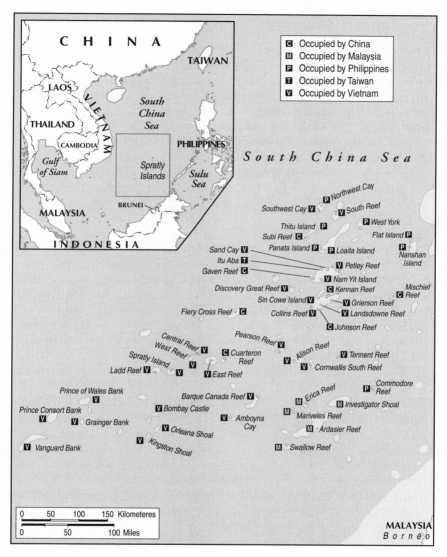

Map 6.2 Spratly Islands

and 1985, long-range patrols were conducted to the South Pole and the Indian Ocean, respectively.[98] Other activities were designed to support China's claims in the Spratlys by "showing the flag" through an increased presence in the area. Regular air patrols over the Spratlys began in 1983.[99] In May 1983, the PLAN conducted the South Sea Fleet's first long-range voyage to the region, which consisted of a supply ship and cargo ship, including 85 naval commanders and 540 operations and navigation systems officers.[100] Well publicized by the Chinese media, the voyage was led by a PLAN deputy commander.[101] Traveling to James (Zhengmu) Shoal, the southernmost feature of the Spratlys, the cruise was designed to familiarize South Sea Fleet officers with the area where they would be conducting future operations.[102] In 1984, the SOA dispatched research ships to the area with State Council approval.[103]

The PLAN's activities in the region and increasing focus on the South China Sea garnered high-level support from civilian leaders. On New Year's Eve 1985, CCP General Secretary Hu Yaobang traveled to the Paracels to visit the troops and civilians stationed there, underscoring senior leaders' support for asserting China's maritime rights. Importantly, naval commander Liu Huaqing accompanied Hu on the trip along with other senior military officials. According to Chinese press reports, one purpose of Hu's visit was to signal China's resolve to defend its territorial claims. During his visit, Hu stated that China "will not permit anyone to seize even one inch of our great country's land."[104]

The decision to establish a physical presence in the Spratlys was made sometime in early 1987. During the fourteenth meeting of UNESCO's Intergovernmental Oceanographic Commission in March 1987, China agreed to build five observation posts as part of a worldwide ocean survey, including one post in the Spratly Islands.[105] Whether China manipulated this meeting to move into the region or was actually invited to do so is unknown. Nevertheless, Chinese sources indicate that it provided diplomatic cover for China's expansion. According to one PLA history, UNESCO's imprimatur provided an "imperial sword" (*shangfang yujian*)

[98] Sha Li and Ai Yi, *Zhongguo haijun zhengzhan jishi* [Record of the Expeditions of China's Navy] (Chengdu: Dianzi keji daxue chubanshe, 1993), 130–142.

[99] Yang, *Dangdai Zhongguo haijun*, 482.

[100] Xu, *Tiemao*, 308.

[101] See the recollections in Lin Daoyuan, ed., *Nansha gaosu women* [What the Spratly Islands Tell Us] (Beijing: Haijun chubanshe, 1988), 3–17.

[102] Xu, *Tiemao*, 309.

[103] Garver, "China's Push," 1008–1009.

[104] Xinhua, 1 January 1986 (Lexis-Nexis); *RMRB*, 2 January 1986, 1. On the importance of this visit, see Xu, *Tiemao*, 308.

[105] *Haijun shi*, 323; Xu, *Tiemao*, 309.

to establish a presence in the region under the auspices of an intergovern-mental organization.[106] With the increasing competition over the Spratlys in the preceding three years, it is likely that China sought this opportunity to legitimate its presence.

Over the next ten months, China conducted a series of surveys and naval patrols to prepare for establishment of the post. In April 1987, two research ships conducted an extensive survey and selected Fiery Cross Reef as the location for the base and observation station.[107] In addition to its large size, this reef was unoccupied and isolated from features held by other states, suggesting that China sought to minimize the diplomatic fallout from its occupation of disputed territory. Also in April, Admiral Liu ordered the South Sea Fleet to conduct the PLAN's first combat patrol in the South China Sea. The goals of the patrol were "to exercise our sovereignty, display our maritime power and integrate war preparedness [*zhanbei*]." Another goal was to "become familiar with the area" because "the Spratlys are our territory, which we will frequently visit from now on."[108] Conducted from May 16 to June 6, the patrol included two "oper-ational exercises" (*zuozhan yanxi*), most likely training for establishing a permanent presence.[109]

In August 1987, the PLAN and SOA submitted a proposal to the CMC and State Council to establish the base and observation station. In Octo-ber and November, ships from the East Sea Fleet conducted a patrol in the area, visiting more than twenty unoccupied reefs.[110] At the same time, a SOA vessel and a naval engineering ship surveyed the waters near Fiery Cross Reef. In November, the CMC and State Council approved the pro-posal and designated the navy as the lead agency with the support of the SOA. The initial plan called for China to occupy a total of nine reefs, including Fiery Cross.[111] In mid-January 1988, an advance party secured Fiery Cross Reef.[112] In the first week of February, a total of eleven ships from the South and East Sea fleets arrived on station, including landing craft, engineering ships with construction materials, and a *Luda*-class guided-missile destroyer.[113] Owing to poor weather, construction did not begin until the end of February.[114]

---

[106] Xu, *Tiemao*, 309.

[107] *Haijun shi*, 323; Xu, *Tiemao*, 309.

[108] Liu, *Liu Huaqing*, 494.

[109] Xu, *Tiemao*, 309.

[110] Xu, *Tiemao*, 309.

[111] Xu, *Tiemao*, 317.

[112] Xu puts the date at January 14, while Lu Ning, citing other Chinese sources, states that it was January 20. See Lu, *Flashpoint*, 88; Xu, *Tiemao*, 310.

[113] *Haijun shi*, 324; Lin, *Nansha gaosu women*, 25.

[114] *Haijun shi*, 324–325.

The March 1988 Clash

Although China may have believed that the remote location of Fiery Cross Reef and its UNESCO mandate would assuage other claimants' concerns, its presence in the region increased tensions and created the conditions for a deadly clash. From a tactical perspective, Fiery Cross Reef was isolated and vulnerable. Reefs on its periphery were unoccupied at the time, but they were near positions under Vietnamese control (see map 6.2). Vietnam's first response, in late January and early February, was to occupy five of those reefs, including three to the south of Fiery Cross and two to the east, in an attempt to form a perimeter around Fiery Cross.[115] Vietnam also began to monitor China's movements in the area, which led to a series of confrontations between the two sides as PLAN units sought to defend China's position. In the course of these confrontations, China and Vietnam raced to occupy more reefs in the surrounding waters.

The first confrontation occurred on January 31, when Vietnam challenged the PLAN vessels at Fiery Cross Reef. Two armed Vietnamese cargo ships with construction materials approached the reef. PLAN ships intercepted these boats and turned them away.[116] After this incident, Vietnam occupied two nearby features, including Ladd (Riji) Reef and Discovery Great (Daxian) Reef (see map 6.2). Vietnam also occupied Tennent (Wumie) Reef in the eastern Spratlys at the end of January.[117]

A second confrontation occurred on February 18. This time, it revolved around Cuarteron (Huayang) Reef, which was located between Fiery Cross and Vietnam's main base in the area, Spratly Island. A PLAN guided-missile destroyer, escort, and transport ship were surveying the area when a Vietnamese minesweeper and armed freighter approached. Both sides dispatched landing parties from the west and east side of the reef, respectively. The Chinese detachment reached the high point first, planting a flag, while the Vietnamese retreated, planting a flag on a wooden post erected on a submerged portion of the reef. When the weather turned, the Vietnamese withdrew, leaving China in control of the reef.[118] On February 25, China occupied its third feature in the area, Gaven (Nanxun) Reef, located to the east of Fiery Cross and near the Taiwan-held Itu Aba Island.[119] In response, Vietnam occupied three addi-

[115] Xu, *Tiemao*, 310.
[116] *Haijun shi*, 326; Xu, *Tiemao*, 311.
[117] Lei, *Nansha*, 204–205.
[118] *Haijun shi*, 326; Xu, *Tiemao*, 311.
[119] Liu, *Liu Huaqing*, 540.

tional features around Fiery Cross Reef: East (Dong) Reef, Alison (Liu-men) Reef, and Cornwallis South (Nanhua) Reef.[120]

As the confrontations intensified, PLAN headquarters dispatched more vessels to the area. On February 22, the "502 task force" (*biandui*) from the South Sea Fleet arrived in the area. On March 5, the East Sea Fleet's "531 task force" arrived, increasing the total number of PLAN ships in the area to fifteen.[121] China was apparently preparing to occupy other vacant features to the east and north of Fiery Cross to create a perimeter around its new base.

A third, and this time violent, confrontation occurred on March 13 and 14. Although Chinese and Vietnamese accounts naturally differ over who arrived first, the confrontation focused on Johnson (Chigua) Reef east of Fiery Cross. Chinese sources state that a PLAN guided-missile destroyer was surveying the reef when three Vietnamese ships approached the area. Anchoring near Johnson and two other reefs, these ships apparently intended to land troops on the vacant reef. Two more PLAN guided-missile destroyers arrived, outgunning the Vietnamese freighters and landing craft. The following morning, each side put troops on the reef, fifty-eight Chinese and forty-three Vietnamese, respectively, each apparently with orders to evict the other.[122] A shoving match broke out, during which shots were fired. Once this occurred, ships from both sides opened fire. With far more firepower, the PLAN ships sank or destroyed all Vietnamese vessels within thirty minutes, killing seventy-four sailors.[123]

To be sure, China's aggressive posture and its decision to establish a presence in the region created conditions for the clash. China's move into the Spratlys compelled Vietnam to attempt to contain China's presence, which increased confrontations between the two sides. Available evidence, however, does not indicate that the clash was part of a Chinese policy to evict other claimants forcefully from occupied features. According to a PLA history, the basic guidelines instructed soldiers "not to fire the first shot; [but] if the enemy occupies our islands, compel (*qiang-xing*) him to leave." They also noted that "the Spratly struggle is a military as well as diplomatic struggle. Strictly grasp this policy."[124] When the confrontation escalated on Johnson Reef, the local Chinese commander ordered the attack on Vietnamese ships before receiving instructions from

---

[120] Lei, *Nansha*, 205.

[121] Xu, *Tiemao*, 311.

[122] Xu, *Tiemao*, 313.

[123] Vietnamese sources are largely consistent with the Chinese account. The main difference concerns who reached the reef first and which side fired first.

[124] Xu, *Tiemao*, 312.

the GSD.[125] After the clash, the CMC rejected a request from local commanders to assault other features under Vietnamese control, even though commanders had apparently already deployed their ships to do so.[126] The CMC's refusal to permit assaults on other islands is consistent with China's strategy for establishing a presence in the area, namely to occupy only vacant features. In this way, China hoped to defend its claims on the cheap. Consistent with this interpretation, in the week following the clash, China occupied two additional vacant reefs, Kennan (Dongmen) and Subi (Zhubi).[127]

Two factors should be stressed. First, unlike in the Paracels, China did not seize the opportunity created by its defeat of Vietnamese forces at Johnson Reef to attack other Vietnamese-held positions, especially prime real estate in the region such as Spratly Island. Second, China also did not occupy three of the features outlined in the initial plan. Most likely, Vietnam occupied these positions after the PLAN appeared at Fiery Cross.

Mischief Reef, 1994

Sometime in the late fall of 1994, China occupied a seventh feature in the Spratlys, the aptly named Mischief Reef. In February 1995, Philippine fishermen reported that China had erected structures on the reef, where Chinese boats were anchored. Although this reef was occupied without armed conflict, it brought renewed attention to the Spratlys dispute and China's potential for aggression. Unfortunately, in contrast with the clashes of 1974 and 1988, Chinese sources on this event are extremely thin, which limits the strength of the conclusions that can be drawn.

One explanation is consistent with the theory presented in this book. China's move into the region, occupation of six features, and clash with Vietnam threatened the position of other claimants, resulting in a spiral of hostility in the South China Sea. Between the March 1988 clash and 1991, Vietnam occupied seven additional features, controlling a total of twenty-five and further consolidating its position in the dispute.[128] In 1992, the China National Offshore Oil Company signed a contract with

---

[125] Lu Ning, *The Dynamics of Foreign-Policy Decisionmaking in China* (Boulder, Colo.: Westview, 1997), 126.

[126] Lu, *Dynamics*, 126–127.

[127] Liu, *Liu Huaqing*, 541.

[128] Collins (Guihan) Reef, Landsdowne (Qiong) Reef, Bombay Castle (Pengbo Bao), Grainger (Lizhun) Bank, Prince of Wales (Guangya) Bank, Vanguard (Wanan) Bank, and Prince Consort (Xiwei) Bank.

an American firm, Crestone, to explore for petroleum in the southwestern Spratlys near Vanguard Bank, which Vietnam had occupied since 1989. Also in 1992, China's National People's Congress passed a law on territorial waters that repeated China's 1951 claim to the Spratlys. In 1993, Brunei issued a formal claim to an EEZ, while Vietnam awarded drilling rights to a consortium of companies including Mobil for exploration blocks west of Crestone's contract area. In May, both China and Vietnam also dispatched survey ships to this contested region. In 1994, competition intensified. Vietnam's PetroChina began to drill in an exploration block within the Creston concession area in May, and China stated in June its intention to begin seismic surveys in the same area. At the same time, the Philippines, with the Alcorn oil company, initiated a major seismic survey of the disputed waters.[129]

Given this heightened competition among the leading three claimants, it is perhaps unsurprising that China occupied an additional feature to strengthen its claim. The occupation of Mischief Reef is consistent with declining claim strength. First and most importantly, Mischief Reef lies in the eastern part of the archipelago. As China's other features are all in the far west, occupation of this reef broadened the scope of waters over which China could claim effective control. Second and perhaps less importantly, the seizure perhaps prevented the formation of an entente between Vietnam and the Philippines. Although both claim sovereignty over the reef, its proximity to the Philippines greatly increased Manila's security concerns, which resulted in a series of bilateral meetings in 1995 between top Chinese and Philippine civilian and military officials.

Bureaucratic politics offers a competing explanation for this occupation. Several strands of circumstantial evidence indicate that the PLAN may have occupied the island without CMC or PBSC authorization. First, the immediate reaction of the PRC embassy in Manila was that the occupation had been "ordered by low-level functionaries acting without the knowledge and consent of the Chinese government."[130] In addition, China's swift diplomatic engagement of the Philippines, which included signing a bilateral code of conduct and financial aid, suggests that it sought to compensate the Philippines for the occupation. Interviews, moreover, indicate that members of the PBSC were "surprised" by the reef's occupation, which, given their membership on the leading small group in charge of foreign policy, suggests that it might have been unapproved.[131] Finally,

---

[129] This paragraph draws on Daniel J. Dzurek, "The Spratly Islands Dispute: Who's on First?" *Maritime Briefing*, vol. 2, no. 1 (1996): 1–67.

[130] "Ramos Orders Philippine Defenses Beefed Up in Spratlys," Japan Economic Newswire, 15 February 1995 (Lexis-Nexis).

[131] Austin, *China's Ocean Frontier*, 91.

an internal circulation bulletin referred to tensions between the Chinese government and military over the Spratly Islands in the years preceding the occupation.[132]

CONCLUSION

Since the establishment of the PRC, China's leaders have used a combination of escalation and delaying strategies to strengthen their relative position in offshore islands disputes. In 1949, China's claims in these conflicts were inferior, as it occupied only some disputed territory in two of four disputes and lacked the naval capabilities to project power over the others. As the importance of offshore islands increased in the 1970s following the worldwide focus on maritime resources, China's claims became increasingly vulnerable. As other claimants increased the number of islands and reefs they occupied, China moved to increase its presence first in the Paracels and then in the Spratlys. The timing of decline in China's claim strength, official histories, and leadership statements explain why and when China has used force in these disputes.

Paradoxically, China's past uses of force in these conflicts suggest that it may be less willing to do so in the future. By using force and occupying contested land, China greatly strengthened its claim in the Paracels and Spratlys. As the 2002 code of conduct declaration demonstrates, China now has a seat at the bargaining table and confidence that its control of some of the territory at stake will ensure that it plays a role in any settlement of the conflict. Moreover, in the fourteen years since its occupation of Mischief Reef, China has not seized any additional features in the Spratlys despite the steady improvement in its naval capabilities. Although China has possessed the means to evict other claimants, it has refrained from such action, as its position in the dispute only grows stronger. Moreover, it sat tight even following Vietnam's occupation of two additional features in 1998 and Malaysia's occupation of two additional features in 1999. This restraint is consistent with my argument, as China's claim strength has greatly improved, reducing the sensitivity to decline and the need to use force. Now, almost all vacant islands and reefs have been occupied by the various claimants, which dampens future competition to control disputed land.

---

[132] Lu Jianren, "Nansha zhengduan ji duice" [Policy Options in the Nansha Dispute], in Yatai yanjiu suo, ed., *Nansha wenti yanjiu ziliao* (Beijing: Zhongguo shehui kexueyuan [internal circulation], 1996).

As White Dragon Tail illustrates, China is most likely to consider compromise in offshore island disputes in response to external threats. Looking forward, however, compromise is unlikely, as whatever external threats occur will have to outweigh the value of petroleum and sea lane security linked to these islands. One possibility for compromise might stem from heightened competition between the United States and China for influence in Southeast Asia. In this scenario, China might be more willing to trade territorial concessions in the Spratlys or even the Paracels for improved ties with regional states. At the moment, however, China has been able to improve ties within the region without offering concessions over the sovereignty of disputed areas.[133]

[133] Michael A. Glosny, "Heading toward a Win-Win Future? Recent Developments in China's Policy toward Southeast Asia," *Asian Security*, vol. 2, no. 1 (2006): 24–57; Philip C. Saunders, *China's Global Activism: Strategy, Drivers and Tools*, Occasional Paper 4 (Washington, D.C.: Institute for National Strategic Studies, National Defense University, 2006); Robert G. Sutter, *China's Rise in Asia: Promises and Perils* (Lanham, M.D.: Rowman and Littlefield, 2005).

Conclusion

THREE MAIN FINDINGS emerge from this study of China's territorial disputes. First, China has not been highly prone to using force in its territorial disputes, the issue over which states are most likely to go to war. China has been more likely to compromise in its territorial conflicts and less likely to use force than many policy analysts assert, theories of international relations predict, or scholars of China expect. China has not become more aggressive in pursuit of many of its claims as it has accumulated economic and military power over the past two decades. Instead, it has compromised frequently and, in some cases, substantially. China has used force in a minority of its disputes, not to pursue broad expansion but to defend the claims it has maintained since 1949. China has fought to protect its core interests, including the territorial integrity of its ethnic minority borderlands, Taiwan's unification with the mainland, and the establishment of a maritime frontier.

Second, counterintuitively, political instability within a state can create strong incentives for peace, not war. In China's many disputes, internal threats to regime security explain the majority of its territorial compromises. Ethnic unrest in China illustrates how internal threats to a state's territorial integrity create incentives for it to cooperate with its neighbors. The 1959 revolt in Tibet, for example, altered the context of China's disputes with its Himalayan neighbors, leading to concessions in conflicts with Burma, Nepal, and India in 1960. In the 1990s, sustained ethnonationalist unrest in Xinjiang created similar incentives for cooperation in disputes with Kazakhstan, Kyrgyzstan, and Tajikistan. In response to these internal threats, China traded territorial concessions for assistance in suppressing the state's domestic foes. Likewise, the absence of ethnic unrest coincides with periods in which China maintained a delaying strategy in its territorial disputes. From the end of the Tibetan revolt to the outbreak of violence in Xinjiang in 1990, China offered no new compromises in its territorial disputes.

Third, decline in bargaining power in a dispute can create strong preventive motivations to use force in territorial conflicts. In its disputes, China has demonstrated a clear sensitivity to negative shifts in its claim strength, using force when it faced militarily powerful opponents that could weaken its position or when it controlled little or none of the land that it claimed. China's homeland disputes illustrate how decline in claim strength creates incentives to use force. China has never used force in its homeland disputes over Hong Kong and Macao. Because it could seize these territories at any time, its bargaining power was never threatened. By contrast, China's leaders have been sensitive to any further decline in their already weak claim over Taiwan, as the PRC does not control any of the disputed land and cannot easily project military power over this area. In the 1950s, China used force to signal its resolve to defend its claims when increased U.S. military support for Taiwan threatened its permanent separation from the mainland. The drop in U.S. support from the 1960s strengthened China's position and reduced incentives for escalation. In the 1990s, amid Taiwan's democratization and the rise of pro-independence political forces, China used force again to signal its commitment to unification when it concluded that the United States backed Taiwan's drive for diplomatic recognition.

EXTENDING THE ARGUMENT

These findings rest on theories of cooperation and escalation in territorial disputes. All things being equal, states prefer to defer and delay the settlement of such conflicts. Nevertheless, offering concessions or using force will be more attractive than delay under certain conditions. A state is more likely to compromise over territory when internal or external threats arise to its strength at home or its position abroad. When facing threats to its security, a state is more willing to trade territorial concessions for improved ties with its neighbors and assistance in countering these other threats.

While threats in a state's overall security environment create incentives for cooperation, shifts in its claim strength or bargaining power in a dispute explain decisions to use force. In territorial disputes, states compete to use military and political means to control disputed land and achieve a favorable negotiated outcome. When one side perceives that it is losing this contest, it is much more willing to use force to counter its decline. A state with a weak claim may encounter an additional incentive to use force when decline in a stronger adversary's position creates a temporary opportunity to strengthen its position by seizing disputed land.

These two theories were tested against one country's many disputes. As argued in chapter 1, the number and diversity of China's disputes provide a fertile laboratory for assessing claims about territorial conflicts. Moreover, China is not an outlier whose behavior requires a special theory. China's willingness to offer concessions or threaten force is statistically indistinguishable from other twentieth-century territorial disputes. Nevertheless, the question of whether the theories presented here can illuminate the sources of cooperation and escalation in other territorial disputes must be examined. To explore the broader relevance of the propositions advanced in this book, this section examines briefly other territorial disputes.

Internal Threats and Cooperation in Territorial Disputes

One might contend that the pacific effects of regime insecurity reflect some factor unique to China. Internal threats to regime security, however, are likely to be a source of cooperation for states that share similar traits with the PRC. Three factors that caused China's regime insecurity are, in fact, common among other states. First, newly established states are likely to face internal challenges to their rule that in turn create incentives for compromise. As the process of state formation often comes at the expense of one or more societal groups, any new state will face lingering internal challenges to its authority. Second, states with authoritarian political systems that concentrate political power in one party or group are also likely to confront internal challenges from disenfranchised actors, creating similar incentives for foreign policy moderation. Third, states composed of multiple ethnic groups are likely to face challenges to their internal authority when minority groups pursue autonomy or independence. When these groups reside near international borders, states can face even more powerful incentives to compromise with their neighbors. Independently, each of these factors is likely to increase incentives for cooperation. When all three are present, the odds of cooperation should rise substantially when neighboring states can provide assistance to strengthen regime security.[1]

The USSR's territorial concessions in the 1918 Treaty of Brest-Litovsk offer one example of a new, authoritarian state using territorial compromises to consolidate its authority at home. Almost immediately following the 1917 October Revolution that brought the Bolsheviks to power, the Soviet Union entered into peace talks with Germany and the Central Powers. For Vladimir Lenin, the new socialist state required time to consolidate its fragile domestic authority that only peace with Germany could provide. Although the concessions in the treaty were hotly debated, Lenin's reasoning prevailed.[2] As he lobbied for ratification, Lenin stated that "whatever respite we may obtain . . . it is better than war, because it gives the masses a breathing-space, because it provides us with an opportunity to correct what the bourgeoisie have done."[3]

---

[1] In the absence of territorial disputes, states with these characteristics should be more likely to pursue compromise over other issues when internal threats to regime security arise.

[2] Adam B. Ulam, *Expansion and Coexistence: The History of Soviet Foreign Policy, 1917–67* (New York: Frederick A. Praeger, 1968), 51–75.

[3] *Collected Works of V. T. Lenin*, vol 27 (Moscow: Progress Publishers 1965), 181–182.

Similarly, Egypt's concessions resulting in the 1978 Camp David Accords and its separate peace with Israel have their roots the social and economic upheaval that this one-party authoritarian state confronted in the mid-1970s. Following the Yom Kippur War, Egypt faced a mounting fiscal crisis and growing social unrest that placed great pressure for change on the state. Peace with Israel and aid from the United States provided one means with which to buffet internal demands for change and increase popular support by devoting more resources to economic development. At Camp David, Egypt traded recognition of Israel for the return of the Sinai Peninsula and a large aid package from the United States that addressed the state's internal problems.[4]

The behavior of many states in Africa after decolonization provides another example of regime insecurity as a source of moderation and compromise in territorial disputes. The combination of new states with limited authority at home and with multiple ethnic groups near their international boundaries (and often across them) dampened conflict and increased cooperation among states in the region. On the one hand, facing these internal challenges, many of the new states in Africa avoided initiating territorial claims in the first place. Following decolonization, far fewer disputes erupted in this region than many had anticipated, as most states were equally vulnerable to each other's claims. On the other hand, many of the disputes that did arise were settled through compromise agreements, often to address domestic concerns.[5] In 1963, for example, Mauritania offered substantial concessions to Mali over the southeastern portion of their border. Mali had supported Mauritanian rebels in the Hodh region, which was also under dispute. Mauritania offered substantial concessions, while Mali ceased its support for the rebels.[6]

External Threats and Cooperation in Territorial Disputes

Although external threats explain only a few of China's compromises, the conditions that give rise to such threats are certainly not unique to China. Rivalry and competition among states are part of the very fabric of international politics and likely to create incentives for cooperation in other

[4] Ibrahim Karawan, "Foreign Policy Restructuring: Egypt's Disengagement from the Arab-Israeli Conflict Revisited," *Cambridge Review of International Affairs*, vol. 18, no. 3 (October 2005): 325–338.

[5] On Africa, see Jeffrey Herbst, *States and Power in Africa: Comparative Lessons in Authority and Control* (Princeton, N. J.: Princeton University Press, 2000); Saadia Touval, *The Boundary Politics of Independent Africa* (Cambridge, Mass.: Harvard University Press, 1972).

[6] Touval, *Boundary Politics*, 249–250.

territorial disputes, especially when regimes are relatively secure from internal threats.

In January 1963, for example, the United States and Mexico settled a long-standing territorial dispute over the Chamizal area between El Paso and Ciudad Juárez. Although the two sides had tried before, this time the international environment had changed for the United States, creating strong incentives for compromise. The revolution in Cuba and failure of the Bay of Pigs invasion had increased the importance of improved U.S. ties with Latin America to counter growing Soviet influence, resulting in President John F. Kennedy's "Alliance for Progress" and enhanced support for the Organization of American States. Territorial compromise in the dispute with Mexico reflected a broader effort to strengthen the U.S. position in the region during the Cold War.[7]

Likewise, the USSR's own rivalry with United States in the mid-1980s resulted in the Soviets' pursuit of compromise with China over their territorial disputes. In his July 1986 speech at Vladivostok, Mikhail Gorbachev indicated that the Soviet Union would accept the *thalweg* principle as the means for delimiting the eastern sector of the border, reversing its position since the 1960s that the boundary lay on the Chinese bank. Given the number of troops deployed along the border, Gorbachev hoped to improve ties with China to strengthen the Soviet Union's position against the United States.

Claim Strength and Escalation in Territorial Disputes

Although declining claim strength has been a central factor in China's decisions to use force over territory, it is certainly not unique to China. The competition to control disputed territory that gives rise to perceptions of declining claim strength is likely to be found in most territorial disputes. In April 1999, for example, Pakistani regular and irregular forces occupied more than seventy positions on the Indian side of the line of control in disputed Kashmir, sparking several months of high-altitude combat. India's consolidation of its political authority in Kashmir was a key factor in the Pakistani decision to use force. In the preceding years, India had managed to suppress the Kashmiri insurgency and hold several rounds of elections that gave new legitimacy to the provincial government, weakening Pakistan's already poor claim. Pakistan concluded that a limited probe might breathe new life into the insurgency, thereby strengthening its otherwise declining position in the dispute.[8]

---

[7] Philip C. Jessup, "El Chamizal," *The American Journal of International Law*, vol. 67, no. 3 (1973): 423–445.

[8] Sumit Ganguly, *Conflict Unending: India-Pakistan Tensions since 1947* (New York: Columbia University Press, 2001).

Declining claim strength provides an alternative explanation of Argentina's April 1982 invasion of the Falkland Islands, a gambit commonly explained as diversionary. In 1980, Argentina suffered a serious setback in negotiations with Britain over the islands' sovereignty when Parliament scuttled a proposal in which Britain would return the islands to Argentina but then lease them back. Over the next two years, Britain rebutted Argentine attempts to place sovereignty on the agenda. When Leopoldo Galtieri assumed leadership of the Argentine military junta in December 1981, the junta sought to counter what they viewed as growing weakness in the dispute by adopting a more rigid negotiating posture and preparing to use force to compel Britain to negotiate.[9] Growing social unrest in Argentina magnified this perception of decline by increasing the importance of achieving tangible progress in the dispute, but Britain's pressure on the junta was decisive, as it weakened Argentina's position in the dispute.

As argued in chapter 1, states with weak or inferior claims may use force when decline in a stronger adversary's power reduces temporarily the cost of seizing contested land. China's own disputes provided no support for this mechanism, but it may have played a role in other conflicts. When Algeria gained its independence in 1962, for example, hostilities erupted with Morocco over the resource-rich Tindouf region. France had transferred administration of this area to Algeria prior to Morocco's own independence in 1956, and Morocco wanted it back. The French withdrawal from Algeria created an opportunity for Morocco to seize the land, which resulted in fighting from July to November 1963.[10]

Likewise, as chapter 2 describes, China's economic difficulties following the Great Leap Forward played a key role in creating perceptions of opportunity for India and Taiwan to make gains in their respective disputes with China. For both Jawaharlal Nehru and Chiang Kai-shek, the mainland's economic crisis suggested a decline in Chinese power and vulnerability to external pressure. China's domestic turmoil appeared to indicate a shift in the local military balance, creating a window of opportunity for India and Taiwan to take action.

Implications for International Relations

Beyond offering theories of cooperation and escalation in territorial disputes, this book holds several implications for the study of international relations more broadly.

[9] Lawrence Freedman and Virginia Gamba-Stonehouse, *Signals of War: The Falklands Conflict of 1982* (London: Faber and Faber, 1990).
[10] Touval, *Boundary Politics*, 120, 256.

First, China's behavior provides support for two noteworthy theories of international relations. China's willingness to cooperate in its territorial disputes during periods of internal unrest and instability supports the theory of omnibalancing, which claims that national leaders will form alliances to balance against the most pressing threat that they face, external or internal. I provide further support for omnibalancing by demonstrating how it applies in one important arena within international relations, namely territorial disputes. This support for omnibalancing suggests that it may be profitably extended to other issues beyond alignment decisions and territorial disputes. More generally, domestic unrest or instability remains an underappreciated source of cooperation in international relations.

Likewise, China's willingness to escalate its territorial disputes in response to perceptions of decline in claim strength offers additional support for preventive war theory. In particular, it demonstrates the utility of the theory in examining why and when states are more likely to use force in specific types of conflicts, not just in response to shifts in their overall position in the international system. Similar analysis may be extended to other domains where deterioration in relative power specific to that domain may create incentives to threaten or use force to halt decline in a state's influence, such as enduring or strategic rivalries.

Second, the examination of China's territorial disputes suggests how scholars can advance the study of international relations. The state-centric approach employed to build my theories of cooperation and escalation provides an alternative framework for integrating the levels of analysis in international relations while treating the state as a unitary actor. Efforts to link the international and domestic levels often select variables from each level and then examine their interaction along the lines of Robert Putnam's two-level games.[11] By shifting the focus to the state as an autonomous actor in both internal and external environments, a state-centric approach adopts a different method, identifying those variables at home or abroad that constrain a state's ability to achieve its goals. This approach does not privilege one level over the other, nor does it limit its analytical focus to any particular level. Moreover, it continues to be useful. In a recent study of border management, for example, George Gavrilis demonstrates that a state's method of extracting resources from society shapes whether it adopts a rigid or flexible approach to policing the flows of people and goods across its borders.[12]

[11] Peter Gourevitch, "The Second Image Reversed: International Sources of Domestic Politics," *International Organization*, vol. 32, no. 4 (Autumn 1978): 881–912; Robert D. Putnam, "Diplomacy and Domestic Politics: The Logic of Two-Level Games," *International Organization*, vol. 42, no. 3 (Summer 1988): 427–460.

[12] George Gavrilis, *The Dynamics of Interstate Boundaries* (Cambridge: Cambridge University Press, forthcoming).

China's willingness to cooperate in many disputes despite its authoritarian political system highlights the importance of moving beyond democracy in the study of domestic political institutions and international relations.[13] As consolidated democracies are still relatively rare, even in those studies that find a positive effect of democracy on certain outcomes, a whole range of variation involving authoritarian states remains unexplained. A state-centric approach provides a framework for investigating how these states behave, as it incorporates factors that shape a state's power both at home and abroad and thus how states calculate the costs and benefits of different foreign policies.

The effects of regime insecurity and decline in claim strength in China's decisions to cooperate or escalate territorial disputes underscore the need to develop more nuanced measures of power in international relations. When states pursue their interests in a specific domain or issue area such as territorial disputes, different components of a state's power are likely to have greater or lesser weight in the decisions that states make beyond their overall capabilities relative to other states in the system. As a result, in seeking to explain how states behave in specific domains, it can be misleading to look only at aggregate power or to overlook a state's internal security.

Third, China's pattern of cooperation and escalation in its disputes offers evidence against several other theories of international relations. To start, China's behavior offers strong evidence against theories that posit a state's internal political conflict as a cause of violent or belligerent foreign policies. According to diversionary war theory and arguments by Edward Mansfield and Jack Snyder about democratization and war, leaders are more likely to escalate crises during periods of domestic political unrest, using tensions abroad to unite and rally society at home.[14] As they give leaders a clear issue over which to mobilize domestic support, territorial disputes offer one arena in which to test propositions about diversion. With many disputes and frequent internal challenges to the state, China in particular offers a series of "easy" cases for diversionary arguments. Yet despite repeated instances of domestic turmoil, China usually pursued cooperation in its territorial disputes, not escalation. That diversionary theory fails numerous tests that it should easily pass can only cast doubt on the theory as a whole.

China's use of force in its territorial disputes nevertheless suggests why internal conflict may be associated with the threat or use of force in some

[13] For one such effort, see Mark Peceny, Caroline C. Beer, and Shannon Sanchez-Terry, "Dictatorial Peace?" *American Political Science Review*, vol. 96, no. 1 (March 2002): 15–26.

[14] Jack S. Levy, "The Diversionary Theory of War: A Critique," in Manus I. Midlarsky, ed., *Handbook of War Studies* (Boston: Unwin Hyman, 1989), 259–288; Edward D. Mansfield and Jack L. Snyder, *Electing to Fight: Why Emerging Democracies Go to War* (Cambridge, Mass.: MIT Press, 2005).

cases. Following Geoffrey Blainey, domestic unrest in one country can shift perceptions of the balance of power between two states, creating a window of opportunity for the weaker party whose position is increased when its stronger adversary appears distracted or consumed by internal challenges.[15] In addition, when a state is challenged by an adversary in a dispute during periods of domestic unrest, force is an attractive response for many reasons apart from diversion. If national leaders conclude that other states are exploiting their weakness, then using force can signal resolve to defend their state's interests.

In addition, China's behavior in its territorial disputes raises questions about offensive realism. This theory claims that a state will pursue expansion when it possesses the capabilities to do so, especially when costs are low and opportunities plentiful. In an offensive realist world, power provides security. A state with a power advantage over others should be more likely to behave aggressively, using its might to achieve its security goals.[16] Although this theory was developed to explain great-power relations, it can be applied to territorial disputes, a core security interest for any state, including great powers such as China. Offensive realism might expect a state to fight frequently over land that would enhance its overall power and for the stronger state in a particular dispute to be more aggressive than the weaker state.

China's behavior, however, is at odds with some of these expectations. To be sure, China has used force in disputes over highly salient territory, such as Taiwan or the Spratly Islands. At the same time, it has compromised frequently in many conflicts where it has enjoyed significant military advantages, especially along its land border. An offensive realist might dismiss this behavior as irrelevant because the territory lacked great economic or strategic value. Nevertheless, China increased its security through compromise, not expansion, by consolidating control over internal frontiers that serve as buffer zones for the most densely populated regions of the country. Likewise, although its power has increased dramatically in the past two decades, China has not become more prone to using force in its disputes. According to one index, China's share of world power increased from 10.8 percent of total world capabilities in 1990 to 13.4 percent in 2001.[17] Yet during this period, China compromised frequently. Perhaps most tellingly, it pursued compromise with Moscow as the Soviet Union grew weaker and then collapsed at the end of 1991

---

[15] Geoffrey Blainey, *The Causes of War* (New York: The Free Press, 1988).

[16] John J. Mearsheimer, *The Tragedy of Great Power Politics* (New York: W. W. Norton, 2001); Fareed Zakaria, *From Wealth to Power: The Unusual Origins of America's World Role* (Princeton, N.J.: Princeton University Press, 1998).

[17] Correlates of War database, from EuGene (v. 3.040).

even though it might have adopted a much more assertive posture instead. At the same time, China has not become increasingly belligerent in its outstanding disputes, especially with India or over strategically important areas in the South China Sea. China has only used force twice since 1990, first with the occupation of Mischief Reef in late 1994 and then during the 1995–96 Taiwan Strait crisis.

China's use of force provides further evidence against offensive realism as well as power transition theory. Contrary to what offensive realism might expect, China has not used force only when it has possessed a military advantage in a dispute. Instead, it has used force to counter decline in its claim strength and bargaining power regardless of whether it possessed a clear military advantage or not. The consistency with which China has used force in response to perceptions of decline and not opportunity is also at odds with power transition theory, which asserts that a rising state is more likely to use force than a declining one, especially when it approaches parity with stronger states in the system.[18]

Arguments about the foreign policies of revolutionary states also find no support in China's behavior in its territorial disputes. In China, radical politics at home failed to produce assertive or belligerent foreign policies in most of its territorial disputes.[19] China not only pursued compromise more frequently than past and current analysts have expected, but in almost every case China did not hitch its territorial claims to its ideological goals.[20] During the early Cold War, for example, China pursued compromise with nonaligned states such as Burma, socialist states such as Mongolia, and allies with the United States including Pakistan.

Finally, China's pattern of cooperation and escalation raises questions about the role of credibility and reputation building in decision making. States are often seen as willing to use force in one area to invest in a general reputation for toughness in order to maintain their credibility and deter states in other areas. Barbara Walter, for example, has argued that a state with multiple territorial conflicts should be reluctant to offer concessions lest it create a reputation for weakness that invites further demands from territorial adversaries.[21] Such a state should also be quite willing to use force against the first adversary that challenges its claims in order to show resolve to deter subsequent challenges.

---

[18] See, for example, A.F.K. Organski, *World Politics* (New York: Knopf, 1958).

[19] See, for example, Stephen M. Walt, *Revolution and War* (Ithaca, N.Y.: Cornell University Press, 1996).

[20] Also, on this point, see Alastair Iain Johnston, "China's Militarized Interstate Dispute Behaviour 1949–1992: A First Cut at the Data," *The China Quarterly*, no. 153 (March 1998): 20–22.

[21] Barbara F. Walter, "Explaining the Intractability of Territorial Conflict," *International Studies Review*, vol. 5, no. 4 (December 2003): 137–153.

With more territorial disputes than any other state since the end of the World War II, China offers a series of easy tests for such claims. Nevertheless, China's willingness to compromise poses a puzzle for these arguments: it repeatedly pursued compromise without any apparent concern for the effect that its concessions would have on its reputation or for appearing weak to other states. This suggests that, under some conditions, states may seek to create reputations for cooperation instead of toughness. Although China did seek to communicate resolve when it used force in some disputes, the target of its aggression was the opponent actively challenging its claim, not other states with which it was disputing territory who might challenge China in the future.

THE SOURCES OF CHINESE FOREIGN POLICY

The study of China's territorial disputes helps illuminate the sources of Chinese foreign policy. In these conflicts, China's paramount leaders have been less important in foreign policy decision making than the state's internal and external security environment.[22] Since 1949, leaders with very different personalities, psychological profiles, and influence within the Chinese political system have adopted or supported roughly the same policies in territorial disputes when confronted with similar threats to the state at home or abroad. Under Mao Zedong and Jiang Zemin, China pursued compromise during periods when the PRC encountered internal threats to regime security, especially ethnic unrest in the frontiers. Similarly, Mao, Deng Xiaoping, and Jiang all used force when China's bargaining power in its disputes declined, though Jiang has done so less violently and frequently. As most uses of force over territory occurred under Mao and Deng, it is possible that these leaders were more disposed to coercion than Jiang. Yet Jiang's leadership coincided with the collapse of the Soviet Union and China's most benign external security environment since 1949, which produced fewer challenges to its territorial claims.

This is not to assert that individual leaders are unimportant. Rather, China's leaders have made key decisions that reflect the imperatives of their state's overall security environment, not personal pathologies. Jiang and Deng would have used force in territorial disputes under the same circumstances as Mao. Deng would have compromised under the same circumstances as Mao and Jiang. The decision to ambush Soviet

---

[22] For arguments on the importance of individual Chinese leaders, see, for example, Chen Jian, *Mao's China and the Cold War* (Chapel Hill: University of North Carolina Press, 2001).

forces in March 1969, however, is perhaps one important exception that cannot be explained fully without appreciating Mao's personality. Given China's intense competition with the United States over Vietnam at that time, it is hard to conclude that a simultaneous armed conflict with the world's other superpower would have enhanced China's security. Mao's own belief in the effectiveness of force likely played a key role in this decision.[23]

In questions of territorial sovereignty, an issue where nationalism might be expected to exert a great influence on foreign policy, nationalism has been less potent than many scholars and observers of China suggest. At no time since 1949 has the PRC issued claims to "lost" territory once ruled or influenced heavily by the Qing, such as the Russian Far East, Mongolia, or parts of Central Asia. The only treaties signed by the Qing that the PRC has sought to overturn were those ceding Macao and parts of Hong Kong. Otherwise, China has accepted the basic delimitations contained in all past agreements. Mao's July 1964 statement that China "had yet to settle its account" over territory ceded to tsarist Russia might be an important exception to this observation. Yet the statement itself is ambiguous, made in the context of Japan's own disputes with the Soviet Union and, in any event, not a clear-cut sovereignty claim. China's policy in its territorial disputes, moreover, never reflected this statement or any deeper irredentist sentiments that it might have reflected.

Since the 1950s, neither the number nor the scope of China's territorial claims has increased. The continuity of China's territorial goals has withstood dramatic changes in China's position in the international system, leadership personalities, and political ideology. Although some of China's goals are revisionist, especially in its homeland and offshore island disputes, importantly, these goals are not new. China has pursued them since the establishment of the PRC in 1949. They reflect a vision of what ought to constitute a modern Chinese state, not interests conditioned by China's position in the international system. Weak or strong, for example, China has sought to unify Taiwan with the mainland and establish a maritime frontier in the South China Sea.

Since the 1990s, scholars and observers of China have noted the increasing prominence of popular nationalism, especially with the decline of socialism as a political ideology. Although it is unclear if nationalism

[23] For similar reasons, China's behavior in territorial disputes suggests that socialist ideology has also been less important than the PRC's broader security environment. China pursued compromise during the "high tide" of socialism in the early 1960s. China also pursued compromise throughout the 1990s when the CCP had abandoned mass mobilization as a tool of domestic politics to pursue Deng's economic reforms. Moreover, even in the early Cold War, China did not prefer to compromise in disputes with socialist states nor did it target nonsocialist states with the use of force.

is in fact increasing, China's behavior in territorial disputes during this period suggests that its impact on foreign policy has been more limited that these arguments imply.[24] The visibility of more nationalistic attitudes within society has not resulted in a more belligerent approach to questions of sovereignty. China has not used force over territory for more than ten years since the 1996 missile tests against Taiwan and has not engaged in combat over territory for more than twenty years since the 1988 clash with Vietnam over Johnson Reef. During this same period, China compromised in nine territorial disputes. Although the central government sought to conceal any details of the concessions it offered, it nevertheless pursued compromise, signed agreements, ratified them, and demarcated its borders on the basis of these documents.

None of this is to claim that nationalism is irrelevant in China's foreign policy or even in its territorial disputes. The persistence of China's desire for unification with Taiwan, its willingness to threaten and use force in this dispute, as well as its resumption of sovereignty over Hong Kong and Macao cannot be explained without reference to nationalism. Moreover, the return of two disputed homeland territories was a clear nationalist achievement. As the state has detailed widely and publicly its claims to the Spratly and Senkaku islands over the past two decades, nationalism may also further reduce the already slim odds of compromise in these disputes because China might be reluctant to relinquish territory it controls such as Fiery Cross Reef. Clear challenges to China's claims in these disputes will likely be met with a rigid if not violent response. Nevertheless, the nationalist pressures held to exist have not translated into increasingly frequent threats to use force or an unwillingness to compromise in territorial disputes. Nor have China's leaders used conflicts over territory to divert public attention from domestic discontent over social issues associated with the turbulence and uncertainty of economic reform. Even in the Taiwan conflict since the early 1990s, a willingness to use force or to make threatening statements has varied with challenges to unification perceived to arise from Taiwan's domestic politics, not China's political instability or nationalist public opinion.

Finally, China's behavior in territorial disputes raises doubts about the strength of a strategic cultural preference for offensive uses of force. When China has used force, it has not sought the annihilation of its opponent,

---

[24] For recent studies of nationalism in China, see, for example, Peter Hayes Gries, *China's New Nationalism: Pride, Politics, and Diplomacy* (Berkeley: University of California Press, 2004); Susan Shirk, *China: Fragile Superpower* (New York, Oxford University Press, 2007). On whether nationalism in China is increasing, see Alastair Iain Johnston, "Chinese Middle Class Attitudes Towards International Affairs: Nascent Liberalization?" *The China Quarterly*, no. 179 (September 2004): 605–606.

nor has it seized large swaths of land that it claims.[25] Likewise, although China has often initiated the use of force, it has not done so when faced with favorable shifts in the balance of power. Instead, China has used force mostly in response to weakness and decline. Finally, in territorial conflicts with India and with Vietnam in the Spratlys, China did not widen its war aims and seize large amounts of contested territory after defeating its opponents decisively on the battlefield. Instead, China has usually exercised restraint following its military victories in territorial disputes, action inconsistent with a preference for offensive action.

One partial exception might be the Spratlys, as China lacked the naval capabilities to occupy features and sustain distant outposts before the early 1980s. Nevertheless, China has been reluctant to attack islands held by other claimants following its occupation of six features in 1988. The early 1990s, for example, might have presented China with an ideal opportunity to target its opponents in the dispute, as the United States appeared to be decreasing its military presence in the region. While competition over the islands became acute in 1993 and 1994, China did not engage in combat despite its improved relative power position. China did seize Mischief Reef, an unoccupied and permanently submerged feature, but it did not take any stronger actions that a preference for offensive uses of force might predict when faced with reduced constraints.

CHINA'S TERRITORIAL FUTURE

Overall, China's many territorial settlements reflect a mostly status-quo approach toward consolidating control of the territory believed to be part of a modern Chinese state. In frontier disputes, China has used compromise to gain recognition of its sovereignty over large ethnic-minority frontiers, areas with latent and open demands for autonomy or independence. When neighbors have sought to challenge China on its land borders, military force has been used, but large amounts of territory have not been seized on the battlefield. Instead, the goal of force was to compel acceptance of China's sovereignty over its frontiers. Moreover, by drafting new boundary agreements and treaties when settling disputes, China has defined with clarity and precision the location of its borders. Some of these texts, especially demarcation protocols to boundary treaties, are hundreds of pages long. Taken together, they reduce ambiguity about the

---

[25] Alastair Iain Johnston, "Cultural Realism and Strategy in Maoist China," in Peter J. Katzenstein, ed., *The Culture of National Security* (New York: Columbia University Press, 1996), 216–270.

extent of China's sovereignty and abandon irredentist claims to territory deemed to be Chinese in the early Qing.

China's willingness to settle many disputes through compromise has important strategic implications for East Asia under the shadow of rising Chinese power. China's concessions have in part enabled the active engagement of the region since the late 1990s that is the hallmark of China's "new diplomacy" and global activism.[26] By settling disputes and eliminating ambiguity about the location of its borders, China has reassured its neighbors about its intentions, lessening the security dilemma as it continues to rise in power. Regional engagement would have been much more difficult to pursue under the shadow of hot territorial conflicts in the region, especially in light of ongoing tensions over Taiwan. Moreover, the imperatives of China's grand strategy of reassurance suggest that these territorial settlements will endure. Abrogating these agreements would raise new questions about China's territorial ambitions along with its willingness to abide by international agreements more generally, both components of reassurance.[27] Given concerns about China's territorial ambitions, violation of any one of these agreements would signal China's "type" as an aggressive state in the region.

China's settlement of the majority of its territorial disputes also reduces future opportunities for violent conflict. If states fight over territory more than any other issue, then China's settlement of seventeen disputes is a positive development. China's past boundary agreements are a remarkably good indicator of peace between China and its neighbors.[28] These agreements are linked to the absence of war with opposing states, as China has not engaged in military conflict over contested areas with any neighbor with whom it has settled a territorial dispute.[29] If China does engage in violent conflict with these neighbors in the future, it is unlikely to occur over disputed territory.

China's territorial dispute behavior suggests more generally that a stronger China might be less prone to using force. In its territorial disputes, China has used force in response to growing weakness or decline.

[26] Evan S. Medeiros and M. Taylor Fravel, "China's New Diplomacy," *Foreign Affairs*, vol. 82, no. 6 (November/December 2003): 22–35; Philip C. Saunders, *China's Global Activism: Strategy, Drivers and Tools*, Occasional Paper 4 (Washington, D.C.: Institute for National Strategic Studies, National Defense University, 2006); David S. Shambaugh, "China Engages Asia: Reshaping International Order," *International Security*, vol. 29, no. 3 (Winter 2004/05): 64–99.

[27] On China's grand strategy, see Avery Goldstein, *Rising to the Challenge: China's Grand Strategy and International Security* (Stanford, Calif.: Stanford University Press, 2005); Saunders, *China's Global Activism*.

[28] On this point, see Johnston, "China's Militarized Interstate Dispute Behaviour."

[29] The one exception concerns clashes on the border with Burma in 1969 involving Burmese communist insurgents. See *NYT*, 8 November 1969, 5.

Paradoxically, then, a strong China might be less likely to use force in its remaining disputes and perhaps in other types of conflicts as well. This does not mean that China will necessarily be more willing to compromise, though it has been quite willing to compromise in many disputes from a position of strength. Nevertheless, a stronger China may not necessarily become more belligerent.

The prospects for China's six unresolved disputes are mixed. In general, good news exists for the region. Four territorial disputes involving China have been effectively neutralized. China reached confidence-building measures in its remaining frontier disputes with India and Bhutan in the 1990s, while negotiations for a final settlement are ongoing and have been conducted without using military threats. In April 2005, India and China signed a further agreement on guiding principles for settling their long-standing dispute.[30] These documents affirm the status quo on the border along the LAC and suggest that a final settlement, if it can be reached, will be largely consistent with the current facts on the ground. The agreements on confidence-building measures reached in the 1990s also reduce the potential for competition in the local military balance and any negative shifts in claim strength that would create incentives for the use of force.

Offshore, the potential for conflict over two of China's outstanding island disputes has been reduced significantly. China has occupied all the disputed Paracels features since its clash with South Vietnam in 1974 over the Crescent Group. Although China is unlikely to relinquish control over the archipelago, Vietnam is equally unlikely to challenge China militarily in this dispute. Moreover, as China continues to rise in power, it may paradoxically be more willing to compromise over some aspect of this dispute with Vietnam, as it will be doing so from a position of strength and thus be able to shape the terms of the agreement. Most likely, such a compromise would occur in response to external threats that China might face elsewhere in the region, which would elevate the importance of diplomatic cooperation with Vietnam. One possibility, for example, might be to compromise over the maritime rights in waters around the Paracels, perhaps sharing the resources in a manner similar to the 2000 fisheries agreement in the Tonkin Gulf.[31]

---

[30] "Agreement between the Government of the Republic of India and the Government of the People's Republic of China on the Political Parameters and Guiding Principles for the Settlement of the India-China Boundary Question," from http://meaindia.nic.in/treatiesagreement/2005/11ta1104200501.htm.

[31] Zou Keyuan, "The Sino-Vietnamese Agreement on Maritime Boundary Delimitation in the Gulf of Tonkin," *Ocean Development & International Law*, vol. 36, no. 1 (2005): 13–24.

Likewise, the hallmark of China's foreign policy in Southeast Asia, the engagement of ASEAN, has led to dampened competition in the Spratly Islands dispute. By agreeing to a code of conduct declaration in 2002 and signing the ASEAN Treaty of Amity and Cooperation in 2003, China has committed to not occupying any additional features in the area and not using force against other treaty signatories, which includes all other parties in the Spratlys dispute except Taiwan. At the same time, having occupied disputed features in 1988 and 1994, China's claim is much stronger than before, and bolstered by its naval power relative to the other claimants, China can be much more confident about achieving its goals in the dispute. China has not occupied a contested feature in more than twelve years and did not respond forcefully when Malaysia occupied two features in 1999. Although China is unlikely to relinquish its claims, it is much more confident about receiving some share of the disputed territory in any negotiated settlement. In 2005, China took perhaps the first step toward such a settlement by signing a joint seismic survey agreement with the Philippines and Vietnam.[32]

Instability nevertheless could increase in the Spratlys for two reasons. First, as the PLA Navy continues to modernize and expand its fleet, it will likely increase the number of patrols in the South China Sea and its presence in the disputed waters. China's strengthening of its position in the dispute would likely be viewed as threatening by the other claimants, and potential for spirals of hostility remains if these states increase their own naval presence around the contested islands and coral reefs. Nevertheless, aggressive action by China against the other claimants in the Spratlys dispute would come at the cost of its diplomatic efforts to engage Southeast Asia and improve ties with ASEAN states. Second, amid contemporary concerns about energy security, the importance of access to petroleum resources grows, including natural gas and oil fields believed to lie underneath the waters around the Spratly Islands. Under these conditions, all claimants are likely to increase their efforts to strengthen their claims, which each is likely to view as offensive and threatening, creating further potential for spirals of hostility and the threat or use of force.

Two disputes, however, threaten conflict and instability in the region. China's dispute with Japan over the Senkaku Islands may be volatile for several reasons. China's claim remains weak, as Japan has controlled the islands since 1972 and international law supports its claim. Japan fields one of the most powerful navies in the world, arguably the strongest in East Asia, and is backed by an alliance with the United States. As a matter of national sovereignty, the islands can easily spark a crisis between China

---

[32] AFP, 14 March 2005 (Lexis-Nexis).

and Japan, one that, as the April 2005 anti–Japan demonstrations in China indicated, would be difficult for both sides to manage.

Yet what is remarkable about this dispute is how conflict has been avoided. China has likely been deterred from using force by Japanese-U.S. naval power in addition to the repercussions that using force would have on China's diplomatic strategy of reassurance. At the same time, although weak, China's claim in the dispute has been stable, owing largely to Japanese efforts to prevent the islands from becoming a source of tension. In February 2005, for example, the Japanese government assumed control of a beacon that a right-wing group had built in 1988, a move that has prevented Japanese citizens from asserting claims by landing on the rocks.[33] China has reciprocated, limiting earlier protests in Beijing over the islands and preventing mainland Chinese activists from seeking to land on the islands. Settlement of the dispute is likely only in the event of a grand bargain amid a broader Japanese-Chinese entente, in which improved bilateral relations outweigh the value of controlling the islands. Nevertheless, even the shared Soviet threat in the 1970s was insufficient to prompt China to drop its claims, which indicates that settlement remains unlikely.

Taiwan is the most conflict-prone territorial dispute involving China. At one level, of course, this is unsurprising, given the importance of unification for China's leaders and likewise autonomy if not independence for many people on Taiwan.[34] So long as the CCP remains in power, and perhaps even if the mainland democratizes, these goals are likely to continue. At the same time, despite all the progress China has achieved in its military reforms, its claim strength and bargaining power in the Taiwan dispute remain weak. It does not control any of the land that it contests and still cannot project power over the island of Taiwan, though it could now conquer the coastal islands, including Jinmen and Mazu. Because of this weakness, coupled with the support for formal independence in Taiwan's domestic politics, China's leaders remain uncertain about the prospects for unification.[35]

[33] *The Japan Times*, 10 February 2005 (Lexis-Nexis).

[34] For more recent analyses on China's Taiwan policy, see Thomas J. Christensen, "Posing Problems without Catching Up: China's Rise and Challenges for U.S. Security Policy," *International Security*, vol. 25, no. 4 (Spring 2001): 5–40; Thomas J. Christensen, "The Contemporary Security Dilemma: Deterring a Taiwan Conflict," *The Washington Quarterly*, vol. 25, no. 4 (Autumn 2002): 7–21; Robert S. Ross, "Navigating the Taiwan Strait: Deterrence, Escalation Dominance and U.S.-China Relations," *International Security*, vol. 27, no. 2 (Fall 2002): 48–85; Allen S. Whiting, "China's Use of Force, 1950–96, and Taiwan," *International Security*, vol. 26, no. 2 (Fall 2001): 103–131. Also see various issues of the *China Leadership Monitor*, http://www.chinaleadershipmonitor.org/.

[35] Recent studies suggest that support on the island for independence may be declining. If true, then the odds of China using force should also decrease. See, for example, Shelly Rigger, *Taiwan's Rising Rationalism: Generations, Politics and "Taiwan's Nationalism,"*

As long as China's position in the dispute remains weak, its leaders will continue to be sensitive to events that appear to reduce the likelihood of achieving unification in the future. Although the impact of Taiwan's domestic politics on cross-strait ties is unpredictable, the U.S. role in the dispute remains a key factor in China's assessments of its claim strength and the utility of using force. Put simply, Chinese perceptions of U.S. support for Taiwan can tip the balance for China's leaders in this dispute. Crises were averted in 1999 and 2002 because the United States signaled that it did not support efforts by Taiwan's presidents to alter the island's standing in the international community. More clearly, further crises have arguably been avoided since President George W. Bush stated in December 2003 that the United States opposes "any unilateral decision by either China or Taiwan to change the status quo. And the comments and actions made by the leader of Taiwan indicate that he may be willing to make decisions unilaterally to change the status quo, which we oppose."[36] Evidently, for China's leaders, incremental efforts by Taiwan to increase autonomy can be managed if they clearly lack the support of other states, especially the United States.

At the moment, China has demonstrated an increasing willingness to live with the status quo across the Strait. Increasing economic and social ties, driven by the growing numbers of Taiwanese who trade with or work on the mainland, have improved assessments of the long-term odds of achieving unification, reducing the short-term incentive to use force. Although a 2000 white paper indicated that China would not wait indefinitely for Taiwan to agree to hold talks over unification, official statements in the past few years reflect more confidence about the future prospects. From Beijing's perspective, ever deepening economic ties between Taiwan and the mainland create dependence that increases the likelihood of unification or at least limits support for formal independence.

Looking forward, one important variable remains: China's growing military power and how it might be used across the Strait. In general, China's military modernization, which since the late 1990s has been focused on developing capabilities to be used in a conflict over Taiwan, has achieved real progress. The question is how these capabilities might be used, as they increase the mainland's ability to coerce the island through blockades and precision-strike attacks even in the absence of an amphibious assault force. From China's perspective, these capabilities strengthen its otherwise weak claim in the dispute, deterring Taiwan's leaders from

---

Policy Studies no. 26 (Washington, D.C.: East-West Center, 2006); Robert S. Ross, "Taiwan's Fading Independence Movement," *Foreign Affairs*, vol. 85, no. 2 (March/April 2006): 141–148.

[36] http://www.whitehouse.gov/news/releases/2003/12/20031209–2.html.

pursuing independence (or at least the Taiwanese people from supporting such efforts). If China's behavior in its other territorial disputes provides any clues to the future of the Taiwan conflict, China will be less likely to use force if its position in the dispute is strong and it remains confident about eventual unification. At the same time, since Taiwan represents a conflict over what is seen on the mainland as homeland territory, China will not be willing to compromise over Taiwan's sovereignty and its place in "one China," however defined. Nevertheless, China's military power may ironically increase its flexibility regarding the form of unification or the potential for negotiations across the Strait.

The consequences of potential conflict over Taiwan cannot be understated. It would almost certainly involve the United States and, given the stakes, would likely involve high levels of force, with long-term consequences for U.S.-China relations and the region. Nevertheless, in terms of China's behavior in territorial disputes, this conflict provides a poor indicator of China's territorial ambitions in the region and its willingness to resort to force in the future. China has settled most of its disputes, dropped potential irredentist claims to Qing land, and neutralized many of its remaining conflicts. China's rising power will create many challenges for East Asia and the world, but its territorial disputes are unlikely to be the leading cause of instability.

Overview of China's Territorial Disputes

FRONTIER DISPUTES

North Korea

China's territorial dispute with North Korea remains largely shrouded in mystery. Because the 1962 boundary treaty was never openly published, little information about the origins of the dispute is available.[1] The dispute stemmed from Japan's occupation of the Korean Peninsula in the late nineteenth century. In the 1895 Treaty of Shimonoseki, China and Japan agreed that the Yalu River would serve as part of the boundary between China and Korea. In 1909, China and Japan further agreed that the Tumen River formed another part of this boundary. For roughly 20 miles around Changbai (Paektu) Mountain, however, the direction of the boundary was unclear, as the peak serves as a watershed for both rivers. Moreover, the 1909 agreement between China and Japan contained contradictory language with respect to the sovereignty of this area.[2]

After 1949, China and North Korea contested the sovereignty of Changbai Mountain. Manchus and Koreans view the mountain, especially its crater lake, as sacred. North Korean communist leader Kim Il-sung claimed to have been born on the slope of the mountain and viewed sovereignty over it as a birthright of the Korean people.[3] A 1713 boundary monument, however, suggested that the mountain lay within China, an ambiguity enhanced by the contradictory language in the 1909 agreement. Estimates of the size of the disputed area range from 467 square kilometers to 1,165 square kilometers, depending on how much of the mountain's eastern slope is included.[4]

The timing of this dispute's initiation is uncertain. Interviews suggest that Kim Il-sung first raised the claim during or soon after the Korean War. North Korea reportedly approached China again in 1960 when Kim

---

[1] Kim Il-sung asked China not to publish the treaty openly.

[2] Department of State, "China-Korea Boundary," *International Boundary Study*, no. 17 (29 June 1962); J.R.V. Prescott, *Map of Mainland Asia by Treaty* (Carlton: Melbourne University Press, 1975), 499–503.

[3] Interview, Beijing, June 2001.

[4] Prescott, *Map*, 500–501. Also see "DPRK-PRC Border Pact Said Confirmed," Yonhap News Agency (Korea), 20 October 1999, in FBIS # FTS19991019001881.

visited Beijing and again through a diplomatic note in 1961.[5] In 1961, both sides repeated claims to Changbai Mountain in official periodicals.[6]

Mongolia

China's territorial dispute with Mongolia was particularly acute because the latter had been part of the Chinese empire since the Yuan dynasty (1271–1378). When the Qing collapsed in 1911, Mongolia declared its independence. A series of agreements acknowledged China's continued suzerainty over Mongolia but also recognized Mongolia's autonomy, which in turn created a vacuum of power that Russia and later the Soviet Union filled. When the Mongolian People's Republic was established in 1924, the Republic of China refused to recognize it. The KMT did recognize Mongolia in 1945 as part of a treaty with the Soviet Union, a status that the PRC affirmed in 1950 through the establishment of diplomatic ties with Ulaanbaatar.[7]

The Chinese-Mongolian border had not been delimited before 1949. In the 1945 agreement recognizing Mongolian independence, the Nationalists included a clause to accept "the existing boundary as the boundary line." The boundary itself was not delimited in this agreement, but Mongolia subsequently claimed, based on this clause, that its border with the PRC was undisputed.[8] Clashes between Nationalist and Mongolian troops occurred in 1947 and 1948 in the western part of the border.[9]

Because of the boundary's topography, estimates of the size of the disputed areas vary. A Chinese scholar states that differences on maps ranged from 50,000 to 190,000 square kilometers.[10] An official Chinese diplomatic history states that the area under dispute was 16,808 square kilometers, an amount that likely refers to the area under negotiation in the spring of 1962.[11] Contested areas included Baogeda Mountain in the east and Beita Mountain as well as the Hongshanzui, Qinghe, and Shengtasi areas in the west adjacent to Xinjiang.

[5] Interview, Beijing, June 2002.

[6] Department of State, "China-Korea Boundary," 1–2.

[7] Department of State, "China-Mongolia Boundary," *International Boundary Study*, no. 173 (14 August 1985); Prescott, *Map*, 90–98.

[8] *DDZGWJ*, 150. Wang Yinqing and Zhaori Getu, eds., *Neimenggu zizhiqu zhi: junshi zhi* [Inner Mongolian Autonomous Region Gazetteer: Military Affairs] (Huhehaote: Neimenggu renmin chubanshe, 2002), 465–468, 471–474.

[9] Wang and Getu, *Neimenggu zizhiqu zhi: junshi zhi*, 465–468, 471–474.

[10] Qu Xing, *Zhongguo waijiao 50 nian* [50 Years of Chinese Diplomacy] (Nanjing: Jiangsu renmin chubanshe, 2000), 219–220.

[11] Wang Taiping, ed., *Zhonghua renmin gongheguo waijiao shi, 1957–1969* [Diplomatic History of the People's Republic of China, 1957–1969] (Beijing: Shijie zhishi chubanshe, 1998), 102.

The dispute between the PRC and Mongolia arose in the early 1950s. In 1953, the two governments signed an agreement on border management, which acknowledged the presence of disputed territory.[12] At the same time, Chinese and Mongolian maps contained contradictory depictions of the border. Local officials held informal talks over the Hongshanzui area in July 1956.[13] Mongolia formally approached China to settle the dispute in 1957 and in 1958 submitted a Soviet map illustrating its depiction of the border.[14]

Soviet Union and Central Asian Successor States

China's most complicated territorial disputes existed with the Soviet Union. Much of the Chinese-Soviet border had been delimited through previous agreements in which the Qing ceded more than 1,500,000 square kilometers of land to Russia. After 1949, disputes arose in areas where the delimitation of these prior agreements was unclear or contradictory, such as Heixiazi (Black Bear) Island.[15] Disputes also arose over areas that China maintained were excluded from previous agreements, such as the Pamir Mountains, which had been allocated to Russia by Britain during the 1895 Pamir Conference (which China did not attend).[16] More generally, both sides often held contradictory viewpoints about the location of the border as determined by the delimitations of these agreements. The border itself was infrequently demarcated, with boundary pillars tens of kilometers apart.[17]

The Chinese-Soviet territorial disputes emerged in the early 1950s. Among China's neighbors, the Soviet Union was a clear referent of Article 55 of the 1949 Common Program, which stated that China would seek to review or revise all prior international agreements. In addition, a 1951 agreement on river navigation indicated an awareness of these disputes

---

[12] Shen Bingnian, ed., *Xinjiang tongzhi: waishi zhi* [Xinjiang Gazetteer: Foreign Affairs] (Wulumuqi: Xinjiang renmin chubanshe, 1995), 266; Wang, *Zhonghua renmin gongheguo, 1957–1969*, 101.

[13] Shen, *Xinjiang tongzhi: waishi zhi*, 266.

[14] Wang, *Zhonghua renmin gongheguo, 1957–1969*, 100.

[15] *DDZGWJ*, 122–123. Tai Sung An, *The Sino-Soviet Territorial Dispute* (Philadelphia: Westminster Press, 1973); Dennis J. Doolin, *Territorial Claims in the Sino-Soviet Conflict: Documents and Analysis* (Stanford, Calif.: Hoover Institution, 1965); George Ginsburgs and Carl F. Pinkele, *The Sino-Soviet Territorial Dispute, 1949–64* (London: Routledge, 1978); Genrikh Kireyev, "Demarcation of the Border with China," *International Affairs*, vol. 45, no. 2 (1999): 98–109; Tsui Tsien-hua, *The Sino-Soviet Border Dispute in the 1970's* (New York: Mosaic Press, 1983).

[16] John W. Garver, "The Sino-Soviet Territorial Dispute in the Pamir Mountains Region," *The China Quarterly*, no. 85 (June 1981): 107–118.

[17] Kireyev, "Demarcation," 98.

when it stated that its provisions applied "irrespective of where the line of the state frontier passes."[18] Confrontations over transborder grazing lands in Central Asia adjacent to Xinjiang began in 1954.[19] Finally, the disputes were mentioned during high-level meetings and official visits, such as Nikita Khrushchev's 1954 visit to Beijing, Zhou Enlai's 1957 trip to Moscow, and Liu Shaoqi's 1960 visit to Moscow.[20]

The actual amount of territory contested by both sides is substantial. Overall, China and the Soviet Union disputed 35,914 square kilometers of land.[21] Disputes in the eastern sector focused mostly on ownership of islands in the Amur and Ussuri rivers comprising roughly 1,000 square kilometers along with Heixiazi and Abagaitu islands, approximately 408 square kilometers in size.[22] In the western sector, the disputes were more complicated. Following the collapse of the Soviet Union in 1991, these conflicts where inherited by the newly independent states in the region. Along the Kazakh border, fifteen disputed sectors totaled 2,420 square kilometers. Along the Kyrgyz border, seven disputed sectors totaled 3,656 square kilometers. Along the Tajik border, three disputed sectors totaled 28,430 square kilometers, including the conflict over the Pamir Mountain region of approximately 28,000 square kilometers.[23]

Afghanistan

China's boundary with Afghanistan is its shortest, stretching only 92 kilometers. Similar to other boundaries in Central Asia, this one had never been delimited by a prior agreement. As the Qing had never accepted the results of the 1895 Russian-British conference on the Pamir Mountains, China disputed the boundary after 1949.[24]

[18] Neville Maxwell, "A Note on the Amur/Ussuri Sector of the Sino-Soviet Boundaries," *Modern China*, vol. 1, no. 1 (1975): 119.

[19] Shen, *Xinjiang tongzhi: waishi zhi*, 284.

[20] Ginsburgs and Pinkele, *Sino-Soviet Territorial Dispute*, 6–16,41; Richard Wich, *Sino-Soviet Crisis Politics: A Study of Political Change and Communication* (Cambridge, Mass.: Harvard University Press, 1980), 26.

[21] In a review of the literature in 1978, Ginsburgs stated that estimates of the disputed area include 38,000 square kilometers, 33,000 square kilometers, and 21,000 square kilometers, depending largely on the size of the Pamir region. Ginsburgs and Pinkele, *Sino-Soviet Territorial Dispute*, 104. Tsui puts the total at roughly 35,000 square kilometers: the eastern sector river island disputes account for 1,000 square kilometers, fifteen Central Asian sectors account for 5,000 square kilometers, and the Pamir Mountains are 28,000 square kilometers. Tsui, *Sino-Soviet Border Dispute*, 73–74.

[22] Kireyev, "Demarcation," 98–109.

[23] Zhang Zhouxiang, *Xinjiang bianfang gaiyao* [Overview of Xinjiang's Frontier Defense] (Wulumuqi: Xinjiang renmin chubanshe, 1999), 135–136.

[24] *DDZGWJ*, 153; Department of State, "Afghanistan-China Boundary," *International Boundary Study*, no. 89 (1 May 1969); Liu Hongxuan, *Zhongguo mulin shi: Zhongguo yu*

In the early 1950s, Chinese maps indicated a claim to approximately 7,381 square kilometers of Afghanistan in the Wakhan Corridor.[25] The first mention of a dispute between China and Afghanistan is unknown. The two countries did not establish diplomatic relations until 1955, but it is likely that the dispute was raised in the negotiations preceding diplomatic recognition. In August 1960, a *People's Daily* editorial referred to "several problems left over by history" in the relationship, a phrase usually used in official Chinese diplomatic statements to refer to territorial disputes with land neighbors.[26]

Pakistan

The border between China and Pakistan had never been delimited in any prior boundary agreement. The dispute centered on the status of the Hunza, a state located around the Hunza River and its tributaries south of the Karakorum watershed.[27] In the eighteenth century, the Mir of Hunza began paying tribute to Chinese authorities in Xinjiang in exchange for grazing rights north of the watershed. In the 1890s, the Hunza was brought under British protection and became a vassal state of Kashmir, but its tributary relationship with China continued. In 1899, the British proposed a boundary line along the watershed, placing the Hunza within British India, but the Chinese government never responded to this proposal. The Mir was still paying gold-dust tribute to China as late as 1936, when the British government of India advised him to stop this practice.[28]

Estimates of the amount of disputed territory differ. In 1954, a map published in China showed more than 100,000 square kilometers of territory in Kashmir as belonging to the PRC as well as a series of strategic

zhoubian guojia guanxi [History of Good-Neighborliness: China's Relations with Peripheral States] (Beijing: Shijie zhishi chubanshe, 2001), 317–318; Prescott, *Map*, 238–241.

[25] "Eloquent Maps," *China News Analysis*, no. 129 (27 April 1956): 6.

[26] *RMRB*, 28 August 1960, 1.

[27] Alastair Lamb, "The Sino-Pakistani Boundary Agreement of 2 March 1963," *Journal of the Australian Institute of International Affairs*, vol. 18, no. 3 (1964); Prescott, *Map*, 231–234. Also, P. L. Bhola, *Pakistan-China Relations: Search for Politico-Strategic Relationship* (Jaipur: R.B.S.A. Publishers, 1986), 92–131; Department of State, "China-Pakistan Boundary," *International Boundary Study*, no. 85 (30 May 1968); Fang Jianchang, "Jindai Zhongguo yu Bajisitan bianjie shi chutan" [Preliminary Discussion of the History of China and Pakistan's Border in Modern Times], *Zhongguo bianjiang shidi yanjiu*, no. 3 (1997): 63–78; Liu, *Zhongguo mulin shi*, 305–306; Mujtaba Razvi, *The Frontiers of Pakistan: A Study of Frontier Problems in Pakistan's Foreign Policy* (Karachi-Dacca: National Publishing House, 1971), 166–193.

[28] Razvi, *Frontiers*, 179. Also, Lamb, "Sino-Pakistani Boundary Agreement."

mountain passes in the region.[29] A map published in 1959 showed roughly 15,000 square kilometers of the Gilgit region (including the Hunza areas) as belonging to China.[30] During the negotiations in 1962 and 1963, however, talks focused on a smaller area, totaling roughly 8,806 square kilometers. The dispute included two drainage areas, grazing fields, a salt mine, seven strategic mountain passes, and the peak of K2, the second-tallest mountain in the world.[31]

The dispute arose shortly after the establishment of the PRC. The first known acknowledgement of the dispute occurred in April 1953, when Pakistan sent a formal protest to China about border violations in the Gilgit region.[32]

India

Excluding the border between Sikkim and Tibet, the Chinese-Indian border had never been delimited clearly. Historically, this desolate and mountainous frontier was not actively administered by either British India, Tibet, or the Qing, nor had it ever been demarcated through the placement of boundary markers.[33] The lack of actual administration formed the crux of the dispute that emerged after Indian independence and the establishment of the PRC. Leaders from both states held opposing views of the location of the customary boundary.[34]

The territorial dispute between China and India concerns three sectors. The eastern sector includes 90,000 square kilometers south of the McMahon Line and north of what China claims as Tibet's customary boundary, effectively the present-day Indian state of Arunachal Pradesh, previously known as the North Eastern Frontier Agency.[35] India claims that the fron-

---

[29] Razvi, *Frontiers*, 169.

[30] Francis Watson, *The Frontiers of China* (New York: Praeger, 1966), 140.

[31] Razvi, *Frontiers*, 177; Anwar Hussain Seyd, *China and Pakistan: Diplomacy of Entente Cordiale* (Amherst: University of Massachusetts Press, 1974), 87.

[32] Razvi, *Frontiers*, 169.

[33] Some agreements did exist, such as the 1842 Tibetan-Kashmir treaty or the documents from the Simla Conference. However, none of these agreements include precise delimitations of the "customary boundary" between the two sides.

[34] *ZYBJ*, 1–111; John W. Garver, *Protracted Contest: Sino-Indian Rivalry in the Twentieth Century* (Seattle: University of Washington Press, 2001), 79–109; Alastair Lamb, *The McMahon Line: A Study in the Relations Between India, China and Tibet, 1904–1914* (London: Routledge & K. Paul, 1966); Alastair Lamb, *The Sino-Indian Border in Ladakh* (Canberra: Australian National University Press, 1973); Neville Maxwell, *India's China War* (New York: Pantheon Books, 1970), 17–64; Wang Hongwei, *Ximalaya shan qingjie: ZhongYin guanxi yanjiu* [Himalayan Sentiments: A Study of Chinese-Indian Relations] (Beijing: Zhongguo zangxue chubanshe, 1998), 23–277.

[35] Wang, *Ximalaya*, 160–162.

tier here was delimited by the McMahon Line drawn at the 1913–14 Simla Conference. China does not recognize the McMahon Line itself or any of the documents from this conference, which it never ratified. In addition, as the line itself was drawn directly on a map, it lacks a precise delimitation.[36] Historically, Tibet had administered the area around Tawang in the far western portion of this sector, where the sixth Dalai Lama was born, and claimed additional areas on the southern slope.[37] After independence in 1947, India moved to assert its authority, slowly administering this region in the early 1950s and in some cases replacing local Tibetan officials.[38]

The western sector includes 33,000 square kilometers adjacent to Xinjiang and the Ali District of Tibet. PLA units first entered this area in 1950 after taking control of Xinjiang and gradually expanded Chinese control throughout the decade.[39] India claims that an 1842 treaty between Tibet and Kashmir established a customary boundary along the Kunlun Mountains to the northeast.[40] China maintains that the border in this region has never been delimited but that a customary boundary has existed along the Karakorum Mountains to the southwest. This region is largely uninhabited but encompasses a key communication route for China, the Xinjiang-Tibet highway, built in 1956.

The central sector, which comprises approximately 2,000 square kilometers, includes a series of mountain passes that lie to the west of the Indian-Tibetan-Nepal trijunction.[41] These passes link many trade and pilgrimage routes that connect India with Tibet. No prior agreement has attempted to delimit this section of the border.

Contention over these three disputed sectors arose in the early to mid-1950s. In 1953, Chinese and Indian diplomats agreed that they would not discuss the boundary in talks over India's trading privileges in Tibet. In 1954, China sent its first demarche to India after a confrontation between Chinese and Indian troops in the central sector.[42] In 1954 and 1956, Zhou Enlai and Jawaharlal Nehru discussed the McMahon Line as well as the border as whole.[43] In 1958, Nehru and Zhou exchanged diplomatic notes that began to detail each side's claims in all sectors.[44]

---

[36] Lamb, *The McMahon Line.*

[37] Maxwell, *India's China War,* 39–64.

[38] Maxwell, *India's China War,* 73.

[39] *ZYBJ,* 43.

[40] Prescott, *Map,* 34–35.

[41] *DDZGWJ,* 181.

[42] *WP,* I, 1.

[43] Subimal Dutt, *With Nehru in the Foreign Office* (Columbia, Mo.: South Asia Books, 1977), 114–116.

[44] *WP,* I.

In addition to the three sectors described above, India also claims territory controlled by China adjacent to Pakistani-held Kashmir. After the signing of the 1963 Chinese-Pakistani boundary agreement, Nehru stated in Parliament that Pakistan had surrendered Indian territory to China, including the Shaksgam Valley.[45] Analysis of this dispute is excluded from this book, as it stems from a prior conflict between India and Pakistan over Kashmir. The 1963 boundary agreement between China and Pakistan was provisional pending the resolution of the Kashmir dispute.

Bhutan

Little is known about China's dispute with Bhutan. The boundary had not been delimited by any prior agreement and was not included in the McMahon Line. The boundary itself was not even surveyed until the early 1970s. In the western sector, 1,128 square kilometers are under dispute.[46] In addition, Chinese and Bhutanese maps show a potential dispute in Bhutan's Gasa region along its northern border with China, an area that might comprise more than 1,000 square kilometers. Due to the limited contacts between China and Bhutan in the early 1950s, it is not known when this dispute was first acknowledged. Nevertheless, it emerged as a secondary issue in China's dispute with India and received prominence when Chinese troops sought to pacify the Tibetan rebellion and moved to seal the border with Bhutan.[47]

Nepal

Although the Himalayas form a natural boundary between China and Nepal, the border itself had never been delimited. Conflicting territorial claims in this region stem from the waxing and waning of Tibetan and Nepali power in the nineteenth century. Many of the areas contested after 1949 arose in the mid-1850s when Nepal invaded Tibet.[48]

[45] Razvi, *Frontiers*, 179.
[46] National Assembly of Bhutan, *Translation of the Proceedings and Resolutions of the 77th Session of the National Assembly of Bhutan* (Thimpu: National Assembly of Bhutan, 1999), 27.
[47] *WP*, I, 96.
[48] Department of State, "China-Nepal Boundary," *International Boundary Study*, no. 50 (30 May 1965); Fang Jianchang, "ZhongNi bianjie chutan" [A Preliminary Investigation of the Chinese-Nepalese Border], *Zhongguo bianjiang shidi yanjiu baogao*, nos. 3–4 (1992): 7–22; Arthur Lall, *How Communist China Negotiates* (New York: Columbia University Press, 1968), 194–201; Prescott, *Map*, 265–271; Yang Gongsu, *Zhongguo fandui waiguo qinlue ganshe Xizang difang douzheng shi* [History of China's Struggle against Foreign Aggression and Intervention in Tibet] (Beijing: Zangxue chubanshe, 1992), 320–325.

After the establishment of diplomatic relations in 1955, China and Nepal disputed two types of territory. The first was grazing areas and villages along the border. The size of these disputed areas have never been discussed officially, but estimates range from 259 to 2,476 square kilometers.[49] Many of these areas were occupied by Nepal after it defeated Tibetan troops in 1854 but were often populated by Tibetans. The largest disputed region was the Nilai area, which comprised approximately 1,200 square kilometers.[50] In other areas, actual administration was simply unclear because both sides claimed jurisdiction or ruled through local leaders. Overall, the two sides contested eleven sectors.[51] The second dispute between the two countries was over Mount Everest. A 1952 government circular indicated Chinese sovereignty over the mountain, which Nepal also claimed.[52]

These disputes between China and Nepal emerged shortly after the establishment of diplomatic relations between the two countries in 1955. In February 1956, Prime Minister Tanka Prasad Acharya raised the issue of disputed areas with Chinese leaders and sought to open talks.[53]

Burma

The majority of the Chinese-Burmese border was delimited in the late nineteenth century through agreements between the British and Chinese governments. The most significant agreements were signed in 1894 and 1897, which delimited the border from the Laos-China-Burma trijunction to the High Conical Peak in the north. Only two areas were not covered by these agreements and subsequently disputed by the two sides. The first was from the High Conical Peak to the India-China trijunction, which included the eastern portion of the McMahon Line. The second was a 257-kilometer portion of the border along the Burmese Wa state in the south, whose delimitation was not agreed on following the 1894 convention and remained in dispute throughout the early twentieth century. An exchange of notes signed by Britain and the Nationalist government in 1941 defined the border in this area, but it was never demarcated.[54]

[49] Lall, *How Communist China Negotiates*, 199; Guy Searls, "Communist China's Border Policy: Dragon Throne Imperialism? " *Current Scene*, vol. 11, no. 12 (15 April 1963): 11.

[50] Yang, *Zhongguo*, 320.

[51] Leo E. Rose, *Nepal: Strategy for Survival* (Berkeley: University of California Press, 1971), 235–236.

[52] Hemen Ray, *China's Strategy in Nepal* (New Delhi: Radiant Publishers, 1983), 25.

[53] S. D. Muni, *Foreign Policy of Nepal* (New Delhi: National Publishing House, 1973), 104.

[54] Prescott, *Map*, 347–353.

The total size of the territory disputed by China and Burma since 1949 is unclear. In the early 1950s, maps published in China showed large parts of Burma, especially in the north, as Chinese territory. The total amount of territory claimed was roughly 67,000 square kilometers, with 55,000 square kilometers in the northern Burmese Kachin state and 12,000 square kilometers in the southern Wa state.[55] In the process of negotiations in the mid-1950s, the scope of contested areas decreased, focusing on four sectors. In the north, China and Burma disputed the location of the boundary from the Izu Razi Pass to the trijunction with India above the Diphu Pass, an area following roughly the McMahon Line and totaling 1,000 square kilometers. Between the High Conical Peak and the Isu Razi Pass, the two sides disputed control of the villages of Hpimaw, Gawlam, and Kangfang, which Britain had annexed in 1911, an area of approximately 482 square kilometers. In the middle, the two sides contested the Nam-Wan Assigned Tract, a 220-square-kilometer area that the Qing had leased to Britain in perpetuity in 1897. In the south, the dispute focused around the Banhong-Banlao tribal region, an area comprising 189 square kilometers. Two smaller areas, 18 square kilometers in size, were also disputed.[56]

The territorial dispute emerged shortly after the establishment of diplomatic relations in 1950 and was raised by Burma's prime minister U Nu in 1954. After several clashes between Chinese and Burmese border forces in late 1955, the two sides began talks in 1956. China was actively patrolling its southern border with Burma to defeat remnant Nationalist troops, who had retreated to Burmese territory in 1950 and were launching periodic raids into Yunnan.[57]

Laos

China's boundary with Laos was one of the few borders that had been delimited in detail and demarcated on the ground before the establishment of the PRC. In agreements reached in 1887 and 1895 between China and France, the two sides delimited the frontier of Indochina, including Laos. Although mostly following different watersheds, the border had been poorly demarcated, with only fifteen boundary markers.[58] After

---

[55] "Eloquent Maps."

[56] *DDZGWJ*, 145–148; "The China-Burma Border," *China News Analysis*, no. 349 (18 November 1960); Department of State, "Burma-China Boundary," *International Boundary Study*, no. 42 (30 November 1964); Wang Shanzhong, "Lunshu Zhonghua renmin gongheguo he Miandian lianbang bianjie tiaoyue" [Discussion of the Boundary Treaty between the People's Republic of China and Union of Burma], *Zhongguo bianjiang shidi yanjiu*, no. 1 (1997): 78–84; Daphne E. Whittam, "The Sino-Burmese Boundary Treaty," *Pacific Affairs*, vol. 34, no. 2 (Summer 1961): 174–183.

[57] *DDZGJD*, 369–379.

[58] Department of State, "China-Laos Boundary," *International Boundary Study*, no. 34 (24 June 1964).

1949, the two sides disputed the location of the boundary in certain areas, contesting approximately 18 square kilometers.[59] It is not known when the first claim was made, but Chinese sources indicate that by 1960 the border was considered to be in dispute.[60]

Vietnam

Like its boundary with Laos, China's boundary with Vietnam was delimited and demarcated through a series of agreements with France. These 1887 and 1895 agreements resulted in the placement of three hundred boundary markers.[61]

Overall, the two sides disputed 164 sectors totaling 227 square kilometers.[62] Most of the disputes arose through divergent interpretations of the Chinese-French agreements. Vietnam also claimed that China had moved one hundred boundary markers during the 1979 war, while China asserted that Vietnam had occupied additional territory after the war. Before 1979, China and Vietnam held one round of negotiations over the land border, but they could not even agree on principles for settling the dispute and then suspended the talks.[63]

After the establishment of the PRC, local officials from both sides acknowledged the presence of disputed areas in 1956. Subsequently, both countries agreed in official correspondence in 1957 and 1958 to maintain the status quo pending a final settlement.[64]

HOMELAND DISPUTES

Hong Kong

The British colony of Hong Kong was established in the late Qing dynasty through three separate agreements. After its defeat in the Opium War, China agreed in the 1842 Treaty of Nanking to cede Hong Kong Island to Britain, a transfer that formed the territorial core of the colony. In

[59] A Sen, ed., *Zhongguo lujiang fengyun lu* [The Stormy Record of China's Territory] (Beijing: Luyou jiaoyu chubanshe, 1993), 24.

[60] Wu Lengxi, *Shinian lunzhan: 1956–1966 ZhongSu guanxi huiyilu* [Ten Years of Polemics: A Recollection of Chinese-Soviet Relations from 1956 to 1966] (Beijing: Zhongyang wenxian chubanshe, 1999), 248.

[61] Department of State, "China-Vietnam Boundary," *International Boundary Study*, no. 34 (15 December 1978); Prescott, *Map*, 447–451.

[62] "Vietnamese Deputy Foreign Minister Interviewed on Land Border Issues with China," *Nhan Dan*, 16 September 2002, BBC Monitoring Asia Pacific, 17 September 2002 (Factiva).

[63] *DDZGWJ*, 338–339.

[64] Guo Ming, ed., *ZhongYue guanxi yanbian sishi nian* [Evolution of Chinese-Vietnamese Relations over 40 Years] (Naning: Guangxi renmin chunabshe [internal circulation], 1992), 143.

1860, China agreed in the Treaty of Peking, after its defeat in the Second Opium War, to cede the tip of the Kowloon Peninsula to Britain. These first two agreements provided for the cession of territory, similar to agreements that the Qing government signed with tsarist Russia.[65] In l898, China in the Convention of Peking leased territory north of Boundary Street in the Kowloon Peninsula to Britain, an area that became known as the "New Territories," along with more than two hundred nearby islands. Overall, the size of the disputed area was 1,092 square kilometers. After 1949, China announced its intention to recover the colony, terminating the lease and recovering the ceded lands as well.

Macao

The Portuguese colony of Macao was originally established without any formal agreement between China and Portugal. In 1553, a Portuguese captain reportedly bribed local Chinese officials for permission to anchor in Macao's harbor and engage in trade. Soon thereafter, the Portuguese began to settle nearby. Initially they rented the land, but in the 1840s Portugal stopped paying rent and evicted the local authorities. This presence was made official in 1887, in the Chinese-Portuguese Treaty of Peking, which provided that "Portugal will administer Macao and subordinate areas in perpetuity, as any other region governed by Portugal."[66] Unlike Britain in Hong Kong, Portugal controlled all of Macao through cession. The size of the disputed area was 28 square kilometers.

Taiwan

The dispute over Taiwan refers to those areas held by the Nationalist government when it retreated to the island following its military defeat on the mainland in the Chinese civil war. As the new PRC government consolidated its control on the mainland, it prepared to invade Taiwan and bring the civil war to an end. Following the outbreak of the Korean War in June 1950 and the dispatch of the U.S. Seventh Fleet to the Taiwan Strait, China postponed plans to retake the KMT-held islands through force, though clashes continued over coastal islands. In total, this dispute accounts for approximately 35,980 square kilometers of land, including the island of Taiwan, the Penghu archipelago in the Taiwan Strait, as well as islands along the coast of Fujian and Zhejiang provinces, including Jinmen and Mazu.

---

[65] *DDZGWJ*, 379–383; Prescott, *Map*, 491–498.
[66] Prescott, *Map*, 489.

OFFSHORE ISLAND DISPUTES

White Dragon Tail Island

Little is known about China's dispute with Vietnam over White Dragon Tail Island. Also known as Bach Long Vi Dao or Nightingale Island, White Dragon Tail lies almost in the middle of the Tonkin Gulf, only 70 nautical miles from Hainan, and is roughly 5 square kilometers in size. It is not known when Vietnam first claimed the territory, but it was under French control during the 1930s. It is also not known whether the PRC issued a formal claim to the island, but it did occupy it after the French evacuated sixty KMT troops who had retreated there when the PLA captured Hainan in 1950.[67] Although the PLA did not occupy White Dragon Tail until August 1955, a small Chinese fishing village had prospered on the island for almost a hundred years.[68] The dispute most likely arose when the PLA took possession of the island.

Spratly Islands

Sovereignty over the islands in the South China Sea commonly known as the Spratly Islands has never been determined in an international agreement. The Spratlys in whole or in part are claimed by China, Taiwan, Malaysia, the Philippines, Vietnam, and Brunei. The Spratlys contain more than 230 features, including 25 islets above the high-tide line in addition to reefs, rocks, and submerged shoals.[69] The largest single feature is Taiping (Itu Aba) Island, which the KMT occupied in 1956 and which comprises approximately 0.46 square kilometers.[70] The total size of all the features is roughly 5 square kilometers.

The PRC first claimed the Spratlys in 1951. During peace treaty negotiations with Japan in San Francisco, Zhou Enlai issued a statement claiming China's sovereignty over the Spratlys and Paracels as well as coastal islands and Taiwan.[71] China's 1958 territorial waters declaration issued during the Jinmen crisis repeated these claims.[72]

[67] Li Dechao, "Bailongwei dao zhengming" [Rectification of White Dragon Tail Island's Name], *Zhongguo bianjiang shidi yanjiu baogao*, vols. 1–2, no. 3 (1988): 22.

[68] Li, "Bailong weidao zhengming," 21–23. The island was under French control until the 1954 Geneva Accord.

[69] Mao Zhenfa, ed., *Bianfang lun* [On Frontier Defense] (Beijing: Junshi kexue chubanshe [internal circulation], 1996), 137.

[70] Dieter Heinzig, *Disputed Islands in the South China Sea: Paracels, Spratlys, Pratas, Macclesfield Bank* (Wiesbaden: Otto Harrassowitz, 1976), 17–19.

[71] For a copy of the statement, see Han Zhenhua, ed., *Woguo nanhai zhudao shiliao huibian* [Collection of Historical Materials on Our Country's South China Sea Islands] (Beijing: Dongfang chubanshe [internal circulation], 1988), 444.

[72] Han, *Woguo nanhai*, 445.

Paracel Islands

China and Vietnam have contested the sovereignty of the Paracels since the early 1950s. The Nationalists have also claimed these islands as part of China. No prior agreement exists for the islands, but they were occupied at various times before 1949 by both France and China. Competing claims are based on historical use and administration, as the islands have provided natural shelter for fishermen in the region.

The Paracel Islands contain twenty-three features, including islands, rocks, reefs, and shoals divided into the Crescent Group in the west and the Amphitrite Group in the east. In total, the features comprise approximately 10 square kilometers of land.[73]

The PRC issued its first claim to the Paracels in 1951 along with its claim to the Spratlys. A PLA garrison established a presence on Woody Island in the Amphitrite Group after the Nationalists left in the spring of 1950.[74] Although China supplied this outpost from Hainan, the first naval patrol of the disputed area was not conducted until 1959.[75]

Senkaku Islands

The Senkaku (Diaoyu) Islands include more than eight features comprising approximately 7 square kilometers. Although Japanese civilians have harvested guano there, Japan has no permanent presence, military or civilian, on these islands.[76] China maintains that the islands reverted to Taiwan after the end of World War II, which abrogated the 1895 Treaty of Shimonoseki, while Japan claims that the islands were never part of the treaty. China did not issue its first claim to the Senkakus until December 1970, after the Nationalists on Taiwan claimed them as being a part of China.[77] It is likely that both the mainland and Taiwan hoped that the United States would not transfer the islands to Japan as part of the Okinawa Reversion Agreement that was concluded in 1971.

---

[73] *DDZGJD*, 646.

[74] Heinzig, *Disputed Islands*, 32.

[75] Zhao Qimin, "Yuanhang qianli, shoujin Xisha" [Ocean Voyage for a Thousand Miles, First Advance to the Parcels], in *Haijun: huiyi shiliao* [Navy: Recollections and Historical Materials] (Beijing: Jiefangjun chubanshe [military circulation], 1999), 424–429.

[76] Zhang Zhirong, ed., *ZhongRi guanxi yu diaoyutai wenti yanjiu lunji* [Research Collection on Chinese-Japanese Relations and the Diaoyutai Problem] (Xianggang: Lizhi chubanshe, 1999), 428.

[77] *RMRB*, 29 December 1970, 1.

Bibliography

Abdulghani, Jasim M. *Iraq & Iran: The Years of Crisis*. London: Croom Helm, 1984.

Accinelli, Robert. " 'A Thorn in the Side of Peace': The Eisenhower Administration and the 1958 Offshore Islands Crisis." In Robert S. Ross and Jiang Changbin, eds., *Re-examining the Cold War: U.S.–China Diplomacy, 1954–1973*. Cambridge, Mass.: Harvard University Press, 2001.

Akino, Yutaka. "Moscow's New Perspectives on Sino-Russian Relations." In Tadayuki Hayashi, ed., *The Emerging New Regional Order in Central and Eastern Europe*. Sapporo: Slavic Research Center Hokkaido University, 1997.

Allee, Todd L., and Paul K. Huth. "When Are Governments Able to Reach Negotiated Settlement Agreements? An Analysis of Dispute Resolution in Territorial Disputes, 1919–1995." In Harvey Starr, ed., *Approaches, Levels, and Methods of Analysis in International Politics*. New York: Palgrave Macmillan, 2006.

Alptekin, Erkin. "The April 1990 Uprising in Eastern Turkestan." *Journal of Muslim Minority Affairs*, vol. 11, no. 2 (1990): 254–256.

Amer, Ramses. "The Sino-Vietnamese Approach to Managing Boundary Disputes." *Maritime Briefing*, vol. 3, no. 5 (2002): 1–80.

Amnesty International. *Secret Violence: Human Rights Violations in Xinjiang*. New York: Amnesty International, 1992.

An, Tai Sung. *The Sino-Soviet Territorial Dispute*. Philadelphia: Westminster Press, 1973.

Austin, Greg. *China's Ocean Frontier: International Law, Military Force, and National Development*. Canberra: Allen & Unwin, 1998.

Ayoob, Mohammed. *The Third World Security Predicament: State Making, Regional Conflict, and the International System*. Boulder, Colo.: Lynne Rienner, 1995.

Azar, Edward, and Chung-In Moon, eds. *National Security in the Third World*. Aldershot: Edward Elgar Publishing, 1988.

Bachman, David M. *Bureaucracy, Economy, and Leadership in China: The Institutional Origins of the Great Leap Forward*. Cambridge: Cambridge University Press, 1991.

Bajpai, G. S. *China's Shadow over Sikkim: The Politics of Intimidation*. New Delhi: Lancer Publishers, 1999.

Barnett, Michael N., and Jack S. Levy. "Domestic Sources of Alliances and Alignments: The Case of Egypt, 1962–73." *International Organization*, vol. 45, no. 3 (Summer 1991): 369–395.

Barnouin, Barbara, and Yu Changgen. *Chinese Foreign Policy during the Cultural Revolution*. New York: Kegan Paul International, 1998.

Baum, Richard. *Burying Mao: Chinese Politics in the Age of Deng Xiaoping*. Princeton, N.J.: Princeton University Press, 1994.

Benson, Linda. *The Ili Rebellion: The Moslem Challenge to Chinese Authority in Xinjiang, 1944–1949.* Armonk, N.Y.: M. E. Sharpe, 1990.

Bernstein, Richard, and Ross H. Munro. *The Coming Conflict with China.* New York: Knopf, 1997.

Betts, Richard K. *Nuclear Blackmail and Nuclear Balance.* Washington, D.C.: Brookings, 1987.

———. "Wealth, Power, and Instability: East Asia and the United States after the Cold War." *International Security,* vol. 18, no. 3 (Winter 1993): 34–77.

Bhattacharjea, Mira Sinha. "China's Strategy for the Determination and Consolidation of its Territorial Boundaries: A Preliminary Investigation." *China Report,* vol. 23, no. 4 (1987): 397–419.

———. "India-China: The Year of Two Possibilities." In Satish Kumar, ed., *Yearbook on India's Foreign Policy, 1985–86.* New Delhi: Sage Publications, 1988.

Bhola, P. L. *Pakistan-China Relations: Search for Politico-Strategic Relationship.* Jaipur: R.B.S.A. Publishers, 1986.

Blainey, Geoffrey. *The Causes of War,* 3rd ed. New York: The Free Press, 1988.

Brook, Timothy. *Quelling the People: The Military Suppression of the Beijing Democracy Movement.* Stanford, Calif.: Stanford University Press, 1998.

Brooks, Stephen G. *Producing Security: Multinational Corporations, Globalization, and the Changing Calculus of Conflict.* Princeton, N.J.: Princeton University Press, 2005.

Brown, Melissa J. *Is Taiwan Chinese? The Impact of Culture, Power, and Migration on Changing Identities.* Berkeley: University of California Press, 2004.

Bu He, ed. *Minzu lilun yu minzu zhengce* [Nationality Theory and Nationality Policy]. Huhehaote: Neimenggu daxue chubanshe, 1995.

Bull, Hedley. *The Anarchical Society: A Study of Order in World Politics.* New York: Columbia University Press, 1977.

Burr, William, ed. *The Kissinger Transcripts: The Top Secret Talks with Beijing and Moscow.* New York: The New Press, 1998.

Bush, Richard C. *Untying the Knot: Making Peace in the Taiwan Strait.* Washington, D.C.: Brookings Institution Press, 2005.

Buszynski, Leszek. "ASEAN, the Declaration on Conduct, and the South China Sea." *Contemporary Southeast Asia,* vol. 25, no. 3 (December 2003): 343–362.

Cabestan, Jean-Pierre. "Taiwan's Mainland Policy: Normalization, Yes; Reunification, Later." *The China Quarterly,* no. 148 (December 1996): 1260–1283.

Cai Xiru, ed. *Bianfang lilun* [Theory of Frontier Defense]. Beijing: Jingguan jiaoyu chubanshe [internal circulation], 1996.

Carlson, Allen. *Unifying China, Integrating with the World: Securing Chinese Sovereignty in the Reform Era.* Stanford, Calif.: Stanford University Press, 2005.

Cha, Victor D. "Hawk Engagement and Preventive Defense on the Korean Peninsula." *International Security,* vol. 27, no. 1 (Summer 2002): 40–78.

Chang, Felix K. "China's Central Asian Power and Problems." *Orbis,* vol. 41, no. 3 (Summer 1997): 401–426.

Chang, Gordon H., and He Di. "The Absence of War in the U.S.-China Confrontation over Quemoy and Matsu in 1954–1955: Contingency, Luck, Deterrence?" *American Historical Review,* vol. 98, no. 5 (December 1993): 1500–1524.

Chang, Luke T. *China's Boundary Treaties and Frontier Disputes: A Manuscript.* New York: Oceana Publications, 1982.

Chang, Maria Hsia. *Return of the Dragon: China's Wounded Nationalism.* Boulder, Colo.: Westview, 2001.

Chang Pao-min. *The Sino-Vietnamese Territorial Dispute.* New York: Praeger, 1986.

Chen Chonglong and Xie Jun, eds. *Haixia liang'an guanxi dashiji* [Chronicle of Cross-straits Relations]. Beijing: Zhonggong dangshi chubanshe, 1993.

Chen Jian. *China's Road to the Korean War: The Making of the Sino-American Confrontation.* New York: Columbia University Press, 1994.

———. *Mao's China and the Cold War.* Chapel Hill: University of North Carolina Press, 2001.

Chen Xueying. *Deng Xiaoping yu Xianggang* [Deng Xiaoping and Hong Kong]. Beijing: Dangdai shijie chubanshe, 1997.

Chen Qimao. "New Approaches in China's Foreign Policy: The Post–Cold War Era." *Asian Survey,* vol. 33, no. 3 (March 1993): 237–251.

Cheng Feng and Larry M. Wortzel. "PLA Operational Principles and Limited War: The Sino-Indian War of 1962." In Mark A. Ryan, David M. Finkelstein, and Michael A. McDevitt, eds., *Chinese Warfighting: The PLA Experience since 1949.* Armonk, N.Y.: M. E. Sharpe, 2003.

Cheng Guangzhong. "Congwei chengnuo fangqi duiTai shiyong wuli: sandai lingdao jiti jiejue Taiwan wenti fangzhen de lishi kaocha" [Never Promising to Renounce the Use of Force: A Historical Examination of the Third-Generation Leaders' Policy for Resolving the Taiwan Problem]. *Junshi lishi,* no. 5 (1999): 37–39.

Cheng, J. Chester, ed. *Politics of the Chinese Red Army.* Stanford, Calif.: Hoover Institution Publications, 1966.

Chung Chien-peng. *Domestic Politics, International Bargaining and China's Territorial Disputes.* London: RoutledgeCurzon, 2004.

"The China-Burma Border." *China News Analysis,* no. 349 (18 November 1960).

Chiozza, Giacomo, and Ajin Choi. "Guess Who Did What: Political Leaders and the Management of Territorial Disputes, 1950–1990." *Journal of Conflict Resolution,* vol. 47, no. 3 (June 2003): 251–278.

Chiozza, Giacomo, and H. E. Goemans. "Peace through Insecurity: Tenure and International Conflict." *Journal of Conflict Resolution,* vol. 47, no. 4 (August 2003): 443–467.

Choucri, Nazli, and Robert Carver North. *Nations in Conflict: National Growth and International Violence.* San Francisco: W. H. Freeman, 1975.

Christensen, Thomas J. *Useful Adversaries: Grand Strategy, Domestic Mobilization, and Sino-American Conflict, 1947–1958.* Princeton, N.J.: Princeton University Press, 1996.

———. "Posing Problems without Catching Up: China's Rise and Challenges for U.S. Security Policy." *International Security,* vol. 25, no. 4 (Spring 2001): 5–40.

———. "The Contemporary Security Dilemma: Deterring a Taiwan Conflict." *The Washington Quarterly,* vol. 25, no. 4 (Autumn 2002): 7–21.

Christensen, Thomas J. "Windows and War: Trend Analysis and Beijing's Use of Force." In Alastair Iain Johnston and Robert S. Ross, eds., *New Directions in the Study of China's Foreign Policy*. Stanford, Calif.: Stanford University Press, 2006.

Cohen, Arthur. *The Sino-Indian Border Dispute*, DD/I Staff Study POLO XVI [Top Secret]. 3 parts. Washington, D.C.: Central Intelligence Agency, 1963, 1964.

Conboy, Kenneth, and James Morrison. *The CIA's Secret War in Tibet*. Lawrence: University of Kansas Press, 2002.

Cong Letian, ed. *Huigu Jinmen denglu zhan* [Reflections on the Battle to Land on Jinmen]. Beijing: Renmin chubanshe, 1994.

Cooper, Scott. "State-Centric Balance-of-Threat Theory: Explaining the Misunderstood Gulf Cooperation Council." *Security Studies*, vol. 13, no. 2 (Winter 2003): 306–349.

Copeland, Dale C. *Origins of Major War*. Ithaca, N.Y.: Cornell University Press, 2000.

Cottrell, Robert. *The End of Hong Kong: The Secret Diplomacy of Imperial Retreat*. London: John Murray, 1993.

Cui Zhiqing, ed. *Haixia liang'an guanxi rizhi (1949–1998)* [Daily Record of Cross-straits Relations]. Beijing: Jiuzhou tushu chubanshe, 1999.

Dalvi, J. P. *Himalayan Blunder: The Curtain-Raiser to the Sino-Indian War of 1962*. Bombay: Thacker and Company, 1969.

Damawat, Tomur. *Lun minzu gongzuo yu minzu wenhua* [On Nationality Work and Culture]. Beijing: Zhonggong zhongyang dangxiao chubanshe, 2005.

Dassel, Kurt, and Eric Reinhardt. "Domestic Strife and the Initiation of Violence at Home and Abroad." *American Journal of Political Science*, vol. 43, no. 1 (January 1999): 56–85.

David, Steven R. "Explaining Third World Alignment." *World Politics*, vol. 43, no. 2 (January 1991): 233–256.

Davies, Graeme A. M. "Domestic Strife and the Initiation of International Conflicts." *Journal of Conflict Resolution*, vol. 46, no. 5 (October 2002): 672–692.

Day, Alan J., ed. *Border and Territorial Disputes*. 2nd ed. Burnt Mill: Longman, 1987.

Dekmejian, R. H. "Soviet-Turkish Relations and Politics in the Armenian SSR." *Soviet Studies*, vol. 19, no. 4 (April 1968): 510–525.

Deng Lifeng, ed. *Zhonghua renmin gongheguo junshi shiyao* [A Brief History of the PRC's Military Affairs]. Beijing: Junshi kexue chubanshe, 2005.

Department of State. "China-Korea Boundary." *International Boundary Study*, no. 17 (29 June 1962).

———. "Burma-China Boundary." *International Boundary Study*, no. 42 (30 November 1964).

———. "China-Laos Boundary." *International Boundary Study*, no. 34 (24 June 1964).

———. "China-Nepal Boundary." *International Boundary Study*, no. 50 (30 May 1965).

———. "China-Pakistan Boundary." *International Boundary Study*, no. 85 (30 May 1968).

———. "Afghanistan-China Boundary." *International Boundary Study*, no. 89 (1 May 1969).

———. "China-Vietnam Boundary." *International Boundary Study*, no. 34 (15 December 1978).

———. "China-Mongolia Boundary." *International Boundary Study*, no. 173 (14 August 1985).

Di Cosmo, Nicola. "Qing Colonial Administration in Inner Asia." *The International History Review*, vol. 20, no. 2 (1998): 24–40.

Diehl, Paul F., and Gary Goertz. *War and Peace in International Rivalry*. Ann Arbor: University of Michigan Press, 2000.

Dillon, Michael. *Xinjiang: Ethnicity, Separatism and Control in Central Asia*. Durham, East Asian Papers, no. 2. Durham, UK: Durham University, 1995.

Directorate for Research. *Luring Deep: China's Land Defense Strategy*, DDB-2610–31–80 [Top Secret]. Washington, D.C.: Defense Intelligence Agency, 1980.

Directorate of Intelligence. *Military Forces along the Sino-Soviet Border*, SR-IM-70–5 [Top Secret]. Washington, D.C.: Central Intelligence Agency, 1970.

———. *Sino-Soviet Exchanges, 1969–84: A Reference Aid*, EA 84–10069 [Top Secret]. Washington, D.C.: Central Intelligence Agency, 1984.

Dmytryshyn, Basil, and Frederick Cox. *The Soviet Union and the Middle East*. Princeton, N.J.: Kingston Press, 1987.

Do, Kiem, and Julie Kane. *Counterpart: A South Vietnamese Naval Officer's War*. Annapolis: Naval Institute Press, 1998.

Doolin, Dennis J. *Territorial Claims in the Sino-Soviet Conflict: Documents and Analysis*. Stanford, Calif.: Hoover Institution, 1965.

Dutt, Subimal. *With Nehru in the Foreign Office*. Columbia, Mo.: South Asia Books, 1977.

Dzurek, Daniel J. "The Spratly Islands Dispute: Who's on First?" *Maritime Briefing*, vol. 2, no. 1 (1996): 1–67.

"Eloquent Maps." *China News Analysis*, no. 129 (27 April 1956).

Fan Shuo. *Ye Jianying zhuan* [Biography of Ye Jianying]. Beijing: Dangdai Zhongguo chubanshe, 1995.

Fang Jianchang. "ZhongNi bianjie chutan" [A Preliminary Investigation of the Chinese-Nepalese Border]. *Zhongguo bianjiang shidi yanjiu baogao*, nos. 3–4 (1992): 7–22.

———. "Jindai Zhongguo yu Bajisitan bianjie shi chutan" [Preliminary Discussion of the History of China and Pakistan's Border in Modern Times]. *Zhongguo bianjiang shidi yanjiu*, no. 3 (1997): 63–78.

Fazal, Tanisha M. *State Death: The Politics and Geography of Conquest, Occupation, and Annexation*. Princeton, N.J.: Princeton University Press, 2007.

Fearon, James D. "Rationalist Explanations for War." *International Organization*, vol. 49, no. 3 (Summer 1995): 379–414.

Feng Qingfu, ed. *Bianjing guanli xue* [The Science of Border Management]. Beijing: Jingguan jiaoyu chubanshe [internal circulation], 1999.

Fewsmith, Joseph. *China since Tiananmen: The Politics of Transition*. Cambridge: Cambridge University Press, 2001.

Fletcher, Joseph. "Ch'ing Inner Asia c. 1800." In John K. Fairbank, ed., *The Cambridge History of China*, vol. 10. Cambridge: Cambridge University Press, 1978.

Fletcher, Joseph. "The Heyday of the Ch'ing Order in Mongolia, Sinkiang and Tibet." In John K. Fairbank, ed., *The Cambridge History of China*, vol. 10. Cambridge: Cambridge University Press, 1978.

Forbes, Andrew D. W. *Warlords and Muslims in Chinese Central Asia: A Political History of Republican Sinkiang, 1911–1949*. New York: Cambridge University Press, 1986.

Fravel, M. Taylor. "Towards Civilian Supremacy: Civil-Military Relations in Taiwan's Democratization." *Armed Forces & Society*, vol. 29, no. 1 (Fall 2002): 57–84.

———. "Regime Insecurity and International Cooperation: Explaining China's Compromises in Territorial Disputes." *International Security*, vol. 30, no. 2 (Fall 2005): 46–83.

———. "Securing Borders: China's Doctrine and Force Structure for Frontier Defense." *Journal of Strategic Studies*, vol. 30, nos. 4–5 (2007): 705–737.

———. "Power Shifts and Escalation: Explaining China's Use of Force in Territorial Disputes." *International Security*, vol. 32, no. 3 (Winter 2007/08): 44–83.

Freedman, Lawrence, and Virginia Gamba-Stonehouse. *Signals of War: The Falklands Conflict of 1982*. London: Faber and Faber, 1990.

Freymond, Jacques. *The Saar Conflict*, 1945–1955. London: Stevens, 1960.

Friedberg, Aaron L. "Ripe for Rivalry: Prospects for Peace in Multipolar Asia." *International Security*, vol. 18, no. 3 (Winter 1993/94): 5–33.

Ganguly, Sumit. "The Sino-Indian Border Talks, 1981–1989: A View from New Delhi." *Asian Survey*, vol. 29, no. 12 (December 1989): 1123–1135.

———. *Conflict Unending: India-Pakistan Tensions since 1947*. New York: Columbia University Press, 2001.

Gartzke, Eric. "The Capitalist Peace." *American Journal of Political Science*, vol. 51, no. 1 (January 2007): 166–191.

Garver, John W. "Chinese Foreign Policy in 1970: The Tilt Towards the Soviet Union." *The China Quarterly*, no. 82 (June 1980): 214–249.

———. "The Sino-Soviet Territorial Dispute in the Pamir Mountains Region." *The China Quarterly*, no. 85 (March 1981): 107–118.

———. "China's Push through the South China Sea: The Interaction of Bureaucratic and National Interests." *The China Quarterly*, no. 132 (December 1992): 999–1028.

———. "The Chinese Communist Party and the Collapse of Soviet Communism." *The China Quarterly*, no. 133 (March 1993): 1–26.

———. "Sino-Indian Rapprochement and the Sino-Pakistan Entente." *Political Science Quarterly*, vol. 111, no. 2 (Summer 1996): 323–347.

———. *Face Off: China, the United States, and Taiwan's Democratization*. Seattle: University of Washington Press, 1997.

———. *The Sino-American Alliance: Nationalist China and American Cold War Strategy in Asia*. Armonk, N.Y.: M. E. Sharpe, 1997.

———. *Protracted Contest: Sino-Indian Rivalry in the Twentieth Century*. Seattle: University of Washington Press, 2001.

———. "China's Decision for War with India in 1962." In Alastair Iain Johnston and Robert S. Ross, eds., *New Directions in the Study of China's Foreign Policy*. Stanford, Calif.: Stanford University Press, 2006.

Gause, F. Gregory. "Iraq's Decisions to Go to War, 1980 and 1990." *The Middle East Journal*, vol. 56, no. 1 (Winter 2002): 47–70.

Gavrilis, George. *The Dynamics of Interstate Boundaries*. Cambridge: Cambridge University Press, forthcoming.

George, Alexander L., and Andrew Bennett. *Case Studies and Theory Development in the Social Sciences*. Cambridge, Mass.: MIT Press, 2005.

Gilpin, Robert. *War and Change in World Politics*. New York: Cambridge University Press, 1981.

Ginsburgs, George. "The End of the Sino-Russian Territorial Disputes?" *The Journal of East Asian Studies*, vol. 7, no. 1 (1993): 261–320.

Ginsburgs, George, and Carl F. Pinkele. *The Sino-Soviet Territorial Dispute, 1949–64*. New York: Praeger, 1978.

Glaser, Bonnie S. "China's Security Perceptions: Interests and Ambitions." *Asian Survey*, vol. 33, no. 3 (March 1993): 252–271.

Gleditsch, Nils Petter. "Armed Conflict and the Environment: A Critique of the Literature." *Journal of Peace Research*, vol. 35, no. 3 (May 1998): 381–400.

Glosny, Michael A. "Heading toward a Win-Win Future? Recent Developments in China's Policy toward Southeast Asia." *Asian Security*, vol. 2, no. 1 (2006): 24–57.

Goddard, Stacie. "Uncommon Ground: Indivisible Territory and the Politics of Legitimacy." *International Organization*, vol. 60, no. 1 (Winter 2006): 35–68.

Goertz, Gary, and Paul F. Diehl. *Territorial Changes and International Conflict*. New York: Routledge, 1992.

Goldstein, Avery. *Rising to the Challenge: China's Grand Strategy and International Security*. Stanford, Calif.: Stanford University Press, 2005.

Goldstein, Lyle. "Return to Zhenbao Island: Who Started Shooting and Why It Matters." *The China Quarterly*, no. 168 (December 2001): 985–997.

Goldstein, Steven M. "Dialogue of the Deaf? The Sino-American Ambassadorial-Level Talks, 1955–1970." In Robert S. Ross and Jiang Changbin, eds., *Re-examining the Cold War: U.S.-China Diplomacy, 1954–1973*. Cambridge, Mass.: Harvard University Press, 2001.

Goncharov, Sergei. "Kosygin-Zhou Talks at Beijing Airport." *Far Eastern Affairs*, nos. 1–2 (1993): 52–65.

Goncharov, Sergei, and Victor Usov. "Kosygin-Zhou Talks at Beijing Airport." *Far Eastern Affairs*, nos. 4–6 (1992): 96–117.

Gong Li. "Liangci Taiwan haixia weiji de chengyin yu ZhongMei zhijian de jiao-liang" [The Causes of the Two Taiwan Strait Crises and Chinese-U.S. Disputes]. In Jiang Changbin and Robert S. Ross, eds., *Cong duizhi zouxiang huanhe: lengzhan shiqi ZhongMei guanxi zai tantao* [From Confrontation to Rapprochement: Reexamining Chinese-U.S. Relations during the Cold War]. Beijing: Shijie zhishi chubanshe, 2000.

———. "Tension across the Strait in the 1950s: Chinese Strategy and Tactics." In Robert S. Ross and Jiang Changbin, eds., *Re-examining the Cold War: U.S.-China Diplomacy, 1954–1973*. Cambridge, Mass.: Harvard University Press, 2001.

Gongan budui: zongshu, dashiji, biaoce [Public Security Troops: Summary, Chronicle of Events, Statistics]. Beijing: Jiefangjun chubanshe [military circulation], 1997.

Gopal, Sarvepalli. *Jawaharlal Nehru: A Biography.* 3 vols. London: Jonathan Cape, 1984.

Gorman, Robert F. *Political Conflict on the Horn of Africa.* New York: Praeger, 1981.

Gourevitch, Peter. "The Second Image Reversed: International Sources of Domestic Politics." *International Organization,* vol. 32, no. 4 (Autumn 1978): 881–912.

Gries, Peter Hayes. *China's New Nationalism: Pride, Politics, and Diplomacy.* Berkeley, Calif: University of California Press, 2004.

Grunfeld, A. Tom. *The Making of Modern Tibet,* revised edition. Armonk, N.Y.: M. E. Sharpe, 1996.

Guo Ming, ed. *ZhongYue guanxi yanbian sishi nian* [Evolution of Chinese-Vietnamese Relations over 40 Years]. Naning: Guangxi renmin chubanshe [internal circulation], 1992.

Guo Ming, Luo Fangming, and Li Baiyin, eds. *Xiandai ZhongYue guanxi ziliao xuanbian* [Selected Materials on Contemporary Chinese-Vietnamese Relations]. Beijing: Shishi chubanshe [internal circulation], 1986.

Gurtov, Melvin, and Byong-Moo Hwang. *China under Threat: The Politics of Strategy and Diplomacy.* Baltimore: Johns Hopkins University Press, 1980.

Hagan, Joe D. "Regimes, Political Oppositions, and the Comparative Analysis of Foreign Policy." In Charles F. Hermann, Charles W. Kegley, Jr., and James N. Rosenau, eds., *New Directions in the Study of Foreign Policy.* Boston: Allen Unwin, 1987.

Haijun shi [History of the Navy]. Beijing: Jiefangjun chubanshe, 1989.

Hale, William. *Turkish Foreign Policy, 1774–2000.* London: Frank Cass, 2000.

Han Zhenhua, ed. *Woguo nanhai zhudao shiliao huibian* [Collection of Historical Materials on Our Country's South China Sea Islands]. Beijing: Dongfang chubanshe [internal circulation], 1988.

Han Zheshi, ed. *Changbai chaoxianzu zizhixian zhi* [Changbai Korean Autonomous County Gazetteer]. Beijing: Zhonghua shuju chubanshe, 1993.

Harding, Harry. "The Chinese State in Crisis." In Roderick MacFarquhar and John K. Fairbank, eds., *The Cambridge History of China,* vol. 15, part 2. Cambridge: Cambridge University Press, 1991.

———. *A Fragile Relationship: The United States and China since 1972.* Washington, D.C.: The Brookings Institution, 1992.

Harris, Lillian Craig. "Xinjiang, Central Asia and the Implications for China's Policy in the Islamic World." *The China Quarterly,* no. 133 (March 1993): 111–129.

Harrison, Selig S. *China, Oil and Asia: Conflict Ahead?* New York: Columbia University Press, 1977.

Hasan, Mushirul, ed. *Selected Works of Jawaharlal Nehru,* second series, vol. 36. New Delhi: Oxford University Press, 2005.

Hassner, Ron E. " 'To Halve and to Hold': Conflicts over Sacred Space and the Problem of Indivisibility." *Security Studies,* vol. 12, no. 4 (Summer 2003): 1–33.

He Di. "Evolution of the People's Republic of China's Policy toward the Offshore Islands." In Warren I. Cohen and Akira Iriye, eds., *The Great Powers in East Asia: 1953–1960*. New York: Columbia University Press, 1990.

———. "The Last Campaign to Unify China: The CCP's Unrealized Plan to Liberate Taiwan, 1949–1950." In Mark A. Ryan, David M. Finkelstein, and Michael A. McDevitt, eds., *Chinese Warfighting: The PLA Experience since 1949*. Armonk, N.Y.: M. E. Sharpe, 2003.

He Dongfang. *Zhang Aiping zhuan* [Zhang Aiping's Biography]. Beijing: Renmin chubanshe, 2000.

He Jihong, ed. *Kezilesu keerkezi zizhizhou zhi* [Kezilesu Kyrgyz; Autonomous Region Gazetteer]. Wulumuqi: Xinjiang renmin chubanshe, 2004.

Heinzig, Dieter. *Disputed Islands in the South China Sea: Paracels, Spratlys, Pratas, Macclesfield Bank*. Wiesbaden: Otto Harrassowitz, 1976.

Hensel, Paul R. "Contentious Issues and World Politics: The Management of Territorial Claims in the Americas, 1816–1992." *International Studies Quarterly*, vol. 45, no. 1 (March 2001): 81–109.

Hensel, Paul R., and Sara McLaughlin Mitchell. "Issue Indivisibility and Territorial Claims." *GeoJournal*, vol. 64, no. 4 (December 2005): 275–285.

Herbst, Jeffrey. *States and Power in Africa: Comparative Lessons in Authority and Control*. Princeton, N.J.: Princeton University Press, 2000.

Hinton, Harold C. *Communist China in World Politics*. New York: Houghton Mifflin, 1966.

Hoffman, Steven A. *India and the China Crisis*. Berkeley: University of California Press, 1990.

Holsti, Kalevi J. *Peace and War: Armed Conflicts and International Order, 1648–1989*. Cambridge: Cambridge University Press, 1991.

Hsiung, James C. "China's Omni-directional Diplomacy: Realignment to Cope with Monopolar U.S. Power." *Asian Survey*, vol. 35, no. 6 (June 1995): 573–586.

Huang Zhengmiao, ed. *Zhejiang sheng junshi zhi* [Zhejiang Province Military Affairs Gazetteer]. Beijing: Difangzhi chubanshe, 1999.

Hucker, Charles O. *A Dictionary of Official Titles in Imperial China*. Stanford, Calif.: Stanford University Press, 1985.

Human Rights Watch. *China: Human Rights Concerns in Xinjiang*. New York: Human Rights Watch, 2001.

Hussain, T. Karki. "India's China Policy: Putting Politics in Command." In Satish Kumar, ed., *Yearbook on India's Foreign Policy, 1989*. New Delhi: Sage Publications, 1990.

Huth, Paul K. *Standing Your Ground: Territorial Disputes and International Conflict*. Ann Arbor: University of Michigan Press, 1996.

———. "Reputations and Deterrence." *Security Studies*, vol. 7, no. 1 (1997): 72–99.

Huth, Paul K., and Todd L. Allee. *The Democratic Peace and Territorial Conflict in the Twentieth Century*. Cambridge: Cambridge University Press, 2002.

———. "Domestic Political Accountability and the Escalation and Settlement of International Disputes." *Journal of Conflict Resolution*, vol. 46, no. 6 (December 2002): 754–790.

Hyer, Eric A. "The Politics of China's Boundary Disputes and Settlements." Ph.D. dissertation, Columbia University, 1990.

Iwashita, Akihiro. *A 4,000 Kilometer Journey along the Sino-Russian Border.* Sapporo: Slavic Research Center, Hokkaido University, 2004.

James, Patrick, and John R. Oneal. "The Influence of Domestic and International Politics on the President's Use of Force." *Journal of Conflict Resolution*, vol. 35, no. 2 (June 1991): 307–332.

Jervis, Robert. "Cooperation under the Security Dilemma." *World Politics*, vol. 30, no. 2 (January 1978): 167–214.

Jessup, Philip C. "El Chamizal." *The American Journal of International Law*, vol. 67, no. 3 (1973): 423–445.

Jetly, Nancy. *India China Relations, 1947–1977: A Study of Parliament's Role in the Making of Foreign Policy.* New Delhi: Radiant Publishers, 1979.

Jiang Zemin. *Lun guofang he jundui jianshe* [On National Defense and Army Building]. Beijing: Jiefangjun chubanshe [internal circulation], 2003.

Jiang Zemin wenxuan [Jiang Zemin's Selected Works], vol. 3. Beijing: Renmin chubanshe, 2006.

Jianguo yilai Mao Zedong wengao [Manuscripts of Mao Zedong since the Founding of the Nation), vols. 7–8. Beijing: Zhongyang wenxian chubanshe [internal circulation], 1992, 1993.

Job, Brian L., ed. *The Insecurity Dilemma: National Security of Third World States.* Boulder, Colo.: Lynne Rienner, 1992.

Johnston, Alastair Iain. "Cultural Realism and Strategy in Maoist China." In Peter J. Katzenstein, ed., *The Culture of National Security: Norms and Identity in World Politics.* New York: Columbia University Press, 1996.

———. "China's Militarized Interstate Dispute Behaviour 1949–1992: A First Cut at the Data." *The China Quarterly*, no. 153 (March 1998): 1–30.

———. "Realism(s) and Chinese Security Policy in the Post–Cold War World." In Ethan B. Kapstein and Michael Mastanduno, eds., *Unipolar Politics: Realism and State Strategies after the Cold War.* New York: Columbia University Press, 1999.

———. "Is China a Status Quo Power?" *International Security*, vol. 27, no. 4 (Spring 2003): 5–56.

———. "Chinese Middle Class Attitudes Towards International Affairs: Nascent Liberalization?" *The China Quarterly*, no. 179 (September 2004): 603–628.

Jones, Daniel M., Stuart A. Bremer, and J. David Singer. "Militarized Interstate Disputes, 1816–1992: Rationale, Coding Rules, and Empirical Patterns." *Conflict Management and Peace Science*, vol. 15, no. 2 (August 1996): 163–213.

Kacowicz, Arie M. *Peaceful Territorial Change.* Columbia: University of South Carolina Press, 1994.

Kao, Ting Tsz. *The Chinese Frontiers.* Aurora, Ill.: Chinese Scholarly Publishing, 1980.

Karawan, Ibrahim. "Foreign Policy Restructuring: Egypt's Disengagement from the Arab-Israeli Conflict Revisited." *Cambridge Review of International Affairs*, vol. 18, no. 3 (October 2005): 325–338.

Karmel, Solomon M. "Ethnic Tension and the Struggle for Order: China's Policies in Tibet." *Pacific Affairs*, vol. 68, no. 4 (1995): 485–508.

Kaul, B. M. *The Untold Story*. Bombay: Allied Publishers, 1967.

Kavic, Lorne J. *India's Quest for Security: Defence Policies, 1947–1965*. Berkeley: University of California Press, 1967.

Kharat, Rajesh S. *Foreign Policy of Bhutan*. New Delhi: Manak, 2005.

Kiang, Ying Cheng. *China's Boundaries*. Lincolnwood, Ill.: Institute of China Studies, 1984.

Kireyev, Genrikh. "Strategic Partnership and a Stable Border." *Far Eastern Affairs*, no. 4 (1997): 8–22.

———. "Demarcation of the Border with China." *International Affairs*, vol. 45, no. 2 (1999): 98–109.

———. "The Serpentine Path to the Shanghai G-5." *International Affairs*, vol. 49, no. 3 (2003): 85–92.

Kissinger, Henry. *White House Years*. Boston: Little, Brown & Co., 1979.

Knaus, John Kenneth. *Orphans of the Cold War: America and the Tibetan Struggle for Survival*. New York: Public Affairs, 1999.

Krasner, Stephen D. *Defending the National Interest: Raw Materials Investments and U.S. Foreign Policy*. Princeton, N.J.: Princeton University Press, 1978.

Kupchan, Charles A. *The Vulnerability of Empire*. Ithaca, N.Y.: Cornell University Press, 1994.

Kwong, Julia. "The 1986 Student Demonstrations in China: A Democratic Movement?" *Asian Survey*, vol. 28, no. 9 (September 1988): 970–985.

Lake, David A. "The State and American Trade Strategy in the Pre-hegemonic Era." *International Organization*, vol. 42, no. 1 (Winter 1988): 33–58.

Lall, Arthur. *How Communist China Negotiates*. New York: Columbia University Press, 1968.

———. *The Emergence of Modern India*. New York: Columbia University Press, 1981.

Lamb, Alastair. "The Sino-Pakistani Boundary Agreement of 2 March 1963." *Journal of the Australian Institute of International Affairs*, vol. 18, no. 3 (1964): 299–312.

———. *The McMahon Line: A Study in the Relations between India, China and Tibet, 1904–1914*. London: Routledge & K. Paul, 1966.

———. *Asian Frontiers: Studies in a Continuing Problem*. New York: Praeger, 1968.

———. *The Sino-Indian Border in Ladakh*. Canberra: Australian National University Press, 1973.

Lampton, David M. *Same Bed Different Dreams: Managing U.S.-China Relations, 1989–2000*. Berkeley: University of California Press, 2001.

Lardy, Nicholas. "The Chinese Economy under Stress, 1958–1965." In John King Fairbank and Roderick MacFarquhar, eds., *The Cambridge History of China*, vol. 14. Cambridge: Cambridge University Press, 1987.

Lattimore, Owen. *Inner Asian Frontiers of China*. New York: American Geographical Society, 1940.

Lebow, Richard N. "Windows of Opportunity: Do States Jump through Them?" *International Security*, vol. 9, no. 1 (Summer 1984): 147–186.

Lee Lai To. *China and the South China Sea Dialogues*. Westport, Conn.: Praeger, 1999.

Leeds, Brett Ashely, and David R. Davis. "Domestic Political Vulnerability and International Disputes." *Journal of Conflict Resolution*, vol. 41, no. 6 (December 1997): 814–834.

Lei Ming, ed. *Nansha zigu shu Zhonghua* [The Spratlys Are China's since Ancient Times]. Guangzhou: Guangzhou junqu silingbu bangongshi [internal circulation], 1988.

Lei Yingfu. *Zai zuigao tongshuaibu dang canmou: Lei Yingfu huiyilu* [Staff Officer at the Supreme Command: General Lei Yingfu's Recollections]. Nanchang: Baihuazhou wenyi chubanshe, 1997.

Leifer, Michael. *ASEAN and the Security of South-East Asia*. London: Routledge, 1989.

Leng Rong and Wang Zuoling, eds. *Deng Xiaoping nianpu, 1975–1997* [Chronicle of Deng Xiaoping's Life, 1975–1997]. 2 vols. Beijing: Zhongyang wenxian chubanshe, 2004.

Levy, Jack S. "Declining Power and the Preventive Motivation for War." *World Politics*, vol. 40, no. 1 (October 1987): 82–107.

———. "The Diversionary Theory of War: A Critique." In Manus I. Midlarsky, ed., *Handbook of War Studies*. Boston: Unwin Hyman, 1989.

Levy, Jack S., and Joseph R. Gochal. "Democracy and Preventive War: Israel and the 1956 Sinai Campaign." *Security Studies*, vol. 11, no. 2 (Winter 2001/2002): 1–49.

Lewis, John Wilson, and Litai Xue. *China Builds the Bomb*. Stanford, Calif.: Stanford University Press, 1988.

Li Danhui. "1969 nian ZhongSu bianjie chongtu: yuanqi he jieguo" [The 1969 Chinese-Soviet Border Conflict: Origins and Outcome]. *Dangdai Zhongguo shi yanjiu*, no. 3 (1996): 39–50.

———. "Dui 1962 nian Xinjiang Yita shijian qiyin de lishi kaocha (xu)" [Historical Investigation of the Origins of the 1962 Yita Incident in Xinjiang (cont.)]. *Dangshi yanjiu ziliao*, no. 5 (1999): 1–22.

Li Dechao. "Bailongwei dao zhengming" [Rectification of White Dragon Tail Island's Name]. *Zhongguo bianjiang shidi yanjiu baogao*, vols. 1–2, no. 3 (1988): 21–23.

Li Fenglin, "ZhongSu bianjie tanpan qinli ji" [Record of My Personal Experiences in the Chinese-Soviet Boundary Negotiations]. *Zhonggong dangshi ziliao*, no. 4 (2003): 25–35.

Li Fusheng, ed. *Xinjiang bingtuan tunken shubian shi* [History of the Xinjiang Production and Construction Corps' Development and Defense of the Frontier]. Wulumuqi: Xinjiang renmin chubanshe, 1997.

Li Hou. *Bainian quru shi de zhongjie: Xianggang wenti shimo* [The End of 100 Years of Humiliation: The Story of the Hong Kong Issue]. Beijing: Zhongyang wenxian chubanshe [internal circulation], 1997.

Li Jiasong, ed. *Zhonghua renmin gongheguo waijiao dashiji, di er juan* [Diplomatic Chronology of the PRC: Volume 2, January 1959–December 1964]. Beijing: Shijie zhishi chubanshe, 2001.

Li Jie. "Changes in China's Domestic Situation in the 1960s and Sino-US Relations." In Robert S. Ross and Jiang Changbin, eds., *Re-examining the Cold War: U.S.-China Diplomacy, 1954–1973*. Cambridge, Mass.: Harvard University Press, 2001.

Li Ke and Hao Shengzhang. *Wenhua dageming zhong de renmin jiefangjun* [The People's Liberation Army during the Cultural Revolution]. Beijing: Zhonggong dangshi ziliao chubanshe, 1989.

Li Li. "Nanwang de shishi, shenke de qishi: wo suo jingli de Xisha ziwei fanji zuozhan" [Memorable Facts, Profound Inspirations: My Personal Experience in the Paracels Self-defensive Counterattack Operation]. In *Zongcan moubu: huiyi shiliao* [General Staff Department: Recollections and Historial Materials]. Beijing: Jiefangjun chubanshe [military circulation], 1997.

Li Lianqing. *Lengnuan suiyue: yibo sanzhe de ZhongSu guanxi* [Hot and Cold Times: The Twists and Turns of Chinese-Soviet Relations]. Beijing: Shijie zhishi chubanshe, 1999.

Li Peisheng and Li Guozhen, eds. *Pingxi Xizang panluan* [Suppression of the Tibetan Rebellion]. Lasa: Xizang renmin chubanshe [internal circulation], 1995.

Li Ping and Ma Zhisun, eds. *Zhou Enlai nianpu, 1949–1976* [Chronicle of Zhou Enlai's Life, 1949–1976]. 3 vols. Beijing: Zhongyang wenxian chubanshe, 1997.

Li Sheng. *Xinjiang dui Su(E) maoyi shi (1600–1990)* [Xinjiang's Trade with the Soviet Union (Russia), 1600–1990]. Wulumuqi: Xinjiang renmin chubanshe, 1993.

Li Xiaobing. "Making of Mao's Cold War: The Taiwan Straits Crisis Revised." In Li Xiaobing and Li Hongshan, eds., *China and the United States: A New Cold War History*. Lanham, Md.: University Press of America, 1998.

———. "PLA Attacks and Amphibious Operations during the Taiwan Straits Crisis of 1954–55 and 1958." In Mark A. Ryan, David M. Finkelstein, and Michael A. McDevitt, eds., *Chinese Warfighting: The PLA Experience since 1949*. Armonk, N.Y.: M. E. Sharpe, 2003.

Li Xing, ed. *Bianfang xue* [The Science of Frontier Defense]. Beijing: Junshi kexue chubanshe, 2004.

Liao Xinwen. "1958 nian Mao Zedong juece paoji Jinmen de lishi kaocha" [A Historical Investigation of Mao Zedong's 1958 Decision to Shell Jinmen]. *Dang de wenxian*, no. 1 (1994): 31–36.

Lieberthal, Kenneth. "The Great Leap Forward and the Split in the Yenan Leadership." In John King Fairbank and Roderick MacFarquhar, eds., *The Cambridge History of China*, vol. 14. Cambridge: Cambridge University Press, 1987.

Lieberthal, Kenneth, and Michel Oksenberg. *Policy Making in China: Leaders, Structures, and Processes*. Princeton, N.J.: Princeton University Press, 1988.

Lin Daoyuan, ed. *Nansha gaosu women* [What the Spratly Islands Tell Us]. Beijing: Haijun chubanshe, 1988.

Liu Hongxuan. *Zhongguo mulin shi: Zhongguo yu zhoubian guojia guanxi* [History of Good-Neighborliness: China's Relations with Peripheral States]. Beijing: Shijie zhishi chubanshe, 2001.

Liu Huaqing. *Liu Huaqing huiyilu* [Liu Huaqing's Memoirs]. Beijing: Jiefangjun chubanshe, 2004.

Liu Shufa, ed. *Chen Yi nianpu* [Chronicle of Chen Yi's Life]. Beijing: Zhongyang wenxian chubanshe, 1995.

Liu Wusheng and Du Hongqi, eds. *Zhou Enlai junshi huodong jishi, 1918–1975 (xia)* [Chronicle of Zhou Enlai's Military Activities]. Vol. 2. Beijing: Zhongyang wenxian chubanshe, 2000.

Liu Xiao. *Chushi Sulian ba nian* [Eight Years as Ambassador to the Soviet Union]. Beijing: Zhonggong dangshi ziliao chubanshe, 1986.

Liu Zhinan. "1969 nian, Zhongguo zhanbei yu dui MeiSu guanxi de yanjiu he tiaozheng" [China's War Preparations and the Study of the Readjustment of Relations with the U.S. and Soviet Union in 1969]. *Dangdai Zhongguo shi yanjiu*, no. 3 (1999): 41–57.

Lo Chi-kin. *China's Policy towards Territorial Disputes: The Case of the South China Sea Islands*. New York: Routledge, 1989.

Lu Hui. *Sanjun shouzhan Yijiangshan* [Three Armed Services First Battle Yijiang-shan]. Beijing: Jiefangjun chubanshe, 1988.

Lu Jianren. "Nansha zhengduan ji duice" [Policy Options in the Nansha Dispute]. In Yatai yanjiu suo, ed., *Nansha wenti yanjiu ziliao*. Beijing: Zhongguo shehui kexueyuan [internal circulation], 1996.

Lu Ning. *Flashpoint Spratlys!* Singapore: Dolphin Press, 1995.

———. *The Dynamics of Foreign-Policy Decisionmaking in China*. Boulder, Colo.: Westview, 1997.

Luthi, Lorenz. *The Sino-Soviet Split*. Princeton, N.J: Princeton University Press, 2008.

Ma Dazheng, ed. *Zhongguo bianjiang jinglue shi* [A History of China's Frontier Administration]. Zhengzhou: Zhongzhou guji chubanshe, 2000.

Ma Dazheng and Liu Ti. *Ershi shiji de Zhongguo bianjiang yanjiu: yimen fazhan zhong de bianyuan xueke de yanjin licheng* [China's Borderland Research in the Twentieth Century: The Evolving History of the Dual Discipline of Borderland Study]. Ha'erbin: Heilongjiang jiaoyu chubanshe, 1998.

Ma Jinan. "Zhongguo jundui jingwai de yichang mimi zhanzheng" [The Chinese Military's Secret War across the Border]. *Dongnanya zongheng*, no. 1 (2001): 11–12.

Ma Xusheng. "Takan bianjie tanpan jiaofeng: zhaohui shiluo de guojiexian (er)" [On-the-Spot Survey of Battles in Boundary Negotiations: Retrieving Lost National Boundaries]. *Shijie zhishi*, no. 12 (2001): 42–43.

MacFarquhar, Roderick. *The Origins of the Cultural Revolution*. 3 vols. New York: Columbia University Press, 1974, 1983, 1997.

MacFarquhar, Roderick, Timothy Cheek, and Eugene Wu, eds. *The Secret Speeches of Chairman Mao: From the Hundred Flowers to the Great Leap Forward*. Cambridge, Mass.: Harvard University, Council on East Asian Studies, 1989.

MacFarquhar, Roderick, and Michael Schoenhals. *Mao's Last Revolution*. Cambridge, Mass.: Belknap Press of Harvard University Press, 2006.

Mandel, Robert. "Roots of the Modern Interstate Border Dispute." *Journal of Conflict Resolution*, vol. 24, no. 3 (September 1980): 427–454.

Mansfield, Edward D., and Jack L. Snyder. *Electing to Fight: Why Emerging Democracies Go to War*. Cambridge, Mass.: MIT Press, 2005.

Mao Zedong waijiao wenxuan [Mao Zedong's Selected Works on Diplomacy]. Beijing: Shijie zhishi chubanshe, 1994.

Mao Zedong wenji [Mao Zedong's Collected Works]. 8 vols. Beijing: Xinhua chubanshe, 1993–1999.

Mao Zhenfa, ed. *Bianfang lun* [On Frontier Defense]. Beijing: Junshi kexue chubanshe [internal circulation], 1996.

Mastanduno, Michael, David A. Lake, and G. John Ikenberry. "Toward a Realist Theory of State Action." *International Studies Quarterly*, vol. 33, no. 4 (December 1989): 457–474.

Maxwell, Neville. *India's China War.* New York: Pantheon Books, 1970.

———. "The Chinese Account of the 1969 Fighting at Chenpao." *The China Quarterly*, no. 56 (December 1973): 730–739.

———. "A Note on the Amur/Ussuri Sector of the Sino-Soviet Boundaries." *Modern China*, vol. 1, no. 1 (1975): 116–126.

McCarthy, Roger E. *Tears of the Lotus: Accounts of Tibetan Resistance to the Chinese Invasion, 1950–1962.* Jefferson, N.C.: McFarland & Company, 1997.

McNeal, Dewardric L. *China's Relations with Central Asian States and Problems with Terrorism.* Washington, D.C.: Library of Congress, Congressional Research Service, 2001.

Mearsheimer, John J. *The Tragedy of Great Power Politics.* New York: W. W. Norton, 2001.

Medeiros, Evan S., and M. Taylor Fravel. "China's New Diplomacy." *Foreign Affairs*, vol. 82, no. 6 (November/December 2003): 22–35.

Meernik, James, and Peter Waterman. "The Myth of the Diversionary Use of Force by American Presidents." *Political Research Quarterly*, vol. 49, no. 3 (September 1996): 575–590.

Meng Zhaobi, ed. *Xinjiang tongzhi: junshi zhi* [Xinjiang Gazetteer: Military Affairs]. Wulumuqi: Xinjiang renmin chubanshe, 1997.

Millward, James. *Beyond the Pass: Economy, Ethnicity and Empire in Qing Central Asia, 1759–1864.* Stanford, Calif.: Stanford University Press, 1998.

Morgan, T. Clifton, and Kenneth N. Bickers. "Domestic Discontent and the Use of Force." *Journal of Conflict Resolution*, vol. 36, no. 1 (March 1992): 25–52.

Morgenthau, Hans J. *Politics among Nations: The Struggle for Power and Peace.* 3rd ed. New York: Knopf, 1960.

Mote, Frederick. *Imperial China: 900–1800.* Cambridge, Mass.: Harvard University Press, 1999.

Muller, David G. *China's Emergence as a Maritime Power.* Boulder, Colo.: Westview Press, 1983.

Mullik, B. N. *My Years with Nehru: The Chinese Betrayal.* Bombay: Allied Publishers, 1971.

Muni, S. D. *Foreign Policy of Nepal.* New Delhi: National Publishing House, 1973.

National Assembly of Bhutan. *Translation of the Proceedings and Resolutions of the 77th Session of the National Assembly of Bhutan.* Thimpu: National Assembly of Bhutan, 1999.

National Intelligence Board. *Chinese Communist Capabilities and Intentions in the Far East*, SNIE 13-3-61 [Top Secret]. Washington, D.C.: Central Intelligence Agency, 1961.

National Intelligence Board. *The USSR and China*, NIE 11–13–69 [Top Secret]. Washington, D.C.: Central Intelligence Agency, 1969.

————. *Communist China's General Purpose and Air Defense Forces*, NIE 13–3-70 [Top Secret]. Washington, D.C.: Central Intelligence Agency, 1970.

————. *Warsaw Pact Forces for Operations In Eurasia*, NIE 11–14–71 [Top Secret]. Washington, D.C.: Central Intelligence Agency, 1971.

Ni Fuhan and Huang Ke, eds. *Heping jiefang Xizang* [The Peaceful Liberation of Tibet]. Lasa: Xizang renmin chubanshe [internal circulation], 1995.

Nie Fengzhi et al., eds. *Sanjun huige zhan donghai* [The Three Armed Services March into Battle in the East China Sea]. Beijing: Jiefangjun chubanshe, 1985.

Niu Jun. "1969 nian ZhongSu bianjie chongtu yu Zhongguo waijiao zhanlue de tiaozheng" [The 1969 Chinese-Soviet Border Conflict and the Restructuring of China's Diplomatic Strategy]. *Dangdai Zhongguo shi yanjiu*, no. 1 (1999): 66–77.

————. "Sanci Taiwan haixia junshi douzheng juece yanjiu" [A Study of Decision Making in Three Military Battles in the Taiwan Strait]. *Zhongguo shehui kexue*, no. 5 (2004): 37–50.

Niu Zhongxun. *Zhongguo bianjiang dili* [China's Frontier Geography]. Beijing: Renmin jiaoyu chubanshe, 1991.

Norbu, Dawa. *China's Tibet Policy*. London: Curzon Press, 2001.

Norbu, Jamyang. "The Tibetan Resistance Movement and the Role of the CIA." In Robert Barnett, ed., *Resistance and Reform in Tibet*. London: Hurst and Company, 1994.

O'Dowd, Edward C. *Chinese Military Strategy in the Third Indochina War: The Last Maoist War*. New York: Routledge, 2007.

Office of National Estimates. *The Soviet Military Buildup along the Chinese Border*, SM-7–68 [Top Secret]. Washington, D.C.: Central Intelligence Agency, 1968.

Office of the Secretary of Defense. *Annual Report to Congress: The Military Power of the People's Republic of China*. Washington, D.C.: Department of Defense, 2005.

Organski, A.F.K. *World Politics*. New York: Alfred A. Knopf, 1958.

Palit, D. K. *War in High Himalaya: The Indian Army in Crisis, 1962*. New Delhi: Lancer International, 1991.

Palmer, David Scott. "Peru-Ecuador Border Conflict: Missed Opportunities, Misplaced Nationalism, and Multilateral Peacekeeping." *Journal of Interamerican Studies and World Affairs*, vol. 39, no. 3 (Autumn 1997): 109–148.

Pang Xianzhi and Jin Chongji, eds. *Mao Zedong zhuan* [Mao Zedong's Biography]. 2 vols. Beijing: Zhongyang wenxian chubanshe, 2003.

Paul, T. V. *Asymmetric Conflicts: War Initiation by Weaker Powers*. Cambridge: Cambridge University Press, 1994.

Payne, S.C.M. *Imperial Rivals: China, Russia, and Their Disputed Frontier*. Armonk, N.Y.: M. E. Sharpe, 1996.

Peceny, Mark, Caroline C. Beer, and Shannon Sanchez-Terry. "Dictatorial Peace?" *American Political Science Review*, vol. 96, no. 1 (March 2002): 15–26.

Pei Jianzhang and Feng Yaoyuan, eds. *Zhou Enlai waijiao huodong dashiji* [Record of Zhou Enlai's Diplomatic Activities]. Beijing: Shijie zhishi chubanshe, 1993.

Perdue, Peter C. *China Marches West: The Qing Conquest of Central Eurasia.* Cambridge, Mass.: Belknap Press of Harvard University Press, 2005.

Petech, Luciano. *China and Tibet in the Early 18th Century: History of the Establishment of Chinese Protectorate in Tibet.* Leiden: Brill, 1972.

Prasad, Niranjan. *The Fall of Towang, 1962.* New Delhi: Palit & Palit, 1981.

Praval, K. C. *The Red Eagles: A History of the Fourth Division of India.* New Delhi: Vision Books, 1982.

Prescott, J.R.V. *Map of Mainland Asia by Treaty.* Carlton: Melbourne University Press, 1975.

Prescott, J.R.V., Harold John Collier, and Dorothy F. Prescott. *Frontiers of Asia and Southeast Asia.* Carlton: Melbourne University Press, 1977.

Putnam, Robert D. "Diplomacy and Domestic Politics: The Logic of Two-Level Games." *International Organization,* vol. 42, no. 3 (Summer 1988): 427–460.

Qi Pengfei. *Deng Xiaoping yu Xianggang huigui* [Deng Xiaoping and the Return of Hong Kong]. Beijing: Huaxia chubanshe, 2004.

Qi Pengfei and Zhang Xiaojing. *Aomen de shiluo yu huigui* [Macao's Loss and Return]. Beijing: Xinhua chubanshe, 1999.

Qian Qichen. *Waijiao shiji* [Ten Stories of a Diplomat]. Beijing: Shijie zhishi chubanshe, 2003.

Qin Wencai. *Shiyou shiren: zai haiyang shiyou zhanxian jishi* [Oil Brigade: The Record of the Battle for Offshore Oil]. Beijing: Shiyou gongye chubanshe, 1997.

Qu Xing. "Shilun DongOu jubian he Sulian jieti hou de Zhongguo waijiao zhengce" [On China's Foreign Policy after the Sudden Change in Eastern Europe and the Disintegration of the Soviet Union]. *Waijiao xueyuan xuebao,* no. 4 (1994): 16–22.

———. *Zhongguo waijiao 50 nian* [50 Years of Chinese Diplomacy]. Nanjing: Jiangsu renmin chubanshe, 2000.

Rasler, Karen A., and William R. Thompson. "Contested Territory, Strategic Rivalries, and Conflict Escalation." *International Studies Quarterly,* vol. 50, no. 1 (March 2006): 145–167.

Ray, Hemen. *China's Strategy in Nepal.* New Delhi: Radiant Publishers, 1983.

Razvi, Mujtaba. *The Frontiers of Pakistan: A Study of Frontier Problems in Pakistan's Foreign Policy.* Karachi-Dacca: National Publishing House, 1971.

Report of the Officials of the Governments of India and the People's Republic of China on the Boundary Question. New Delhi: Ministry of External Affairs, 1961.

Rigger, Shelly. *Taiwan's Rising Rationalism: Generations, Politics and "Taiwan's Nationalism."* Policy Studies no. 26. Washington, D.C.: East-West Center, 2006.

Robinson, Thomas W. *The Sino-Soviet Border Dispute: Background, Development and the March 1969 Clashes.* Santa Monica, Calif.: RAND Corp., 1970.

———. "The Sino-Soviet Border Conflict." In Stephen S. Kaplan, ed., *Diplomacy of Power: Soviet Armed Forces as a Political Instrument.* Washington, D.C.: The Brookings Institution, 1981.

———. "China Confronts the Soviet Union: Warfare and Diplomacy on China's Inner Asian Frontiers." In Roderick MacFarquhar and John K. Fairbank, eds., *The Cambridge History of China,* vol. 15, part 2. Cambridge: Cambridge University Press, 1991.

Romberg, Alan D. *Rein In at the Brink of the Precipice: American Policy toward Taiwan and U.S.-PRC Relations*. Washington, D.C.: Henry Stimson Center, 2003.

Rose, Leo E. *Nepal: Strategy for Survival*. Berkeley: University of California Press, 1971.

Ross, Robert S. *The Indochina Tangle: China's Vietnam Policy, 1975–1979*. New York: Columbia University Press, 1988.

———. *Negotiating Cooperation: The United States and China, 1969–1989*. Stanford, Calif.: Stanford University Press, 1995.

———. "The Diplomacy of Tiananmen: Two-Level Bargaining and Great-Power Cooperation." *Security Studies*, vol. 10, no. 2 (Winter 2000/2001): 139–178.

———. "The 1995–1996 Taiwan Strait Confrontation: Coercion, Credibility and the Use of Force." *International Security*, vol. 25, no. 2 (Fall 2000): 87–123.

———. "Navigating the Taiwan Strait: Deterrence, Escalation Dominance and U.S.-China Relations." *International Security*, vol. 27, no. 2 (Fall 2002): 48–85.

———. "Taiwan's Fading Independence Movement." *Foreign Affairs*, vol. 85, no. 2 (March/April 2006): 141–148.

Rossabi, Morris. *China and Inner Asia: From 1368 to the Present Day*. New York: PICA Press, 1975.

Rupen, Robert A. "Mongolia in the Sino-Soviet Dispute." *The China Quarterly*, no. 16 (October–December 1963): 75–85.

Russett, Bruce. *Grasping the Democratic Peace*. Princeton, N.J.: Princeton University Press, 1993.

Samuels, Marwyn S. *Contest for the South China Sea*. New York: Methuen, 1982.

Saunders, Philip C. *China's Global Activism: Strategy, Drivers and Tools*. Occasional Paper 4. Washington, D.C.: Institute for National Strategic Studies, National Defense University, 2006.

Saunders, Phillip C., and Erica Strecker Downs. "Legitimacy and the Limits of Nationalism: China and the Diaoyu Islands." *International Security*, vol. 23, no. 3 (Winter 1998/1999): 114–146.

Sawhney, Pravin. *The Defence Makeover: 10 Myths That Shape India's Image*. New Delhi: Sage Publications, 2002.

Schweller, Randall. "Neorealism's Status-Quo Bias: What Security Dilemma?" *Security Studies*, vol. 5, no. 3 (Spring 1996): 90–121.

———. "The Progressiveness of Neoclassical Realism." In Colin Elman and Miriam Fendius Elman, eds., *Progress in International Relations Theory: Appraising the Field*. Cambridge, Mass.: MIT Press, 2003.

———. *Unanswered Threats: Political Constraints on the Balance of Power*. Princeton, N.J.: Princeton University Press, 2006.

Scobell, Andrew. *China's Use of Military Force: Beyond the Great Wall and the Long March*. New York: Cambridge University Press, 2003.

Searls, Guy. "Communist China's Border Policy: Dragon Throne Imperialism?" *Current Scene*, vol. 11, no. 12 (15 April 1963): 1–22.

Segal, Gerald. *Defending China*. Oxford: Oxford University Press, 1985.

———. *China Changes Shape: Regionalism and Foreign Policy*. Adelphi Paper no. 287. London: International Institute for Strategic Studies, 1994.

Sen, A, ed. *Zhongguo lujiang fengyun lu* [The Stormy Record of China's Territory]. Beijing: Luyou jiaoyu chubanshe, 1993.

Seyd, Anwar Hussain. *China and Pakistan: Diplomacy of Entente Cordiale.* Amherst: University of Massachusetts Press, 1974.

Sha Li and Ai Yi. *Zhongguo haijun zhengzhan jishi* [Record of the Expeditions of China's Navy]. Chengdu: Dianzi keji daxue chubanshe, 1993.

Shakya, Tsering. *The Dragon in the Land of the Snows: A History of Modern Tibet since 1947.* New York: Penguin Compass, 1999.

Shambaugh, David S. "China Engages Asia: Reshaping International Order." *International Security,* vol. 29, no. 3 (Winter 2004/05): 64–99.

Shen Bingnian, ed. *Xinjiang tongzhi: waishi zhi* [Xinjiang Gazetteer: Foreign Affairs]. Wulumuqi: Xinjiang renmin chubanshe, 1995.

Shen Weiping. *8.23 paoji Jinmen* [August 23 Shelling of Jinmen]. Beijing: Huayi chubanshe, 1998.

Shephard, John Robert. *Statecraft and Political Economy on the Taiwan Frontier, 1600–1800.* Stanford, Calif.: Stanford University Press, 1993.

Shi Bo. *1962: ZhongYin dazhan jishi* [Record of the China-India War]. Beijing: Dadi chubanshe, 1993.

Shi Yuanhua. "Lun xin Zhongguo zhoubian waijiao zhengce de lishi yanbian" [On the Historical Evolution of New China's Peripheral Foreign Policy]. *Dangdai Zhongguo shi yanjiu,* vol. 7, no. 5 (2000): 38–50.

Shi Zhongquan. *Zhou Enlai de zhuoyue gongxian* [Zhou Enlai's Great Contributions]. Beijng: Zhonggong zhongyang dangxiao chubanshe, 1993.

Shichor, Yitzhak. "Separatism: Sino-Muslim Conflict in Xinjiang." *Pacifica Review,* vol. 6, no. 2 (1994): 71–82.

Shipp, Steve. *Macau, China: A Political History of the Portuguese Colony's Transition to Chinese Rule.* Jefferson, N.C.: McFarland & Company, 1997.

Shirk, Susan L. *China: Fragile Superpower.* New York: Oxford University Press, 2007.

Sidhu, Waheguru Pal Singh, and Jing-dong Yuan. "Resolving the Sino-Indian Border Dispute." *Asian Survey,* vol. 41, no. 2 (March/April 2001): 351–376.

Simmons, Beth A. *Territorial Disputes and Their Resolution: The Case of Ecuador and Peru.* Peaceworks no. 27. Washington, D.C.: United States Institute of Peace, 1999.

———. "Rules over Real Estate: Trade, Territorial Conflict, and International Borders as Institution." *Journal of Conflict Resolution,* vol. 49, no. 6 (December 2005): 823–848.

Smith, Warren W. *Tibetan Nation: A History of Tibetan Nationalism and Sino-Tibetan Relations.* Boulder, Colo.: Westview, 1996.

Snyder, Scott, Brad Glosserman, and Ralph A. Cossa. *Confidence Building Measures in the South China Sea.* Honolulu: Pacific Forum CSIS, 2001.

Song Liansheng and Gong Xiaohua. *Duizhi wushi nian* [Fifty Years of Confrontation]. Beijing: Taihai chubanshe, 2000.

Spence, Jonathan. *The Search for Modern China.* New York: W. W. Norton, 1990.

Stolper, Thomas E. *China, Taiwan, and the Offshore Islands: Together with Some Implications for Outer Mongolia and Sino-Soviet Relations.* Armonk, N.Y.: M. E. Sharpe, 1985.

Su Yongwen, Qiu Xinyan, and Xia Zhongchun, eds. *Aletai diqu zhi* [Altay Prefecture Gazetteer]. Wulumuqi: Xinjiang renmin chubanshe, 2004.

Su Yu wenxuan [Su Yu's Selected Works]. 3 vols. Beijing: Junshi kexue chubanshe, 2004.

Suettinger, Robert L. *Beyond Tiananmen: The Politics of U.S.-China Relations, 1989–2000*. Washington, D.C.: The Brookings Institution, 2003.

Sun Cuibing, ed. *Yunnan shengzhi: junshi zhi* [Yunnan Provincial Gazetteer: Military Affairs]. Kunming: Yunnan renmin chubanshe, 1997.

Sun Xiao and Chen Zhibin. *Ximalaya shan de xue: ZhongYin zhanzheng shilu* [Himalayan Snow: Record of the China-India War]. Taiyuan: Beiyue wenyi chubanshe, 1991.

Suri, Jeremi. *Power and Protest: Global Revolution and the Rise of Detente*. Cambridge, Mass.: Harvard University Press, 2003.

Sutter, Robert G. *China's Rise in Asia: Promises and Perils*. Lanham, M.D.: Rowman and Littlefield, 2005.

Swaine, Michael D. "Chinese Decision-Making Regarding Taiwan, 1979–2000." In David M. Lampton, ed., *The Making of Chinese Foreign and Security Policy in the Era of Reform*. Stanford, Calif.: Stanford University Press, 2001.

Swaine, Michael D., and Ashley J. Tellis. *Interpreting China's Grand Strategy: Past, Present, and Future*. Santa Monica, Calif.: RAND, 2000.

Tang Jiaxuan, ed. *Zhongguo waijiao cidian* [Dictionary of China's Diplomacy]. Beijing: Shijie zhishi chubanshe, 2000.

Teiwes, Frederick C., and Warren Sun. *China's Road to Disaster: Mao, Central Politicians and Provincial Leaders in the Unfolding of the Great Leap Forward, 1955–1959*. Armonk, N.Y.: M. E. Sharpe, 1999.

Teng, Emma J. *Taiwan's Imagined Geography: Chinese Colonial Travel Writing and Pictures, 1683–1895*. Cambridge, Mass.: Harvard University Press, 2004.

Thatcher, Margaret. *The Downing Street Years*. London: HarperCollins, 1993.

Tian Zengpei, ed. *Gaige kaifang yilai de Zhongguo waijiao* [China's Diplomacy since Reform and Opening]. Beijing: Shijie zhishi chubanshe, 1993.

Toft, Monica Duffy. *The Geography of Ethnic Violence: Identity, Interests, and the Indivisibility of Territory*. Princeton, N.J.: Princeton University Press, 2003.

Touval, Saadia. *The Boundary Politics of Independent Africa*. Cambridge, Mass.: Harvard University Press, 1972.

Tretiak, Daniel. "The Sino-Japanese Treaty of 1978: The Senkaku Incident Prelude." *Asian Survey*, vol. 18, no. 12 (December 1978): 1235–1249.

Tsui Tsien-hua. *The Sino-Soviet Border Dispute in the 1970's*. New York: Mosaic Press, 1983.

Tulchin, Joseph S. *Argentina and the United States: A Conflicted Relationship*. Boston: Twayne, 1990.

Tzou, Byron N. *China and International Law: the Boundary Disputes*. New York: Praeger, 1990.

Ulam, Adam B. *Expansion and Coexistence: The History of Soviet Foreign Policy, 1917–67*. New York: Frederick A. Praeger, 1968.

Van Evera, Stephen. "The Cult of the Offensive and the Origins of the First World War." *International Security*, vol. 9, no. 1 (Summer 1984): 58–107.

———. "Hypotheses on Nationalism and War." *International Security*, vol. 18, no. 4 (Spring 1994): 5–39.

———. *Causes of War: Power and the Roots of Conflict*. Ithaca, N.Y.: Cornell University Press, 1999.

Vasquez, John A. *The War Puzzle*. New York: Cambridge University Press, 1993.

Vasquez, John, and Marie T. Henehan. "Territorial Disputes and the Probability of War, 1816–1992." *Journal of Peace Research*, vol. 38, no. 2 (2001): 123–138.

Voskresensky, Alexei. "Some Border Issues Unsolved." *New Times*, no. 19 (1991): 26–27.

Wachman, Alan M. *Why Taiwan? Geostrategic Rationales for China's Territorial Integrity*. Stanford, Calif.: Stanford University Press, 2007.

Wagner, R. Harrison. "Bargaining and War." *American Journal of Political Science*, vol. 44, no. 3 (July 2000): 469–484.

Waijiao bu, ed. *Zhonghua renmin gongheguo bianjie shiwu tiaoyue ji: ZhongA ZhongBa juan* [Collection of Treaties on the PRC's Boundary Affairs: China-Afghanistan, China-Pakistan]. Beijing: Shijie zhishi chubanshe [internal circulation], 2004.

———, ed. *Zhonghua renmin gongheguo bianjie shiwu tiaoyue ji: Zhong-Yin ZhongBu juan* [Collection of Treaties on the PRC's Boundary Affairs: China-India, China-Bhutan]. Beijing: Shijie zhishi chubanshe [internal circulation], 2004.

———, ed. *Zhonghua renmin gongheguo bianjie shiwu tiaoyue ji: ZhongHa juan* [Collection of Treaties on the PRC's Boundary Affairs: China-Kazakhstan]. Beijing: Shijie zhishi chubanshe [internal circulation], 2005.

———, ed. *Zhonghua renmin gongheguo bianjie shiwu tiaoyue ji: ZhongJi juan* [Collection of Treaties on the PRC's Boundary Affairs: China-Kyrgyzstan]. Beijing: Shijie zhishi chubanshe [internal circulation], 2005.

———, ed. *Zhonghua renmin gongheguo bianjie shiwu tiaoyue ji: ZhongTa juan* [Collection of Treaties on the PRC's Boundary Affairs: China-Tajikistan]. Beijing: Shijie zhishi chubanshe [internal circulation], 2005.

———. *Zhonghua renmin gongheguo bianjie shiwu tiaoyue ji: ZhongYue juan* [Collection of Treaties on the PRC's Boundary Affairs: China-Vietnam]. Beijing: Shishi chubanshe [internal circulation], 2004.

Walder, Andrew G., and Yang Su. "The Cultural Revolution in the Countryside: Scope, Timing and Human Impact." *The China Quarterly*, no. 173 (March 2003): 75–99.

Walt, Stephen M. *The Origins of Alliances*. Ithaca, N.Y.: Cornell University Press, 1987.

———. *Revolution and War*. Ithaca, N.Y.: Cornell University Press, 1996.

Walter, Barbara F. "Explaining the Intractability of Territorial Conflict." *International Studies Review*, vol. 5, no. 4 (December 2003): 137–153.

Waltz, Kenneth N. *Theory of International Politics*. New York: McGraw-Hill, 1979.

Wang Bingnan. *ZhongMei huitan jiunian huigu* [Reflections on Nine Years of Chinese-American Talks]. Beijing: Shijie zhishi chubanshe, 1985.

Wang Chenghan. *Wang Chenghan huiyilu* [Wang Chenghan's Memoirs]. Beijing: Jiefangjun chubanshe, 2004.

Wang, David D. *Under the Soviet Shadow: The Yining Incident*. Hong Kong: The Chinese University Press, 1999.

Wang Enmao wenji [Wang Enmao's Collected Works]. Beijing: Zhongyang wenxian chubanshe, 1997.

Wang Hongwei. *Ximalaya shan qingjie: ZhongYin guanxi yanjiu* [Himalayan Sentiments: A Study of Chinese-Indian Relations]. Beijing: Zhongguo zangxue chubanshe, 1998.

Wang Shangrong. "ZhongYin bianjing ziwei fanji zuozhan shijian de zongcan zuozhan bu" [The GSD's Operations Department during the Chinese-Indian Border Counterattack in Self-defense]. In *Zongcan moubu: huiyi shiliao* [General Staff Department: Recollections and Historical Materials]. Beijing: Jiefangjun chubanshe [military circulation], 1997.

———. "Xin Zhongguo dansheng hou jici zhongda zhanzheng" [Several Major Wars after the Emergence of New China]. In Zhu Yuanshi, ed., *Gongheguo yaoshi koushushi* [An Oral History of the Republic's Important Events]. Changsha: Henan renmin chubanshe, 1999.

Wang Shanzhong. "Lunshu Zhonghua renmin gongheguo he Miandian lianbang bianjie tiaoyue" [Discussion of the Boundary Treaty between the People's Republic of China and Union of Burma]. *Zhongguo bianjiang shidi yanjiu*, no. 1 (1997): 78–84.

Wang Shuanqian, ed. *Zouxiang 21 shiji de Xinjiang: zhengzhi juan* [Xinjiang Moving toward the 21st Century: Politics]. Wulumuqi: Xinjiang renmin chubanshe, 1999.

Wang Taiping, ed. *Deng Xiaoping waijiao sixiang yanjiu lunwenji* [Collected Papers on the Study of Deng Xiaoping's Diplomatic Thought]. Beijing: Shijie zhishi chubanshe, 1996.

———, ed. *Zhonghua renmin gongheguo waijiao shi, 1957–1969* [Diplomatic History of the People's Republic of China, 1957–1969]. Beijing: Shijie zhishi chubanshe, 1998.

Wang Wenrong, ed. *Zhanlue xue* [The Science of Military Strategy]. Beijing: Guofang daxue chubanshe, 1999.

Wang Yan. *Mubiao, Yijiangshan—Wojun shouci luhaikong lianhe duhai denglu zuozhan jishi* [Target, Yijiangshan: Record of Our Army's First Land, Sea, and Air Joint Amphibious Landing Operation]. Beijing: Haichao chubanshe, 1990.

———, ed. *Peng Dehuai nianpu* [Chronicle of Peng Dehuai's Life]. Beijing: Renmin chubanshe, 1998.

Wang Yinqing and Zhaori Getu, eds. *Neimenggu zizhiqu zhi: junshi zhi* [Inner Mongolian Autonomous Region Gazetteer: Military Affairs]. Huhehaote: Neimenggu renmin chubanshe, 2002.

Wang Zhongxing. "60 niandai ZhongYin bianjing chongtu yu Zhongguo bianfang budui de ziwei fanji zuozhan" [The 1960s Chinese-Indian Border Conflict and the Counterattack in Self-defense of China's Frontier Defense Troops]. *Dangdai Zhongguo yanjiu*, no. 5 (1997).

Wang Ziwen, ed. *Fujian shengzhi: junshi zhi* [Fujian Provincial Gazetteer: Military Affairs]. Beijing: Xinhua chubanshe, 1995.

Watson, Francis. *The Frontiers of China*. New York: Praeger, 1966.

Way, Christopher R. "Political Insecurity and the Diffusion of Financial Market Regulation." *The ANNALS of the American Academy of Political and Social Science*, vol. 598, no. 1 (2005): 125–144.

Wei Ling and Sun Jiewan. *Deng Xiaoping waijiao sixiang tanjiu* [Research on Deng Xiaoping's Diplomatic Thought]. Beijing: Zhongyang wenxian chubanse, 2000.

Wei Mingsen. "Xisha ziwei fanji zhan" [Paracels Counterattack in Self-defense]. In *Haijun: huiyi shiliao* [Navy: Recollections and Historical Materials]. Beijing: Jiefangjun chubanshe [military circulation], 1997.

Wei Zhongli and Song Xianchun, eds. *Guonei anquan baowei* [Safeguarding Internal Security]. Beijing: Jingguan jiaoyu chubanshe [internal circulation], 1999.

Whiting, Allen S. *China Crosses the Yalu: The Decision to Enter the Korean War.* New York: Macmillan, 1960.

———. *The Chinese Calculus of Deterrence: India and Indochina.* Ann Arbor: University of Michigan Press, 1975.

———. "China's Use of Force, 1950–96, and Taiwan." *International Security*, vol. 26, no. 2 (Fall 2001): 103–131.

Whitney, Joseph. *China: Area, Administration and Nation Building.* Department of Geography Research Paper no. 123. Chicago: University of Chicago, 1970.

Whittam, Daphne E. "The Sino-Burmese Boundary Treaty." *Pacific Affairs*, vol. 34, no. 2 (Summer 1961): 174–183.

Wich, Richard. *Sino-Soviet Crisis Politics: A Study of Political Change and Communication.* Cambridge, Mass.: Harvard University Press, 1980.

Wiens, Herold J. *China's March toward the Tropics.* Hamden, Conn.: Shoe String Press, 1954.

Winchester, Michael. "Beijing vs. Islam." *Asiaweek*, vol. 23, no. 42 (1997): 31.

Wishnick, Elizabeth. *Mending Fences: The Evolution of Moscow's China Policy from Brezhnev to Yeltsin.* Seattle: University of Washington Press, 2001.

Wohlforth, William Curti. *The Elusive Balance: Power and Perceptions during the Cold War.* Ithaca, N.Y.: Cornell University Press, 1993.

Wolff, David. " 'One Finger's Worth of Historical Events?' New Russian and Chinese Evidence on the Sino-Soviet Alliance and Split, 1948–1959." *Cold War International History Project Working Paper*, no. 30 (2000).

Woodman, Dorothy. *The Making of Burma.* London: The Cresset Press, 1962.

Wu Lengxi. *Yi Mao zhuxi: wo qinshen jingli de ruogan zhongda lishi shijian pianduan* [Remembering Chairman Mao: Fragments of Certain Major Historical Events Which I Personally Experienced]. Beijing: Xinhua chubanshe, 1995.

———. *Shinian lunzhan: 1956–1966 ZhongSu guanxi huiyilu* [Ten Years of Polemics: A Recollection of Chinese-Soviet Relations from 1956 to 1966]. 2 vols. Beijing: Zhongyang wenxian chubanshe, 1999.

Wu Shicun. *Nasha zhengduan de youlai yu fazhan* [Origin and Development of the Nansha Disputes]. Beijing: Haiyang Chubanshe [internal circulation], 1999.

Xiao Xinli, ed. *Mao Zedong yu gongheguo zhongda lishi shijian* [Mao Zedong and Major Historical Events of the Republic]. Bejiing: Renmin chubanshe, 2001.

Xie Yixian. *Zhongguo dangdai waijiao shi (1949–1995)* [History of China's Contemporary Diplomacy (1949–1995)]. Beijing: Zhongguo qingnian chubanshe, 1997.

Xing Guangcheng. "China and Central Asia: Towards a New Relationship." In Yongjin Zhang and Rouben Azizian, eds., *Ethnic Challenges beyond Borders: Chinese and Russian Perspectives of the Central Asia Conundrum*. New York: St. Martin's Press, 1998.

———. "China and Central Asia." In Roy Allison and Lena Jonson, eds., *Central Asian Security: The New International Context*. Washington, D.C.: The Brookings Institution, 2001.

Xinjiang tongzhi: gongan zhi [Xinjiang Gazetteer: Public Security]. Wulumuqi: Xinjiang renmin chubanshe, 2004.

Xu Ge. *Tiemao gu haijiang: gongheguo haizhan shiji* [Steel Anchors Consolidating Maritime Frontiers: Record of the Republic's Naval Battles]. Beijing: Haichao chubanshe, 1999.

Xu Tao and Ji Zhiye, eds. *Shanghai hezuo zuzhi: xin anquan guan yu xin jizhi* [Shanghai Cooperation Organization: New Security Concept and New Mechanism]. Beijing: Shishi chubanshe, 2002.

Xu Yan. *Jinmen zhi zhan* [Battle for Jinmen]. Beijing: Zhongguo guangbo dianshi chubanshe, 1992.

———. *ZhongYin bianjie zhizhan lishi zhenxiang* [The True History of the Chinese-Indian Border War]. Hong Kong: Cosmos Books, 1993.

———. "*Neimu*" *da baoguang* [Revealing the Secrets of "Inside Stories"]. Beijing: Tuanjie chubanshe, 1994.

———. "1969 nian ZhongSu bianjie de wuzhuang chongtu" [The 1969 Armed Conflict on the Chinese-Soviet Border]. *Dangshi yanjiu ziliao*, no. 5 (1994): 2–13.

———. "Jiefang hou woguo chuli bianjie chongtu weiji de huigu he zongjie" [A Review and Summary of Our Country's Handling of Border Conflicts and Crises after Liberation]. *Shijie jingji yu zhengzhi*, vol. 3 (2005): 16–21.

Xu Zehao. *Wang Jiaxiang zhuan* [Wang Jiaxiang's Biography]. Beijing: Dangdai Zhongguo chubanshe, 1996.

———, ed. *Wang Jiaxiang nianpu* [Chronicle of Wang Jiaxiang's Life]. Beijing: Zhongyang wenxian chubanshe, 2001.

Xue Jundu and Lu Nanquan. *Xin Eluosi: zhengzhi, jingji, waijiao* [New Russia: Politics, Economics, Diplomacy]. Beijing: Zhongguo shehui kexue chubanshe, 1997.

Yan Xuetong. "Shiyan Zhongguo de anquan huanjing" [Preliminary Analysis of China's Security Environment]. *Dangdai guoji wenti yanjiu*, no. 4 (1994): 35–41.

Yanbian Chaoxianzu zizhizhou zhi [Yanbian Korean Autonomous Prefecture Gazetteer]. Beijing: Zhonghua shuju chubanshe, 1996.

Yang Chengwu. "Xizang panluan" [The Tibetan Rebellion]. In *Zongcan moubu: huiyi shiliao* [General Staff Department: Recollections and Historical Materials]. Beijing: Jiefangjun chubanshe [military circulation], 1997.

Yang Gongsu. *Zhongguo fandui waiguo qinlue ganshe Xizang difang douzheng shi* [History of China's Struggle against Foreign Aggression and Intervention in Tibet]. Beijing: Zangxue chubanshe, 1992.

————. *Cangsang jiushi nian: yige waijiao teshi de huiyi* [Ninety Years of Great Changes: A Special Envoy's Recollections]. Haikou: Hainan chubanshe, 1999.

Yang Guoyu, ed. *Dangdai Zhongguo haijun* [Contemporary China's Navy]. Beijing: Zhongguo shehui chubanshe, 1987.

Yang Kuisong. *Mao Zedong yu Mosike de enen yuanyuan* [Personal Feelings between Mao Zedong and Moscow]. Nanchang: Jiangxi renmin chubanshe, 1999.

————. "The Sino-Soviet Border Clash of 1969: From Zhenbao Island to Sino-American Rapprochement." *Cold War History*, vol. 1, no. 1 (August 2000): 21–52.

Yang Qiliang. *Wang Shangrong jiangjun* [General Wang Shangrong]. Beijing: Dangdai Zhongguo chubanshe, 2000.

Yang Qinhua. "Zhongguo gongchandang he Zhongguo zhengfu jiejue Taiwan wenti zhengce de youlai ji fazhan" [Origins and Development of the CCP and Chinese Government's Policy for Resolving the Taiwan Problem]. *Zhonggong dangshi ziliao*, no. 53 (1994): 65–80.

Yao Zhongming. "Zhou Enlai zongli jiejue ZhongMian bianjie wenti de guanghui yeji" [Premier Zhou Enlai's Glorious Achievement in Settling the Chinese-Burmese Border Problem]. In Pei Jianzhang, ed., *Yanjiu Zhou Enlai: waijiao sixiang yu shijian* [Studying Zhou Enlai: Diplomatic Thought and Practice]. Beijing: Shijie zhishi chubanshe, 1989.

Ye Fei. *Ye Fei huiyilu* [Ye Fei's Memoirs]. Beijing: Jiefangjun chubanshe, 1988.

Ye Zhangyu. "Zhonggong diyidai lingdao jiti jiejue Xianggang wenti zhanlue jueci de lishi kaocha" [Historical Examination of the CCP's First-Generation Leaders' Strategic Decisions for Resolving the Hong Kong Problem]. *Dangdai Zhongguo shi yanjiu*, vol. 14, no. 3 (2007): 46–53.

Yin Qiming and Cheng Yaguang. *Diyi ren guofang buzhang* [First Minister of Defense]. Guangzhou: Guangdong jiaoyu chubanshe, 1997.

Yin Zhuguang and Mao Yongfu. *Xinjiang minzu guanxi yanjiu* [Research on Nationality Relations in Xinjiang]. Wulumuqi: Xinjiang renmin chubanshe, 1996.

You Ji. "Changing Leadership Consensus: The Domestic Context of the War Games." In Zhao Suisheng, ed., *Across the Taiwan Strait: Mainland China, Taiwan and the 1995–1996 Crisis*. New York: Routledge, 1999.

Yu Manfei and Lin Xiaoguang. "50 nian lai Zhongguo gongchandang duiTai zhengce de fazhan bianhua" [Development and Transformation of the CCP's Policy toward Taiwan over the Past 50 Years]. *Zhonggong dangshi ziliao*, no. 69 (1996): 137–159.

Yu Yan. *Wushi nian guoshi jiyao: junshi juan* [Summary of 50 Years of State Affairs: Military Affairs]. Changsha: Hunan remin chubanshe, 1999.

Zacher, Mark W. "The Territorial Integrity Norm: International Boundaries and the Use of Force." *International Organization*, vol. 55, no. 2 (Spring 2001): 215–250.

Zakaria, Fareed. *From Wealth to Power: The Unusual Origins of America's World Role*. Princeton, N.J.: Princeton University Press, 1998.

Zhai Qiang. *The Dragon, the Lion, and the Eagle: Chinese-British-American Relations, 1949–1958*. Kent, Ohio: Kent State University Press, 1994.

Zhai Zhirui and Li Yuzhuang. *Jinmen jishi: wushi niandai Taihai weiji shimo* [Jinmen Record: The Whole Story of the 1950s Taiwan Strait Crisis]. Beijing: Zhonggong zhongyang dangxiao chubanshe, 1994.

Zhang Baijia. "Cong 'yi bian dao' dao 'quan fang wei': dui 50 nianlai Zhongguo waijiao geju yanjin de sikao" [From "Lean to One Side" to "Omnidirection": Reflections on the Evolution of China's Foreign Policy Structure over the Past 50 Years]. *Zhonggong dangshi yanjiu*, no. 1 (2000): 21–28.

———. "The Changing International Scene and Chinese Policy toward the United States, 1954–1970." In Robert S. Ross and Jiang Changbin, eds., *Re-examining the Cold War: U.S.-China Diplomacy, 1954–1973*. Cambridge, Mass.: Harvard University Press, 2001.

———. "Jiushi niandai de Zhongguo neizheng yu waijiao" [China's Domestic Politics and Diplomacy in the 1990s]. *Zhonggong dangshi yanjiu*, no. 6 (2001): 29–34.

Zhang Lijun. "Building Peaceful Borders." *Beijing Review*, vol. 49, no. 25 (June 2006): 10.

Zhang Shu Guang. *Deterrence and Strategic Culture: Chinese-American Confrontations, 1949–1958*. Ithaca, N.Y.: Cornell University Press, 1992.

———. *Economic Cold War: America's Embargo against China and the Sino-Soviet Alliance, 1949–1963*. Stanford, Calif.: Stanford University Press, 2001.

Zhang Tong. "DuiYin ziwei fanji zhan qianhou de huiyi" [Recollections of the Counterattack in Self-defense against India]. In Pei Jianzhang, ed., *Xin Zhongguo waijiao fengyun* [New China's Diplomatic Storms]. Beijing: Shiji zhishi chubanshe, 1990.

Zhang Tongxin and He Zhongshan. *'Yiguo liangzhi' yu haixia liang'an guanxi* ["One Country Two Systems" and Cross-straits Relations]. Beijing: Zhongguo renmin daxue chubanshe, 1998.

Zhang Xiaoming. "China's 1979 War with Vietnam: A Reassessment." *The China Quarterly*, no. 184 (December 2005): 851–874.

Zhang Zhen. *Zhang Zhen huiyilu* [Zhang Zhen's Memoirs]. Beijing: Jiefangjun chubanshe, 2003.

Zhang Zhirong, ed. *ZhongRi guanxi yu diaoyutai wenti yanjiu lunji* [Research Collection on Chinese-Japanese Relations and the Diaoyutai Problem]. Xianggang: Lizhi chubanshe, 1999.

———. "ZhongYin guanxi de huigu yu fansi: Yang Gongsu dashi fangtan lu" [Review and Reflections on Chinese-Indian Relations: Record of an Interview with Ambassador Yang Gongsu]. *Dangdai yatai*, no. 8 (2000): 17–25.

———. *Zhongguo bianjiang yu minzu wenti: dangdai Zhongguo de tiaozhan jiqi lishi youlai* [China's Frontier and Nationality Problems: Contemporary China's Challenges and Their Historical Origins]. Beijing: Beijing daxue chubanshe, 2005.

Zhang Zhouxiang. *Xinjiang bianfang gaiyao* [Overview of Xinjiang's Frontier Defense]. Wulumuqi: Xinjiang renmin chubanshe, 1999.

Zhao Qimin. "Yuanhang qianli, shoujin Xisha" [Ocean Voyage for a Thousand Miles, First Advance to the Parcels]. In *Haijun: huiyi shiliao* [Navy: Recollections and Historical Materials]. Beijing: Jiefangjun chubanshe [military circulation], 1999.

Zhao Shenying. *Zhang Guohua jiangjun zai Xizang* [General Zhang Guohua in Tibet]. Beijing: Zhongguo zangxue chubanshe, 2001.

Zhao Suisheng, ed. *Across the Strait: Mainland China, Taiwan and the 1995–1996 Crisis*. New York: Routledge, 1999.

———. "Changing Leadership Perceptions: The Adoption of a Coercive Strategy." In Zhao Suisheng, ed., *Across the Taiwan Strait: Mainland China, Taiwan and the 1995–1996 Crisis*. New York: Routledge, 1999.

Zheng Shan, ed. *Zhongguo bianfang shi* [History of China's Frontier Defense]. Beijing: Shehui kexue wenxian chubanshe, 1995.

Zheng Zhiyun and Li Min, eds. *Yumin xianzhi* [Yumin County Gazetteer]. Wulumuqi: Xinjiang renmin chubanshe, 2003.

"Zhengge Xizang pingpan san nian" [Three Years of Suppression throughout Tibet]. *Zhongguo diming*, vol. 1, no. 115 (2004): 38–40.

Zhonggong Xizang dangshi dashiji, 1949–1966 [Chronicle of Major Events in the History of the CCP in Tibet, 1949–1966]. Lasa: Xizang renmin chubanshe, 1990.

Zhonggong zhongyang zuzhibu, ed. *Zhongguo diaocha baogao: xin xingshi xia renmin neibu maodun yanjiu* [China Investigative Report: Research on Internal Contradictions of the People under New Circumstances]. Beijing: Zhongyang bianyi chubanshe, 2001.

Zhou Enlai junshi wenxuan [Zhou Enlai's Selected Works on Military Affairs]. Beijing: Renmin chubanshe, 1997.

Zhou Enlai waijiao wenxuan [Zhou Enlai's Selected Works on Diplomacy]. Beijing: Zhongyang wenxian chubanshe, 1990.

Zhou Liming. "Lengzhan hou Laowo de duihua zhengce" [Laotian China Policy after the Cold War]. *Dangdai yatai*, no. 9 (2000): 19–24.

Zhou Zhihuai. "Guanyu 1995–1996 nian Taihai weiji de sikao" [Reflections on the 1995–1996 Taiwan Straits Crisis]. *Taiwan yanjiu jikan*, no. 2 (1998): 1–7.

Zhu Tingchang. "Lun Zhongguo mulin zhengce de lilun yu shijian" [On the Theory and Practice of China's Good-Neighbor Policy]. *Guoji guancha*, no. 2 (2001): 12–18.

———, ed. *Zhongguo zhoubian anquan huanjing yu anquan zhanlue* [China's Peripheral Security Environment and Security Strategy]. Beijing: Shishi chubanshe, 2002.

Zhuang Chaoqun, ed. *Xinjiang Tongzhi: shengchan jianshe budui zhi* [Xinjiang Gazetteer: Production and Construction Corps]. Wulumuqi: Xinjiang renmin chubanshe, 1998.

Zinberg, Yakov. "The Vladivostok Curve: Subnational Intervention into Russo-Chinese Border Agreements." *Boundary and Security Bulletin*, vol. 4, no. 3 (1996): 76–86.

Zou Keyuan. "Maritime Boundary Delimitation in the Gulf of Tonkin." *Ocean Development & International Law*, vol. 30, no. 3 (1999): 235–254.

———. "The Sino-Vietnamese Agreement on Maritime Boundary Delimitation in the Gulf of Tonkin." *Ocean Development & International Law*, vol. 36, no. 1 (2005): 13–24.

Index

Note: Page numbers in **bold** indicate illustrations